Laurence Sterne
The Early & Middle Years

Arthur H. Cash

Laurence Sterne

The Early & Middle Years

LONDON

Methuen & Co Ltd

MCMLXXV

First published 1975 *by Methuen & Co Ltd*
11 *New Fetter Lane, London* EC4P 4EE
© 1975 *Arthur H. Cash*
Printed in Great Britain by
W & J Mackay Limited, Chatham

ISBN 0 416 82210 X

Distributed in the USA by

HARPER & ROW PUBLISHERS, INC.

BARNES & NOBLE IMPORT DIVISION

for
Dess Mitchell Cash

Contents

Illustrations

Plates to the Appendix on Portraits of Sterne
between pp. 304–305

I. THE INFALLIBLE MOUNTEBANK, OR QUACK DOCTOR
From a comic broadside

II. THOS. BRIDGES *&* LAWRENCE STERNE, AS MOUNTEBANSK
Engraving by Charles John Smith after an oil, now lost

III. MEZZOTINTO ENGRAVING BY EDWARD FISHER,
AFTER REYNOLDS

IV. LINE ENGRAVING BY JOHN BARLOW, AFTER REYNOLDS

V. WATER COLOUR AND CHALK BY CARMONTELLE
The copy in the National Portrait Gallery

VI. OIL PORTRAIT BY AN UNKNOWN HAND

VII. CARICATURE IN OIL BY THOMAS PATCH

VIII. ENGRAVING BY PATCH,
ELABORATED FROM HIS OIL CARICATURE

BUST BY JOSEPH NOLLEKENS
IX. The copy in Shandy Hall
X. The copy in the National Portrait Gallery

UNAUTHENTIC PORTRAITS
XI. Attributed to Francis Cotes
XII. Attributed to Thomas Gainsborough
XIII. Attributed to Allan Ramsay
XIV. Attributed to Christopher Steele

YORK MINSTER
Engraving after a painting by Joseph Baker, *c.* 1750
back endpaper

Preface

If Momus's glass were only fixed in the human breast, observed Tristram Shandy,

> nothing more would have been wanting, in order to have taken a man's character, but to have taken a chair and gone softly, as you would to a dioptrical bee-hive, and look'd in,——view'd the soul stark naked; ——observ'd all her motions,——her machinations;——traced all her maggots from their first engendering to their crawling forth;—— watched her loose in her frisks, her gambols, her capricios; and after some notice of her more solemn deportment, consequent upon such frisks, &c.——then taken your pen and ink and set down nothing but what you had seen, and could have sworn to:——But this is an advantage not to be had by the biographer in this planet.

Consequently, Tristram found it wellnigh impossible to write about his father and his Uncle Toby. How much more difficult to write the history of a man when he has been dead for 200 years. A quixotic undertaking. One can only search diligently after such traces as remain, try to establish some 'facts', and do one's best to weave them into a story, haunted the while with a thought: though a biographer may amass more factual knowledge than he has of his nearest neighbour, he cannot know his man in another way as well as he can know a stranger after two minutes of casual conversation in the street. I am familiar with Sterne's face, but have never seen its changing expressions, have taken the measure of his form, but never observed his gestures, have read his words, but never heard his intonations. The historic Sterne, like his own Tristram, is the 'sport of small accidents', for his story must be read in a haphazard trail of letters, legal documents, political pamphlets, prejudiced memoirs, frivolous anecdotes – anything which the goddess Chance has seen fit to preserve.

These I could at least examine for myself, trying to winnow the fact from the opinion, of whatever bias, and I could look at the facts afresh to see what story could be found in them. To do so with an open mind, I have tried to free myself from the judgements of previous biographers and from the traditions about Sterne which prevailed in the early years of this century. In 1853 Thackeray published his vitriolic lecture on Sterne in *English Humourists of the Eighteenth Century*. Thackeray was shocked, or pretended to be shocked, at Sterne's infidelities to his wife. Sterne in love would weep and snivel, but 'it could not be expected that a gentleman with such a fountain at command should keep it to *arroser* one homely old lady, when a score of younger and prettier people might be refreshed from the same gushing source'. What really bothered Thackeray, I have always suspected, was not Sterne's restlessness in marriage, but the fact of a clergyman taking up the part of a lover, 'quoting the Lord's Prayer, with a horrible baseness of blasphemy, as a proof that he had desired not to be led into temptation'. The remark, like many in the lecture, is inaccurate. But no matter: Thackeray might have forgiven all had Sterne not taken 'his personal griefs and joys, his private thoughts and feelings to market, to write them on paper, and sell them for money'. Eleven years later, Percy Fitzgerald brought out the first full-length biography of Sterne (1864, revised 1896 and 1904). So kind was Fitzgerald to Sterne's memory, so uncritical and sympathetic, that inevitably one sees his study of Sterne as a reaction against Thackeray. Wilbur Cross was more objective. He first urged Fitzgerald to modify his enthusiasm, and when Cross came to write his own *Life and Times of Laurence Sterne* (1909, revised and expanded 1925 and 1929), he tried to avoid a censorious tone. But Cross was excited about the newly discovered memoir of Sterne by John Croft, a man who disliked Sterne almost as much as Thackeray. Little wonder that Cross's objectivity sometimes failed. 'Full justice, I daresay, has not yet been done to Sterne', he wrote to an admirer. 'In spite of every endeavour, Thackeray's portrait still intrudes upon my imagination, though I know it to be untrue in all essential details. I feel that the way has been merely pointed out to a biographer who can write of Sterne, unhampered by Victorian traditions.'[1] Sterne's first two biographers were men of high integrity, but it was an uphill struggle in their times to give a fair and balanced account of a naughty priest. So I have set aside their biographies while writing my own. What faults of the present age may be embodied in

[1] Letter dated New Haven, 10 October 1909, to Charles Marchant in London. In the collection of Kenneth Monkman at Shandy Hall.

my work I cannot say, but at least my generation does not expect a man to doff his libido when he dons his priestly robes, nor a writer of fiction to keep secret his personal life. Seeing no need to attack or defend Sterne, I have tried to do neither.

I have used the biographies of Fitzgerald and Cross in another way – to indicate where materials on Sterne might lie. For this I am more deeply in their debt than my notes suggest. But how much larger my debt to L. P. Curtis, whose searches after Sterne far outstripped those of his teacher, Cross. Curtis is the greatest of all explorers into Sterne's history, the discoverer of innumerable documents, and the scholar-detective who separated from a large and confused body of letters those which were genuinely Sterne's and those which had been forged by William Combe and others. He was painstaking and astonishingly accurate. But, out of respect for his teacher, no doubt, Curtis wrote no biographical study except his short *Politicks of Laurence Sterne* (1929). His other discoveries were recorded in a few articles and the massive notes to his edition, *Letters of Laurence Sterne* (1935). I myself have found a number of new records, especially in the ecclesiastical archives of York and the Public Record Office. I have the advantage of James Kuist's discovery of the memoir of Sterne by his former servant, Richard Greenwood. Kenneth Monkman, Hon. Secretary of the Laurence Sterne Trust and Hon. Curator of Shandy Hall, has kindly shared with me a number of documents he has found. Others will be brought to light with the publication of Monkman's own book on Sterne's early writing career. Still, most of the documents I cite were found first by L. P. Curtis. 'Tell me, ye learned, shall we for ever be adding so much to the *bulk*——so little to the *stock*?'

Acknowledgements

This book was conceived in the chill of York Minster Library, more years ago than I like to think. At that time, there was no heat in the old stone chapel which housed the bulk of the collection, and the place smelled strongly of mould. Elizabeth Brunskill, semi-retired, Bernard Barr, newly in charge, Mr Gyopay the bookduster, Canon Reginald Cant, chancellor and librarian of the dean and chapter, and I, the sole researcher, would huddle over coffee in Miss Brunskill's sorting room amid the boxes of ecclesiastical court records, and we would talk about York and the minster and Sterne. They were so interested in Sterne's history and so very generous to me – patiently answering my questions, telling me where to search, digging up unknown documents – that it became impossible *not* to try my hand at a new biography. The Minster Library is warmer now, and dry, and fully staffed and well used. But I treasure the memory of those exciting cold days and the kindness of my friends.

The trail led to the York City Library, where I was assisted by Morris Smith and Joyce Fowkes. From there to the Borthwick Institute, where the late Norah K. Gurney made me welcome and Ann Rycroft and Neville Webb piled my desk with folio records of the Archbishops of York – records which thirty-five years before Curtis had found in old closets in the basement of Bishopthorpe Palace. The Cambridge University Library shortly afterwards became my headquarters, and there I had the services of a friendly staff and the companionship of an accomplished Sternian, J. C. T. Oates, who has helped me on more problems than I could possibly enumerate. Miss H. E. Peek opened the university archives. Freda Jones helped me with the archives of Jesus College and tactfully informed me that my early notions about eighteenth-century Cambridge were all wrong. I went often to London to work in the British Museum and the Public Record Office. One day I went to Fleet Street, to the Old Cheshire Cheese, to meet a stranger who seemed to have been everywhere before me. Since then Kenneth Monkman has become my principal adviser; he has generously shared his extensive knowledge of Sterne and read with care early and late drafts of this book. In due time I returned to Yorkshire to meet Canon Harry Broughton, then vicar of Coxwold, who showed me the church and the parish registers and introduced me to his neighbour, that energetic and most kind lady, the late Marion Egerton. Mrs Egerton filled the gaps in my knowledge of local history and took me to Shandy Hall, then a ruin, to Newburgh Priory and Skelton Castle. At the priory, Captain V. M. Wombwell invited me to look at the papers of his ancestor, Lord Fauconberg, and Mrs Wombwell and Mrs Egerton helped me to sort through them. Winsome Ringrose-Wharton and I looked for the papers of her ancestor, John Hall-Stevenson; if we did not find much, it was a delight to be in 'Crazy Castle'. The late Francis Wilson, vicar of Sutton-on-the-Forest, and Margaret Wilson became my hosts and friends. Philip Ward helped me with the Sutton parish registers, and John Hutchinson with those of Stillington. Sister Loyola gave me access to the muniments of the Bar Convent. Ursula Lascelles shared her family's records of 'Panty' Lascelles. Mr and Mrs Ronald Pontefract showed me about Elvington Hall; Mr and Mrs E. Anthony Spenser took me through Woodhouse. I was introduced to Halifax and Hipperholme by Peter Facer, and the staffs at the Yorkshire Archaeological Society Library and the Halifax Public Library helped me with their archives and local collections. I worked at the Sheepscar Library, Leeds, and the Sheffield Central Library. I was made welcome at the North Riding Registry of Deeds by Samuel Wilkinson, and by M. C. K. Croft-Andrews of the North Riding Record Office. Eventually I went to Ireland, where I was assisted by the late Travers Nuttall, his brother the late Freeman Nuttall, and Hugh Jameson, rector of Annamoe. For the help of all these people, more than I could possibly name individually, I am grateful.

In subsequent years, I have had the advice and assistance of several scholars. Chief among these is L. P. Curtis, who cheered me on in my endeavours and patiently read and commented upon an early draft. Lodwick Hartley also made suggestions about this early version and sent me new information. Dr E. A. Gee taught me much about the history of Yorkshire houses; John Harvey helped with details of York topography; Kenneth Craven brought to my attention the materials on Richard Spence; and D. M. Smith sent me documents. I have had the advice and encouragement of Harlan Hamilton, George Kahrl, Roy Wiles, Alan Charity and my former teachers, now my friends, Allen Hazen and James Clifford.

I am grateful for help given by the Bodleian Library staff, the staffs of the National Portrait Gallery, the Royal Academy of Arts, the Huntington Library, the Morgan Library, the Folger Library, the Boston Public and New York Public Libraries, the university libraries at Harvard, Yale, Princeton, Columbia, Colorado State University, and the library of my own New Paltz College. I wish to thank the Huntington Library for permission to quote from the Elizabeth Montagu papers; Lord Fitzwilliam, his trustees, and the City Librarian for allowing me to quote from the Wentworth-Woodhouse Muniments in the Sheffield City Libraries; Lord Brownlow, their owner, and Peter Walne of the Hertfordshire Record Office for permission to quote from the Egerton papers. I am grateful for the permission I have received from the Greater London Council as Trustees of the Iveagh Bequest, Kenwood, to reproduce Highmore's portrait of Dean Fountayne and his bride; from W. S. Lewis to use Patch's engraving of 'Sterne and Death'; the Master and fellows of Jesus College, Cambridge, to use Patch's original painting and the so-called Ramsay portrait of Sterne; and from the Prints Division, New York Public Library, Astor, Lenox and Tilden Foundations, to reproduce Barlow's engraving after Reynolds's portrait of Sterne; and from Dr Calvin H. Plimpton to publish the portrait attributed to Cotes. The photograph of Kenneth Monkman's copy of the Nollekens bust was made by Mr Monkman and is reproduced by his kind permission. I have been unable to trace the owner of the Reynolds portrait of Stephen Croft; it is here reproduced from a photograph in the files of the National Portrait Gallery. My quotations from L. P. Curtis's edition of *Letters of Laurence Sterne* are by permission of the Clarendon Press, Oxford. My thanks to the Bobbs-Merrill Co., Inc., for permitting my quotations from James A. Work's edition of *Tristram Shandy*. I have been supported in my research by a grant from Colorado State University Research Funds and a sabbatical leave from Colorado State University, by a research grant and a faculty fellowship from the Research Foundation of the State University of New York.

Lastly, I wish to thank Katharine Waugh for proof-reading, Veda Strachen and Barbara Sammons for typing, and Dorothy and Hilarie Cash for their support and help. I am grateful to the Master and fellows of St Catharine's College, Cambridge, for their hospitality during the 1964–5 academic year.

Cambridge, as from New Paltz, New York,
18 February 1974.

Short Titles
& Abbreviations

Unless otherwise indicated, books cited in this study were published in London. Wherever possible, Sterne's letters and major works are cited parenthetically; the editions used are included in the short-title list.

Sources used in several chapters are cited by short title, distinguishable in the notes because printed in roman capitals and roman small capitals.

Other sources are given a full reference, with standard use of italics, when first cited in a given chapter; second and subsequent references within the chapter are simplified. No use has been made of the Modern Language Association system of abbreviations for periodicals, though some periodicals are included in the short-title list.

ACT BOOK – *Act Book (Institutions) 1710–62, 1733–44, 1744–55, 1755–68.* MS records of the Archbishops of York, at the Borthwick Inst.

ANECDOTES – *Literary Anecdotes of the Eighteenth Century*, ed. John Nichols, 9 vols, 1812–15.

ANONYMOUS LETTER – Anonymous letter, dated 15 April 1760, describing the writer's visit to Sterne in June 1759, as published by Wilbur L. Cross from a clipping of the *St. James Chronicle* (presumably the first publication) in *Works*, 12 vols bound as 6, New York and London: Clonmel Society, 1904, III, ii, 24–32. (A second publication appeared in the *European Magazine*, March 1792, pp. 169–70.)

ANSWER – [John Fountayne], *An Answer to a Letter Address'd to the Dean of York, in the Name of Dr. Topham*, York, 1758.

BM – British Museum.

BARR – C. B. L. Barr, *Laurence Sterne's Borrowings from York Minster Library, 1741–1754.* Unpublished list prepared by the assistant librarian in charge, York Minster Library, for the Laurence Sterne Bicentenary Conference, 1968.

BEST – G. F. A. Best, *Temporal Pillars: Queen Anne's Bounty, the Ecclesiastical Commissioners, and the Church of England*, Cambridge, 1964.

Borthwick Inst. – Borthwick Institute for Historical Research, York.

BURN – Richard Burn, *Ecclesiastical Law*, 2 vols, 1763.

CANNON – Richard Cannon, *Historical Record of the Thirty-Fourth, or the Cumberland Regiment of Foot*, 1844.

CHAPTER ACTS – MS minutes book of the dean and chapter of York, at the Minster Library.

CHAPTER DEEDS – *Register of Deeds, 1728–47, 1747–68*. MS record of the dean and chapter, at the Minster Library: W g–h.

CLAY – J. W. Clay, 'The Sterne family', YAJ, XXI (1911), 91–107. Genealogy.

CLEVELAND COURT – *Archdeaconry of Cleveland Court Books, 1734–74*. MS record of the ecclesiastical court, at the Borthwick Inst.

CLIMENSON – *Elizabeth Montagu: The Queen of the Blue Stockings: Her Correspondence from 1720 to 1761*, ed. Emily J. Climenson, 1906.

COLEY REGISTER – *The Nonconformist Register, of Baptisms, Marriages, and Deaths, Compiled by the Revs. Oliver Heywood & T. Dickenson . . . Generally Known as the Northowram or Coley Register*, ed. J. Horsfall Turner, Brighouse, 1881.

CROFT – John Croft, 'Anecdotes of Sterne vulgarly Tristram Shandy', in *Whitefoord Papers, Being the Correspondence and other Manuscripts of Colonel Charles Whitefoord and Caleb Whitefoord from 1739 to 1810*, ed. W. A. S. Hewins, Oxford, 1898, pp. 223–35.

CROSS – Wilbur L. Cross, *The Life and Times of Laurence Sterne*, 3rd ed., New Haven, 1929, reissued, New York, 1967.

CURIOUS COLLECTION – *A Curious and Interesting Collection of Papers, Printed and Manuscript*. Scrapbook once belonging to John Towneley, later to Robert Davies, at York Minster Library.

CURTIS – L. P. Curtis, notes to LETTERS.

DNB – *Dictionary of National Biography*.

DEALTARY LETTERS – One letter by Sterne and five by the Reverend Dr Thomas Newton addressed to the Reverend John Dealtary, at the Bodleian Library: ENG. LETT. d. 122 (published in part by L. P. Curtis, 'New light on Sterne', *Modern Language Notes*, LXXVI (1961), 498–501).

DRUMMOND RETURNS – *Archbishop Drummond's Visitation Returns, 1764.* MS at the Borthwick Inst.

East Riding Deeds – Records at the East Riding Registry of Deeds, Beverley.

EGERTON LETTERS – Letters and papers of the Reverend Dr Henry Egerton, among the family papers of Lord Brownlow, housed at the Hertfordshire County Record Office (published in part by Arthur H. Cash, 'Some new Sterne letters', TLS, 8 April 1965, p. 284).

ENGLISH ARMY LISTS – Charles Dalton, *English Army Lists and Commission Registers, 1661–1714*, 6 vols, 1892–1904.

FORTESCUE – John W. Fortescue, *A History of the British Army*, 13 vols, 1910–30.

GEORGE I'S ARMY – Charles Dalton, *George the First's Army, 1714–1727*, 2 vols, 1910–12.

GRAY – Arthur Gray, MS notes on the members of Jesus College, Cambridge, at the college archives office.

GRAY AND BRITTAIN – Arthur Gray and Frederick Brittain, *A History of Jesus College Cambridge*, Cambridge, 1960.

GREENWOOD – Richard Greenwood, a former servant of Sterne's, as interviewed by Joseph Hunter. MS in Hunter's hand, at BM: Add. MSS 24446, fols. 26–7 (edited and published by James Kuist, 'New light on Sterne: an old man's recollections of the young vicar', *PMLA*, LXXX [1965], 549–53).

HAS – *Transactions of the Halifax Antiquarian Society*, volumes dated but un-numbered.

Halifax Library – Halifax Central Public Library.

HAMMOND – Lansing van der Heyden Hammond, *Laurence Sterne's 'Sermons of Mr Yorick'*, New Haven, 1948.

HARGROVE – William Hargrove, *History and Description of the Ancient City of York*, 2 vols, York, 1818.

HERRING RETURNS – *Archbishop Herring's Visitation Returns, 1743*, ed. S. L. Ollard and P. C. Walker, 5 vols, 1927–31 (Yorkshire Archaeological Society Record Series, LXXI [1927], LXXII [1928], LXXV [1929], LXXVII [1930], LXXIX [1931]).

Huntington Library – Henry E. Huntington Library and Art Gallery, San Marino, California.

HUTTON–FOUNTAYNE LETTERS – Correspondence of Archbishop Matthew Hutton and Dean John Fountayne, MS bound under the title

1749/50 Correspondence between the Archbishop & Dean respecting the Appointment of a Residentiary, in the hands of Fountayne, Sterne, and others. At York Minster Library.

ILLUSTRATIONS – *Illustrations of the Literary History of the Eighteenth Century*, ed. John Nichols, 8 vols, 1817–58.

INSTITUTIONS – *Institutions (Commissions) 1731–1742*. MS records of the Archbishops of York, at the Borthwick Inst.

LPS – Proceedings of the Leeds Philosophical Society.

LAWTON – George Lawton, *Collectio Rerum Ecclesiasticarum de Dioecesi Eboracensi*, 2 vols paginated as one, 1840.

LETTER TO THE DEAN – [Francis Topham], *A Letter Address'd to the Reverend the Dean of York*, York, 1758.

LETTERS – *Letters of Laurence Sterne*, ed. L. P. Curtis, Oxford, 1935.

MARRIOTT – Anecdote of Sterne told by Dr Marriot [?Randolph Marriott, DD] to W. Hazlett [?William Hazlitt], *Monthly Repository of Theology and General Literature*, III (1808), 376–7.

MEMOIRS – 'Memoirs of the Life and Family of the Late Rev. Mr. Laurence Sterne', in LETTERS, 1–9.

Minster Library – Library of the dean and chapter of the Cathedral of York.

MINSTER REGISTERS – 'Register of burials, marriages, and baptisms in York Minster', ed. Robert H. Skaife, YAJ, I (1869–79), 226–330 [burials]; II (1871–3), 321–70 [marriages]; III (1874–5), 81–146 [marriages]; VI (1880–1), 385–95 [baptisms].

N&Q – *Notes and Queries*.

NEWBURGH PAPERS – Papers and letters of Thomas Belasyse, Fourth Viscount and First Earl Fauconberg, in the possession of Captain Victor Malcolm Wombwell, at Newburgh Priory, Coxwold. Recently, the bulk of these papers was given to the North Riding Record Office, Northallerton: shelved as 'Wombwell papers'.

North Riding Deeds – Records at the North Riding Registry of Deeds, Northallerton.

POLITICKS – L. P. Curtis, *The Politicks of Laurence Sterne*, Oxford and London, 1929.

PRO – Public Record Office, London.

PYLE – Edmond Pyle, *Memoirs of a Royal Chaplain, 1729–1763*, ed. Albert Hartshorne, New York and London, 1905.

QUARTER SESSIONS – *Quarter Session Records*, ed. J. C. Atkinson (North Riding Record Society, VIII), 1890.

REPLY – [Francis Topham], *A Reply to the Answer to a Letter Lately Addressed to the Dean of York*, York, 1759.

ROMANCE – [Sterne], *A Political Romance, Addressed to – ——, Esq; of York*, York, 1759 [sometimes called *The History of a Good, Warm Watch-coat*], the copy at York Minster Library (has been reissued in facsimile, with an introduction by Kenneth Monkman, by the Scolar Press, Menston, Yorkshire, 1971).

SENTIMENTAL JOURNEY – *A Sentimental Journey through France and Italy by Mr. Yorick*, ed. Gardner D. Stout, Jr, Berkeley and Los Angeles, 1967.

SERMONS – *Sermons of Mr. Yorick* and *Sermons by the Late Rev. Mr. Sterne*, ed. Wilbur L. Cross, in *Works*, New York and London, 1904, V, i–ii.

SEVEN LETTERS – *Seven Letters Written by Sterne and His Friends*, ed. W. Durrant Cooper, 1844.

SKAIFE – Robert H. Skaife, *Civic Officials of York and Parliamentary Representatives*. MS at the York Public Library.

STERNE, HAMLET, AND YORICK – Kenneth Monkman, 'Sterne, Hamlet, and Yorick: some new material', in WINGED SKULL, 112–23.

STERNE'S MOTHER – Arthur H. Cash, 'Who was Sterne's mother?', N&Q, CCXII (1967), 162–9.

SYKES – Norman Sykes, *Church and State in England in the XVIIIth Century*, Cambridge, 1934.

TLS – *Times Literary Supplement*.

TINDAL – N[icholas] Tindal, *The Continuation of Mr. Rapin de Thoyras's History of England, from the Revolution to the Accession of King George II*, 2 vols [numbered III, IV in the continuous series], 1732–45, reissued 1751.

TRISTRAM SHANDY – *The Life and Opinions of Tristram Shandy, Gentleman*, ed. James Aiken Work, New York, 1940.

VENN – John Venn and J. A. Venn, *Alumni Cantabrigienses*, 10 vols, Cambridge, 1922–54.

West Riding Deeds – Records at the West Riding Registry of Deeds, Wakefield.

WINGED SKULL – Arthur H. Cash and John M. Stedmond (eds.), *The Winged Skull: Papers from the Laurence Sterne Bicentenary Conference*, Kent, Ohio, 1971, simultaneously published in London under the title, *The Winged Skull: Essays on Laurence Sterne*.

WINSTANLEY – D. A. Winstanley, *Unreformed Cambridge: A Study of Certain Aspects of the University in the Eighteenth Century*, Cambridge, 1935.

Y AJ – *Yorkshire Archaeological and Topographical Journal*, name changed with
    Vol. XIII (1895) to *Yorkshire Archaeological Journal*.
YORK PRESS – Robert Davies, *A Memoir of the York Press*, Westminster,
    1868.

The Sterne family:
a sketch pedigree

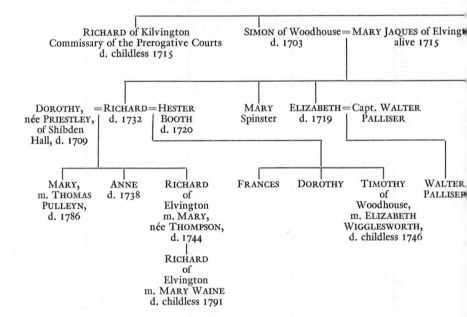

RICHARD STERNE
Archbishop of York
d. 1683

RICHARD of Kilvington
Commissary of the Prerogative Courts
d. childless 1715

SIMON of Woodhouse = MARY JAQUES of Elving
d. 1703   alive 1715

DOROTHY, = RICHARD = HESTER   MARY   ELIZABETH = Capt. WALTER
née PRIESTLEY,   d. 1732   BOOTH   Spinster   d. 1719   PALLISER
of Shibden   d. 1720
Hall, d. 1709

MARY,   ANNE   RICHARD   FRANCES   DOROTHY   TIMOTHY   WALTER
m. THOMAS   d. 1738   of   of   PALLISER
PULLEYN,   Elvington   Woodhouse,
d. 1786   m. MARY,   m. ELIZABETH
                     née THOMPSON,   WIGGLESWORTH,
                        d. 1744   d. childless 1746

                        RICHARD
                          of
                       Elvington
                     m. MARY WAINE
                     d. childless 1791

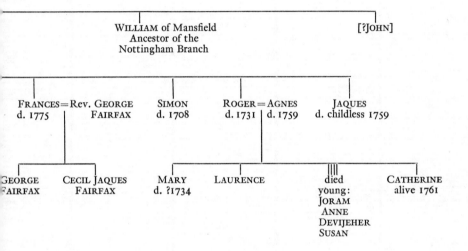

WILLIAM of Mansfield
Ancestor of the
Nottingham Branch
      [?JOHN]

FRANCES=Rev. GEORGE   SIMON   ROGER=AGNES   JAQUES
d. 1775   FAIRFAX   d. 1708   d. 1731 | d. 1759   d. childless 1759

GEORGE   CECIL JAQUES   MARY   LAURENCE   died   CATHERINE
FAIRFAX   FAIRFAX   d. ?1734   young: alive 1761
                                                   JORAM
                                                   ANNE
                                                   DEVIJEHER
                                                   SUSAN

I

Birth
& Early Childhood
1713–1724

'I wish either my father or my mother, or indeed both of them, as they were in duty equally bound to it, had minded what they were about when they begot me.' The comic opening sentence of *Tristram Shandy* contains, in a sense, the whole of the story, for it announces the triumph of good humour over despair. It also suggests the author's life and temperament. Laurence Sterne had his own share of 'pitiful misadventures and cross accidents', which may have generated in his imagination the ironic universe of *Tristram Shandy*, but he never surrendered to despondency. 'He has,' a friend said, 'and happy for him it is that he has, such a spring of good spirits in himself.'[1] Though at times he would complain, always in the end he would choose to laugh at life.

His misfortunes, like those of his small hero, began *ab ovo*. His tall, spare frame, the poverty of his childhood, and his anomalous social position were determined when he was begotten – which would have been in February 1713 at Dunkirk. The father-to-be, Roger Sterne, was a twenty-one year old ensign in Chudleigh's regiment of foot and a veteran of many battles in Flanders during the wars of Queen Anne. By birth and education he was a gentleman, though his prospects were meagre. His rank was the lowest in the army; he was cut off from his family and penniless. His wife, Agnes, having grown up in camps and barracks, knew little of the world but the military life. By comparison with her husband she was of low birth, the daughter, as Sterne said, of 'a noted sutler', a provisioner who followed the troops.[2]

The war had been stopped – at least for British soldiers. In 1711 the Tory

[1] DEALTARY LETTERS, fol. 133v.
[2] In STERNE'S MOTHER, I have given the argument, too detailed and involved to be repeated here, for accepting Sterne's

ministry of Harley and Bolingbroke had secretly decided to seek a separate peace with France. Marlborough, the soldiers' hero, was displaced as commander-in-chief by the Duke of Ormonde, a Jacobite, who began, as Sterne put it in *Tristram Shandy*, 'playing the devil in *Flanders*' (VIII, xix, 562). In July of 1712, Ormonde commanded the British troops to pull back from the siege of Quesnoy, deserting their allies. Orders were issued for a reduction of regiments, orders carefully calculated to weed out the Whig colonels and generals. Chudleigh's regiment was one of those marked for disbandment – for dishonour, it must have seemed to Roger and Agnes Sterne. The common troops, understanding only the shame of defection and the disgrace to their dead comrades, were ready to mutiny. The Dutch and Flemish citizens were outraged and at the point of riot. Nevertheless, the regiments were dispatched to the ports.[1]

The author of such a book as *Tristram Shandy* surely would have been aware that he was conceived at Dunkirk and was there *in utero* during the signing of the ignominious Treaty of Utrecht, which left a scar upon the heart of Tristram's Uncle Toby. To the end of his life Uncle Toby 'never could hear *Utrecht* mentioned . . . without fetching a sigh, as if his heart would break in twain'. The destruction of Dunkirk fortress in compliance with the treaty – a pivotal event in the novel – was begun in actuality before Sterne's parents left. As they sailed out of the harbour bound for Ireland, they would have heard the explosions being set off by the French engineers – the demolition woefully and drolly re-enacted in miniature by Captain Toby Shandy and Corporal Trim, the end of their wars upon the bowling green, the end of Uncle Toby's long sustaining dream.[2]

'At Clonmel in the south of Ireland . . . I was born November 24th, 1713, a few days after my mother arrived from Dunkirk.'[3] His parents had gone to Clonmel, Sterne said, so that his mother could be with her family, the Nuttalls. Exactly where she lay in is uncertain, but local tradition points to a house in Mary Street, now a roofless ruin with grasses and wild flowers

---

statement that his mother 'was the Daughter of no Other than a poor Suttler who followed the Camp in Flanders' (LETTERS, 40). I there take exception to the argument of the late Thomas Sadlier, Ulster King of Arms, passed on by CURTIS, 5–6, 7, that she was the daughter of Captain Christopher Nuttall.

[1] FORTESCUE, I, vi, 551–5; II, vii, 3–5; Geoffrey Holmes, *British Politics in the Age of Anne*, 1967, p. 28.

[2] TRISTRAM SHANDY, 457–8, 463–5. Unless otherwise indicated, movements and engagements of Chudleigh's regiment from CANNON.

[3] Sterne's statements about his birth and early life from MEMOIRS.

growing along the edges of its irregular walls.[1] Laurence was probably baptized in the Protestant church, St Mary's, only a few hundred yards away, though the parish registers for the time are lost.

'My birth-day was ominous to my poor father, who was, the day after our arrival, with many other brave officers broke, and sent adrift into the wide world with a wife and two children.' Besides this infant son, Roger and Agnes had a year old daughter. The order which broke the regiment was signed in London on the very day of Sterne's birth.[2] Roger would be continued on half pay, but he had barely managed to keep his wife and child alive before. He had to face the situation squarely. 'He left Ireland', said Sterne, 'as soon as I was able to be carried, with the rest of his family, and came to the family seat at Elvington, near York, where his mother lived.' Only despair would have driven Roger to take his wife and children across the treacherous winter Irish Sea to ask help from a proud mother. Mrs Mary Sterne was not unkind, but she held to the traditions of her station. She was a widow of sixty-one and mistress of Elvington in her own right.[3] How could she accept Agnes as her daughter?

In *Tristram Shandy*, Sterne would poke fun at his family – 'for these four generations, we count no more than one archbishop, a *Welch* judge, some three or four aldermen, and a single mountebank' (VIII, iii, 542) – though the archbishop and aldermen were real enough. They, and especially the archbishop, had set the Yorkshire Sternes apart from the older, less distinguished family.[4] Roger's grandfather, Dr Richard Sterne, Archbishop of York, had been a national hero. During the Civil War, Dr Sterne, then Master of Jesus College, Cambridge – 'the greatest of the Masters', he is called by the college historians[5] – rose to fame as a leader of the Cambridge

[1] William P. Burke, *History of Clonmel*, Waterford, 1907, p. 478; a photograph of the ruin in WINGED SKULL.

[2] PRO: WO. 26/15, p. 31.

[3] Mrs Mary Sterne, née Jaques, was baptized 26 May 1653: Elvington parish registers at Borthwick Inst. CLAY was mistaken in saying that she died in 1708, an error repeated by Sterne scholars: notes of the Reverend Sutton Squire and a deed of 1714/15, both cited below, show that she was alive. Probably she was alive in 1717, the time of the last legible record of the family in the badly damaged registers.

[4] Genealogical charts in *Visitations of Norfolk*, ed. Walter Rye, 1891, p. 267; *Familiae Minorum Gentium*, ed. John W. Clay, 1895, pp. 516–17; *Visitations of Cambridge*, ed. John W. Clay, 1897, pp. 58, 122 (Harleian Soc. Pub., XXXII, XXXVIII and XLI). CLAY traces the Yorkshire branch from Archbishop Sterne and prints from extant wills.

[5] GRAY AND BRITTAIN, 72. For a description of portraits of Dr Sterne at the college and at Bishopthorpe Palace, see John Ingamells, *Catalogue of Portraits at Bishopthorpe Palace*, York (Borthwick Inst.), 1972, pp. 54–5.

loyalists. Contemporary accounts tell of his collecting and smuggling to the king a treasure of silver plate from the halls of sundry colleges. Cromwell, infuriated, marched upon Cambridge, arrested the leaders, and a few days later allowed them to be paraded in London and stoned by the rabble. The Master of Jesus was locked in the Tower and later transferred to a coal ship, where he was tortured by being forced below deck with a crowd of prisoners deprived of food, water and sanitation, the airholes purposely plugged. For his heroism, Charles II at the Restoration presented him to the bishopric of Carlisle and soon thereafter translated him to the see of York.[1] But Richard Sterne soon wore out his greatness. His services at York were not particularly praiseworthy, and he is said to have 'minded chiefly the enriching his family'.[2]

At the archbishop's death in 1683, family leadership fell to his eldest son, Richard Sterne, squire of Kilvington, Member of Parliament for Ripon, and commissary (judge) of the Exchequer and Prerogative Courts of the Arch-bishop of York – the most wealthy spiritual court in the north, which one day Laurence Sterne would represent in his satirical *Political Romance* as the great, warm watch-coat. This second patriarch was still alive when Sterne was born, but old and childless. When he died, Kilvington was sold out of the family; his will and his wife's divided their wealth between a Notting-hamshire branch, descendants of William Sterne, the archbishop's third son, and the Yorkshire branch, descendants of Simon Sterne, the second son.[3]

The Sterne family appears at this distance much like other families of the gentry in the seventeenth and early eighteenth centuries. They were linked by blood and marriage in a loose federation of brothers, children, wives and husbands under the leadership of the most powerful male. They stuck to-gether in business, politics and decisions about marriage – until Roger Sterne broke the pattern. If the men tended to marry slightly below their

[1] John LeNeve, *Lives and Characters . . . of All the Protestant Bishops*, 2 vols, 1720, I, ii, 241–57; Edmund Carter, *History of the University of Cambridge*, 1753, pp. 187–9; DNB.

[2] Gilbert Burnet, *History of My Own Time*, ed. Osmund Airy, 2 vols, Oxford, 1897–1900, II, 430. Francis Drake, in *Eboracum*, 1736, pp. 464–5, said that the archbishop 'would have deserved a larger encomium than most of them, had he not demised *Hexgrave* in *Nottinghamshire*, to his son and his son's wife, from this see'. He is praised by Joseph Nicholson and Richard Burn, *History and Antiquities of the Counties of Westmorland and Cumberland*, 2 vols, 1777, II, 288–90.

[3] CLAY; VENN. The purchase of Kilvington: North Riding Record Office: ZB. a. Ralph Thoresby in his *Diary*, ed. Joseph Hunter, 2 vols, 1830, I, 154, described this Richard Sterne as 'very good company'.

station, all but Roger wed heiresses who brought wealth into the group. The girls married as they could, but always to political and religious allies.

Simon Sterne, the father of the Yorkshire branch, being the archbishop's second son and the father of Roger Sterne, never came to enjoy the position of family head because his older brother outlived him. He had little wealth in his own right, but he had accommodated himself to the condition of a younger son. Reared from the age of ten or twelve at Bishopthorpe Palace, he was sent to Jesus College in the high status of fellow commoner. He took no degree, but went on to acquire the polish of the town as a member of Lincoln's Inn. With such qualifications he had little trouble marrying into a wealthy family, whose upper-middle-class values he cheerfully adopted. It was his wife's family, the Jaqueses, who bought the estate of Woodhouse, near Halifax, to which Simon took his wife and son in 1688. In Halifax, though he must have managed farmlands, he became something of an industrialist, operating the coal pits and corn mill on the estate. He was, however, no great financial success, and when he died in 1703, 'having undergone a severe Salivation for a cancer in the mouth', he left what little property he owned outright to his three younger sons. Why should he worry about the eldest, Richard, who would inherit half the Sterne fortunes and all those of the Jaqueses?[1]

His expectations were indeed fulfilled, and in time the mantle fell to the third Richard Sterne, Roger's older brother, who would play an important part in the childhood of Laurence Sterne. This Richard's seat was still Woodhouse, where he chose to live out his life in the fine old Tudor house which, despite its name, was built of stone.

In the winter of 1713–14 Ensign Sterne did not take his family to his brother's. Since their father's death, Roger and the younger children had lived with their mother on another estate, at Elvington, in the East Riding of Yorkshire. Sterne exaggerated when he referred to Elvington as the 'family seat'. It had been the seat of the Jaques family, and Roger's mother, the last of that line, had not inherited it until her middle years. None of the Sternes had lived there until Mrs Mary Sterne took her younger children to Elvington in 1704.

The Jacqueses were not of the indigenous, agrarian gentry. They made their first fortunes in the city, exemplifying a common pattern in the north

[1] CLAY; VENN; COLEY REGISTER, 233; *Records of the Honourable Society of Lincoln's Inn*, 2 vols, 1896, I, 314. His failure to mention Woodhouse in his will indicates that Simon did not own it outright.

during the seventeenth century – rich merchants or industrialists displacing the older rural families, buying up estates and planting their sons with one foot in the country and one in the city.[1] Elvington had been bought by Sir Roger Jaques, merchant, alderman, and chief magistrate of York, who was knighted by Charles I.[2] His wife, born Mary Rawdon, also from a line of prosperous York merchants, is delightfully captured in her brother's auto-biography – an exuberant and slightly pretentious lady of the successful bourgeoisie.[3] The son of this couple, Roger Jaques, Esq., lived as the squire of Elvington; and Mary Sterne, who was his daughter, had been reared as a typical Yorkshire gentlewoman. When she inherited the estate from an older brother,[4] she was living with her husband and children at Woodhouse, where she remained until her husband's death. In 1704 she left Woodhouse to her eldest son, who had just married, and took her three daughters and three younger sons to the home of her childhood.

A letter of Mrs Sterne's, written shortly after they arrived at Elvington, brings to mind the trite image of the hen clucking over her chicks. She was writing to James Lister of Halifax, an old friend who was also the family apothecary, and she speaks of his prescriptions for her sick daughter, Mary (called Molle), and for her new daughter-in-law, whom she had left at Wood-house suffering from an abscessed tooth:

> . . . I retourn you my harty thanks for ye care you have of my childer   I bles god Molle is much better   I hope with your hillp in a Lettell time may wear out ye distim^r [distemper]   She is at York with my Brother   Your young bride hes her face swelld   yet I got her

---

[1] Edward Hughes, *North Country Life in the Eighteenth Century*, 1952.

[2] Pedigree and sketch of Sir Roger Jaques in SKAIFE; Robert Davies, 'An Episode in the Municipal History of . . . York', YAJ, V (1877–8), 55, n. 5.

[3] *Life of Marmaduke Rawdon*, ed. Robert Davies, 1863, p. 25 and *passim*; pedigree of Rawdon on p. xli. Her will in *Abstracts of Yorkshire Wills*, ed. John William Clay (Yorkshire Archaeological Association Record Series, IX), 1890, p. 118.

[4] Elvington passed successively from Sir Roger Jaques to (1) his son, Roger Jaques, Esq.; (2) his grandson, also Roger Jaques (Mary's brother), who died childless in 1680; (3) William Jaques, possibly a younger brother (baptized at Elvington 1654), or more probably an uncle of Mary's, who would have been holding the estate in trust. The uncle was buried at Elvington in 1707, but he (or Mary's brother) had already established in 1700 a trust leaving the estate to Simon Sterne, Mary or their son Richard, whoever should survive: East Riding Record Office: DDFA 4/4; East Riding Deeds, N/393/862. Various wills of the family are among the Jaques family papers at the Yorkshire Archaeological Association Library, Leeds: MS 679.

bloded   I disir you to send her something to purge her with for she is
so swelld that thay could not pull out the tooth   I am much obliged
to you for your frind shept [friendship] to dicke . . .[1]

Some of this orthography can be put down to Yorkshire dialect, but not all.
It would appear that gentlewomen of rural Yorkshire were not much encouraged to study the printed word.

Elvington Hall in Mrs Sterne's time was a modest brick house, not nearly
so large and fine as it appears today. Originally the public road ran within a
few feet of the north side, where today there are gardens. But the lovely
view to the south remains – lawns sloping down to the rich ings, or fields,
along the River Derwent, across which can be seen the steeple of Sutton-on-
Derwent church. Only the avenue of Dutch elm trees is now missing – and a
magnificent avenue it must have been, as one judges from the enormous
stumps still to be seen. The estate itself, lying a few miles south-east of York,
was large, including numerous tenant cottages, farmlands, woodlands and
fisheries.[2]

Roger Sterne, who had lived at Elvington from the age of about twelve,
must have understood early that such riches were not his. He had come into
the world an impoverished gentleman who would derive little benefit from
his birth unless he were willing to support the pre-eminence of his brother
Richard of Woodhouse. In the winter of 1708–9, when he was – probably –
sixteen,[3] he decided to leave home. During the previous summer he had lost
his brother Simon.[4] He had nothing in common with his younger brother,
Jaques. From what we know of their later lives, it is difficult to imagine
Roger and Jaques as anything but Tom Jones and Blifil. Roger was still at

[1] Halifax Library: Lister Letters, 1649–
1730.
[2] The house is that still called Elvington
Hall and occupied by the present owner,
Mr Ronald Pontefract. It can be identified
positively by tracing the sequence of
owners back to Mrs Sterne: East Riding
Deeds, E/273/487, N/393/862, R/219/517,
R/225/531, R/336/815, AU/590/981, HQ/
80/85; deeds and memorials at the East
Riding Record Office, DDFA 4/1, DDFA
4/4; DPX 4; the Ordnance Survey map of
1854 (surveyed in 1850), sheet 192; and
J. J. Sheahan and T. Whellan, *History and
Topography of the City of York*, 2 vols,
Beverley, 1856, II, 617. Dr E. A. Gee,

Investigator for the Royal Commission on
Historical Monuments, who examined the
house, reported that the only part surviving from 1704 is that with low ceilings on
the north; the only visible interior feature
is a stop-chamfered ceiling beam in the
room east of the north entrance hall.
[3] Lacking any record of Roger's birth,
I accept the traditional date of 1692.
Jaques Sterne was born 1695/6: VENN.
[4] This brother, not noticed by CLAY or
any other genealogist, was buried at
Elvington on 22 August 1708. The will of
Simon Sterne, the father, is worded in a
way to suggest that he had more than
two younger sons.

Elvington in November 1708, as we know from a note by the rector of the parish: 'Mr Roger Stern paid me twenty Shillgs on the 2^d day of November 1708 for the Tith of the Mask in the year 1708 – My servant James Homs took two tith piggs together of Madam Stern on the 30th of Octob^r 1708.' (The Reverend Sutton Squire was anxious to establish a precedent about the tithes on the field curiously called 'the Mask' and for several years made notes in the parish registers about his collections.) The family may have urged Roger to go to Cambridge where he could claim one of the Sterne scholarships at Jesus College, established by his grandfather,[1] for they were made readily available to any member of the family who wanted one. Jaques would soon do that. But Roger was an active, athletic sort, and probably he had no taste for studies. He heard the bells ring for Marlborough's victories at Landen, Drusen, Ostend and Dendermond. He wanted to go to the wars.

Richard Sterne, who could well have afforded it, did not buy his brother a commission. Perhaps Roger quarrelled with his family. Whatever the details, he left home in the spring and joined the army without a commission. Probably he was enrolled as a volunteer by some recruiting detachment from Hamilton's regiment of foot, later, with a change of colonels, to be called Chudleigh's.[2] The regiment had lost so many men in Flanders that it was withdrawn from the fierce front so that it could be built up to full strength. Detachments would have been sent to England in search of recruits. Since no records were kept, one can only surmise that Roger joined as a volunteer, a special category for young gentlemen who hoped to win the commissions they could not purchase. As such, he would have been treated as a fellow by the officers except, of course, on the drillfield or battlefield, where he would take orders like any common soldier. The usual practice, before the Duke of Ormonde put a stop to it, was to replace officers lost in battle with the best-qualified men on the spot. So desperate was the need for officers during the last years of the war that most soldiers who could read and write eventually were given field commissions – if they survived long enough. A gentleman volunteer was an obvious choice.

By the autumn of 1709, Hamilton's had acquired a full contingent, but most of the men were raw recruits. Presumably they were trained that

---

[1] *My Lord of Yorke's Statutes*, MS at Jesus College archives: TRU. 3. 1. In 1677, the archbishop and his eldest son established a scholarship at Corpus Christi College, Cambridge, from which the archbishop had graduated.

[2] Sterne was mistaken when he said in the MEMOIRS that his father had belonged to Handaside's regiment: CURTIS, 5.

winter. In the spring, Roger must have marched with the regiment, now under the personal command of Marlborough, to the French frontier, taking part in the passing of Pont-à-Vendin. At the siege of Douai the men 'were fully employed . . . in the trenches, carrying on the approaches, repulsing the sallies of the garrison, and storming the outworks, which occasioned considerable loss'.[1] By the time the fortress surrendered, 82 officers and men of Hamilton's had been killed, 130 wounded. The regiment was given no rest, but was ordered on to join the main army at Villers-Brulin during the siege of Béthune.

Roger was commissioned, it seems certain, in the place of some officer who had died at the bloody siege of Douai. That fortress capitulated on 27 June, and Roger's commission was signed in London on 1 July 1710.[2] The young man who received this news during the siege of Béthune was a seasoned soldier, aged eighteen.

Ensign Sterne commanded a platoon that year at the sieges of Aire and Saint-Venant. The campaign of that summer, says the historian, was 'by military men, esteemed very extraordinary in this respect, that our men were about a hundred and fifty days in open trenches, a thing said to be without example'.[3] Laurence Sterne, who grew up among these military men, hearing their talk of those terrible days, had a somewhat different notion. One recalls Corporal Trim's commentary upon prayer:

> When a soldier . . . an' please your reverence, has been standing for twelve hours together in the trenches, up to his knees in cold water, ——or engaged . . . for months together in long and dangerous marches; ——harrassed, perhaps, in his rear to-day;——harrassing others tomorrow;——detached here;——countermanded there;——resting this night out upon his arms;——beat up in his shirt the next;—— benumbed in his joints;——perhaps without straw in his tent to kneel on;——must say his prayers *how* and *when* he can.   (VI, vii, 421)

The next year Roger was engaged in one of Marlborough's most brilliant actions, the passing of Arleux, when the troops made a forty-mile push in eighteen hours. Hamilton's then took up a position in the siege of Bouchain, which capitulated in September.

The men were repairing the damaged fortress when Roger and Agnes were married. The wedding took place, Sterne said in the 'Memoirs', on 25

[1] CANNON, 18.
[2] PRO: Ind. 5431, fol. 149.
[3] TINDAL, IV, 175; FORTESCUE, I, vi, 542–50.

September (old style) 1711. Nine and a half months later, on 10 July 1712, at some unknown inn of Lille, Agnes gave birth to a daughter, whom she named Mary.[1]

Sterne was confused about his mother's origins, and his two statements on the matter are in some respects contradictory. He said, for instance, that her father, the sutler, had been in Flanders during Queen Anne's wars; but that is not likely. The man, whatever his name, probably followed his trade in Flanders during the earlier wars of William, and probably Agnes was born in Flanders. Soon thereafter the sutler died, and his widow, possibly a French or Flemish woman, remarried, this time to Captain Christopher Nuttall, who took her and her daughter to Ireland. Captain, later Major, Nuttall had three sons who at one time or another served beside him in Brewer's regiment of foot. He owned property in Dublin, and his sons had interests in Jamaican plantations.[2] Agnes was proud to look upon herself as a member of a military family. Little wonder that she should twice marry soldiers.

Agnes married first a certain Captain Hebert, 'of a good family', and came with him to Flanders, where he died or was killed. She soon met and married Roger. 'N. B.', noted Sterne in the 'Memoirs', 'he was in debt' to Agnes's father. All evidence considered, one must doubt the remark. The sutler was long dead, and Roger could hardly have known Captain Nuttall, who was stationed in England during the entire period of Roger's army service. Sterne probably fabricated the point to excuse his father's rash marriage. He wrote the 'Memoirs' for his daughter, who had never known her military grandfather but could well remember her grandmother as the foolish, grasping woman she later became. More likely, Roger Sterne at his wedding had congratulated himself upon winning the ideal soldier's wife, schooled in the military life and traditions, resourceful and resolute. Probably she was a fine looking woman.[3] Still, her class was well below his. She had no education, no social polish, no grasp of the obligations which held together a family such as the Sternes. Whether Roger intended it or not, his choice of a wife would be seen as a defiance of his family.

---

[1] The only known records of the wedding and the births and deaths of the children, including Sterne's birth, are in MEMOIRS; almost certainly Sterne took them from a family bible.

[2] STERNE'S MOTHER; cf. MEMOIRS, LETTERS, 40–1.

[3] Her beauty is presumed upon the evidence that her two daughters who reached maturity were beautiful. GREENWOOD said so of Catherine, and Sterne in MEMOIRS of Mary. He also remarked how handsome was her half-brother.

However shocked Mrs Mary Sterne may have been when she met Roger's wife, she could not very well shut the door upon this unfortunate couple with their two infants, penniless, and worn down by their long travels. She made arrangements for them to stay at Elvington, but not in the Hall. As a deed of the following year indicates, Roger Sterne, 'Gentleman', lived in one of the tenant houses. Laurence spent most of his first seventeenth months in a cottage at Elvington.

Agnes would have met all of her husband's family during this period. She may have gone with them to Halifax in September 1714 when Richard Sterne, Esq., was married for a second time. But the eldest brother never became her friend: when she was widowed and in need, he flatly refused to help. No doubt she also met the youngest brother, Jaques, who would have come home in the winter of 1714-15 after completing his BA degree at Jesus College. The two older girls, Mary – or Molle – and Frances, were living with their mother; and the youngest, Elizabeth Palliser, as we shall see, had returned with her husband. Frances was then being courted by the Reverend George Fairfax, whom she married on 10 August 1715. The Fairfaxes settled at the rectory of Washingborough in Lincolnshire, where they befriended Molle, who never married and lived with them; and they helped Jaques, who began his career in the church as Mr Fairfax's curate.[1] We know of no subsequent connection between this couple and Sterne's parents. The Elvington parish registers also bespeak Agnes's estrangement from the family. Elizabeth Palliser was brought to bed of a son at Elvington in November 1716. The following summer, Frances Fairfax brought her sick child home: he was buried there on 2 August 1717. But Agnes was to bear her children in inns and barracks and to bury most of them wherever the fortunes of a military life might place her.

Mrs Mary Sterne may well have been happy to see all of her children and grandchildren within so brief a span, but she had no intention of enriching any of them except her eldest. During this very year she precluded the need for a will by assigning Elvington and her other properties to Richard.[2] The traditions of primogeniture were deeply rooted. Her decision probably implies nothing at all about her opinion of the other children. No doubt she considered that Roger and Jaques had been unusually well treated by their father, who had left his own property, certain lands at Otley and Danby

[1] GRAY. The marriages: COLEY REGISTER. Molle's life with the Fairfaxes: East Riding Deeds, N/174/385.

[2] East Riding Deeds, E/273/487, dated 18 February 1714/15.

Wiske, to be divided among his younger sons – now reduced in number to two. By the terms of Simon's will, however, Roger could not claim his half until Jaques reached the age of twenty-one. He would be poor for two more years.

Nevertheless, Agnes and Roger may have had a pleasant social life during this period. They were part of a tiny community of Whig army officers stranded in the country. Roger's youngest sister, Elizabeth, had married Captain Walter Palliser of Saunderson's marines, and they too had come to Elvington when the captain was put on half pay. He is mentioned in the deed of that year as 'Walter Pallister Esquire', also possessed of some part of Mrs Sterne's estate, probably another cottage. The couple baptized their first child at Elvington church on 22 February 1714/15. Walter's brother, Captain Hugh Palliser, also on half pay, was living at nearby Ellerton.

These military brothers, considerably older than Roger, must have been romantic figures to him in his youth; it may be that their example had inspired him to join the army. They had a small estate at Ellerton, close to Elvington, and Captain Walter Palliser had been courting Roger's sister before Roger left home. The captain had been commissioned since 1693 and had seen service at Gibraltar, Spain, the West Indies, Maryland and Nova Scotia. Hugh Palliser (who became the father of the famous Admiral Hugh Palliser) had been an officer since 1696; he bore scars on either cheek from wounds received at Almanza fighting against the Duke of Berwick, bastard son of the Pretender.[1]

Politics must have been much discussed among these restless men so recently dismissed from their profession for political reasons. The Pallisers' history leaves little doubt of their Whiggish views. Roger's position is implied from the regiment he joined – one created by William III to fight the Pretender. Among its original officers was no less a Whig than Sir Richard Steele.

Within months a shift of the political wind raised their hopes of re-entering the service. The Tory ministry collapsed after the death of Queen Anne in August 1714. The ministry which replaced it contained many Whigs

---

[1] Memoir of the Palliser family in W. O. Cavenagh, 'Castle-town Carne and its owners', *Journal of the Royal Society of Antiquaries of Ireland*, Consecutive Series XLI (1911), 246–58; XLII (1912), 34–43. The brothers' military careers: ENGLISH ARMY LISTS, III, 31; IV, 141, 185, 284; V, 139–40, 261; GEORGE I'S ARMY, I, 357. Their property at Ellerton: William Paver, *Supplement to Consolidated Yorkshire Visitations*, 3 vol. MS at BM: Add. MSS. 29650–2, II, 104. Hugh Palliser signed Mrs Sterne's deed of 1714/15 as a witness.

friendly to the old army, including Robert Walpole as paymaster. Marlborough was soon reinstated as captain general, and by September, when King George landed in England, the government was scurrying about to prepare for a Jacobite invasion. By January 1715 reports were arriving from Scotland of a rebel army in the highlands. Marlborough countermanded the crippling clause in the Mutiny Act which had confined each regiment to a particular small district. In March, Walter and Hugh Palliser were re-commissioned as captains, this time in Will's regiment of foot.

On 20 June Chudleigh's regiment was ordered to be raised, and in July all half-pay officers were commanded to hold themselves in readiness. The day before that order, on 22 July, Roger's commission, with those of his fellow officers in Chudleigh's, had been signed in Westminster. In the words of Laurence Sterne, echoing the military talk of his childhood, 'our household decamped with bag and baggage for Dublin'.[1]

Roger had been summoned to Dublin because his regiment belonged to the Irish Establishment of the army. Agnes was probably delighted to return to the town where she had lived off and on as a child. She would be able to rejoin the Nuttalls, and they would both be among old friends. There were diversions of all sorts in the lively, Protestant-dominated town. It was, in fact, the Dublin we associate with Jonathan Swift, who had recently taken up residence there as Dean of St Patrick's. Still, the couple must have known that Roger could remain in Dublin only a short time. The officers' first task would be to recruit the rank and file, and for that they would return to England. Because Catholics could not be enlisted, no regiment could hope to find enough men in Ireland, not even in the Pale of Dublin.

Whether in barracks or lodgings, Agnes settled the family, probably expecting her husband to be away only a short while. In due time the officers were convened, at Dublin Castle, no doubt, and soon thereafter set off for Guildford, in the south of England. On 27 September 1715 Chudleigh's regiment, considerably enlarged, was ordered to Plymouth via Winchester, Blandford and Exeter, 'To March in Two Divisions Viz^t The Second the Day after the First, And to rest the Sundays and every Third or Fourth day on their March, as the Officer in Chief shall see occasion'.[2] But the rebellion grew rapidly, and major battles were fought at Preston and Sheriffmuir. In December, when it was learned that the Pretender had landed in Scotland, a

[1] MEMOIRS; FORTESCUE, II, vii, 4–6; PRO: Ind. 5430, fol. 58; Ind. 5431,   fol. 149; SP. 44/176, fol. 197; WO. 26/15, fol. 31.
[2] WO. 5/20, fol. 106.

decision was made not to return Chudleigh's to Ireland, but to send them directly north as soon as they were ready.

Agnes packed her things and sailed for Liverpool, where she expected to meet them. They were not there. 'In a sad winter, my mother and her two children followed him, travelling from Liverpool by land to Plymouth (Melancholy description of this journey not necessary to be transmitted here).' Sterne's vivid idea of this difficult trek could not have been directly recalled; he remembered, rather, his mother's talk of it. Well she might talk of her trials, pregnant for the third time, travelling with two babes through strange, hostile country trying to find her husband. 'She laid in at Plymouth of a boy, Joram.' The baby must have been born in some inn, for barracks were rare in England. Wherever there were troops, the soldiers' families huddled in the inns, an annoyance to the local people, who considered the children a nuisance and their fathers a threat to English liberty.

Fate, however, put an unexpected end to the rebellion: the Spanish fleet bringing the main Jacobite force was wrecked by a storm. Agnes may have felt her prayers answered in this event; her husband could only have felt frustrated. Before long the ministry, embarrassed by the large number of troops on their hands, began again to reduce them. On 12 October 1716 Chudleigh's was marched to Exeter under orders to remain quiet and not to disturb the citizenry. Possibly the family followed. In March, when the Assize Court was meeting, the regiment retired into the country to avoid the anger of the mob. Roger learned in May that Chudleigh's was to be cut down in size, though not disbanded. He soon found himself in command of a comically grotesque company made up mostly of corporals and drummers. In the spring the officers took the men to Appledore, and thence to Bideford, where they set sail for Dublin.[1] 'My mother, with three of us . . . took ship at Bristol, for Ireland, and had a narrow escape from being cast away by a leak springing up in the vessel. – At length, after many perils, and struggles, we got to Dublin.'

After two years of moving about, Dublin must have seemed a haven. What is more, it lay in Roger's power at last to do something for this brave little family. Jaques Sterne had recently reached the age of twenty-one, and the two brothers had come into that modest fortune left by their father. No legal papers remain to tell the story, but obviously Roger borrowed heavily against the lands he inherited or sold them outright. He leased a town house

---

[1] WO. 5/21, fols. 6–7, 96; WO. 5/22, fols. 52–3; WO. 55/346, fol. 335.

in Dublin and began playing the prodigal. He must have spent almost everything: it was to be the last time he or Agnes would live in a genteel manner. 'My father took a large house,' Sterne wrote, 'furnished it, and in a year and half's time spent a good deal of money.' The slightly acid tone probably reflects his mother's bitterness. Not yet four when they returned to Dublin, Laurence would have remembered little of this period of comfort. It did not last long.

In December 1718 war was declared against Spain, and by April the family was 'all unhinged again'. The regiment was ordered to Bath. By June it was in Bristol – and being moved out of town for the fair, first, and then for the assizes. In July they marched to Norton St Philip and two weeks later to Portsmouth to embark for the Isle of Wight.[1] Agnes and the children, who set out with Roger, were soon separated from him: 'We accompanied the regiment, and was driven into Milford Haven, but landed at Bristol, from thence by land to Plymouth again, and to the Isle of Wight.'

Up to this point, Sterne's memoir seems to have been pieced together from recollected conversations and a family bible. From the summer of 1719, when he was approaching the age of six, it is drawn more and more from his own memory. 'I remember', he wrote, 'we stayed encamped some time before the embarkation of the troops.' He remembered too the sadness of that time: 'in this expedition from Bristol to Hampshire we lost poor Joram – a pretty boy, four years old, of the small-pox.'

'My mother, sister, and myself, remained at the Isle of Wight during the Vigo Expedition.' As it turned out, the Vigo Expedition was the whole of the war. The English troops landed on the Spanish west coast and took up positions before the town of Vigo. The citizens surrendered, though the citadel held out for three days, losing half their men in the shelling. The English lost two officers and four men. Next, they marched to Pontavedra, only to be met by the city magistrates offering the keys. They then sailed for home.[2]

Agnes, meanwhile, had given birth to a daughter. 'We had poor Joram's loss supplied during our stay in the Isle of Wight, by the birth of a girl, Anne.' Unfortunately, Chudleigh's was not returned to the island; instead, it was landed in the south of Ireland.

. . . the regiment had got back to Wicklow in Ireland, from whence

[1] WO. 5/23, fols. 93, 153, 157, 161, 166.
[2] TINDAL, IV, 604–5; FORTESCUE, II, vii, 10. The Vigo garrison fell on 10 October and the English troops embarked on 27 October. Anne Sterne was born on 23 September.

my father sent for us. . . . We embarked for Dublin, and had all been cast away by a most violent storm; but through the intercessions of my mother, the captain was prevailed upon to turn back into Wales, where we stayed a month, and at length got into Dublin, and travelled by land to Wicklow, where my father had for some Weeks given us over for lost.

A treaty was signed with Spain three months later, beginning a long peace for England which, welcome as it was to their wives and children, must have been dreary indeed to the men of Chudleigh's regiment.

Probably Laurence's strongest recollections of Wicklow were of English children swarming through and about the barracks, playing, fighting, and being scolded by their mothers. Most of the families were content, for the soldiers generally agreed that the barracks of Ireland were much better accommodation than the crowded inns of England. For a gentleman such as Roger they must have been a trial. But Roger, as his son said, was not often given to complaining. He put his family in Wicklow barracks for the next year.

Agnes bore her fifth child there, a boy named Devijeher, 'after Colonel Devijeher', Sterne said, probably taking his information from the family bible. It was a tradition in the army to compliment a fellow officer by naming a son for him. The friend so honoured by Roger and Agnes was Abraham Devisscher (as the name is spelled in the army lists). The two men had served together as ensigns while they were still bachelors, but Devisscher had been fortunate (or perhaps wealthy) enough to be promoted to captain and then to lieutenant-colonel.[1]

The naming of this child suggests that Roger was by now emotionally withdrawn from his family. Like so many soldiers of that time, he seems to have substituted one familial society for another, the military brotherhood for the extended family. It was indeed a family of soldiers that Laurence grew up in. To the end of his life he would feel at home with military men.

The thirty officers of the regiment with their ladies held themselves stiffly apart from the riotous crew of common soldiers with their crowd of wives, concubines and ragged children. Among the enlisted men, Laurence would have known best those who acted as servants to the officers. Did one of them, one wonders, walk with a stiff leg and wear upon occasion a

---

[1] CURTIS, 6. I take the spelling from Ind. 5431, fol. 148.

Montero cap? Both groups were governed by the officers sitting in council under the presidency of Colonel Chudleigh. When called upon, they would act as a panel of judges, an investment company, or an athletic club. Because the populace in both England and Ireland was, for different reasons, hostile to the army, the officers were forced to look after their own. They pooled their pay, invested some of it and divided the rest according to their own scheme. Their investments made up a pension fund for their widows and children, and for this purpose the government gave them the pay of a mythical officer called 'The widow's man'. (A more regularized scheme of pensions was introduced later, before Agnes became a widow.) They shared their goods and labour and generally treated each other as blood brothers. It must be said, however, that this sort of *esprit de corps* had reached its peak under Marlborough in Queen Anne's wars. During the long peace of Walpole, when Sterne was growing up, it tended to break down. More and more often those officers who could afford it went off to their homes or to London, leaving the troops in the hands of their less fortunate comrades.

Roger's duties during this period would have been primarily disciplinary. The ranks, especially in times of peace, were filled with riffraff, scoundrels and blockheads who fought with each other at the drop of a hat and deserted whenever they grew restless. The problem was compounded in Ireland where these lawless Englishmen looked upon the Catholic Irish as the enemy and perpetrated the worst crimes against them without a qualm of conscience. When they were caught, their officers tried them at courts martial. Since they had no access to prisons, these military judges were constrained to use various tortures as punishment.

> Was it *Makay*'s regiment, quoth my uncle *Toby*, where the poor grenadier was so unmercifully whipp'd at *Bruges* about the ducats?
> ——O Christ! he was innocent! cried *Trim* with a deep sigh.——
> And he was whipp'd, may it please your honour, almost to death's door.   (IV, iv, 275)

Actually, whipping was the mildest punishment. The bludgeoning euphemistically called 'gauntleting' sometimes resulted in death, and there was an increased use of picketing, about which Trim had some knowledge. A picketed soldier was, in effect, crucified, though not to the point of death: he was hanged by one wrist in such a manner that he could relieve his agony

only by resting his bare feet on the upturned points of spears. Public hang-
ings were common.[1]

Since the point of these cruelties was to inspire the men with fear, the
regiment was forced to witness them. Laurence probably saw such sights;
if not, he would have known about them. Still, many children in the
eighteenth century were exposed to similar cruelties. Nothing seems to
have shaken his affection for soldiers. The military was, he once commented,
'a profession which makes bad men worse'; nevertheless, it was an old
soldier, Uncle Toby, whom he represented as formed 'of the best and
kindliest clay . . . all gentle, generous and humane'[2] – perhaps the most
believable good man in English fiction.

One link with Roger's past and family was unbroken in Ireland – the
Pallisers. Captain Hugh Palliser was recommissioned some time before 1722
in Roger's regiment.[3] More interesting is the presence of the eldest brother
in that family, Colonel Thomas Palliser, now retired from his long military
career and living north of Wicklow at Castletown Carne. The Pallisers,
being brothers-in-law to Roger's sister, probably were considered members
of the family. The older man was in his sixties when Laurence would have
come to know him. In rough outline, he is strikingly suggestive of Uncle
Toby. Perhaps Laurence even called him 'Uncle Thomas'. At least he heard
him called that by his cousin, the younger Walter Palliser, with whom
Sterne later attended college. Like Uncle Toby, the Colonel was a native of
the North Riding of Yorkshire who had served many years as a captain of
Grenadiers. He had fought in the siege of Limerick; perhaps he was the
source of those realistic details about that muddy siege told in the novel by
Corporal Trim (V, xl, 398–402). Colonel Palliser had served in Flanders
during the wars of both William and Anne, taking part in many battles
which poor, disabled Uncle Toby could only play out on his bowling green.
He was, moreover, a religious man, as one judges from his gift of a silver
chalice to the Protestant church at Castletown Carne. To be sure, in many
important respects he was unlike Sterne's character, being more practical,
political and wealthy. He was serving as Member for Fethard in the Irish
Commons and planning to build his new house, eventually called Portobello,
on a large tract on Durbards Island granted him by the Crown out of the
lands seized from the Duke of Ormonde. This old soldier lived to within a

[1] FORTESCUE, I, vi, 575–80; II, vii,   SENTIMENTAL JOURNEY, 170.
32–5.   [3] PRO: Ind. 5432, fol. 115.
[2] TRISTRAM SHANDY, IX, xxii, 626;

few years of Sterne's writing of *Tristram Shandy*, dying in 1756 well over the age of ninety. Sterne's character was not modelled upon any single historical person, but old Colonel Palliser comes closer to him than anyone else in Sterne's known life.[1]

Agnes too had her 'relations' – the Nuttalls. One can well imagine how delighted she was to be invited for a long stay in the country with one of them. 'We decamped', wrote Sterne, 'to stay half a year with Mr Fetherston, a clergyman, about seven miles from Wicklow, who being a relation of my mother's, invited us to his parsonage at Animo.' Thomas Fetherston, curate of the combined parishes of Derralossory and Annamoe, was married to the former Mary Nuttall, Agnes's step-sister. They lived in a long, ramshackle thatched cottage close to the River Suir. It was in ruinous condition, with rotting floors and timbers, kept damp by frequent floods of the river.[2] The cottage is gone now, though the barns and well are still there, not far from the present parsonage. There is hardly any village in the parish of Annamoe. The old cottage stood in the country among lovely wooded hills and pastures. Laurence, then seven, must have passed an idyllic spring here playing with his sister and cousins.

Close to the parsonage is a stone bridge, and on the other side may be found the remains of a mill. Here, according to local tradition, Laurence had the miraculous accident of which he later spoke with some pride: 'It was in this parish, during our stay, that I had that wonderful escape in falling through a mill-race whilst the mill was going, and of being taken up unhurt – the story is incredible, but known for truth in all that part of Ireland – where hundreds of the common people flocked to see me.' It is possible, of course, that the boy imagined the incident, appropriating to himself a similar myth about Archbishop Sterne.[3] Nevertheless, the ruins of the

[1] An obituary in the *London Magazine*, 1756, p. 612, asserts erroneously that he died aged 107. My account is based upon Cavenagh; his will at the Minster Library, Hailstone BB. 23; and Philip Herbert Hore, *History . . . of Wexford*, 5 unnumbered vols, 1901, *passim*. The theory that Uncle Toby is modelled upon the eccentric Captain Robert Hinde (1720–86), who built miniature fortifications, is fanciful. Captain Hinde did not retire from the army until 1763 and did not begin his hobby until after Sterne's death: [Mary F. Curling], 'Traditions of Sterne and Bunyan', *Macmillan's Magazine*, XXVIII (1873), 238–41, followed by Reginald L. Hine, *Hitchin Worthies*, 1932, pp. 165–84. See also N&Q, Fourth Series XII (1873), 40.

[2] STERNE'S MOTHER. A petition dated 1729, now in the Annamoe church files, describes the cottage and its ruinous condition.

[3] According to Ralph Thoresby, *Diary*, II, 15, when the archbishop as a boy was playing near a mill, he fell into the sluice: 'there was but one board or bucket wanting in the whole wheel, but a gracious

mill – a race, paved sluice box, rotting wheel and buckets – show at least a possibility of the event. It would have been almost certain death for an adult to have fallen into the machine, but a small boy might have survived had he been swept into the wheel so as to be caught lying prone in one of the buckets.

In the summer or autumn of 1721 Chudleigh's regiment was moved to Dublin. Roger and Agnes followed. Little Devijeher, a sickly child, was so weak they feared he could not survive the journey. He was left behind 'at nurse at a farmhouse near Wicklow'. At Dublin, 'we lay in the barracks a year'. How hard it must have been for Agnes, living meanly in Dublin where so short a time before she and Roger had occupied their own house and used their own furniture.

During the year in Dublin barracks, Sterne said, 'I learned to write, &c.' Possibly John Vincicombe, the regimental chaplain,[1] gave Laurence his first lessons. There is another, more interesting possibility: that his first teacher was named Lefever, the man who inspired the famous story of Lieutenant Le Fever and his son. Richard Griffith, a minor Irish writer who spent some time with Sterne during the autumn of 1767, said that Sterne told him as much. Sterne added, said Griffith – though the words could hardly be Sterne's – that 'it was he who imbued my soul with humanity, benevolence, and charity'.[2] The account is so patently improbable that Sterne's previous biographers have understandably ignored it. The army lists, however, throw the matter into a new light: they record a Lieutenant Rowland Lefever in Chudleigh's regiment. True, the first listing is for 1724, a few months after Laurence was sent to school in England, but that does not necessarily indicate that Laurence could not have known him. The record was made *after* the lieutenant joined the regiment. Besides, army lists were often inaccurate or incomplete. There is also a possibility that two men, a father and son, are represented in the name of Rowland Lefever, which continues on the lists for forty years – an extremely long service for one man.[3] In *Tristram Shandy* it is the son of Lieutenant Le Fever who is

Providence so ordered it, that the void place came down at that moment.' Thoresby also told how the boy miraculously survived a fall from a church steeple.
[1] Named in PRO: SP. 44/176, fol. 197. From this period, no official records of the regiment survive: they were lost in the 1922 burning of the Irish Public Record Office.

[2] *The Posthumous Works of a Late Celebrated Genius, Deceased*, 2 vols, 1770, I, 20. I have not seen the original London edition, but have consulted the pirated Dublin edition of the same year.
[3] GEORGE I'S ARMY, II, 412; PRO: Ind. 5433, fol. 75 (for 1730); Ind. 5434, 5438–9, 5441–4, 5446–9, 5451–5. For another theory that Le Fever was modelled

suggested as a tutor for Tristram. No certain conclusion emerges from the fragmentary evidence, though it increases the possibility that, in writing about the devout, trusting Lieutenant Le Fever and his son, 'free, and generous, and bountiful, and brave' (VI, v, 415), Sterne was moved by a recollection of some admired soldier and his son.

Devijeher grew stronger, and during the summer of 1722 Roger fetched him back to the family. But then little Anne grew sick and died: 'This pretty blossom fell at the age of three years, in the Barracks of Dublin – she was, as I well remember, of a fine delicate frame, not made to last long, as were most of my father's babes.'

In the autumn the regiment was ordered to Carrickfergus in the north. 'We all decamped, but got no further than Drogheda, thence ordered to Mullengar, forty miles west, where by Providence we stumbled upon a kind relation, a collateral descendant from Archbishop Sterne, who took us all to his castle and kindly entreated us for a year.' No one has yet identified this kind relative – who must have been more distantly related than Sterne thought. Although it often has been asserted that the prominent Irish family of Stearne descended from Archbishop Sterne, no convincing evidence has been presented.[1]

In March of 1723 their generous host sent them off to join the regiment

---

upon the son of a schoolmaster of Portarlington, Co. Queens, see *Willis's Current Notes*, July 1855, p. 50.

[1] Probably their host was related through a common ancestor earlier than the archbishop. The outstanding Irish family of Stearne included John Stearne, MD, founder of the Irish College of Physicians; John Stearne, Dean of St Patrick's and Bishop of Clogher, the friend of Swift's; and Major-General Robert Stearne. They are sometimes said to descend from the youngest son of the archbishop, named John, who is shown on Joseph Hunter's pedigree in *Familiae Minorum Gentium* and named by CLAY. But I am doubtful that such a son ever reached maturity since nothing else is known of him and he is not mentioned in his father's will. But, if he did mature and migrate to Ireland, he would have been too young to found the Irish family. The archbishop's youngest

son could have been born no earlier than 1650 and therefore could not have been the great-grandfather of the Bishop of Clogher, who was born in 1660: see T. W. Blecher, *A Memoir of John Stearne, M.D.*, Dublin, 1865, BM: U. 24. 35. Percy Fitzgerald, in 'Sterne and his day', *Dublin University Magazine*, LX (1862), 179–92 (first of a series of articles, the author identified in Vol. LXIII [1864], 328–38), reported the researches of John O'Donovan, LLD, who said that the Irish family descended from John Sterne of Stapleford, who came to Ireland as an official to Theophilus Buckworth, Bishop of Dromore (d. 1652). John the son of the archbishop, reported Fitzgerald, also came to Ireland and left descendants there, but the name was lost because there were no male descendants. Fitzgerald changed his account slightly in his *Life of Laurence Sterne*, 2 vols, 1864, I, 20–6.

at Carrickfergus, 'loaded with kindness, &c. – a most rueful and tedious journey had we all, in March, to Carrickfergus, where we arrived in six or seven days'. The hardships were too much for Devijeher; in Carrickfergus he died, aged three. 'Another child sent to fill his place, Susan; this babe too left us behind in this weary journey.' Laurence was left with only one childish companion, Mary, his older sister who had been born in Flanders. Four other children were dead. Yet another girl would be born to his parents after Laurence left them – Catherine. She would live to see her brother famous, but would be sadly estranged from him.

Laurence reached his tenth birthday while the family was moving about northern Ireland. Then he was taken to England, never to live with them again.

Mothers play no important part in Sterne's novels. This would not be worth remarking except that Sterne so openly identified himself with his narrator-protagonist, Tristram, whose history is traced from his conception. Mrs Shandy performs her painful role in childbirth; beyond that, nothing in the barely sketched character suggests Agnes Sterne. A quiet, browbeaten woman, Mrs Shandy 'went out of the world at last without knowing whether it turned *round*, or stood *still*' (VI, xxxix, 472). Sterne's picture of his real mother in the 'Memoirs' is also a sketch, but of a vastly different woman. The few bold, unadorned strokes reveal her suffering, forbearance, and the great strength which, if it allowed her to survive her harsh life, probably alienated her son.

Tristram and Yorick, as we see him in *A Sentimental Journey*, are most warmly and spontaneously affectionate toward young women, often hapless young women, or toward older men who are often soldiers. Laurence's most gratifying childish love, this pattern suggests, was for his sister and father. Mary was sometimes called Maria,[1] a name Sterne gave to the lovely, wistful girl of both his novels who was driven mad by disappointment in love. It was a fate his poor sister would eventually suffer. His father Laurence described in the 'Memoirs' thirty-six years after his death:

My father was a little smart man – active to the last degree, in all exercises – most patient of fatigue and disappointments, of which it

[1] So named in the papers of administration granted to Agnes Sterne in Ireland after her husband's death: seen by Fitz-gerald before they were destroyed with other Irish records and described in *Life*, I, 81.

pleased God to give him full measure – he was in his temper somewhat rapid, and hasty – but of a kindly, sweet disposition, void of all design; and so innocent in his intentions, that he suspected no one; so that you might have cheated him ten times in a day, if nine had not been sufficient for your purpose.

2

Hipperholme,
Halifax & Skircoat
1724–1733

In the autumn of 1723 or the spring of the following year, 'I forget which,' Sterne wrote, 'my father got leave of his colonel to fix me at school – which he did near Halifax, with an able master; with whom I staid some time.' Sterne neglected to say which of the two schools near Halifax he attended, that at Heath, situated between the town and his uncle's estate, Woodhouse, or the more distant school east of Halifax in the village of Hipperholme. Thanks to the researches of Thomas Cox, the Halifax antiquarian, we can be certain Laurence attended Hipperholme, sometimes walking the long distance from Woodhouse and stopping to visit his uncle's relations, the Listers, who lived at Shibden Hall, also to the east of Halifax.[1] His 'able master' at Hipperholme School was Nathan Sharpe, a close friend of the

---

[1] *A Popular History of the Grammar School of Queen Elizabeth at Heath*, Halifax, 1879, pp. 103–8. Because Heath School is closer to Woodhouse, early scholars assumed that Sterne had attended there. Cox, himself a master of Heath, challenged the assumption primarily from two evidences. The master of Heath in Sterne's day, Thomas Lister, was a grumpy old man hated by the pupils, an 'old little good for naught fellow', as a contemporary put it, surely not Sterne's 'able master'. Secondly, Cox interviewed an eighty year old lady, Miss Marion Lister (only distantly related to the master of Heath), who lived at Shibden Hall on the opposite side of Halifax in the direction of Hipperholme. According to Cox, Miss Lister 'distinctly remembers her father telling her that Laurence Sterne used to walk to Hipperholme School from his uncle's house along an ancient footpath which formerly ran through the yard of Shibden Hall'. Some of the letters from which Cox gathered his evidences are now at the Borthwick Inst.: R. Bp. G. 2. 3/10–31; others can be found in transcript in the John Lister commonplace book: Halifax Library, JN/3. John Watson, in *History and Antiquities of the Parish of Halifax*, 1775, did not include Sterne's name in his list of outstanding alumni of Heath School.

Sterne family, related to Laurence's uncle by marriage. Uncle Richard must have encouraged the arrangement and agreed to look after the boy. But he did not pay Laurence's expenses: those were carried by the school, and years later, when Sterne received his first living, a bill for his entire schooling was presented to him.[1] Neither did Laurence live regularly with his uncle at Woodhouse, but with Mr Sharpe or, if space were short, with one of the cottagers of Hipperholme village.[2] Roger may have been poor, but he was able to place his son in a good school, to give him family protection and some contact with six cousins – motherless cousins, it should be added, for Uncle Richard had by this time lost his second wife. Arrangements completed, Roger departed for Ireland. Laurence would never see his father again.

Both Hipperholme and Skircoat, the township in which Woodhouse lay, were included in the sprawling parish of Halifax. The town itself was the centre of England's wool industry, and the entire area was industrialized after the manner of that age. All year long, trains of pack animals trudged up and down the small, steep mountains on narrow paved strips laid beside the wider dirt roads, impassable in wet weather.[3] The Calder River turned the machines of the fulling mills, and the mountains supplied the dyers with coal and swift water. The hillsides were dotted with 'manufacturies', tiny family-operated enterprises, located to take advantage of the numerous spring-fed rills. To Daniel Defoe, the quick little streams, bright with dye, darting from house to house and across the road, the racks of coloured cloth hanging to dry and reflecting the sun, seemed 'the most agreeable Sight I ever saw'. Defoe, caught up in the romance of industry, was delighted to see women and children carding and spinning, 'all employed from the youngest to the oldest, scarce any thing above four Years old, but its Hands were sufficient for its own Support'.[4] Laurence would also have been aware of the coal miners with blackened faces and deep coughs, some of them boys his own age, who spent their lives digging pits by hand straight downwards to a depth where they were forced to stop for lack of oxygen.[5]

[1] LETTERS, 39–40.
[2] Although Sterne may have walked to Hipperholme on weekends, the village is too remote from Woodhouse for daily walking. Mr Peter Facer, formerly of Hipperholme School, now of Colne School, kindly supplied information on eighteenth-century boarding practices.

[3] C. Clegg, 'Coaching days', HAS, 1923, pp. 123–58.
[4] A Tour thro' the Whole Island of Great Britain, 2nd ed., augmented by Samuel Richardson, 3 vols, 1738, III, 77–9.
[5] W. B. Trigg, 'Halifax coalfields', HAS, 1930, pp. 117–58.

The Leeds road, which Laurence walked from Hipperholme to Halifax, led directly into the town market square. There he would have seen an ancient cross, possibly the market cross which came to his mind when writing *Tristram Shandy* (VI, xiv, 433), and beyond it the large, Gothic parish church where his grandfather lay buried. On one of the stone columns in the nave was a small wooden plaque commemorating Simon Sterne's gift to the parish of religious books collected originally by Archbishop Sterne.[1] Close to the main entrance he may have dropped a penny into a box held by a wooden statue labelled 'Old Tristram'. It still stands there, life-size and painted in strong life colours, a representation of a bearded beggar or poor-house inmate presenting a box for coins, above which appear the words 'Remember the Poor'. In Sterne's novel, Walter Shandy maintains that of all Christian names *Tristram* is the 'lowest and most contemptible', and he would frequently demand whether anyone 'had ever heard tell of a man, call'd *Tristram*, performing any thing great or worth recording?——No——, he would say,——TRISTRAM!——The thing is impossible.' Since the word *shandy* meant in Yorkshire 'a little crackbrained', 'Tristram Shandy' may have suggested to Sterne something like 'poor fool'.[2]

There was a pillory in the market place, a stocks, and a small courthouse. Laurence would have heard about a scandal connected with that building which implicated his late grandfather. If he were moved to pity by the sight of malefactors pinned in the pillory, he had already passed, or would pass, depending on his direction, a far worse sight: at the top of Beacon Hill in plain sight of the road was a gibbet from which swung from time to time the rotting bodies of felons.[3]

On Saturdays the market square was crowded with working families and buyers from all over England and even the Continent. The butchers' shambles would then be transformed into a bright bazaar with the woollens

[1] H. P. Kendall, 'Binroyd in Norland', HAS, 1913, pp. 179–92; T. W. Hanson, 'Halifax parish church: the library', HAS, 1909, pp. 288–98; Hanson, 'Halifax parish church library', HAS, 1951, pp. 37–47. The collection was recently given by the parish to York Minster Library.

[2] TRISTRAM SHANDY, I, xix, 55; Canon Savage, 'Halifax parish church: the 17th century woodwork', HAS, 1908, pp. 351–95. As Kenneth Monkman shows in WINGED SKULL, 280, the word *shandy* meant in 1691 'wild'; by 1788 it had come to mean 'a little crack-brained; somewhat crazy'. This leaves open the question raised a century ago whether Sterne's book itself affected the meaning of the word: 'Jaydee', in N&Q. Second Series XII (1861), 250, and answer by 'TB', p. 298. Etymologically, the name Tristram means 'sad'.

[3] R. Eccles, 'Halifax beacons', HAS, 1923, pp. 189–96.

laid out for display. In a nearby hall would be a massive auction of goods opened and closed by a timed bell and conducted according to strict rules, much like those of a modern stock exchange.[1]

From all this bustle, Hipperholme was removed. It was a peaceful village, half way up a mountain and surrounded by rolling fields and high forests. The master's house – probably the only school building – had been located in the village since 1660, but the spirit was imparted by Coley Chapel, one of several ancient chapels of ease belonging to Halifax parish. Its curates had founded the school and originally conducted the classes there.[2] Since then the mastership was customarily held by the curate of Coley. Laurence went to daily prayers in this stone chapel, a romantic near-ruin standing by itself on a south-east slope. For years the entire Sterne family had frequented Coley Chapel, drawn by the beauty of the place, probably, and by their friendship with Mr Sharpe. Here they brought their children to be baptized, and here most of the children returned to be married.

Nathan Sharpe was a kindly man in his middle years. He had been reared at Hipperholme, educated at Jesus College, Cambridge, and returned as master of the school in 1697. He promptly married Anne Priestley of Halifax, a first cousin to Richard Sterne's wife – his first wife, then still alive. To celebrate his good fortune, he 'made a great feast . . . invited 200 persons'. The story was told by Oliver Heywood, the dissenting minister of Hipperholme, who added, 'the like sumptuous work hath not been known in our country'.[3] Perhaps the master was maintaining a certain tradition of worldliness in his family. Another Nathan Sharpe, possibly an uncle, had quarrelled with a debtor, said Heywood, had got drunk, fallen off a bridge, and

[1] [Samuel Midgley], *Halifax and Its Gibbet-Law*, 1708, pp. 5-15 and *passim*. This competent history was pirated by John Bentley, a clerk of Richard Sterne's justicial court, who published it under his own name.

[2] Peter Facer, 'A short history of Hipperholme Grammar School', HAS, 1970, pp. 49-70. The seventeenth-century house or houses which Sterne knew are no longer standing.

[3] 'History of Coley Chapelry', in *Northowram: Its History and Antiquities*, ed. Mark Pearson, Halifax, 1898, p. 59. VENN was mistaken in saying that Sharpe became master in 1703, which was the date of his curacy: his nomination to the mastership, dated 11 November 1697, at Borthwick Inst.: R. VI. N. 526. The marriage record in COLEY REGISTER, dated January or February 1697/8, styles him master. VENN and Heywood both say that his wife was the daughter of Francis Priestley. Francis was brother to Thomas Priestley, Dorothy's father. Dorothy married (1) Samuel Lister of Shibden Hall and (2) Richard Sterne. See Jonathan Priestley's memoir of the family in *Yorkshire Diaries and Autobiographies*, ed. Charles Jackson (Surtees Soc. Pub. LXXVII), Durham, 1886.

drowned. Yet another man of that name, perhaps the master's grandfather, died in 1679 of a disease which afflicted his mouth because, as Heywood explained, he was 'wont to be a great swearer, curser'.[1] This man had been 'tenant of Coley Chappel', that is, the assistant curate. Sterne's master may have served in that capacity for a time: he was not preferred to the actual curacy until 1703. Nathan Sharpe's conviviality, the success of his son, who had a good living and became a royal chaplain,[2] and his fast friendship with the Whiggish Sternes suggest that he was of the worldly, politic clergy of moderate religious views, the sort of parson his bright young pupil would become.

Woodhouse was also in a peaceful setting, cut off from Halifax by a broad hill covered with wild moors in which were many treacherous coal pits. A steep path, now called Woodhouse Lane, led from the moors to the uncle's house, and past it down to the Calder River. The estate, spread over the side of the valley, included several smaller houses, some coal pits, and on the river a corn mill called Sterne Mill. The house itself, though not exceptionally large, was a fine old Tudor stone house, three storeys high, rearing box-like among the trees. It is still there and still occupied.[3]

When Laurence first arrived, his uncle's house was kept by Mary and Anne, aged nineteen and twenty. They and Richard, the heir, were the children of the first wife, née Dorothy Priestley. Young Richard, who was later kind to his cousin, may have been in school with Laurence for one year: the next year he entered Jesus College. Then there were two younger girls and Timothy, aged five, children by the second wife, née Hester Booth. Their life was typical of the rural gentry. Cousin Richard and later Timothy rode to hounds. Their father ran horses in the Wakefield races and once won a plate of fifteen guineas. The squire subscribed to Theobald's *Shakespeare* and was interested enough in his family to employ a researcher – a 'hawker

---

[1] *Oliver Heywood*, ed. J. Horsfall Turner, Brighouse, 4 vols, 1881-5, II, 140 and *passim*.

[2] The Reverend Abraham Sharpe, curate of Sowerby Bridge Chapel, probably was Nathan's son. Cox said that he and Richard Sterne called one another 'cousin', and a memorial book at Halifax Library, AB/12, shows that he came from Hipperholme. Perhaps he was the Reverend Abraham Sharpe who became Rector of Londesborough and Market Weighton:

obituary, *Gentleman's Magazine*, 1736, p. 553. Not to be confused with the famous mathematician, Abraham Sharp of Little Horton.

[3] The house, built in 1589, was once the home of Nathanial Waterhouse, the benefactor of the parish. It has since come to be called 'Wood Hall', probably to distinguish it from 'Lower Woodhouse', across the road, which originally belonged to the estate: R. Bretton, 'Wood Hall, Skircoat', HAS, 1955, pp. 19-32.

herald' – to supply him with a proper coat of arms, the starling-crested arms his nephew would one day make famous through *A Sentimental Journey*. Possibly the family, or some of them, spent winters at York, where Richard Sterne had a house in Peasholme-Green.[1]

Laurence's uncle was a pillar of the Walpole interest at Halifax, a justice of the peace, and a governor of schools and workhouses.[2] A dignified, confident man, he took his family responsibilities seriously and bore his sorrows manfully. Although he quarrelled with the Listers over the rights to Shibden Hall estate, which his first wife brought temporarily under his control, he was not stubborn: later, he was a close friend of that family.[3] As a disciplinarian, he could be firm. Acting as a justice, he once ordered a poor widow, Dorothy Mawd, and her son, Samuel, to be whipped along the public highway for two miles as punishment for stealing several pieces of wood for their fire.[4] No doubt he shared the general view that cruelty was necessary if order were to be preserved, and probably his children and nephew accepted that opinion without question. Uncle Richard provided Laurence with a good model of a gentleman, typical in most ways, though perhaps unusually conscientious and upright.

The gentry of Halifax, however, were scarcely distinguishable from the middle class, to whose values and attitudes Laurence was constantly exposed. The Listers, for instance, though masters of a fine old estate, had been apothecaries for several generations. Their boys, with whom he probably went to school, were enterprising sorts who later went fortune-hunting in Virginia. Dr Thomas Nettleton of Hague Hall, near Woodhouse, was intimate with his uncle. This physician, an active Whig and author of

[1] Advertisement, *York Mercury*, 9 March 1724, p. 11; ILLUSTRATIONS, III, 222; 'Journal of John Hobson', in *Yorkshire Diaries and Autobiographies*, ed. Charles Jackson (Surtees Soc. Pub. LXV), Durham, 1877, p. 284; [Percy Fitzgerald], 'Sterne and his day', *Dublin University Magazine*, LX (1862), 554–5.

[2] The record of his life is too full to present in detail. See especially Trigg; Watson; John Lister, 'History of Shibden Hall in the early eighteenth century', HAS, 1936, pp. 1–25; Tom Sutcliff, 'Some old Warley houses', HAS, 1918, pp. 33–67; and several of his letters among the Lister Letters at Halifax Library.

[3] Dorothy was left Shibden Hall for use during her lifetime by her first husband, Samuel Lister. Although the Lister family made several unsuccessful attempts to repossess the estate, Dorothy kept possession even after she was remarried to Richard Sterne. The couple lived there briefly, but moved to Woodhouse when Mrs Mary Sterne and the younger children moved to Elvington.

[4] I have not been able to locate the original of this court order, reproduced by Tom Sutcliff in 'Woodhall and Copely Hall', HAS, 1904–5, pp. 251–62.

moral tracts, came from a Puritan family and is reported to have been a close friend of Daniel Defoe's.[1] Laurence would have associated with the children of the families of Booth and Priestley, related to his uncle through two marriages; both had recently risen to prominence through their successes in the wool industry. Uncle Richard himself probably remained in Halifax because of business interests. We know that he operated Sterne Mill and several coal pits.[2] Though he must have managed farmlands, the poor farming conditions of the Calder Valley would not have held him there. He could easily have moved to Elvington, where the land was rich. The middle-class traditions of the Rawsons and Jaqueses, one concludes, were diluted but not completely washed out of the Sternes.

As one might expect of an industrial community, many Halifax families were descendants of Puritans and continued their ethical and religious traditions. There were at least sixty Quaker families in the parish, some of them living at Hipperholme village.[3] In later years, Sterne the clergyman would express a tolerance of Quakers, 'a harmless quiet people', but he would preach against any worship which sought divine inspiration through ecstasy: when a man combines prayer with fasting and mortification of his body, 'is it a wonder, that the mechanical disturbances and conflicts of an empty belly, interpreted by an empty head, should be mistook for the workings of a different kind from what they are?' (SERMONS, II, 74). Sterne was preaching primarily against Methodism, a movement which arose during his middle years, but he may also have been recalling the Presbyterians of Halifax. There were 300 or more families of nonconforming Presbyterians in the parish. Many of their fathers had been converted by the Reverend Oliver Heywood of Hipperholme, the celebrated preacher and inveterate scribbler, a delightful and courageous man who left the stamp of his personality upon the entire parish. Heywood's evangelical prayer meetings, if not extreme, were distinctly emotional: 'John Butterworth prayed solidly and tenderly,' he wrote, 'Thomas Bently prayed

---

[1] Watson, 470. On Nettleton, see J. Horsfall Turner, *Halifax Books and Authors*, Brighouse, 1906, pp. 32–3; William Cudworth, *Life and Correspondence of Abraham Sharp*, 1889, Chapter XIV. Nettleton's Whiggism is revealed in his letter to Lord Irwin of 5 September 1741, at the Sheepscar Library, Leeds: Temple Newsam Papers, PO/10/9.

[2] Trigg; Sutcliff, 'Some old Warley houses', HAS, 1918, pp. 33–67. According to local tradition, the little girl in Wordsworth's poem 'Lucy Gray' was drowned at Sterne Mill.

[3] HERRING RETURNS, II, 32–3; IV, 227–9; COLEY REGISTER.

zealously and importunately, James Wadington prayed understandingly and affectionately, Michael Stead (a blind man) prayed pertinently and savourily.'[1]

On the other hand high church Anglicanism was well represented at Halifax in the person of the vicar, Thomas Burton, who was suspected of Popery and Jacobitism. He once got into difficulties with Walpole's ministry for a sermon on the thesis that kings are not accountable to their subjects because their power and authority are not derived from the people.[2] But Archbishop Sterne's high church monarchism had been modified by his Halifax descendants, who had become Whigs in politics and moderates in religion. Their friends, the Priestleys, Booths and Listers, though descended from Puritans, had moved into this same middle road. Laurence would have been encouraged to respect the established church as an institution and would have been reminded often that his great-grandfather had helped to revise *The Book of Common Prayer* – in such a way as to exclude both Catholics and Calvinists.[3] But probably the clerical hero most often held up to him was the moderate and popular John Tillotson, Archbishop of Canterbury from 1691 to 1694, who had been born in a family of poor clothiers at Haugh End, Sowerby, just down the road from Woodhouse. Sterne would eventually embrace the traditions of Latitudinarianism established by Tillotson and, like many other preachers, he would borrow liberally from Tillotson's lucid, orderly sermons.[4] Mr Burton would have had little opportunity to prose-lytize any child in the Sterne family. Curiously, Burton then held the prebend of Givendale at York Minster, a stall which eventually would be given to Laurence Sterne – an evidence of the swing of the York church toward Latitude and Whiggism.

Richard Sterne was at constant odds with the vicar over politics, and seriously so, for Jacobitism was no dead issue. Beacon Hill took its name from a great pile of timbers to be set afire in case of attack. It had been lit during the uprising of King James's supporters in 1689, and it would burn again during the Jacobite rebellion of 1745. Whether or not the vicar was an actual Jacobite, he was certainly a Tory. He worked for a makeshift coalition of opponents to Walpole called the 'Country Interest' – disaffected Whigs,

[1] *Autobiography, Diaries, Anecdote*, III, 147.

[2] Turner, *Halifax Books*, 48. On Burton's career and politics: Watson, 372.

[3] Order of Charles II forming a com-mittee of bishops for this purpose at Borthwick Inst.: R. 11.

[4] HAMMOND, 155–76. Tillotson's in-fluence: SYKES, 257–68; L. P. Curtis, *Anglican Moods of the Eighteenth Century*, New York, 1966, pp. 34–44.

old-fashioned Tories and 'country gentlemen'.[1] Richard Sterne and his brother, Jaques, in York, were allies of the Archbishop of York, Lancelot Blackburn, a key figure in Walpole's hegemony in the north of England. Jaques, beginning his rise in the church, was then serving as Blackburn's chaplain. The brothers were second-generation Whigs. Although their grandfather, the archbishop, had kept quiet during the exclusion controversy – suspiciously, some said – their father, Simon, had taken a stand for Whiggism and the enthronement of William and Mary, playing a small part in the general Whig seizure of power structures in 1688.[2] At the parish level, this meant gaining control over public-service institutions – schools, hospitals or alms houses – which offered their governors opportunities to barter services for political support. Simon was one of the Whigs who took control of Heath School and of workhouses for poor boys at Sowerby and Halifax. In subsequent years, the vicar had won back much of that control and worked against Walpole in election contests. His name had become anathema to Archbishop Blackburn, who readily admitted that he kept an eye on Mr Burton's health, 'on account of the very great advantage it might be to His Majesty's service . . . if I should live to see that vicarage filled with a proper incumbent, as well disposed to the interest of the government, as it had hitherto been by one incorrigibly set against it'.[3] The difficulties derived largely from the industrial history of Halifax. The original large estates in the area had been broken up and sold piecemeal for those small family factories. Consequently there was an unusually large number of landholders qualified to vote – 6,000 by one estimate – all of them free of economic pressures from the gentry. Because they fell easily under the influence of their vicar, Mr Burton commanded a large block of votes.

Unfortunately, no records have come to light of the struggle – as it surely was – between Richard Sterne and Thomas Burton during the county election of 1727. But we know about two lesser skirmishes for control of local institutions.

Shortly before Laurence came to Halifax, a scandal had broken out about

[1] Cedric Collyer, 'Yorkshire elections of 1734', LPS, VII (1952–5), 53–82.
[2] J. H. Plumb, *Origins of Political Stability*, 1967, pp. 63–5. James II abdicated on 11 December and the declaration was presented to William and Mary on 13 February 1688/9. Simon Sterne's nomination as a governor of Heath School was made during this interval; it is dated 15 January 1688/9: Borthwick Inst., R. Bp. G. 2. 3/7–9. Simon's services on the boards of the workhouses: H. P. Kendall, 'Sowerby workhouse', HAS, 1956, pp. 61–7.
[3] Quoted by Collyer, p. 59.

the misconduct of Simon Sterne, when he was alive, and his contemporaries on the board of Halifax workhouse. These governors had 'fraudulently' misused the endowment funds to build a schoolhouse in Halifax market square which was never used for training boys at all: it became a courthouse for hearings before the justices of the peace, of which Simon was one. The current board, led by the vicar, had managed to get a judgement against the heirs of the older governors, and Richard Sterne had been charged with a double portion of the cost: he was ordered to compensate for the crimes of both his father and the first husband of his first wife. The heirs fought the case so successfully that they goaded Mr Burton into a rash move. He had himself sworn in as a justice and commenced a prosecution of his own. Uncle Richard and his colleagues proved that he was acting illegally and convinced the courts that a new charter was needed. The charter gave control to Archbishop Blackburn, and Burton ended by paying heavy court costs.[1] In 1727 the two men fought again, this time for control over the grammar school at Heath. The archbishop initiated the action. He appointed Richard Sterne to a board hitherto controlled by the vicar and ordered an investigation of the management. The squire soon exposed the deplorable condition of the school and the misuse of its funds. He began to press the governors to fill eleven vacancies on the board with 'Men of Worth, & of the Establisht Church, & . . . Entire friends to the Government'. Mr Burton boycotted the meetings, threw up every block he could and, when the quarrel grew hot, refused the sacraments to Mr Sterne. Eventually Uncle Richard, with the help of his father-in-law, Timothy Booth, put up money for a new charter, broke the hold of the vicar and hired a new master.[2]

Archbishop Blackburn, recognizing the sort of allies he had in the Sternes, made Richard a governor also of Hipperholme School and, in 1729, assisted Jaques to the prebend of Apesthorpe in York Minster. Laurence, though he would not have followed these developments closely, grew up expecting institutions, the church in particular, to be highly politicized.

[1] A full account of the case in *The History of the Town and Parish of Halifax*, 1789, by a certain Reverend Nelson, pp. 634–9. Although this is a poor book, much of it copied from Watson, this particular account probably represents original research. John Lister, the antiquarian, seems to have known the original documents, which he recorded in his commonplace book.

[2] Cox. Documents and letters relating to Heath School at Borthwick Inst.: R. Bp. G. 2. 3/7–31; copies in the John Lister commonplace book. During the next dozen years the school improved little: see the note by the Reverend George Legh in HERRING RETURNS, II, 32–3.

Adult men undertook political fights as a natural course of events, and those with whom he associated himself, his uncles, his master, were called 'friends of the government'. He may have been encouraged to think that his own education was made possible by his family's loyalties and entailed an obligation to the Walpole ministry.

Laurence was not a 'free scholar'; his education was not gratis, as it might have been for a boy with no family. But probably he was made aware that he must perform satisfactorily if he were to stay. Although we have no record of the statutes of Hipperholme School, they survive for Heath School, probably much the same sort of rules. 'If any [free] scholler upon due proof first had shall be found altogether negligent or uncapable of learning at the discretion of the Master he shall be returned to his friends to be brought up in some other honest trade & exercise of life.' Since there were many boys in the streets of Halifax wearing the uniforms of the work-houses, the lesson probably was not lost on Laurence.

If the curriculum at Hipperholme were similar to that at Heath, Laurence read primarily Virgil, Cicero, Horace and Caesar. He was expected to compose and deliver orations in Latin. He studied Hesiod and Homer, and he wrote verses in Greek. Then there was the catechism, which he learned by rote. One recalls Walter Shandy's strictures on rote learning, demonstrated by Trim's reciting his catechism (V, xxxii, 392–3). In time, Laurence was instructed in Hebrew grammar and logic. Beyond this basic course there may have been instruction in writing and arithmetic for those students whose families would pay an extra fee.

One thing about Laurence's accomplishments as a scholar is clear: he became an excellent Latinist. 'Slawkenbergius's Tale' in *Tristram Shandy* was composed in English and then a part translated into very good Latin.[1]

It is obvious from his novels how dearly Laurence loved classical literature. There is a touching passage in Uncle Toby's 'apologetical oration' on war when the old soldier speaks of his school days:

> When we read over the siege of *Troy* . . . was I not as much concerned for the destruction of the *Greeks* and *Trojans* as any boy of the whole school? Had I not three strokes of a ferula given me, two on my right hand and one on my left, for calling *Helena* a bitch for it? Did any one of you shed more tears for *Hector*?   (VI, xxxii, 461)

[1] The opinion of Mr Aloys Skoumal, Lecturer in Translation, University of Prague. Mr Skoumal has been unable to find an original for 'Slawkenbergius's Tale', though, as he points out, one may yet appear.

Would not Laurence have had feelings like these, associating the war of Troy with his father? In *A Sentimental Journey*, he had Yorick recall how Virgil had helped him to 'cheat expectation and sorrow of their weary moments':

> . . . as I have a clearer idea of the elysian fields than I have of heaven, I force myself, like Eneas, into them – I see him meet the pensive shade of his forsaken Dido – and wish to recognize it – I see the injured spirit wave her head, and turn off silent from the author of her miseries and dishonours – I lose the feelings for myself in hers – and in those affections which were wont to make me mourn for her when I was at school.   (225)

No doubt he was a sensitive boy, but perhaps not unusually so. There seems to be nothing abnormal about Laurence's school book, which came to light and was described by Percy Fitzgerald. This was a Latin textbook, *Synopsis Communium Locorum ex Poetis Latinis Collecta*. Unfortunately it has since been lost again. 'It was a soiled, dirty book', said Fitzgerald,

> every page scrawled over with writing, sketches, repetitions of his own name and those of his fellows. Everywhere is repeated 'L. S., 1728,' the letters being sometimes twisted together in the shape of a monogram. On the title-page, in faint brown characters, was written, in straggling fashion, the owner's name: 'Law: Sterne, September ye 6, 1725'. We also find some of his schoolfellows' names, such as 'Christopher Welbery,' 'John Turner' (a Yorkshire name), 'Richard Carre, ejus liber,' 'John Walker,' with 'Nickibus Nunkebus,' 'rorum, rarum,' &c. Then there is a stave of notes, with the 'sol fa,' &c. written below, and signed 'L.S.' Then we come on this: 'I owe Samuel Thorpe one halfpenny, but I will pay him to-day.' On another page we read 'labour takes panes,' 'John Davie,' 'Bill Copper,' the latter, no doubt, a school nickname. But on nearly every page of this dog-eared volume is displayed some rude drawing or sketch done after the favourite schoolboy rules of art. One curious, long-nosed, long-chinned face has written over it, 'This is Lorence,' and there is certainly a coarse suggestion of the later chin and nose of the humorist. There are ladies' faces, owls, and cocks and hens, &c.; a picture of 'a gentleman,' so labelled underneath; and several, as we might expect, of soldiers – one especially, in the curious sugar-loaf cap seen in the picture of 'March to Finchley,' with the wig, short stock gun and its strap. We

find also some female faces, early evidence, perhaps, of our hero's later tastes. Then we come on the words, 'A drummer,' 'A piper,' and this compliment, 'puding John Gillington.' Sometimes the name which figures everywhere is spelled 'Law: Stern – his book.'[1]

All in all, it seems likely that Laurence was happy and successful at school. In later years he treasured one memory of Mr Sharpe. 'Cannot omit mentioning this anecdote of myself, and school-master', he wrote in the 'Memoirs'.

He had had the cieling of the school-room new white-washed – the ladder remained there – I one unlucky day mounted it, and wrote with a brush in large capital letters, LAU. STERNE, for which the usher severely whipped me. My master was very much hurt at this, and said, before me, that never should that name be effaced, for I was a boy of genius, and he was sure I should come to preferment – this expression made me forget the stripes I had received.

Early in 1727 Roger Sterne's regiment was called into action. He, Agnes and their daughters had been living all this while in Londonderry. Now the regiment was ordered to Gibraltar to meet the threat of an attack by Spain. Wives and families would remain in Ireland. Under Colonel Robert Hayes, one of their own veterans who had purchased the command from Chudleigh, they reached the fortress on 26 March.[2] The posture of the Spanish forces turned out to be mostly bluff. They withdrew after a few border skirmishes. After the years of Walpole's peace, the incident was of great interest in England, and Laurence might have read numerous accounts in the *Leeds Mercury* or the *York Courant*.

There followed melancholy news from both Gibraltar and Londonderry. Hayes's regiment was retained on the Rock as part of the garrison – a notoriously unhealthy post. The barracks were inadequate, and the men suffered from exposure and dysentery.[3] In northern Ireland there was a dreadful famine. The army wives and families had adequate food, but about them were thousands of peasants dying of starvation.[4]

Perhaps because Roger's nerves were on edge, perhaps because of a Shandian streak in his nature, he quarrelled with a fellow officer about a

[1] *Cornhill Magazine*, New Series XIX (1892), 482–3.
[2] PRO: Ind. 5431, fol. 147; CO. 137/53, fol. 320; CANNON, 22–3.
[3] FORTESCUE, I, vi, 563–4; II, vii, 44–5.
[4] *York Courant*, 14 January 1728/9.

goose. In the end, they fought a duel. 'My father', said Sterne, 'was run through the body by Captain Phillips.'[1] To a friend, Sterne described the duel in detail. The captain, goes this report,

> put his rapier with such vigour through [Ensign] Sterne's person, that he actually pinned him to the wall behind. Then, with infinite presence of mind, the 'little smart man' begged of Captain Philips, with much courtesy, that before withdrawing his blade, he would have the courtesy to brush off any plaster adherent to the point.[2]

The wound left him with an 'impaired constitution', said Sterne, but he was not relieved of his duties. Colonel Hayes and other officers who could afford the journey returned to England from time to time, but Roger did not.[3]

On 12 October 1730 the Duke of Newcastle signed an order sending the regiment directly from Gibraltar to Jamaica, where an uprising of slaves had alarmed the colonial government. Seven weeks later six transports crowded with soldiers in gay spirits and good health were riding at anchor off Port Royal. They had little or no understanding of the situation they had been called to correct. The vast numbers of slaves in Jamaica bred a chronic fear among their masters, which led in turn to atrocious brutalities. Rebellious blacks were regularly burned alive. Such treatment had the opposite of the intended effect, and large numbers of slaves ran off to the untracked interior, where they formed well-organized societies, the Maroons. But the colonials were a disorganized lot. They had already sent two parties of their own volunteers against the runaways; the first had lost itself in the tropical forests and grown so sick they were unfit for action, and the second had mutinied and murdered their commander. At Port Royal the government had neither stocked provisions nor arranged quarters for the troops they had requested. 'It has been said, the Runaway Negroes have been troublesome,' wrote Colonel Thomas Townsend, 'altho I do not find there is so much in that as has been reported, & if it were, as they have a 120 Miles of Mountain

[1] Identified by CURTIS, p. 7, as Michael Phillips; cf. GEORGE I'S ARMY, II, 413.

[2] 'This I have on the authority of Mr. Waterton, the well-known naturalist, whose father knew Mr. Sterne well': Percy Fitzgerald, Life of Laurence Sterne, 2 vols, 1864, I, 79. On the acquaintance of Charles Waterton (1782–1865) of Welton Hall, Yorkshire, with Sterne, see Letters of Charles Waterton, ed. R. A. Irwin, 1955, p. 131.

[3] York Courant, 27 October 1730. CANNON was mistaken in saying that the regiment returned to England: the order sending them to Jamaica, PRO: CO. 91/1.

to range in, it seems very impracticable to destroy them. The People do not seem to value them much; nor do they for the most part seem well pleased at our coming.'[1]

Six companies from Hayes's, including Roger and his men, were dispatched to the town of Port Antonio on the north side of the island, reported to be a trouble spot. Colonel Hayes wrote from there in February, 'The Affair of the Blacks I look upon to be a Ram, for I can find no body that has either seen or felt them, in a wrathfull way. . . . I know no Business I have here except to sacrifice my Health and impoverish my Fortune.' Companies were soon dispatched to posts all over the island, sometimes isolated from each other by fifty or more miles – 'no such thing as a Surgeon going from quarter to quarter here without Wings'.

'I dare say a great many will never meet again', wrote Townsend. 'Our men already begin to have Feaver & Fluxes, and yesterday we buried Capt. Bellenden.' The blacks were nowhere, and the epidemic raged among the men. Toward the end of March Colonel Cornwallis wrote to his brother:

> One can't set four & twenty hours without hearing of some of the Corps either Sick or Dead. I am sure there is not an Officer here but with pleasure would go into the most desperate siege than stay in this damned unwholesome place, for then one should have a Chance to gain some Credit or die honourably, here no Service to be done of Consequence, no Reputation to be gained.[2]

Four days later the melancholy Cornwallis took charge, for Colonel Hayes was dead.

Roger lingered at Port Antonio. In May a group of citizens from Port Royal and Kingston, discouraged by disease and failing business, hired a ship and sailed around to Port Antonio with the thought of settling there. They found the town inhabited chiefly by soldiers, all sick. Rather than land, they turned about and set sail for Virginia. In England, on 9 March, a commission was made out for Roger Sterne to be lieutenant in the place of Thomas Batton, who had died. It was not approved until 12 May. News of his promotion may have reached Roger before, as his son wrote, the fever 'took away his senses . . . and made a child of him'. For a month or two he walked about continually, without complaining, 'till the moment he sat

[1] PRO: CO. 137/53, fols. 313v, 320, 326; FORTESCUE, II, vii, 37–40; *York Courant*, 12 January 1730/1. Transcripts of letters relating to the Jamaica expedition may be found in CO. 137/19, Pt. I.
[2] CO. 137/53, fols. 320–320v, 323–4.

down in an arm chair, and breathed his last'. Lieutenant Roger Sterne died at Port Antonio on 31 July 1731.[1]

How Laurence bore his grief we do not know, but he seems to have found little comfort in his mother, whom he now saw for the first time in five years. She came from Ireland with her two daughters, seeking to settle Roger's inconsequential estate and to make arrangements to live henceforth in England. Her 'Clamourous & rapacious Temper' only alienated the Sterne family anew. The little sister, Catherine, four or five years old, Laurence had never seen before. But in Mary, his old playmate, now nineteen, he found a warm and sympathetic friend – or so the wording of the 'Memoirs' suggests. Turning eighteen himself, he knew how to appreciate Mary's sweetness and beauty.

Agnes Sterne went on to York, seeking papers of administration for the estate, only to be told she must take them out in Ireland. She also asked her brothers-in-law to help her obtain a dispensation from the government to draw her pension on the English Establishment, rather than the Irish, to which Roger's regiment belonged. Richard declined, possibly because he dreaded her living in England, and Jaques would not suffer her to see him.[2] There was nothing she could do but return to Ireland.

Laurence remained with Mr Sharpe another year. His last emotional tie with the family in Ireland was soon broken. Mary, Sterne said in the 'Memoirs',

> was most unfortunate – she married one Weemans in Dublin – who used her most unmercifully – spent his substance, became a bankrupt, and left my poor sister to shift for herself, – which she was able to do but a few months, for she went to a friend's house in the country, and died of a broken heart. She was a most beautiful woman – of a fine figure, and deserved a better fate.

Agnes was eventually granted the administration papers in Ireland.[3] She

[1] CO. 137/53, fol. 368. Sterne was mistaken in saying that his father died in March. Roger Sterne's promotion: CO. 137/53, fol. 336; WO. 25/18, fol. 45. The refugees from Port Royal: *York Courant*, 18 May 1731.

[2] LETTERS, 35. Jacob Costobadie, who told Sterne how his mother had acted in York, was then assistant registrar to the archbishop, the person to whom Sterne's mother would go seeking papers of administration.

[3] Fitzgerald, *Life*, I, 81, described these papers, which presumably he saw. They have since been destroyed. He dated them 18 August 1732, but a brief record at Somerset House indicates that the administration was opened in April and concluded in August 1733: Administrations AA, 1733.

opened an embroidery school and began to draw her pension of £20 a year. According to reports, she and Catherine 'lived well', and the Sterne brothers probably had a good conscience. Laurence seems to have put his mother out of his mind.

Uncle Richard's health was failing. In September 1732 he made his will, leaving Elvington to young Richard and Woodhouse to Timothy. A month later, on 9 October, he died during a journey to York.[1] What was Laurence to do now? Years later when he thought back, he described himself as 'without one Shilling in the World, and I may add, *at that time* without one Friend in it'. He turned to his Uncle Jaques, who 'absolutely refused giving me any aid'. Sterne's later comment to Jaques is biting: 'I think you were the best Judge of What You had to do in Such a Case, & were only Accountable to God and Your own Conscience.' Then, like a blessing, a friend and patron appeared, 'my Cosin Sterne of Elvington who became a father to Me, & to whose Protection *then*, I cheifly owe What I now am'.[2] Sterne remained grateful for the rest of his life. Long after Cousin Richard's death, he told in the 'Memoirs' how he had stayed in school "till by God's care of me my cousin Sterne, of Elvington, became a father to me, and sent me to the university &c. &c.'

Richard, still unmarried, had just left Jesus College. He took no degree, but very few young squires did. Degrees at Jesus were for professional men, clergy for the most part. Richard knew that his impoverished cousin would have to take that road. Laurence did not arrive at Cambridge, however, until November 1733. The intervening year he probably spent at Elvington. The family at Woodhouse was breaking up. The girls and Timothy were soon settled at Bradford, and Woodhouse was leased to a certain John Lodge.[3] Sterne probably spent the year helping his cousin take charge of his new estate. Two young bachelors in charge of Elvington – it suggests a pleasant period.

Nathan Sharpe died in the spring of that year.[4] Thus was severed Sterne's last link with Halifax and Hipperholme. So far as we know, he never returned there again.

[1] COLEY REGISTER, 311; CLAY.
[2] LETTERS, 34–5.
[3] Borthwick Inst.: R. Bp. G. 2. 3/31.

[4] Died 9, buried 12 May 1733, aged fifty-two years and ten months: Watson, 441; VENN concurs with the date but gives his age as fifty-eight.

3

Cambridge
1733–1737

Sterne was registered *in absentia* at Jesus College, Cambridge, on 6 July 1733 – or rather, misregistered: they first had his name down as Henry.[1] With all the confusion in the family following the death of Uncle Richard and the delays in settling the legacies, Sterne entered the university somewhat late. He was nearly twenty.

Cousin Richard would have had no hesitations about the college. Since their ancestor had distinguished himself as Master of Jesus, Sternes of each generation had returned there – Simon, Uncle Jaques and Cousin Richard himself. It had also been the college of their teacher, Nathan Sharpe. Financially, it would be a bargain because Sterne could have one of the scholarships established by the archbishop – if available. None *was* available when he arrived, but one would be forthcoming. So the young squire had his cousin's name put 'on the boards' in the summer of 1733. Sterne actually arrived, as the *Steward's Account* shows, on 11 November.[2]

The town of Cambridge had grown little since the Middle Ages. Jesus College stood at its north edge, surrounded by open, treeless fields, across which could be seen distant windmills. The medieval and Stuart buildings where Sterne lived and studied have a great charm for us, though Sterne probably found them old and inconvenient. The brick buildings of the entrance court he might have thought passably modern, but he would have looked upon the heavy stone chapel as crude compared to the light, perpendicular-gothic chapel of King's – especially since the nave of the Jesus chapel had been awkwardly blocked off to be used as part of the

[1] College *Register*, in the college archives.
[2] College archives, A/C. 7. 5. Sterne, who remembered dates badly, said in the MEMOIRS that he went to the university in 1732.

Master's Lodge. The library, hall, and other rooms about a small inner court, once the cloister of the nunnery of St Radegund, were medieval timber structures of a sort all too common in Sterne's youth, and all too often dilapidated.

The college had been founded in 1496 by John Alcock, Bishop of Ely, who tyrannically deposed the nuns of St Radegund, seized and rebuilt their buildings, and endowed his new college with all their property. Its heyday had been during the Mastership of Richard Sterne in 1634–44. He had freed the college of debt, revised the curriculum and brought a disgruntled group of fellows into harmony. He was also responsible for the greatest architectural changes, having raised the subscriptions for the purchase of a chapel organ and the building of the chambers on the north side of the entrance court. Under Richard Sterne's leadership Jesus College, alive with intellectual ferment, had grown to be the second largest college in Cambridge. It had been much more exciting in those days than when Laurence Sterne attended.[1]

The university was relatively quiet, though it was only a calm between the stormy days of Dr Richard Bentley and the political takeover by the Duke of Newcastle when he was made chancellor in 1746. As an institution it was archaic. To some degree it still is, but was much more so then. It was entangled in the outmoded *Statutes of Queen Elizabeth*, volumes of legal precedents, traditional prerogatives, and ecclesiastical laws unreformed since Henry VIII. The colleges, most of them under equally antique laws, still showed many characteristics of the medieval priory. The fellows were in holy orders; supposedly they devoted their lives to worship and study – for the glory of God – and suffered students to live among them as a favour. The university sent its own representatives to Parliament, and fellows belonged to no city, borough or shire. They governed their own territories as 'liberties' and disciplined their members in 'peculiar' ecclesiastical courts lying outside the purview of the bishops. But the real power lay in the hands of those who made the appointments, and often they were not even associated with the university: groups of electors or individual patrons – the king, or the Bishop of Ely (in the case of the Mastership of Jesus), or some other high official. A clever legalist like Richard Bentley, Master of Trinity, could take

---

[1] General information about Jesus College from GRAY AND BRITTAIN; J. G. Sikes and Freda Jones, 'Jesus College, Cambridge', in *Victoria History . . . Cambridgeshire*, III, 1959, pp. 421–8. Architectural information from the drawing published by David Loggan in *Cantabrigia Illustrata* [1690]; and Robert Willis and John Clark, *Architectural History of . . . Cambridge*, 3 vols, Cambridge, 1886, II, 173–4.

advantage of this confusion to usurp appointments and to tyrannize the fellows of his college.[1]

The perfection of political bribery at Cambridge had to await the coming of Newcastle, but it was certainly a political battleground when Sterne was there. Fifteen years before, Chancellor Macclesfield had tried to reform the university to make it a sound prop for Walpole's ministry – instruction in political theory and constitutional law, of course, but also, in Macclesfield's plan, pensions for fellows 'to encourage them to serve the government' and choice preferments for the 'well-affected'. Although as a reform the plan fell through, the political preferments were *de facto* and it was common to pay off political favours with scholarships for the children of the ministry's friends.

For all that, Cambridge was still one of the great intellectual centres of Europe. It trained an enormous proportion of the English clergy, though its professional degrees of law and medicine were inferior. It was strong in classics and related disciplines such as rhetoric and morals, and it kept abreast of modern philosophy, giving a strong emphasis to the study of Locke and Newton. A Cambridge education went far toward equipping a young man for the life of a gentleman, and the gentry sent its sons in large numbers with no thought of a practical education and often without intending them to stay on for a degree.

Jesus College itself was at a low point. The Master, Dr Charles Ashton, was old and studious and seldom seen. He had the reputation of being very learned in religious history, but like George Eliot's Mr Casaubon, he compiled voluminous notes without publishing anything. Nevertheless, he had the respect of the university, and when other college heads were attacked in a satirical poem, the *Capitade*, he was spared:

> Ashton the wise, the learn'd, the ag'd, the good,
> Whose soul unmov'd, Temptation hath withstood.

Sterne, who evidenced in *Tristram Shandy* (V, xxxii, 393) a distrust of patristic or Talmudic studies, probably was disappointed by the dull

[1] General information about the university as a whole from WINSTANLEY; Christopher Wordsworth, *Social Life at the English Universities in the Eighteenth Century*, Cambridge, 1874; Wordsworth, *Scholae Academicae: Some Account of the Studies at the English Universities in the Eighteenth Century*, Cambridge, 1910; James Henry Monk, *Life of Richard Bentley*, 1830; and D. A. Winstanley, *The University of Cambridge in the Eighteenth Century*, Cambridge, 1922.

fellows brought in by this scholarly old man. Certainly, Ashton's old-fashioned Toryism tended to isolate Jesus from the rest of the university, which was steadily moving toward support for the Walpole ministry. Earlier, the college had lost active young Whigs such as Thomas Herring and Matthew Hutton, both destined to become Archbishops of York and Canterbury. Nevertheless, there must have been an undercurrent of opposition to the Master, and Sterne may have been quietly encouraged by the political stance of his family. Lynford Caryl, one of Sterne's tutors, was a key man in Newcastle's later control.

Academically, the college had suffered from Ashton's reluctance to encourage the modern sciences. No fellow had distinguished himself in mathematics, physics or law; and the students did not perform well enough in examinations to maintain a good reputation for Jesus. From being one of the three largest colleges when Ashton took charge, it had dwindled to one of the smallest.

The religious atmosphere at Jesus was neither puritanical nor liberal: it was strictly a high church college, excluding dissenters by statute. Its chief function was to train poor boys for the priesthood, and it had amassed a number of endowed scholarships specifically designated for sons or orphans of poor clergymen. Its actual graduates almost always took holy orders. Young squires, such as Sterne's cousin, continued to come to Jesus, but few completed a degree. Most of the students had grown up in rural parsonages and would return to that life. Probably it never crossed anyone's mind that young Laurence Sterne could become anything but a clergyman.

During his first eight months at Jesus, Sterne was a 'sizar', but that was normal at the college because most of the boys enrolled initially in that group. There has been considerable misunderstanding of the Cambridge sizars, because they are assumed to have lived like the Oxford servitors: in fact they were much better off, more like modern students in the United States who work their way through college. They were never asked to do hard manual labour, but made extra money waiting on table, acting as clerks for the library or chapel, or doing secretarial work for fellows and wealthy students. They considered it a privilege that they were excused from meals in the hall, which were expensive, and were allowed to take snacks in the buttery – a practice called sizing. They had no rooms, but slept in the garrets over the fellows' rooms. To be a sizar was not degrading at Jesus, where everyone understood that the best students usually came from that group. Most of the scholarships were given to sizars, and from the scholars were selected the fellows. True, the majority of fellows had a slow rise; nevertheless the best preferments in the hands of the colleges went to them, and the rare spectacular careers began there. This had been the route of some of the most celebrated men of the university – Richard Bentley, for example, or Isaac Newton; and about half the bishops of the established church had begun as impoverished fellows of Cambridge or Oxford. Thomas Gray was speaking of the sizars at Peterhouse when he described them as 'Graziers' Eldest Sons, who came to get good Learning, that they may all be Archbishops of Canterbury'.[1]

Socially the sizars mixed freely with the intermediate class of students, the 'pensioners', who made up the majority throughout the university. A sizar of Jesus wrote in 1741, 'the difference between sizar and pensioner, either as to the expence or manner of living, [is] (in our Society at least) next to nothing.'[2] It is not likely that Sterne saw much of the wealthy 'fellow commoners' or the 'noblemen' – if indeed anyone was registered in this last rank during Sterne's time at Jesus. Fellow commoners ate at high table and shared the combination room with the fellows, and they had the privilege of 'huddling' – that is, faking – their examinations. Gray described them as 'imitatours of the Fellows, or else Beaux, or else nothing'. But this group was small and did not much affect the spirit of the college: Sterne probably paid little attention to them during his first two years there.

Sterne was poor but not destitute. His cousin allowed him £30 a year. That seems a sizeable allowance when we recall that most assistant curates got by on that or less; but country living with its free fuel and garden produce was less expensive than at Cambridge, where costs were rising sharply during the mid-century. In any event, Sterne did not long remain a sizar.

On 30 July 1734, a certain Mr Hall vacated one of the Sterne scholarships, and Laurence was elected to take his place. Archbishop Sterne had designed the scholarships for poor boys of Yorkshire or Nottinghamshire, and Sterne qualified by both his poverty and birth.[3] It is doubtful, however, that academic prowess entered into the fellows' considerations, for it seems to

---

[1] Gray's comments about Cambridge are taken from his two letters to Horace Walpole, 31 October and 17 November 1734, written soon after he was enrolled at Peterhouse: *Correspondence*, ed. Paget Toynbee and Leonard Whibley, 3 vols, Oxford, 1935, I, 3–7.

[2] Ralph Heathcote, quoted by WIN-STANLEY, 201.

[3] College *Register*. CROSS, 27, questioned his qualifications because he was born in Ireland, but a soldier's child belonged to his father's parish.

have been understood that any descendant of the archbishop could claim the scholarship. Jaques Sterne had received one, and may well have needed it; and Sterne's Cousin Richard had availed himself of one – though it is hard to imagine his being pressed for funds. Two younger cousins, George Fairfax and Walter Palliser, would soon become Sterne scholars.

Sterne now became a 'scholar', a class distinct from both pensioners and sizars. He had lost the right to work for extra money but, as the record called *My Lord of Yorke's Statutes*[1] shows, he began to draw at once his share of the profits from the endowment, which amounted in the long run to a total of £27. 15s. 0½d. – roughly £11 a year. Since no one could live on such an income, an endowed scholarship was always augmented with a 'foundation scholarship', which provided room and board. Sterne thus was given a room of his own, though probably an inferior one, and 1s. 3d. a week for his 'commons' – a meat dish served in the hall twice a day. He would have paid for vegetables and puddings out of his own pocket – except on feast days – and probably bought the usual student breakfast of bread and beer.

It appears that Sterne's friendships during his first two years at Cambridge were among students of his own class. The name of Frederick Keller appears next to that of Laurence Sterne on virtually all of the college and university documents. That in itself hardly proves friendship, but the fact that they elected to take their master's degrees on the same day suggests a plan to be together and to celebrate after the ceremony. Keller was the son of a deceased clergyman and had received one of the Rustat scholarships for boys in that plight. His late father, a German, had served as a Lutheran priest before coming to England, when he was ordained in the established church. Young Keller turned out the best scholar of the group, winning the admiration of old Dr Ashton and, consequently, a fellowship as soon as he graduated. Eventually Dr Ashton bequeathed Keller his massive volumes of notes – more of a burden than a boon. It was years before poor Keller finally brought out an edition of Justin Martyr's *Dialogues* with annotation by the former Master.[2] After such promise, his career was dismal. He hung on at the college for thirteen years, trying to support an impoverished mother the while, and waiting for a patron. Finally he became tutor to Francis Willoughby, son of Baron Middleton, and through the baron's influence got two livings. Like his patrons, Dr Ashton and the Willoughbys, he was an

[1] College archives, TRU. 3. 1.
[2] Τοῦ ἁγίου Ἰουστίνου . . . ἀπολογιαι ὑπερ Χριστιανων. S. *Justini Apologiae pro* *Christianis, Graece et Latine. Interpretationem* . . . *accommodavit et annotationes adjecit C. Ashton*, Cambridge, 1768.

old-fashioned Tory, but his years of dependency upon the powerful and rich seem to have turned him into a Uriah Heep. In several letters to the Duke of Newcastle asking for further preferment, he fawns and flatters obnoxiously. The tone of his letters changes entirely after Francis Willoughby became the baron: in these he blusters and threatens to advise the young lord to withhold his support from Newcastle. A third living was finally given him – probably to shut him up – but not until he had been kept on tenterhooks for many years. If Sterne could have foreseen this career – and he probably could, because it was typical – he would have had little interest in a fellowship.[1]

Another young man who went through all the registrations and lectures and examinations with Sterne was Peter Torriano. He too met Sterne and Keller on the day they took their master's degrees. Peter was the son of a London merchant and had been educated at the well-known Merchant Taylors' School. Perhaps his father was abroad. His mother had recently died in Holland. In any event, he received a scholarship and began to prepare for the church.[2]

In 1735 two first cousins of Sterne's showed up at Jesus – Walter Palliser and George Fairfax – and both soon were possessed of Sterne scholarships. How much he had in common with young Fairfax is unknown. George, the son of Roger Sterne's older sister, Frances, and her husband, the Reverend George Fairfax, had grown up in the parsonage at Washingborough, Lincolnshire. One imagines that Sterne liked the other cousin. Walter was the son of Roger Sterne's younger sister, Elizabeth, and Captain Walter Palliser, since promoted to lieutenant-colonel. The boy had lost his mother at an early age and, presumably, grown up among soldiers. They must have talked about Elvington, where Walter was born, of barracks life, and old 'Uncle Thomas' Palliser in Ireland. Sterne would have remembered well Walter's other uncle, Captain Hugh Palliser, from the days when he had served with Roger Sterne. If the captain ever stopped at Cambridge and, according to the custom, sent word to his nephew to meet him in some ale house or coffee house, Sterne would have gone along to see the old scarred soldier.

[1] VENN; GRAY; Keller's letters to Newcastle at BM: Add. MSS 32726, fol. 205; 32732, fol. 176; 32876, fols. 122–3; 32882, fol. 488; 32886, fols. 248–9; 32896, fols. 316–17; 32901, fol. 456; 32929, fols. 121–2; 33072, fol. 247; 35616, fol. 197; obituary, *Gentleman's Magazine*, 1785, p. 748.
[2] VENN; GRAY.

These young men may have taught each other a good deal during their Cambridge years, as bright students do everywhere, but the academic standards of the university as a whole were very low – much below those of many modern universities. Students had an opportunity for a sound education on their own initiative, but the demands made upon them were few.

They may have attended a few lectures by professors, though it is unlikely that attendance was ever required. Professorships were often sinecures, the rewards for political loyalty in many cases.[1] The colleges had all the responsibility for instruction, and they operated on the theory that undergraduates would live in a scholarly society of fellows from whom they would learn by observing. The theory seldom worked because the scholarly abilities and accomplishments of Cambridge fellows were usually low. Thomas Gray called them 'sleepy, drunken, dull, illiterate Things'. Few were ever permitted to give courses of instruction, though occasionally they took on a pupil who could afford to pay. Their life was generally empty and dull. Though fellows were ordained, they seldom had the experience of parochial duties. Marriage was prohibited for all but heads of colleges; so the fellows' personal lives were sometimes wayward. Most of them came from poor, rural families, and the most polite society they had known was that of an occasional well-bred student. Their manners were boorish and their gluttony notorious. Exceptions there certainly were: David Hartley had been a fellow of Jesus, though he had resigned in 1730 over a religious question. But most were mediocre men who had no higher ambition than to win the loyalties of some wealthy fellow commoner, to become his mentor, and to win preferment in the church through the sponsorship of his family.

Virtually all of Sterne's instruction was by the successive tutors of Jesus College. There was only one tutor at a time because the college was so small. The fellows who won tutorships were considered quite successful. The post was sometimes a stepping-stone to the mastership, and it was lucrative because every student paid a tuition fee. But it was demanding. The tutor had the duty of preparing the young men for their university examinations. He looked after their finances, received their bills and accepted the responsibility if the bills were not paid. Sterne was educated under four successive tutors.[2]

[1] WINSTANLEY, 5–6.
[2] College *Register*; university archives: *Supplicats*, 1734–7, 1737–40; VENN;

GRAY; Caryl's obituary, *Gentleman's Magazine*, 1781, p. 295.

The first of these was Charles Cannon, a man of thirty about whom we know little. He died at the college soon after Sterne began studies with him. Cannon was succeeded by the gifted Lynford Caryl, eventually to become Registrar of the University and, in 1758, Master of Jesus. Caryl was one of those unrecognized great men of his age – politically active but so fair-minded that he kept the respect of the entire university. Meticulous and scholarly, he was the first man to put in order the archives of Jesus College and of the chapter at Canterbury; energetic and imaginative, he would attract excellent fellows to Jesus and build it up again to one of the leading colleges at Cambridge. A portrait at Jesus shows a stocky man with clear, intelligent eyes and a firm jaw. He had come to Jesus an impoverished son of a deceased clergyman. By the time he died he was a wealthy man with many preferments. Caryl, it seems, did not fail to keep track of the interesting career of his former pupil: in 1760 he subscribed to Sterne's sermons. Caryl moved on to other duties, and the pupils were taken over late in 1734 or early the next year by a young man who had only recently graduated – Richard Oakeley. He may have been substituting for Caryl since he did not hold the position long. Oakeley was not particularly distinguished in his later career, which was typical: he held on at Jesus for twenty-three years until he had sufficient preferments, dying in 1784 the parson of three parishes. The last of Sterne's tutors was John Bradshaw, a substantial man who had held a fellowship since 1722 simultaneously with the vicarage of Comberton, near Cambridge. We know few details about his life. Sterne may have received some instruction from one or two others. The tutors could hire lecturers for those subjects in which they themselves did not feel qualified. Because they had to pay these assistants out of the tuition fees, the practice was all too rare.

All indications are that the lectures were exceedingly dull, even those of Caryl, who was very slow of speech[1] – no more than a continuation of the grammar school drills with a dry presentation of information to be learned by rote. Sterne probably found them less stimulating than his studies with Nathan Sharpe at Hipperholme. 'Sciences', said Walter Shandy, 'may be learned by rote, but Wisdom not' (V, xxxii, 392). The lectures were held in the hall, which doubled as classroom and dining room, the students studying at tables from which they had just dined. Cleanliness was not often a virtue at Cambridge: in one college hall the floor was covered with sawdust which

[1] Gilbert Wakefield, *Memoirs*, 1804, pp. 63–119.

was turned over when it got too dirty, and turned again, and again, until it was carried out in the spring the colour of charcoal.

We have little knowledge of the curriculum. At most colleges classics were read in the original languages, and the scholars were expected to become proficient in Latin and Greek. Modern languages were not studied, except on the side. Mathematics was emphasized because few students had any training in it before they arrived at Cambridge. Philosophy, an amorphous subject, included geography, ethics and the natural philosophy we would call science. At Cambridge, Plato was pre-eminent among ancient authors, Locke and Newton among modern.

Formal logic and classical rhetoric were studied with a view to mastering them as practical skills. Sterne, though he had the highest respect for rhetorical skill, was not certain it could be taught in this manner. Walter Shandy was a natural rhetorician:

> Persuasion hung upon his lips, and the elements of Logick and Rhetorick were so blended up in him . . . that NATURE might have stood up and said,——'This man is eloquent.' . . . I well remember, [says Tristram] when he went up along with me to enter my name at *Jesus College* in ★★★★,——it was a matter of just wonder with my worthy tutor, and two or three fellows of that learned society, ——that a man who knew not so much as the names of his tools, should be able to work after that fashion with 'em.   (I, xix, 52–3)

Despite Ashton's interest in training youth for the church, undergraduates at Jesus were taught no theology; that subject was to be saved for postgraduate study. So Sterne's professional training was confined to a little civil law, that branch under which fell ecclesiastical law. But no one who hoped to be ordained could scamp the duty of attending every Sunday the university sermons at Great St Mary's, which may have given them the basics of theology.

Sterne would have been encouraged to read on his own and would have had the time for it. Those hours probably provided the best part of his education at Cambridge. Filtered through the ingenious forged Sterne letters of William Combe comes a comment upon this matter which very probably is genuine in substance, perhaps even in wording. In Combe's version, Sterne says of Lynford Caryl, 'He used to let me have my way when I was under his direction, and that showed his sense, for I was born to travel out of the common road and to get aside from the highway path and he had sense enough to see it and not to trouble me with trammels.'[1]

In recommending reading, his tutors followed Daniel Waterland's *Advice to a Young Student*, first published 1706, but reprinted 1730 and 1740. In *Tristram Shandy* Sterne labelled Yorick's philosophical learning, 'Waterlandish knowledge' (VI, xi, 427). Waterland, a celebrated moralist and theologian, was a tutor at Magdalene College. After opening with such maxims as 'Avoid idleness, otherwise called lounging', he gets down to study methods: spend mornings and evenings on philosophy and afternoons on classics, 'as requiring less coolness'. Divinity, as one might expect, is a study for Sunday and holidays. To prepare oneself in classics, he recommends Terence, Virgil and Cicero to be read 'over and over again as models', especially Cicero, a model for the orations the student must perform as part of his examinations. Greek classics are also on his lists – Xenophon, Sophocles, Thucydides, Aristotle, but especially Plato. In the philosophy of law, it is Puffendorf and Grotius; in morality, Malebranche and Stillingfleet. In fact, many modern writers are recommended by Waterland – Descartes, Whiston, Boyle, Samuel Clarke; and he repeatedly mentions the importance of Locke and Newton. In short, Waterland's recommendations cover most of the authors whom any self-respecting gentleman would have wanted to read. Sterne borrowed in his sermons from several divines on Waterland's list, in fact, from Waterland himself; and he referred in *Tristram Shandy* to some of the philosophers. He may have read them first at Cambridge. Other writers who influenced him profoundly – Shakespeare, Cervantes, Rabelais, Swift, Pope – were ignored by the tutors. These were the popular authors, read for delight. No one thought to lecture on them.

In 1735 Sterne matriculated, not late (as has been said), but on the schedule of Jesus College, which trained students two or three years before presenting them as bona fide members of the university.[2] Thereafter, he prepared for his examinations.

Early in 1736, when his tutor thought him ready, his name was entered in the *Supplicats*. The 'Acts' (or 'Exercises') were so constantly modified during the first half of the century that we cannot know how demanding they were for Sterne; probably they were easy. He was given two weeks' notice when he would appear in the Schools, and he responded by submitting

[1] Letter No. 2, dated 17 July 1764, in *Original Letters of the Late Reverend Mr. Laurence Sterne*, 1788. Harlan Hamilton believes the sentence is Sterne's: see his 'William Combe and the *Original Letters . . .*', *PMLA*, LXXXII (1967), 420–9, esp. n. 24.

[2] University archives: *Matriculations*; cf. CROSS, 27.

to the moderator three questions upon which his acts were to be based. Two of these were mathematical; the third, 'the moral question', was traditionally taken from Locke or Samuel Clarke. Since Sterne could decide which of these would be debated first, we can guess that he chose Locke. On the appointed day, he mounted a rostrum and faced his opponent across the room, another student, on his own rostrum. Sterne opened the debate by reading in Latin an essay on the first question. The opponent then presented a syllogistic argument against Sterne's statement, to which Sterne responded in Latin, casting his reply as well as he could in the terms of formal logic. The debate went on until the moderator was satisfied. Debates on the other questions against a second and third opponent followed, but they were short. A few weeks later Sterne would have appeared at the Senate House for his university examinations (later called the Senate-House examinations). Since these evolved from hollow rituals at the beginning of the century to the difficult Tripos of the next century, we judge that they had at least some substance when Sterne took them. The procedure was informal: any regent of the university could appear and ask the students any question he wished, but traditionally a mathematical question. His last examination 'by the Father of the College' was completely meaningless. Dr Ashton – if he acted in the typical way – would have told the candidates ahead of time what he would ask and what they should reply. The purpose of the little farce was only to fulfil one of the outmoded statutes of the university. No objections being raised to Sterne's performances, he was allowed to take the Oaths of Supremacy and Allegiance and to sign the university *Subscription Book*. His name was then entered in the *Grace Book* and his degree was thereby assured.[1]

Ultimately, one has to judge the value of Sterne's Cambridge education by his mature work. Forty or fifty years ago, hardly anyone would have thought to describe him as a philosophical novelist, yet such is the prevailing opinion today. No less a critic than Sir Herbert Read has called him 'one of the world's greatest humanists'.[2] It is difficult to imagine any author attaining that compliment whose years at the university had not been profitable.

He had almost a full year more to remain in college: his degree would not be granted until January, and he would linger on for another two months

[1] Documents at the university archives. Examinations: WINSTANLEY, 43–57; Wordsworth, *Scholae Academicae*, 36–8.

[2] Foreword to Arthur H. Cash's *Sterne's Comedy of Moral Sentiments*, Pittsburgh, 1966.

after that. But no more lectures in the hall. His time was to be spent in reading theology to prepare for the master's degree. He may have done that. His last year, however, was almost certainly a time for diversions – such as he could afford.

Financially it was a difficult time, with expenses 'too Scantily defray'd', he wrote, 'by my Cosin Sterne . . . & the last Year not pay'd'. Cousin Richard, now married and rearing a family, had fallen into debt. Sterne had to borrow. The college *Steward's Account*, which records small sums lent to students for pipes or candles or coals, does not contain Sterne's name. One infers that he needed more than the steward was prepared to lend and had to turn to some wealthy student. He would not clear this troublesome debt for several years.[1]

Almost certainly the person from whom he borrowed was his new friend John Hall, who would later change his name to John Hall-Stevenson. Hall registered at the college on 16 June 1735. Significantly, Sterne made only one comment about his Cambridge experience in the 'Memoirs': "'Twas there I commenced a friendship with Mr. H[all], which has been most lasting on both sides.' Hall was to become Sterne's crony in their bachelor years, the whet to his wit, the intimate friend who shared his troubles. Critics of eighteenth-century literature, playing the popular game of identifying fictional characters as actual people, assumed that Sterne had represented Hall as Eugenius, the faithful, prudent counsellor of *Tristram Shandy* and *A Sentimental Journey*. If so, it was a joke: Eugenius is a stock character, the confidant, quite unlike Hall, who was never very prudent or wise. He was, however, faithful, in his odd way, and in so far as Sterne captured in the character the archetype of the friend, he may have had Hall in mind. If Eugenius represented Hall, then the famous tragicomic scene of Yorick's death in *Tristram Shandy* accurately prophesied how Sterne's friend would comfort him in his final illness.[2]

Hall arrived at the college a young squire of seventeen. Sterne was a sophisticated twenty-one. By Sterne's standards, Hall was very wealthy. It is surprising that their friendship developed since Hall enrolled as a fellow commoner. Few of that class took up with scholars. Hall, however, would not have considered himself a jot better born than Sterne. His father, Joseph

[1] LETTERS, 40. Evidence of Cousin Richard's debts inherited by his son can be found in the 'Sterne family papers': Halifax Library, shelf mark 2352-5.

[2] TRISTRAM SHANDY, I, xii. On 19 March 1768, the day after Sterne's death, Henry Lord Belasyse wrote from London to his father, Lord Fauconberg, 'Mr Hall attended him [Sterne] throughout his Illness': NEWBURGH PAPERS.

Hall, a prosperous lawyer of Durham, had no distinguished ancestry. His mother's family was more romantic: for two centuries they had lived in a venerable ruin in the far north of Yorkshire called Skelton Castle. Hall's uncle, Lawson Trotter, a Jacobite, sold it to Hall's father. Hall himself inherited it when he was only thirteen.[1] He was well bred, but his claims to aristocracy came primarily from his mother, whereas Sterne, despite the obscurity of his mother, had the surname of a celebrated ancestor. Intellectually and artistically he was decidedly Sterne's inferior, though he was not without ability. He read widely and collected an excellent library at Skelton – since dispersed – but he was not a genuine scholar. He took no degree and probably intended none. His later publications were tasteless. He wrote third-rate verse and talked entertainingly because it delighted him to do so. He was handsome, as one sees from the Philippe Mercier painting at Skelton probably dating from 1740. In his middle age he showed the 'courteous manner' of a 'highly-accomplished and well-bred gentleman'.[2] Sterne may have learned much about social grace from him. The self-conscious talk of 'urbanity' in *A Sentimental Journey* suggests that Sterne cultivated it deliberately. And certainly Hall, who had many family connections and was by nature gay and gregarious, introduced Sterne to a wider circle of acquaintances than he would have had otherwise.

They were soon addressing one another as 'cousin', a term of endearment which they were to continue for the rest of Sterne's life; and it appears that Sterne was soon helping Hall with his studies. A romantic image of these two reading together under a great walnut tree has become traditional. There was such a tree, well over a century old, which filled up the inner court of Jesus College, formerly the cloister.[3] Study under that tree was not particular to these two. It was so large and the court in which it grew so small that no one could escape studying under it – the point of Hall's later verses on the tree:

> At CAMBRIDGE many years ago,
> In Jesus, was a Walnut-tree;

[1] DNB; VENN; SEVEN LETTERS, 22–3; GRAY; CURTIS, 114; J. W. Ord, *History and Antiquities of Cleveland*, 1846, pp. 252–8; Robert Surtees, *History and Antiquities of Durham*, 4 vols, 1816–40, II, 291–2.

[2] Alexander Carlyle, *Autobiography*, 3rd ed., 1861, p. 454; LETTERS, 140.

[3] GRAY AND BRITTAIN say that records of the tree go back to Elizabethan times. Loggan, however, does not show a tree in the inner court in his print of 1690, possibly because it would have blocked the view of the buildings. See also CROFT. Hall's verse from 'My Cousin's Tale', in *Crazy Tales*, 1762, pp. 16–17.

The only thing, it had to shew,
    The only thing, folks went to see.

Being of such a size and mass,
    And growing in so wise a College,
I wonder how it came to pass,
    It was not call'd the Tree of Knowledge.

    . . . . . .

Tho', in the midst of the quadrangle,
    They ev'ry one were taught their trade;
They ev'ry one were taught to wrangle,
    Beneath its scientifick shade.

It overshadow'd ev'ry room,
    And consequently, more or less,
Forc'd ev'ry brain, in such a gloom,
    To grope its way, and go by guess.

Sterne would have introduced his young friend to such pastimes as were available to him, many of which differed little from those of Cambridge students today. Cricket, football and bowls were all being played. Punting on the Cam was as popular then as now. It is amusing to imagine 'Lorry Slim', as he later called himself, standing at the rear of the flat boat, his 'thin, dry, . . . rarified' figure, 'tolerably strait made, and near six feet high' (which you know, madam, was exceptionally high in those under-nourished days), imperfectly covered with a windblown black gown, his small face with red lips and nose 'an inch at least longer than most of my neighbours' showing under a large, round Tudor cap such as undergraduates then wore.[1] Sterne cut a comical figure in the world, though less in his physical person, which was attractive to women, than in his droll manner.

If there was a music society at Jesus, Sterne would have been a member. He delighted all his life to 'fiddle', as he called it, and a bass viol was among his effects.[2] Where else would he have learned to play stringed instruments? Hall and Sterne would also have found college musical concerts interesting because of the guests: townspeople came, bringing their daughters. 'As to the concerts we frequently have in our halls,' wrote a student in 1750,

[1] Wordsworth, *Scholae Academicae*, 24;   [2] LETTERS, 441; MEMOIRS. LETTERS, 240-1.

do they not in some measure contribute, by bringing us into company, to the wearing off that rust and moroseness which are too often contracted by a long continuance in college? And though these meetings are frequented by some, so entirely on account of the company and conversation, that it has been declared that the concert would have been excellent, if there had been no MUSIC in it, yet in general we shall find it otherwise. . . . As to FIDDLING in particular, for my part, I see no absurdity in attracting the eye of the fair by displaying a white hand, a ring, a ruffle, or a sleeve to advantage.[1]

The town of Cambridge, however, was much rougher then. Prostitution was flagrant, and students gambled despite the university prohibitions. They went to cockfights and enjoyed themselves at frequent bullbaitings. They drank and quarrelled and fought in the streets, sometimes with each other and sometimes with townsmen. Little wonder that private instructors in the arts of boxing and wrestling did a thriving business in Cambridge. Sterne and Hall had ample opportunity to get into trouble, but they never did – that we know of. If they permitted themselves forbidden pleasures, they got away with it. The record of the Court of the Vice-Chancellor, to which student malefactors were brought, shows no charge against them.[2] Sterne, of course, would have watched his step: the archbishop had stipulated that a Sterne scholar who was 'notoriously vicious or debauched in his conversation' would lose the scholarship.

Hall's wealth and rank, however, opened opportunities for pleasure which Sterne could not have had on his own. One assumes that Hall often treated his friend because in later years he won a strong reputation for hospitality and generosity.

Very probably they made some excursions to London. Sterne's letters during his triumphal visit to the capital in 1760 suggest that he was familiar with London. We know Hall went there because on 21 November 1735, a few months after he enrolled at Jesus, he was admitted to the Inner Temple.[3] It was not uncommon for students at the university to be enrolled simultaneously at one of the inns of court. Few studied any law: they simply used the inns as clubs and stayed there during their London adventures. Membership admitted them to the Court of St James. In later years

[1] Quoted by Wordsworth, *Social Life,* 202–3.
[2] University archives: *Act Book of the Vice-Chancellor's Court.*
[3] *Admissions to the Inner Temple 1660–1750,* a transcript of the original records at the Inner Temple Admissions Office.

Hall had a house in Westminster where 'he lived as other men of the world do whose philosophy partakes . . . of Epicurius'.[1] Of the situations at Cambridge and at the Temple, Hall concluded that Cambridge was the more valuable. Many years later he wrote to his grandson,

> I should . . . recommend Cambridge as a place infinitely preferable to ye Temple, and particularly on account of ye connexions you may form with young gentlemen of y^r own [age] of ye first rank, men y^t you must live with hereafter: it is the only time of life to make lasting, honourable, and useful friendships. . . . You will observe too y^t ye same income, which will do for ye Temple but which will only serve you to associate with very *middling* company in London, is sufficient for ye first at Cambridge.[2]

Since Hall was interested in the 'first' company at Cambridge, we may assume that he invited Sterne into it when he could. He probably was a member of the Combination-Room Club of Jesus, made up of fellows and fellow commoners, but it is unlikely that he could have introduced a scholar into that group very often. Sterne, of course, might have had his own club, for we know that there were clubs at Jesus for students of his rank. One of them was a club of Rustat scholars, who spent their money on punch, wine and the services of bedmakers.[3]

Hall would have been freer to take Sterne to the Union Coffee House in Jesus Lane, which normally was patronized by fellow commoners. If they were not happy there, the town was full of coffee houses, so popular that they had driven out most of the ale houses. In effect, the coffee houses became political clubs where newspapers were read and political issues debated, the forerunners of the present student union. Roger North, writing early in the century, was shocked at their proliferation:

> . . . it is become a custom after chapel to repair to one or other of the coffee-houses (for there are divers) where hours are spent in talking; and less profitable reading of newspapers, of which swarms are continually supplied from London. And the scholars are so greedy after news (which is none of their business), that they neglect all for it; and it is become very rare for any of them to go directly to his chamber after prayers without doing his suit at the coffee-house;

[1] ANECDOTES, III, 86-8.
[2] SEVEN LETTERS, 17.
[3] *Rustat Accounts:* college archives, TRU. I. 9.

which is a vast loss of time grown out of a pure novelty, for who can apply close to a subject with his head full of the din of a coffee-house?[1]

In the coffee houses Sterne and Hall would have been drawn to the company of young Yorkshiremen of like political sentiments. Since there were fewer than 500 students at the university, they would have had no difficulty distinguishing such allies.

One was John Fountayne, whom Sterne latter spoke of as an 'Old Friend & College Acquaintance'. This young pensioner of St Catherine's Hall was the second son of the squire of Melton, near Hull, a stalwart of Sir Robert Walpole. John Fountayne would eventually become Sterne's dean at York Minster.[2] They probably got to know Edwin Lascelles, son of the squire of Harewood and Stank. He would marry Hall's neighbour, Anne Chaloner of Guisborough. In later years he would serve as Member of Parliament for Scarborough and then for Northallerton.[3] Another friend was Joseph Bridges of St John's College, who ended up with several livings in and about York and became a vicar choral (as the subchanters of York Minster were called). He was 'intimately acquainted' with Sterne in those years, and his wife was close to Sterne's wife.[4] Thomas Gilbert of Skinningrave, close to Skelton, was later a friend of Hall's, dedicating to him his little volume, *Poems on Several Occasions* (1747). He must have impressed the group, for he was already a fellow – of Peterhouse. Gilbert was in love with one of Hall's cousins.[5]

It is not unlikely that Gilbert introduced Hall and his friends to Thomas Gray, for the poet was then an undergraduate of Peterhouse. They may have known slightly Gray's friend Horace Walpole, registered at King's – though not often there. The politically minded students of Cambridge must have been very curious about the son of the 'Prime Minister', as Walpole was jokingly called at the university. Hall later corresponded occasionally with Horace Walpole.[6] But the overrefined Gray and Walpole might not

[1] *Lives of the Norths*, ed. Augustus Jessopp, 3 vols, 1890, II, 292.

[2] DNB; VENN; LETTERS, 33; CURTIS, 28; BM: Add. MSS 32712, fols. 93–4.

[3] VENN; CURTIS, 410; university archives: *Matriculations*. Edwin Lascelles, created Baron Harewood in 1790, subscribed to Sterne's *Sermons* and *A Sentimental Journey*.

[4] VENN; CROFT; CURTIS, 59; Robert Forsyth Scott, *Admissions to . . . St John . . . Cambridge*, 1882–1931, III, 450.

[5] See in his volume, 'Verses writ on a Glass, under the Name of Miss Trotter of Durham'. His career: VENN; CURTIS, 226. He subscribed to the *Sermons*, 1766.

[6] SEVEN LETTERS.

have been comfortable among the rougher young men of Yorkshire, any or all of whom might have made one of that Cambridge party which wounded young Gray's sensibilities:

> Imagine me pent up in a room hired for the purpose, & none of the largest, from 7 a-oclock at night, till 4 in the morning! 'midst hogsheads of Liquor and quantities of Tobacco, surrounded by 30 of these creatures, infinitely below the meanest People you could even form an Idea off; toasting bawdy healths & deafned with their unmeaning Roar.

It is not unrealistic to suggest that future dignitaries of the church might take part in such rowdy parties. It was a very worldly church these men would enter. When Sterne and Bridges were first associated with York Minster, Archbishop Blackburn was still in the see of York. About him Edmond Pyle told the story, 'that on the occasion of a visitation at St. Mary's, Nottingham, he ordered pipes and tobacco and liquors to be brought into the vestry "for his refreshment after the fatigues of confirmation"'.[1] Sterne, though he drank little himself, was never put off by heavy drinking. In his later years he did not smoke, though he had tried it. He loved, rather, the atmosphere associated with that vice: 'my brain', he once wrote,

> will not bear Tobacco, inasmuch as the fumes thereof do concoct my conceits too fast so that they would be all done to rags before they could be well served up – the heat however at 2^d hand, does very well with them . . . I cannot smoak wth You, yet to shew you, I am in full harmony with you, I'll fiddle you a grave movement whilst you pipe it in your way & Hall shall dance a Saraband to us with a pair of bellows & Tongs.[2]

Sterne was quite capable of crude language among his clerical friends. He opened one letter of 1762 to Dr Henry Egerton, Chancellor of Hereford and Treasurer of Bangor, with 'Phelps is a son of a Bitch'. (It was said good-naturedly about Richard Phelps who had dared to tell Egerton that Sterne was not looking well.)[3] Even a smutty joke from his undergraduate days about the saint patroness of Jesus College found its way into *Tristram*

[1] PYLE, 81.
[2] LETTERS, 122. His moderation in drinking: GREENWOOD.

[3] EGERTON LETTERS, AH 2237.

Shandy: 'the pricks which enter'd the flesh of St. *Radagunda* in the desert'. St Radegund is said to have mortified her flesh by applying to it a heated metal cross armed with sharp points.[1] John Fountayne did not completely give up the student art of profanity when he became Dean of York Minster. In his anger he did not hesitate to bestow '*coarse Language and scandalous Appellations*' upon Dr Francis Topham, the pompous Didius of *Tristram Shandy*. The lawyer thought Fountayne 'crude' and 'undistinguished', and his friends at the minster a set of 'warm and violent Men'. You 'have filled your Mouth with much *coarse Language*', complained Topham, 'which it must be allowed you have *discharged* upon the Doctor [i.e., himself] in the *greatest Abundance*, and *most plentiful Manner.*'[2]

Fountayne and his circle of clergy at York were socially versatile, displaying polished manners in public, but in private masculine gatherings reverting to the habits of Cambridge undergraduates. What to succeeding generations sometimes has looked like a split in Sterne's personality between sentimentality and bawdy was probably no more than a refusal to compartmentalize his manners in this way. Sterne, unlike his associates at York, was willing to play up for comic effect the contrast between the manner of the priest and that of the jester. In doing so he disregarded the 'understrapping Virtue of Prudence'. 'I'm sure with regard to Discretion,' he once wrote, 'tho' I have no great communications with her – I had always a regard for her at the bottome – She is a very honest Woman; & I should be a brute to use her ill – only I insist upon it, she must not spoil good company.'[3]

Puerile comedy, however, plays only a small part in Sterne's letters and novels. The dominant note, as modern critics are well aware, is a gaiety touched by melancholy – a humour verging upon tragedy. That too may have roots in Sterne's Cambridge experience. 'I remember', says Tristram, addressing his own animal spirits,

when DEATH himself knocked at my door——ye bad him come

[1] TRISTRAM SHANDY, VIII, xvii, 557; cf. 251. See the compliment to *Tristram Shandy* cast as a mock legal document, dated 19 February 1760, and signed by six Cambridge fellows and undergraduates, including Thomas Twining, BM: Add. MSS 39929, fol. 1. On 18 March 1968 the undergraduates of Jesus College commemorated the bicentenary of Sterne's death with a non-stop, around-the-clock reading in the hall of *Tristram Shandy* and *A Sentimental Journey*. They were so delighted that the following Sunday they commenced in the chapel a non-stop reading of his sermons.

[2] LETTER TO THE DEAN, 13; REPLY, 7, 47–8.

[3] LETTERS, 76, 118.

again; and in so gay a tone of careless indifference, did ye do it, that he doubted of his commission——

'——There must certainly be some mistake in this matter,' quoth he.

Now there is nothing in this world I abominate worse, than to be interrupted in a story——and I was that moment telling *Eugenius* a most tawdry one in my way, of a nun who fancied herself a shell-fish, and of a monk damn'd for eating a muscle, and was shewing him the grounds and justice of the procedure——

'——Did ever so grave a personage get into so vile a scrape?' quoth Death. Thou hast had a narrow escape, *Tristram*, said *Eugenius*, taking hold of my hand as I finish'd my story——   (VII, i, 479–80)

In writing the passage Sterne was probably recalling his first discovery, at Cambridge, of the disease which would eventually take his life – call it tisick, consumption, or (in modern terms) pulmonary tuberculosis. Telling Hall about a similar attack he suffered at Paris in 1762, he recalled what had happened at college: 'I had the same accident I had at Cambridge, of breaking a vessel in my lungs. It happen'd in the night, and I bled the bed full.'[1] Duty, gaiety, mortality: Cambridge prepared Sterne to become a humorist.

His degree was granted, presumably, in January 1736/7, for it was the custom to hold Commencement exercises that month. It was hardly a joyful time. The foundation scholarship had been taken away the month before,[2] and with a degree he could no longer hold a Sterne scholarship. He was penniless and without a patron. Hall had left for his 'grand tour'.

There was no escaping it any longer: Sterne would have to make up his mind now whether or not to be ordained. Today it is popular to say that impecunious eighteenth-century gentlemen usually entered the church because there was nothing else for them. It is not *quite* so simple. Jonathan Swift had a long career as a private secretary before he was ordained. Others sought positions as stewards, went to Westminster looking for a place in the government, or to London to seek admission into some merchant house. Sterne might have run up debts trying these, but they were possible had he wanted to avoid the church. In the end, he chose ordination.

The question of whether or not he was sincerely religious is hardly worth

[1] LETTERS, 180.
[2] Entry for 16 November 1736 in the college *Register*. The last entry for Sterne in *My Lord of Yorke's Statutes* is for Lady-day, 1737.

raising. Almost everyone of that time was. The clergy who attacked atheists from the pulpit had seldom met one. Sterne met an atheist once – or rather, a man whom everyone assumed to be an atheist – David Hume, and promptly engaged him in a public debate about miracles.[1] Rather thoughtless aspersions have been cast upon Sterne's religious convictions, but not by anyone who has looked into his sermons.

The question of whether his *moral* character qualified him for the priesthood is considerably more interesting. True, he never acquired the reputation for licentiousness of some London clergy, such as Samuel Johnson's cousin, Cornelius Ford, or became debauched in that really shocking eighteenth-century fashion demonstrated by his later friends, John Wilkes and Sir Francis Dashwood. But Sterne wore the wrong colour for a sinner of even slight degree, at least for an indiscreet one. It probably was a mistake to take up parochial duties, which confined him to a life too narrow for his restless, gay spirit.

Nevertheless, Sterne decided to enter the church. As any other indigent student who had made that decision would, he asked the fellows of his college for aid. He probably hoped for a place in Yorkshire, but the Jesus College sphere of influence was Cambridgeshire and its surrounding counties. They knew of nothing, it seems, in the north. Sterne was finally forced to settle for a job close by. On 6 March at Buckden Hall, near Huntingdon, he was admitted to the Order of Deacons by Richard Reynolds, Bishop of Lincoln, and licensed to the assistant curacy of St Ives. This settled, he went back to Jesus for a final month, dining in hall until 9 April, the day before Easter of 1737.[2]

[1] LETTERS, 218–19.
[2] *Steward's Account*. Ordination and licensing: the bishop's *Register* at the castle, Lincoln; BM: Add. Chart. 16158.

Early Career
& Marriage
1737–1741

As assistant curate of St Ives, Sterne was at the bottom of 'the hill of preferment', as he later called it,[1] a hill which only a few climbed easily. The church allowed many graduates of Cambridge and Oxford to remain assistants for twenty years or more, sometimes without the dignity of priest's orders. Often they lived in abject poverty, a state which had little or no redeeming moral value for most churchmen. Sterne had known kind clergy, such as Mr Featherston of Annamoe, and devout priests, such as Dr Ashton, but rarely had he met a man of God whose life was rigorously ascetic – except perhaps one or two Halifax dissenters whom he scorned. Although the Wesley brothers and George Whitfield had already held their quiet prayer meetings at Oxford, the evangelical Methodist movement was not yet under way. The clergy whom Sterne knew best were usually responsible, sincerely religious men, but unabashedly worldly in their personal lives. The important thing for a man in Sterne's position was to get a living as soon as possible: under normal circumstances a living could not be taken away, and so provided the cornerstone for a fortune. But livings were bestowed by the Crown, the bishops, or a hodgepodge of individuals and chartered bodies – usually without any regard for the qualifications of the candidate.[2]

Sterne probably wished he could purchase a living – a common practice which entailed no sense of shame since it denoted family prestige. His cousin, Walter Palliser, appears to have had that good fortune. He was

[1] LETTERS, 406.
[2] Norman Sykes, *Edmund Gibson*, Oxford, 1926, Chapter IV; L. P. Curtis, *Anglican Moods of the Eighteenth Century*, New York, 1966; HERRING RETURNS, Introduction; BEST, 46–8 and *passim*; SYKES, Chapter V.

ordained a priest immediately upon graduation and stepped into the vicarage of East (or Great) Drayton, Nottinghamshire. His father and uncle had retired from the army and established themselves as squires in that neighbourhood. Later Walter added two more livings in the area, where he spent the rest of his comfortable life.[1]

For Sterne, or any impoverished man who aspired to the priesthood, there was only one path – as J. H. Plumb put it, 'a well-placed patron and unwavering devotion to politics'.[2] For centuries the powerful had bartered church livings for political support, but no one so systematically and thoroughly as Walpole. Sterne appeared on the scene at the end of the 'golden age of Church-Whig alliance'.[3] Although, as time proved, his commitment to Walpole was not deep, Sterne would have thought himself fortunate in his family's political history, especially in that of his Uncle Jaques, who had laboured arduously for Walpole and, as a result, had risen to prominence in York as precentor of the minster and Archdeacon of Cleveland.

Still, it must have been obvious to Sterne and his other cousin at Cambridge, George Fairfax, that winning the patronage of their uncle would not be easy. George was in the better position because Jaques had some obligations to his parents: the senior George Fairfax had once employed Jaques as his curate and had harboured his unmarried sister, Mary, or Molle. Nevertheless, young George would have to wait six years for his first living and not until his third is there evidence of Uncle Jaques's help. On 28 April 1746 George was presented to the vicarage of Shirton (or Sturton), Nottinghamshire, by the dean and chapter of York, in a meeting where Dr Sterne was one of three voting members.[4] Family influence in return for

[1] VENN; HERRING RETURNS, IV, 6, 42; ACT BOOK, 1733–44, fols. 142–3. The Palliser brothers at Kirk Deighton and North Deighton: DNB, on Admiral Hugh Palliser; Samuel Lewis, *Topographical Dictionary of England*, 1835, on Kirk Deighton; West Riding Deeds, NN/695/1001; ENGLISH ARMY LISTS, IV, 141; V, 139.

[2] *Sir Robert Walpole: The Making of a Statesman*, 1956, p. 71. Walpole's influence over the church: Plumb, *Sir Robert Walpole: The King's Minister*, Boston, Mass., 1961, pp. 92–9. For Plumb's thesis that Walpole's systematic bribery 'cemented the political system': *Origins of Political Stability*, Boston, Mass., 1967.

[3] A period which ended when Edmund Gibson, Bishop of London, broke with Walpole in 1737: SYKES, 36.

[4] CHAPTER ACTS. His career may be traced in GRAY; ACT BOOK, 1744–55, fols. 60, 80–2; 1755–68, fol. 359. His younger brother, Cecil Jaques Fairfax, was admitted to St John's, Cambridge, in June 1745, licensed assistant curate to his brother in 1750, and made a fellow of St John's in 1752: GRAY; ACT BOOK, 1744–55, fol. 269; Robert Forsyth Scott, *Admissions to . . . St. John*, Cambridge, 1882–1931, III, 115.

favours: that was a normal pattern, though Jaques was in no hurry to carry it out. Laurence, who had no claims upon him at all, would have to perform or promise his own favours, and they would have to be political.

Sterne took up his duties at St Ives on Easter Sunday 1737. It is doubtful that he preached that day, but he must have attended services in the large, handsome parish church. We can imagine how, afterwards, the vicar, William Pigot, introduced the slim young gentleman from Cambridge to three stalwart farmers, the churchwardens. If the vicar thought to link Sterne's name with the former Master of Jesus College, there would have been light talk about Richard Sterne's opposition to Oliver Cromwell, who had been a farmer in this community and had served as a churchwarden himself.

Sterne made no entries in the parish registers of St Ives. Probably, beyond the usual duties of visits and secretarial work, he preached whenever Mr Pigot needed relief. He may have stayed there only four or five months. During the summer an opportunity of some sort was opened by the college: on 4 August the fellows made a note that testimonial letters had been written for 'Dominus Sterne'.[1] How long he stayed with Mr Pigot after that can only be guessed.

On 18 February 1737/8, Sterne was licensed assistant curate for the parish of Catton in the East Riding of Yorkshire.[2] He was nominated by the new rector of Catton, Richard Sowray, a graduate of Jesus College. Mr Sowray, after waiting fifteen years for a living, had suddenly been given two – Catton and Askham Richard, in the West Riding.[3] He probably discovered that he could not serve both personally and applied to his old college for an assistant.

Again Sterne left no record in the parish registers, but we can be reasonably certain that he preached regularly and had most of the responsibilities at Catton. Mr Sowray lived at Askham Richard. Sterne's salary was £30 a year – hardly a princely income, but about top for an assistant curate in Yorkshire. Where he lodged, we do not know. He was only a few miles from Elvington, but Cousin Richard had leased the estate and was living in York.

It did not take Dr Jaques Sterne long to discover his promising nephew. On 2 April 1738, possibly six months after Sterne arrived at Catton, but only six weeks after his licence there, his name appeared on the parish registers of Sutton-on-the-Forest, of which he would soon be the vicar.[4]

[1] College *Register*.
[2] INSTITUTIONS, fol. 17; ACT BOOK, 1710–62, fol. 82.
[3] HERRING RETURNS, I, 8, 47, 149.
[4] Parish registers, now being kept by the Sutton churchwardens.

The Reverend John Walker of Sutton, who was seriously ill, must have appealed for help to his superior, the Archdeacon of Cleveland, who was, of course, Dr Sterne. Uncle Jaques called in his nephew. Mr Walker recovered enough to make one further entry in the registers; the others, all in the burial record, are in Sterne's hand. In four months Sterne buried ten parishioners, the last of whom was Mr Walker himself.

On 15 August Archbishop Lancelot Blackburn granted letters demissory to Laurence Sterne to be collated to the vicarage and to receive priest's orders. The archbishop was himself the patron of the living, but we can hardly doubt that he was honouring the request of his friend and ally, Jaques Sterne: as Laurence explained in the 'Memoirs', 'I then came to York, and my uncle got me the living of Sutton'. The archbishop should have ordained Sterne himself, but he was so negligent of his duties that York-shiremen had to go elsewhere for that rite. Sterne set out across the north of England to Chester, where on 20 August he was ordained by Samuel Peploe, Bishop of Chester, in a special service held in the bishop's chapel.[1] It probably is an error in the entry, but it appears from the parish registers that Sterne returned from Chester to Sutton that very day and sometime before midnight administered for the first time a sacrament – the baptism of Robert, son of William Greaves.

On 24 August the archbishop signed a parchment 'collation', and the next day a group of villagers gathered outside the church for the ceremony of induction. Richard Musgrave, parson of nearby Stillington (as well as Marton and Farlington Chapel), was in charge. Philip Harland had stepped across from Sutton Hall and stood scowling, for the squire would have been angered that this nephew of a Whig politico should be thrust upon his village. Following an ancient ritual, Mr Musgrave took Sterne's hand and laid it upon the large key standing in the door to All Hallow's church. While Sterne stood thus, Mr Musgrave read out the 'instrument' of the arch-bishop.[2] Then Sterne unlocked the door, walked in and to the back, seized the rope and tolled the bell. The document was signed, hands were shaken all around, and Sterne had become vicar of Sutton-on-the-Forest.

As soon as he found a moment to himself, Parson Sterne took down the baptismal register and wrote in print capitals at the top of a clean page: 'The Revd Mr Laur: Sterne, Vicar'. He had not presumed to act as the incumbent when he had baptized William Greaves's son five days before,

[1] INSTITUTIONS, fol. 29; BM: Add.   [2] BM: Add. Chart. 16159.
Chart. 16160; CURTIS, 8–9.

but had entered that record at the bottom of Mr Walker's list. On his own list he recorded eight more baptisms that year.

The village of Sutton-on-the-Forest, or Sutton-Galtres, as it was sometimes called, stood amid cleared fields beyond which were bogs and patches of forest – the remains of the great Forest of Galtres. The area was flat and damp. It bordered an ancient Roman road running north from York which, eight miles from town, made an un-Roman sharp turn to the right into Sutton village; another road to the left led to the smaller village of Huby, formerly a separate parish but now combined with Sutton. Close to this corner, facing each other across the road, stood the church and Sutton Hall, the house of the squire.

The Hall, which is still there, is a handsome brick house, surrounded by trees, gardens and a brick wall. The front drawing room, the upstairs back parlour, the garden wall which turns sharply at the corner strongly suggest Shandy Hall, not Sterne's later house at Coxwold, which he jokingly called Shandy Hall, but the house in his novel. Sutton had been the seat of the Harlands for a century. In the church, every monument which can be made out today was raised in honour of some member of that family. One of them preserves the memory of a Harland ancestor who, like the ancestral Sir Roger Shandy of the novel, fought in the Battle of Marston Moor.[1]

The church stood in a small quadrangle, bounded on the east by a dilapidated thatched house – the parsonage. The crudely built square tower of the church dated from the fourteenth century, the stone nave from the fifteenth. It was a small but pleasant church, though very damp, and it opened upon a fine expanse over which Sterne looked to the main entrance of Squire Harland's house.

Philip Harland was a Tory. Five years older than Sterne, he had matriculated at Queen's College, Oxford, and registered at Gray's Inn. His opposition to Walpole was decidedly active, and he was a heavy contributor to that opposition charity at York, the public hospital.[2] His father, Richard, formerly the squire, but now living in York where he practised law, was also an old-fashioned Tory who had campaigned hard for the Country

---

[1] A plaque in Sutton church honours Richard Harland, d. 1689, as a veteran of Marston Moor, but it was not erected until 1766, five years after the appearance of Vol. III, wherein Walter Shandy mentions his ancestor (p. 205).

[2] *An Account of the Public Hospital*, York, 1743, a volume at Minster Library, Hailstone B 8; numerous articles in *York Courant* on the hospital. Harland served on the Grand Jury twice: *York Courant*, 18 March 1739/40 and 15 March 1742/3; CURTIS, 50.

Interest in 1734.[1] During the past two decades the Harlands had controlled every single vote in the village except that of the late vicar. To be sure, the deanery of Bulmer, in which Sutton lay, was a stronghold of the Country Interest,[2] but Sutton was of particular importance because it had more voters than most villages of its size. A century before, sixty yeoman families had been granted freeholds in compensation for common land lost in an enclosure; so now sixty farmers of Sutton and Huby were voters.[3] They worked daily with the Harlands and were happy to vote with them.

Sterne's major political task, we can hardly doubt, was to try to win some of these votes for the Ministerial Party. But he would also have been expected to look after the financial interests of the church which were being threatened by the Harlands and their farming friends. Both Richard and Philip Harland had been trying out the new techniques of farming within enclosed fields, and their several closes had hemmed in the church lands and lowered their value. The old vicar, a virtual Mr Quiverful with a large family to support from one mediocre living, had been helpless to stop them. In fact he could not even give the archbishop a satisfactory account of what was happening. At one point, His Grace had been constrained to send a spy into the village to size up the political and economic situation, one James Borwick.[4] Little wonder that Sterne, the new representative of the archepiscopacy and the party of Walpole, should write in his 'Memoirs', 'as to the Squire of the parish, I cannot say we were upon a very friendly footing'.

Sterne's parish duties were not very demanding at this period, and there was nothing he could do for the archbishop at once. The crop on the church glebe was being harvested for Mrs Walker, and she and her numerous brood were still living in the parsonage. Eventually they found a cottage and stayed on in Sutton, one of the boys growing up to become a curate for Sterne. A local tradition says that Sterne lived for a time in Church Farm, west of the church, renamed in his honour a century ago 'Laurence House Farm'. Perhaps he had rooms there during this period. Almost certainly he also had lodgings in York and spent much of his time there. For his travels

---

[1] Buried at Sutton 16 May 1750; served as an officer of the castle and judge of the quarter sessions: QUARTER SESSIONS, 25 July 1732; 22 July 1746; *York Courant*, 16 May 1749; POLITICKS, 12.

[2] Cedric Collyer, 'Yorkshire elections of 1734', LPS, VII (1952–5), 53–82.

[3] Thomas Gill, *Vallis Eboracensis*, 1852, pp. 407–13; LAWTON, 462–4; *Victoria County History . . . York: North Riding*, II, 196–202.

[4] Borwick to Archdeacon Thomas Haytor, 7 February 1733/4, in the Church Commissioners file, Borthwick Inst.

back and forth he would have bought a horse, perhaps a handsome one, and a 'demi-peak'd saddle, quilted on the seat with green plush', such as Parson Yorick had bought 'in the pride and prime of his life' (I, x, 18–19).

In April 1739 Sterne hired an assistant curate, Richard Wilkinson. It was an unusual move, considering that he had only one living, and debts besides. Probably he was encouraged by his uncle, who had an eye to the coming political campaign. Jaques may have thought his nephew could best serve by making himself known. In any event, Sterne established many friendships in Yorkshire during this period. From April 1739 until he let Mr Wilkinson go two years later, it is virtually certain he lived in York.

The old city of York seems small today, and charming. Its great minster, the intact medieval wall, mellow timber houses, handsome brick Georgian houses, and that crazy little street called the Shambles, we value for their quiet beauty and as a link with the past. Sterne as a young man must have seen it as a buzzing centre of commerce, associated in his mind with his own Jaques and Rawdon ancestors. He was aware of the crowded roads and the sloops tied up at the wharves. York had a nautical air then, when ocean-going ships sailed up the Ouse, and the streets were full of mariners. He would have been fully aware that the king's officers ruled the north of England militarily and judicially from York Castle, that the archbishops from their palace at Bishopthorpe governed all the Northern Province of the Church of England.

Sterne lodged in the vicinity of the minster, almost certainly, in the area dominated by clergy which lay within the north corner of the old wall. Much of that section was included in the Liberty of St Peter, a political entity governed by the dean and chapter. A portion of the Liberty was cut off physically – the Minster Yard, defined by walls, houses and gates which were kept locked at night. The crowded buildings within have mostly been cleared away now and replaced with gardens. Then a great many people lived in the Minster Yard. The portion belonging to the archbishopric, north-west of the Minster, with its tumbledown gothic buildings, had been leased for a century or more to the Irwin family and was being used for many profane purposes. An ancient cloister (a small section of which still stands) had been turned into a makeshift theatre, and the old chapel of the archbishops was being used as a hay barn – the very chapel which has since been converted into the fascinating minster library. Between these and the Minster was 'Lord Irving's Square', now a broad expanse of grass, then a jumble of rotting stone, the remains of medieval buildings. One of the minster gates opened into the north end of Stonegate (-*gate* as a suffix in Yorkshire means 'street' – a Norse word). Here stood the shop of Charles Pearson who made clerical gowns and riding habits. Except for the modern display windows, Stonegate looks much the same now as then. The narrow street behind it, Grape Lane (a dialectal rendering of Grope Lane), was the street of the prostitutes. Another minster gate opened into Lop Lane (now Duncombe Place), which was beginning to look modern with new houses and a street lamp.

On the south side of the town, Micklegate and Castlegate had rows of fine new houses built by rural gentry who found it cheaper to spend their leisure time at York than at London. The city purposely courted them for their money and tried to develop suitable diversions. Outside Micklegate Bar (one of the fortified gates in the city wall) were the broad, level fields called Knavesmire, because executions took place there. The gentry raced their horses over these fields, and Race Week (which still goes on) had become a gay festival of every August which brought noble and gentle families from all over England to enjoy the excitement of the races and the round of entertainments and balls.

The York assembly rooms, designed by the celebrated Earl of Burlington, had only recently been built. Many thought the ballroom the finest in England, but others found its Corinthian columns too heavy for the room. A contemporary complained that the behooped ladies sitting behind them might as well have 'hid themselves in the cloisters of a cathedral'. The ballroom, wrote Tobias Smollett,

> might be converted into an elegant place of worship; but it is indiffer-ently contrived for that sort of idolatry which is performed in it at present: the grandeur of the fane gives a diminutive effect to the little painted divinities that are adored in it, and the company, on a ball-night, must look like an assembly of fantastic fairies, revelling by moon-light among the columns of a Grecian temple.[1]

It is unlikely Sterne could have afforded a subscription to the assembly rooms, and there is no reliable evidence that he was a member before the period of his fame. But many of his neighbours subscribed, and he must have gone at times as a guest. Would his friends not have been astonished

[1] *Humphry Clinker*, 1771, II, Matthew Bramble's letter of 4 July; Arthur Young, *A Six Months Tour through the North of England*, 4 vols, 1770–1, I, 182–5.

to know that thirty years later the ladies and gentlemen of the assembly rooms would be doing a country dance named, in Laurence Sterne's honour, 'the Tristram Shandy'?[1]

There were other, free entertainments. Arthur Young much admired the walk being built along the river, winding at the midway point through a grove of trees. In one direction he could see open meadows; in the other the impressive arch of Ouse Bridge; 'the sloops, barges, boats, and business of the river, are most lively objects for this very agreeable walk'. If the weather was unseasonable, there was the nave of the minster, where the fashionable went to promenade round and round beneath the high arches.

Theatrical companies came and went. That of Thomas Keregan played in the makeshift theatre in the Minster Yard. One of the members, John Arthur, tried to raise a subscription for a permanent company, explaining that he would take care to select actors and actresses who 'might be as sociable off the stage, as entertaining on it'. Another theatre, in Mint Yard, gave its patrons good return for their money, offering *Romeo and Juliet* (songs between the acts) combined with the pantomime, *Merlin: or, the British Enchanter*.[2]

Sterne probably played his viol with a musical society, perhaps also a violin. One acquaintance reported that a decade later he was playing first violin with such a group, very likely the music club which met at the George Inn in Coney Street.[3]

Sterne would have attended many Sunday services at the minster, or the evensongs, when the choirboys sang like angels over the richer voices of the paid 'song-men' – as indeed they still do. But having many friends among the clergy of other York churches, he might have attended almost anywhere. He must have had experiences similar to that of another young bachelor clergyman, Edmond Pyle:

> I had like to have lost my heart at York. It is a terrible thing to have such a place in the church as I have; – nothing but ladies by dozens (& very pretty ones) on the right hand or the left, or in front of my stall. But, through mercy, having the service to read, I was forced to look, at

[1] R. Grundy Heape, *Georgian York*, 1937, p. 47. The *York Courant* regularly listed prominent people who attended the Race Week balls at the assembly rooms, and some subscribers are named in the *Assembly Rooms: Minute Book*, a MS at the York Public Library.

[2] YORK PRESS, 189–91; handbill at BM: 1878. d. 19.

[3] MARRIOTT; *York Courant*, 29 September 1742.

least, as much upon the rubrick of the book as upon that of their cheeks![1]

Sterne's acceptance at York was made easy by his name. Cousin Richard, now living in a house in Castlegate, made him welcome.[2] A little later Richard would move to Fulford, or Gate Fulford, south of the city, presumably to pursue his hobby of gardening. He was a member of a fashionable gardener's club, and once served as major-domo for their Florist Feast, complete with a flower-decked parade through the city.[3] Richard was not very intellectual, and his wife was so poorly educated that she could not sign her name. But he was proud of his family and honoured their founder by paying for the plate of Archbishop Sterne's monument in Dr Francis Drake's *Eboracum* (1736), the great history of York and its minster.[4] Although Richard was heavily in debt to his Uncle Jaques and to his brothers-in-law,[5] he stabled a chestnut hunter and kept two 'couple' of beagles. At least once he served on the Grand Jury.[6]

We have no specific evidence which would connect Sterne with his Cousin Timothy, Richard's younger half-brother. Timothy had a townhouse in York, though he lived primarily at Shipley, near Bradford. Timothy turned out to be such an imprudent man that one imagines that Sterne would have found him amusing. His highest accomplishments were services as a Grand Juror – once – and as a governor of the Bradford grammar school. At the age of fifteen he married a Miss Wigglesworth. But he loved horse-racing and gambling, and within a few years he would squander his entire inheritance, including Woodhouse and the estates of the Booth family.[7]

[1] PYLE, 168.

[2] The evidence that Sterne saw his cousin socially during this period is indirect: a year after Richard's death, his widow, Mary, was remarried at Sutton on 10 October 1745, to John Baird of Leith, merchant. Possibly she was living with Sterne and his wife, but more probably she had come to be married by Sterne out of a personal attachment to him. Necessarily her friendship with him would have developed during this period. This Mary (mistakenly called Ann by CLAY) was the daughter of a Bradford attorney named Thompson, but she regularly signed all legal documents with the mark of 'X'. She married (1) William Swaine of Bradford;

(2) Richard Sterne; (3) John Baird of Leith, with whom she settled at Brayton, near Selby: 'Sterne family papers' at Halifax Library, shelf mark 2352–5.

[3] *York Courant*, 24 July, 7 August 1739; 22 January 1739/40; 8 April 1746. MINSTER REGISTERS, YAJ, XV, 147–8.

[4] P. 465.

[5] 'Sterne family papers'.

[6] *York Courant*, 18 March 1739/40; his will in CLAY.

[7] CLAY; *York Courant*, 29 July 1740; 20 November 1744; 8 April 1746; 24 November 1747; administration of the goods of Timothy Sterne, 13 January 1746, at the Borthwick Inst. He is noticed by Tom Sutcliff, 'Some old Warley houses', HAS,

It may have been something of a problem for Sterne to see much of these cousins without losing favour with Uncle Jaques, for both Richard and Timothy had broken the family's political tradition and gone over to the Country Interest. Nevertheless, Sterne probably shared with them the family sorrows and joys. He may have attended the funeral of Richard's sister Anne, who died a spinster in the spring of 1738, and the baptism, followed two days later by the funeral, of a little girl born to Mary and Richard on 2 June of that year and named Anne for her late aunt. A more joyful occasion was the birth of Richard's heir, the fifth Richard Sterne, born at the Castlegate house in January of 1739/40.[1]

Sterne saw a great many people other than his family. The Red Lyon Inn near Monk Bar was a favourite place where he sometimes received his mail.[2] He must have passed many hours at the George Inn, in Coney Street, where the Walpole party held their meetings. In his earliest known letter, dating from November 1739 and addressed to the Reverend John Dealtary, rector of Skirpenbeck, he speaks of receiving fourteen letters in a three-week period.[3] His manner in a social gathering was always winning: 'A man of prodigious wit', his servant said, '& the entertainment of every company.'

John Hall was back from the Continent, and Sterne spent some time in his company at Skelton Castle and probably in York. There may have been revels with other young men, perhaps their old Cambridge friends. But Sterne 'never drank to excess', said Greenwood, his servant: 'he usually after dinner took one glass of wine, of which he drank half, & filled his glass with water for the rest.' Probably it was women, not wine, which hurt Sterne's reputation. It was whispered about that he 'delighted in debauchery'. That was how Matthew Robinson passed on the gossip he had heard from Dr Henry Goddard,[4] a young physician living at Foston, not far from Sutton.

In July 1740 the names of Peter Torriano, Frederick Keller and Laurence

---

1918, pp. 33–67; and H. W. Harwood, 'Four Midgley farms', HAS, 1939, pp. 213–16. The report that he served as a governor of Heath School, Halifax, probably arises from a confusion of Timothy Sterne with his grandfather, Timothy Booth; the very full record of the school at the Borthwick Inst. makes no mention of him. C. D. Webster, in 'Halifax attorneys', HAS, 1963, pp. 69–87,

identifies his wife as the daughter of William Wigglesworth, attorney of Slaidburn.

[1] *York Courant*, 22 January 1739/40. CLAY misdates the birth as 22 February.
[2] LETTERS, 46. The inn has only recently disappeared; not to be confused with the present Red Lyon in Fossgate.
[3] DEALTARY LETTERS, fols. 141–2.
[4] CLIMENSON, I, 73.

Sterne appeared together in the *Grace Book* of Cambridge;[1] presumably they had become Masters of Arts on the first Tuesday of July, the traditional Commencement Day for those receiving graduate degrees. They were supposed to have been studying theology for the previous year, and they would have presented letters testimonial asserting that they had led scholarly, studious and morally upright lives since receiving their first degrees. The master's was legally an earned degree, but the examinations were 'huddled'. Sterne privately enacted some sort of charade before the Proctor so that the university could say that the statutes had been complied with. The ceremony itself was farcical. Each 'inceptor' came forward, took the hand of the Proctor, and swore that he would reside at Cambridge for five years, would teach daily in the Schools, and would teach at no university but Cambridge or Oxford. The society which placed so heavy an emphasis upon vows as to make the right to hold office and to vote depend upon them quietly encouraged its best-educated men to break their word.[2]

We can imagine how the three friends, now 'regent masters', celebrated that evening. Sterne then returned to York, and the next time he was out at Sutton-on-the-Forest he proudly wrote in the parish register, 'Laurence Sterne Created Master of Arts at Cambridge July – 1740 – '.

He was not, however, completely free of his obligation to the university. He was expected to continue his study of theology and to return a year later for another exercise called 'dissing', or sometimes 'cursus disputationis'. Curiously, the university did not neglect this posterior examination, though its content escaped recording. Sterne did return to Cambridge, as the *Steward's Account* shows, in June 1741.[3] Torriano was there too, and Keller, of course, as a fellow.

To our knowledge, this was his last visit to Cambridge. Probably at this time he brought a gift to Jesus College, a portrait of Archbishop Sterne. The painting still hangs in the hall, a poor copy of the portrait at Bishop-thorpe Palace. An inscription on the frame says only that it was a gift to the college of Laurence Sterne, an alumnus.

It was the last time Sterne would see Torriano. This young man had served for three years as an assistant curate at Whittlesford, close to Cam-

[1] University archives, fol. 495.
[2] WINSTANLEY, 62–4.
[3] College archives, A/C. 7. 5. Sterne was charged full rate for meals for three weeks following Midsummer Day, though he need not have been present during that entire period.

bridge, but it seems he was not happy in a clerical career. He was preparing to marry and to go fortune-hunting in Jamaica. He was destined to die in Jamaica soon after his arrival.[1]

On 6 January 1740/1, the *York Courant* announced that the Reverend Laurence Sterne would succeed Dr Samuel Baker as prebendary of Givendale in the minster. Dr Baker was to become chancellor of the cathedral. On the sixteenth, Archbishop Blackburn signed the collation. Sterne owned in the 'Memoirs' that his uncle had obtained this post for him also. It would not be long before they would open a newspaper war against the Country Interest.

On Monday the nineteenth, Dean Richard Osbaldeston, the Reverend Thomas Lamplugh, and the Reverend Robert Reynolds gathered in the icy chapter house for the ceremony of induction.[2] Normally the winter meetings of the chapter were summarily adjourned to the vestry, where there was a fire, but this one had to be held in the chapter house and the choir. Sterne 'appeared personally in his Choir Habits', and the chapter formally

> . . . admitted him the said Laurence Sterne in his proper person to the Canonry in the said Cathedral Church and to the prebend of Givendale . . . together with all its rights members and appurten-ances by the Delivery of a Book and Bread and receiving him their Brother and Canon in the said Church by the kiss of Charity which doing the said Laurence Sterne took the Oaths of Symony and the accustomed Oath . . . of the Church of England . . .

The kiss of charity was corporal and a good deal more real than the Oath of Symony. It seems not to have worried Sterne that in the course of accepting a preferment in exchange for political work he swore never to buy or sell any church office: the eighteenth-century clergy raised no such questions. This part of the ceremony made Sterne a 'canon'. He still had to be made a 'prebendary', and for that purpose the little group marched into the draughty minster and back to the choir, where they were met by one of the vicars choral, the Reverend John Fuller. Mr Fuller, acting as the archbishop's representative, now installed Sterne in the original sense of that word: he placed him in the stall of the choir reserved for the prebendaries of Given-dale. They then marched back into the chapter house for another oath, and

[1] GRAY; VENN.
[2] CHAPTER ACTS; INSTITUTIONS, fol. 55; ACT BOOK, 1710–62, fol. 103.

The summons, schedule, and induction papers at Minster Library: Box D 1.

'the said Laurence took his place in the Chapter'. Then, with the said Laurence acting as a member, they went through the entire ceremony again to induct Dr Baker into the chancellorship. They must have been half frozen by the time they got to the vestry.

The simultaneously held offices of canon and prebendary are puzzling to us, used as we are to a more streamlined church. The canonry was the older office, dating from the early Middle Ages when the dean and his subordinate priests (who obeyed the Canon Law) performed their one major duty, singing the praises of God, independently of any bishop. The later, espiscopally organized church corrected that: the Archbishops of York traded control of the chapter for tracts of land given to each canon for his personal use. Thus he became a prebendary, for the word *prebend* means a portion of church income. Although for a time the archbishops ruled absolutely, during the Reformation much of the power was returned to the dean and chapter. In Sterne's time, a new member of the chapter was appointed by a concurrence of the archbishop with the dean and chapter.[1] What he is called depends upon local custom. In eighteenth-century York, he was a *prebendary*, though today at York the title of *canon* is used.

Sterne's only official duties were to preach in the minster on the fifth Sunday after Epiphany and the twenty-sixth after Trinity.[2] He sometimes has been blamed for not participating more often in chapter meetings, but that arises from a misunderstanding. Chapter business was conducted by a small clique of residentiaries and prebendaries living in York. Although Sterne had a legal right to take part, it would have been a presumption to do so without an invitation from the residentiaries.

Sterne probably had cause to complain as he later did of 'the Expences of coming into my Preferments'.[3] An assortment of fees had to be paid to the archbishop's registrar, the dean and chapter registrar, to this person and that. The clergy were continually plagued with fees in any sort of legal proceeding or preferment, and those associated with the minster were unusually high. So Sterne's elevation was a gamble which made him particularly interested in the potential returns of the stall.

The 'prebendal estate' which went with Givendale included a large tract

---

[1] Sterne may have understood these matters from reading Edmund Gibson's *Codex*, which he once borrowed from the Minster Library: BARR. They are explained admirably in BURN.

[2] A schedule of the sermons is to be found in a little book at the Minster Library, Thomas Ellway, *Anthems: for Two, Three, Four, Five, Six, Seven, and Eight Voices*, 2nd ed., York, 1753.

[3] LETTERS, 40.

of land at Poppleton and another at Givendale. Officially, Sterne now became the lord of the manor of Givendale. But both tracts had long been leased to the family of the Earl of Carlisle, of Castle Howard, and so long as the lease remained in force Sterne's income would be precisely £10 a year.[1] The leasing of land in eighteenth-century York was a gambling game: leases were drawn, not for a specified period of years, but for the length of life of 'the longest liver' among the people named on the lease. Givendale, as most estates associated with the dean and chapter, was leased for three lives. When the last of those three people died, the lease would expire. It could then be renewed or made out to another party, but for the new lease Sterne would collect a large 'fine'. The prebendaries of York counted themselves lucky if they were able to collect a fine once during their tenure.

These churchmen, naturally enough, kept an eye on the health of the people named on their leases, and those in the inner circle of the cathedral watched carefully the condition of lessees of those prebends which might soon change hands. Of the three people named in the Givendale and Poppleton deed, two were already dead and the third was very ill – facts which Dr Jaques Sterne must have known very well when he sought this preferment for his nephew. The longest liver was Charles Howard, Viscount Morpeth, a twenty-three year old nobleman who was being talked about as a candidate for Knight of the Shire in the Country Interest. All the politicos were watching his delicate health. Despite an advanced consumptive illness, the young man was elected, but he died a few weeks later, on 9 August 1741. His death precipitated the contested by-election in which Sterne would play an active part.

On 12 November Sterne renewed the lease of the entire prebendal estate to Lord Morpeth's father, the Earl of Carlisle. He must have collected a fine of about £150 – quite a sum for Sterne, whose living returned only about half that every year.[2] One must not read any sinister meaning into the fact that Sterne was dealing with the leader of the Country Interest. It was unthinkable not to renew a lease to the party who was farming the land – so

---

[1] Legal documents related to Givendale estates are at the office of the Church Commissioners, London: Files 13,876, 2,812; and at the Borthwick Inst.: 'Givendale prebendal estates: deeds 1697–1797'.

[2] Dean Osbaldeston's renewal of the lease upon lands at Fangfoss to Lord Carlisle, mentioned below, was recorded in *Deanery Leases*, Minster Library: S 3 (5) a, fol. 27. Carlisle paid a fine of £121, but the annual rent came to only £8. 1s. 6d. The annual rent for Givendale estate was £10. If the proportion of rent to fine was the same for both transactions, Carlisle would have paid Sterne a fine of £150.

long as they were willing to pay the fine. At this very time, Dean Osbaldeston, a leader of the Ministerial Party, renewed to Lord Carlisle the lease of Fangfoss, in the dean's prebendal estate. Although politics in Yorkshire was not very gentlemanly, business was.

Four years after completing his BA degree, Sterne was well established. 'He seated himself quietly in the lap of the church; and if this was not yet covered with a fringed cushion, 'twas not naked.' (For once, Dr John Hill's hackwork biography of 1760 rings true.)[1] His status as prebendary would hardly have impressed men of power, for it carried no patronage. Nevertheless, it gave him local prestige and a respectable title to the outside world. 'Direct for me, *Prebendary of York*', he would write on his business correspondence. His income, though below average for the clergy, was better than one might expect for a young man. It would improve before long.

He was now in a position to get married – something he had been thinking about for a year. In the autumn of 1739 he had fallen in love with a lady whose identity he disguised. Who 'Miss C——' might be is a mystery, as are the circumstances surrounding this love affair. Sterne alluded to them in that earliest-known letter addressed to the Reverend John Dealtary.[2] 'I never wishd for your Company so much in my life as Just now,' Sterne wrote,

I have a thousand things I want to talk over with you, which are only fit for Conversation, & cannot well be committed to paper: I must let you know this much; That you have now received a Letter from one of the most miserable and Discontended Creatures upon Earth; Since I writ last to you, I have drawn Miss C—— into a Correspondence; in the Course of which together with her Consistency in acting towards me, since the beginning of this affair; I am convinced she is fixed in a resolution never to marry, and as the whole summ of happiness I ever proposed was staked upon that single Point, I see nothing left for me at present but a dreadful Scene of uneasiness & Heartache.

There is something in my Case very extraordinary and out of the Common Road which I must not venture to Acquaint you with by Letter for fear of Accidents &c—— I could easily be eloquent in my wishes for others; since now I have nothing left, to wish for myself; If a hasty Prayr for y^r wellfare will show my sincerity, 'May you Enjoy a life of uninterrupted Calmness & repose unruffled either with pas-

[1] *Royal Female Magazine*, 1 May 1760, as reprinted in *London Chronicle*, 3–6 May 1760.

[2] DEALTARY LETTERS, fols. 141–2.

sions or Disappoi[n]tm^{ts} or, if the wish is too extravagant, & it must be supposed, that some of the ten thousand different heartaches, I am struggling with, must one time or other be y^r lot; Then 'May you find a friend ready to hear & pity you; whom both honour & humanity may Instruct to act towards you with sincerity and good nature. It probably happens well for you that I have a great many letters to answer this Post; otherwise I should not know how to give over. I am in great hast

Y^{rs} Affectionatly

L. Sterne

His letter about Miss C—— was written from Skelton Castle; he and Hall had just returned from Durham where, probably, they had visited Miss Anne Stevenson of Manor House. Two months later, on 12 February 1739/40, the *York Courant* announced, 'Last Week John Hall, of Skelton-Castle, Esq.; was married to Miss Stevenson, a young Lady of 25,000 l. Fortune. The Ceremony was perform'd by the Rev. Mr. Sterne of Sutton-Forest' – interesting enough news to be carried the next week in the *London and Country Journal*.

Anne's portrait, at Skelton Castle, shows a pretty, dark-haired girl of a sweet expression. Nine months later she bore a son, also named John, and the following year a second son, Joseph-William. Hall-Stevenson (who had added his wife's surname to his own in order to win her fortune) may have been happy in these years, though later he was disgruntled about his marriage.

The pattern now taking shape in Sterne's life is recognizable. He had grown tired of the bachelor life; his closest friend had married an attractive and wealthy girl; he had decided to take that step himself but had been rejected. He was ripe for another love.

'At York I became acquainted with your mother', Sterne wrote to his daughter in the 'Memoirs', 'and courted her for two years – she owned she liked me, but thought herself not rich enough, or me too poor, to be joined together.' If we take the words strictly, they indicate that he was courting his future wife at the same time as Miss C——; that may be the case, though Sterne was often inaccurate in the chronology of his own history.

Elizabeth Lumley in the winter of 1739/40, if that was when Sterne met her, was twenty-five years old and living in her own house in Little Alice Lane within the Minster Yard. It would seem that after the death of her parents, when she was fifteen, guided no doubt by some relative or guardian, she had invested part of her modest fortune in this house and moved there. The churchwardens of St Michael le Belfrey, the parish church of the area, left a record of a house belonging to a 'Mrs Lumley', which they assessed annually for taxes from 1731 to 1740. The house changed hands before the 1741 assessment, made after Elizabeth was married.[1] It must have been one of several timber houses which then stood opposite St William's College within the afternoon shadow of the minster and just inside the east minster gate, an ideal location for a young woman interested in young clergymen. With whom she lived we do not know, but one feels certain she had a proper companion. 'Tho' she was but a homely woman, still she had many Admirers, as she was reported to have a Fortune, and she possessed a first rate understanding', said John Croft. Her cousin, Matthew Robinson, implied that she was no beauty in his comment upon the problems she would face upon her marriage: 'What hopes our relation may have of settling the affections of a light and fickle man I know not, but I imagine she will set about it not by means of beauty but of the arm of flesh.'

Elizabeth came from a good family, but her father, the Reverend Robert Lumley, was a man of unpleasant disposition and spendthrift habits. With little or no fortune of his own, he married a wealthy widow and quickly ran through hers. Elizabeth's mother, born Lydia Light, had first married Thomas Kirk, a well-known virtuoso and the squire of Cookridge Hall in Adel, near Leeds, who left her the estate at his death. Cookridge was a handsome place with formal gardens and a labyrinth, famous in its time, containing '65 centres' and '300 Views'. Lumley had no certain occupation when he married Mrs Kirk and moved into Cookridge, where Elizabeth was baptized on 13 October 1714. They lived in great luxury and had a constant succession of visitors, but it appears their fortune was inadequate to that life. Lumley was offered the living of Bedale, in the North Riding, which he was happy to have since it was one of the most wealthy livings in Yorkshire. They sold Cookridge to the Duchess of Buckingham and moved into the parsonage at Bedale where they continued to spend money as fast as it came in. When Lumley died a few years later, in April 1729, he left only a small fortune. His wife died shortly afterwards, leaving two teenage girls with

[1] Minster Library: *St. Michael le Belfrey Account Book, 1730–1752*. The marriage register of the minster identifies her as living in 'Little Alice Lane, within the Close of the Cathedrall'. The street, then called Little Alice Lane for a diminutive woman who had kept an ale house there, has now been given the bland name of College Street.

meagre incomes and expensive tastes, ill equipped to become the helpmeets of the struggling parsons they married.[1]

Lydia, the younger sister, was the first to marry. She was pretty and likeable and not very discreet. She married the Reverend John Botham, at the time only an assistant curate. Botham was an unimaginative man with a puritan streak oddly contrasting with his love of luxury. Through wealthy relatives of his (an uncle, Henry Legg, became Chancellor of the Exchequer in 1754), they knew many people in polite society and were tempted into living beyond their means. They soon became destitute, objects of the charity of relatives.[2]

After Sterne began to pay his court, Elizabeth went for a long visit to the Bothams in Staffordshire where, Sterne said in the 'Memoirs', 'I wrote to her often'. Three of those letters to 'my L', as he called Elizabeth Lumley, survive.[3] In the earliest, Sterne's expressions of love are warm and romantic

[1] For the date of Lumley's death, misrecorded by VENN and others, see *York Courant*, 22 April 1729. Other information on the family from CLIMENSON, I, 55 and *passim*; MINSTER REGISTERS, YAJ, II, 321; *Registers of the Parish Church of Adel* (Thoresby Soc., V), 1907, p. 120; Ralph Thoresby, *Ducatus Leodiensis; or the Topography of . . . Leeds*, 2nd ed., 1816, pp. 157-62, 187-8.

[2] CLIMENSON, I, 180-1, 230-1; II, 54-5; CURTIS, 435.

[3] LETTERS, 16-19. CURTIS, 12-16, gives his reasons for believing that a fourth letter of this group (No. I in his edition) was forged by Lydia Sterne from passages in Sterne's *Journal to Eliza*. I agree that we cannot accept the letter in the form which Lydia gave to it in her edition of 1775 (where it appears as the second letter), though I am doubtful that the *Journal* was Lydia's source. Previous to the appearance of his LETTERS, Professor Curtis had published his opinion of Letter I in TLS, 23 June 1927. He was answered by Margaret R. B. Shaw on 21 July 1929, and 6 June 1935. Miss Shaw, who argued for the authenticity of the letter, continued her case in *Laurence Sterne: The Making of a Humorist*, 1957. Recently, her opinion has been supported on new grounds by Duke Maskell, 'The authenticity of Sterne's first recorded letter', N&Q, CCXV (1970), 303-7. (See also Edwin Clark, 'Sterne's letters are a mystery', *New York Times Book Review*, 15 January 1928, pp. 1, 25.) The controversy is of interest to philologists because, if the letter is genuine, it contains the earliest recorded use of the word *sentimental*: B. Sprague Allen, 'The dates of *sentimental* and its derivatives', *PLMA*, XLVIII (1933), 303-7. Claude Rawson, University of Warwick, in a detailed analysis (not yet published) argues convincingly that the question is still open, though he declines to pronounce upon the authenticity of the letter. Rawson's analysis suggests a hypothesis as yet unexamined by any of these scholars: the letter in question, I would suggest, was modelled, not upon the *Journal to Eliza*, but upon a letter to Mrs Draper in Sterne's hand, now lost. As we know, letters which Sterne wrote concurrently with the *Journal* frequently contain remarkably close parallels to that document, not necessarily because Sterne was copying from one to the other, but possibly because the ideas and phrasing were fresh in his mind. Lydia, according to my hypothesis, would have found the letter to Mrs Draper among her

– perhaps blindly romantic, since love promises escape from the world, rather than strength with which to face it:

> Yes! I will steal from the world, and not a babbling tongue shall tell where I am – Echo shall not so much as whisper my hiding place – suffer thy imagination to paint it as a little sungilt cottage on the side of a romantic hill – dost thou think I will leave love and friendship behind me? No! they shall be my companions in solitude, for they will sit down, and rise up with me in the amiable form of my L.[1]

The next letter is considerably more controlled, giving the impression that the lover finds it hard to shake off the habits of a sermonist: '. . . my L. has lodged an indictment against me in the high court of Friendship – I plead guilty to the charge, and intirely submit to the mercy of that amiable tribunal . . . a too easy pardon sometimes occasions a repitition of the same fault.' He follows with two little sermons, the first on how people excuse their moral faults – suggestive of his famous sermon, *The Abuses of Conscience* – and the second on the topic of 'parsimony in esteem'. Again he declares a romantic faith in the natural goodness of man, a recurrent theme of his sermons: 'nature never made an unkind creature – ill usage, and bad habits, have deformed a fair and lovely creation.' He is lonesome: 'return – return – the birds of Yorkshire will tune their pipes, and sing as melodiously as those of Staffordshire' – not a very good line for Laurence Sterne, but he had not yet found his idiom.

The last letter is sombre. He tells Elizabeth about the death of an older friend and consoles her upon a similar loss. As to love, it is a bit ominous that Sterne has offended her again: 'What could tempt me to it! but if a beggar

father's effects at Shandy Hall. I suspect that Lydia never saw the *Journal*, or else she would have destroyed it after making what use she wished of it. Probably Sterne took the *Journal* to London and left it at his death in the hands of a friend (Mrs James?), and thus it was separated from his other papers. In any event, Lydia, I suggest, found a letter to Mrs Draper, changed the date, altered the names of the servants to disguise what she was doing, and readdressed it to her mother. Ultimately, I agree with Professor Curtis that Lydia tampered with her father's papers in order to distract the public from his affection for Eliza Draper and to pay a compliment to her mother, though I disagree with him about her original source. The other three of the letters addressed to Elizabeth Lumley, Curtis decided, 'may be accepted with less caution'. I too accept them, having no good reason to do otherwise. The style in some passages seems unworthy of Sterne, but Sterne wrote in many styles.

[1] Cf. SENTIMENTAL JOURNEY, 115–16.

was to knock at thy gate, wouldst thou not open the door and be melted with compassion. – I know thou wouldst, for Pity has erected a temple in thy bosom.'

Pity may have been an easy emotion for Elizabeth, but its temple was really in the breast of her fiancé. Obviously, Sterne was fascinated by the emotion long before he began to write fiction. In the 'Memoirs', he took care to explain how pity had played a key role in this courtship. At Elizabeth's return from Staffordshire, he said,

> she fell into a consumption – and one evening that I was sitting by her with an almost broken heart to see her so ill, she said, 'my dear Lawrey, I can never be yours, for I verily believe I have not long to live – but I have left you every shilling of my fortune;' – upon that she shewed me her will – this generosity overpowered me. – It pleased God that she recovered, and I married her in the year 1741.

The incident cannot have precipitated Sterne's proposal, for he had long been begging Elizabeth to marry him. But it remained in his memory as one of the most significant moments of the courtship.

In later years, when a distance grew between the husband and wife, Sterne felt himself drawn to other women who evoked his pity. Eliza Draper was in poor health and was trapped in a hopelessly unhappy marriage. He created a fictional character of this sort in Madame de L*** of *A Sentimental Journey*, and in one scene has Yorick anticipate the 'moral delight' of sitting beside her all night drying her tears while he listens to 'the sickening incidents of a tale of misery' (pp. 145-6). Consumption, which was Elizabeth's disease as well as his own, had a special fascination. Sterne was later moved by and attracted to Miss Sarah Tuting, who was dying of consumption. 'The gentle Sally T----', he wrote in a letter to her,

> is made up of too fine a texture for the rough wearing of the world – some gentle Brother, or some one who sticks closer than a Brother, should now take her by the hand, and lead her tenderly along her way – pick carefully out the smoothest tracks for her – scatter roses on them – & when the lax'd and weary fibre tells him she is weary – take her up in his arms——
>
> I despise Mankind, that not one of the race does this for her – You know what I have to say further——but adieu.   (p. 224)

Without attempting the hopeless task of making a psychological analysis of a man dead for two centuries, one can still point out an obvious pattern in this character. Men who long for a weak woman to love and care for are sometimes worried about their masculinity: they are attracted to women whose limited demands will pose no threat. The thought is reinforced by Tristram Shandy, the first novel in our literature which gives a central place to the theme of impotency. This is not to say that Sterne was actually impotent; but he may have suffered anxieties about his adequacy – altogether a different matter.

If Sterne thought he was marrying a weak woman whom he could love pityingly and care for tenderly, he was naïve. Elizabeth had a very different side which was well known to her peers. We have an excellent witness in her cousin, Elizabeth Robinson, who became the famous bluestocking, Elizabeth Montagu. (Mrs Montagu's father and Elizabeth Lumley's mother were half-brother and sister, children of one mother by her two marriages.)[1] Elizabeth Robinson was younger, closer in age and affection to Lydia Lumley, with whom she carried on a long correspondence. Though she had grown up in York and lived in the Great House in the Minster Yard, she left that city before Elizabeth Lumley moved there and avoided her when she returned for visits. But in later years Mrs Montagu had a vivid memory of her cousin, whom she described as 'very absurd' in her manner of making enemies, 'but her Father was of ye same sort'. 'She was always taking frump at somebody & forever in quarrels & frabbles.'[2] On another occasion she wrote,

> M[rs] Sterne is a Woman of great integrity & has many virtues, but they stand like quills upon the fretfull porcupine, ready to go forth in sharp arrows on ye least supposed offence; she w[d] not do a wrong thing, but she does right things in a very unpleasing manner, & the only way to avoid a quarrel with her is to keep a due distance. I have not seen M[rs] Sterne since I was a girl in hanging sleeves, but I know her character well.[3]

Sterne and Elizabeth would not have a happy life together.

In speculating upon this ill-fated love, one must guard against over-simplification. His later history does not suggest that Sterne simply fell out of love when he discovered his wife's faults. On the contrary, it suggests that for most of their years together Sterne and Elizabeth continued to love

[1] CLIMENSON, I, p. 1 ff.
[2] Letter to her sister, Sarah Scott, 11 April 1765, MS at Huntington Library: MO 5820.
[3] Letter to Leonard Smelt [?September 1768], MS at Huntington Library: MO 4999.

each other in some sense despite frequent, violent quarrels. Their life to-gether was a torment because their antagonisms were accompanied by an ambivalent attraction. We see this with remarkable clarity in the description of them by John Croft: 'Sterne and his Wife, tho' they did not *gee* well to-gether for she used to say herself, that the largest House in England cou'd not contain them both, on account of their Turmoils and Disputes, they were every day writing and addressing Love Letters to one another.' No doubt the very fact that Elizabeth could *write* accounts for much of the attraction. Educated women were rare, and Sterne, in later years, found him-self drawn to bluestocking types such as Mrs Montagu, Elizabeth Vesey and Eliza Draper.

Once the engagement was declared, the thought of a wedding did wonders for Elizabeth's recovery. 'I never saw a more comical letter than my sweet cousin's, with her heart and head full of matrimony', Elizabeth Robin-son wrote to her sister; 'pray do matrimonial thoughts come upon *your recovery*? for she seems to think it a symptom'. Even planning household economies had become thrilling to Elizabeth. They had consulted Dr Jaques Sterne and upon his advice entrusted her small estate to Sterne's hands.[1] They were moving to Sutton where they could live frugally.

> I do not comprehend what my cousin means by their little desires [wrote Elizabeth Robinson]; if she had said little stomachs, it had been some help to their economy, but when people have not enough for the necessaries of life, what avails it that they can do without the super-fluities and pomps of it? Does she mean that she won't keep a coach and six, and four footmen? What a wonderful occupation she made of courtship that it left her no leisure nor inclination to think of any thing else. I wish they may live well together.[2]

They were married in the minster on 30 March 1741, the day after Easter. Although we have no details of the wedding celebration, it must have attracted some attention: the cathedral was not parochial, and only a few weddings were allowed, to people of some status. This bridegroom had recently become a member of the chapter and entered the political lists on the side of the predominantly Whig clergy. The dean himself performed the ceremony,[3] as Sterne proudly noted in his own parish register at Sutton:

[1] LETTERS, 39–40.
[2] CLIMENSON, I, 74.
[3] The entry in the MINSTER REGIS-

TERS, YAJ, III, 93, reads, 'The Reverend Mr Lawrence Sterne and Mrs. Elizabeth Lumley, of Little Alice Lane, within the

Laurence Sterne A M. Vicar of Sutton on the Forest and Prebendary of York, was married by the Revd Dr Osbaldeston Dean of York to Elizabeth Lumley, the 30th Day of March 1741 (being Easter Munday) in the Cathedral——

By Licence

A popular comic story of Sterne's getting up in the pulpit the morning after the wedding and preaching upon the text, 'We have toiled all the night and have taken nothing', is obviously apocryphal: the wedding was on Monday, not Saturday.[1] Neither can one accept John Croft's fiction that Elizabeth herself popped the question in the assembly rooms, from which 'they went off directly . . . and were married'. There was no hasty elope-ment. A lot of unhistorical flotsam collects about the figure of Sterne.

Elizabeth Robinson was soon passing on the news of the wedding. 'Mr. Sterne has a hundred a year living, with a good prospect of better prefer-ment. He was a great rake, but being japanned and married, has varnished his character.' She did not know how thin was the varnish.

The joys of the honeymoon were followed by hard work. Sterne's lodgings had to be closed and Elizabeth's house sold. By early May they were at Sutton-on-the-Forest. Elizabeth found no 'little sungilt cottage on the side of a romantic hill'; it was a run-down house on the boggy flats north of the Great Forest. It would be their home for the next nineteen years.

Close of the Cathedrall. (Lic. Mar^d by Richd Osbaldeston, the Dean).' At the Borthwick Institute, among the Dean and Chapter of York Marriage Bonds and Allegations, may be found Sterne's alle-gation (what we might call an application for the marriage licence) and bond (an agreement to forfeit £200 if he failed to complete the marriage), both dated 28 March 1741, and signed by Sterne – shelf mark D/C. MB.1741.

[1] CURTIS, 15, attributes the story to John Seward. It appeared also in the so-called 'Joe Miller's' jest-book of 1793, *The History, Witty Questions, and Answers of that* *Noted Philosopher, the Miller of Whittingham Mill*; another version in *Spirit of English Wit; or, Post Chaise Companion*, 5th ed. [18--], p. 345. John Croft told another story in his own jest-book, *Scrapeana: Fugitive Miscellany*, 1792, p. 32: 'Mr. S----- meeting a Lady in the street the day after he was married; she wished him joy. On which S. replied, "I thank you kindly, Madam, but I have had quite enough."' Biographers have sometimes rifled *Scrapeana* for stories of Sterne, but it is no more than a jest-book, for which Croft claimed no historic validity.

Politics

1741—1742

The first issue of the *York Gazetteer* appeared on 10 March 1741, three weeks before Elizabeth and Laurence were married. Dr Jaques Sterne, it would seem, put up the money for this newspaper, the first in Yorkshire to support the Walpole party; Laurence provided most of the writing talent. Sterne probably welcomed the opportunity to repay the man who had obtained for him his living and prebend: 'my uncle and myself were then upon very good terms', he said in the 'Memoirs'. But it is hard to imagine his generating much enthusiasm for a ministry which had been responsible for the Jamaican fiasco of 1731, and he found it difficult to work with his uncle. In the end the partnership would turn into a disaster. 'He quarrelled with me afterwards', Sterne said of his uncle, 'because I would not write paragraphs in the news-papers – though he was a party-man, I was not, and detested such dirty work: thinking it beneath me – from that period, he became my bitterest enemy.'[1]

Sterne could hardly have helped but compare his father – simple, athletic and courageous – to his present mentor – shrewd, energetic, combative in the political lists. Jaques's history was as opposite from that of Roger as can be imagined. While his brother was fighting in Flanders, Jaques had taken up the family scholarship at Jesus College. In the crisis of 1714, when England withdrew from the war, when Bolingbroke and Ormonde were setting up the nation for a Jacobite takeover, Jaques witnessed an attempted counter-coup at Jesus College. Two slightly older friends tried – unsuccess-fully – to wrest control of the college from its Tory master, Dr Ashton.[2] The Whigs, when securely in power, amply rewarded these young

[1] In his letter to his uncle of 1751 (LETTERS, 41), Sterne implied that their quarrel began at this time: he spoke of ten years of persecution.

[2] GRAY AND BRITTAIN, 110.

champions. Thomas Herring became, in time, Bishop of Bangor, Archbishop of York and Archbishop of Canterbury; Matthew Hutton succeeded him in each post. But Jaques, perhaps cheated by his youth and undergraduate status, did not play a major role in the Jesus College revolt, and was destined to enjoy a less spectacular career.

After a brief period in Nottinghamshire serving as curate to his brother-in-law, George Fairfax, Jaques withdrew temporarily from the church. He came to York, where he courted and won a wealthy widow sixteen years older than he. She was the daughter of Sir John Goodrick, Bart., of Ribston, though not his heiress, as some have thought, but the heiress of her first husband, Charles Mosley. She had no children by either marriage. Jaques was soon in control of a good deal of land, most of it in the West Riding, but he was too restless to settle into a life of leisure.[1] In 1720, shortly after his wedding, he was ordained. In 1723 he became rector of Rise – propitious name. To this village in the East Riding he moved with his wife, where he began to rebuild the rectory in that impeccable taste he showed whenever it came to material objects.[2] But his unbounded, perhaps manic, energy took him back to Cambridge, where in 1724 he took the degree of Doctor of Laws – an earned degree at that time, which gave him excellent credentials for legal work within the church.

A rabid Whig, Jaques soon became chaplain and political henchman to the archbishop whom the Whigs had recently placed at York, Lancelot Blackburn. In 1729, two years after a bitter county election campaign, he received the additional livings of Hornsey and Hornsey-cum-Riston, as well as the prebend of Apesthorpe at the minster (exchanged in 1731 for that of Ullskelf). He was a leader in the last-ditch political battle of 1734, for which he received unusual rewards – an additional prebend at Southwell Cathedral, the archdeaconry of Cleveland, and the precentorship of York (a preferment which required him to exchange his prebend for that of Driffield). He immediately 'protested residence' and was received by the dean and chapter as a canon residentiary. His income from these benefices came to over £900 per annum.[3] His total income can only be guessed. He turned over his

[1] CLAY; *Dugdale's Visitations of Yorkshire*, ed. J. W. Clay, Exeter, 1894, pp. 56–7. On Jaques Sterne's land holdings: West Riding Deeds, NN/695/1001; OO/746/1063; PP/453–454/671; SS/25/38; UU/213–214/290–1.
[2] ACT BOOK, 1710–62, fol. 87. On the

rectory: George Poulson, *History and Antiquities of the Seigniory of Holderness*, 2 vols, 1840, I, 415. The dining room which Jaques added to Gray's Court is universally admired.
[3] J. Sterne to Newcastle, 24 November 1752, BM: Add. MSS 32730, fols. 285–6.

parishes to curates and moved to York, where he leased from Bacon Morritt the 'Little House in the Minster Yard', traditionally occupied by high churchmen. It was part of a complex which included the Treasurer's House and the 'Great House', now called Gray's Court. Eventually, in 1742, he bought the larger portion and moved into the Great House.[1]

His influence in the church was now considerable. As Archdeacon of Cleveland, he was chief administrator of the northern quarter of the diocese and chief judge of its ecclesiastical court. As precentor and residentiary, he became the chief business manager of the minster. We see him, in the minster records of this period, bustling off to London to inspect the chapter properties there, signing leases, collecting fines, paying off workmen and songmen, supervising repairs of the minster fabric. Since the chapter had numerous advowsons, his patronage was sought by many. Most penniless young clergymen would have sold their souls to the devil for such an uncle.

A month before the *Gazetteer* appeared, Sterne had preached a special sermon at the minster upon the request of the dean and chapter. The day was 4 February, 'being ye time appointed by his Majesty for a Public Fast'.[2] The fast was occasioned by the declaration of war in December against France and her allies. Walpole's long peace policy had failed at last. Yielding to popular demand, he had allowed the nation to be drawn into, first, a relatively minor naval war with Spain, and then the growing European conflagration, the War of the Austrian Succession. Walpole's hold was weakening. Many older Whigs, angered by the shift of policy, withdrew their support, and those who had cried for the war now began to complain of

On his professional career: CLAY; GRAY; VENN; CURTIS, 29; HERRING RETURNS, II, 88–90; III, 35–6; ACT BOOK, 1733–44, fols. 28, 56–8; 1744–55, fol. 262; CHAPTER ACTS, 29 October to 8 November 1735; 8–13 April 1750; 29 May 1755.

[1] A tradition persists at York that he lived in the Little House, but the only documentary evidence I have discovered is in Dr John Burton's *British Liberty Endanger'd*, 1749, p. 14. Speaking of an incident in 1745, Burton referred to Jaques Sterne as 'a Tenant of B[aco]n M[o]rr[i]ts'. Matthew Robinson (father to Elizabeth Montagu) sold the Little House to Bacon Morritt and the other two parts (the Great House and Treasurer's House) to Edward Finch. At Finch's death in 1742, Jaques bought the Great House and Treasurer's House for £1,200. But perhaps he had not yet moved into the Great House in 1745, although he was there the next year. In 1752, he sold the Treasurer's House to Dr Francis Topham, for an unknown sum; and in 1757, sold the Great House for £2,000. The Treasurer's House is now a museum; the Great House is now occupied by St John's College. See Mrs Edwin Gray, *Papers and Diaries of a York Family, 1764–1839*, 1927, esp. p. 3.

[2] Minster Library: *St. Peter's Account-book, 1720–69*, 12 February 1740/1.

rising taxes and poor management. Everyone wondered whether the Parliament to be dissolved in March might be the last in which Walpole could find sufficient support.

Sterne, in his brief political career, was active in a regular election and a by-election, both of critical importance because their outcomes might mean the retention or fall of Walpole. The regular election, following the dissolution of Parliament, involved two seats for Knights of the Shire – representatives of the entire county – and other seats for various boroughs, including the city of York. Sterne and his uncle were primarily concerned with the county elections, though keenly interested in all of them. The by-election of the winter of 1741–2 was to choose a single Knight of the Shire. Only weeks after the regular election a seat won by young Lord Morpeth was vacated by his untimely death. The contest to elect his successor was the climax of Sterne's adventure into politics.

Elections in which people actually voted were rare; usually representatives were chosen by nomination alone. Only when two opposing groups nominated candidates was there a contest followed by a poll. Contested elections were expensive and had to be paid for by local gentlemen.

Modern historians are generally agreed that by the middle of the century there were no genuine political parties in England, no discrete, cohesive, disciplined in-group and out-group institutions. The Whig and Tory parties had been very real in the reign of Anne, but during the long period of the 'Whig oligarchy' the party system disintegrated. At mid-century, there was much use of the names *Tory* and *Whig*, but no real organizations behind the words.[1]

Sterne entered politics on the side of a temporary organization of Walpole supporters. His uncle might refer to their group as Whigs, but the opposition called them sneeringly the 'Court Party' or, when they were of a mind to be more accurate, the 'Ministerial Party'. In Yorkshire, supporters of Walpole had a more valid claim upon the word *party* than others because they used some bold devices of organization which effectively unified their efforts.

[1] Throughout this chapter, I depend upon L. P. Curtis's invaluable POLITICKS. My information on county politics is taken in part from Cedric Collyer's articles, 'The Rockinghams and Yorkshire politics, 1742–1761', *Publications of the Thoresby Society*, XLI (1946–53), 352–82; 'Yorkshire elections of 1734', and 'Yorkshire elections of 1741', LPS, VII (1952–5), 53–82, 137–52. For national politics, I depend upon Sir Lewis Namier, 'Monarchy and the party system', in *Personalities and Powers*, New York, 1955, pp. 13–38; Namier, *The Structure of Politics at the Accession of George III*, 1963; J. H. Plumb, *The Origins of Political Stability*, Boston, 1967; and Geoffrey Holmes, *British Politics in the Age of Anne*, New York, 1967.

Their opposition was a disorganized, heterogeneous group of old-fashioned Tories (some few of whom were quiet Jacobites), disaffected Whigs, disappointed place-seekers, and rural squires of an independent cut. The squires dominated and gave the name to this group – 'the Country Interest'. There had been a 'Country Party' of sorts ever since the reign of William and Mary; Walter Shandy identified himself with these fiercely independent squires, drawn together by a distrust of courts and government. The Country Interest of the 1740s, a larger group of dissidents, hated taxes, dissenters, 'placemen' and the army. It was against their nature to form a genuine party organization, and usually it was immaterial to them whether their fellows called themselves Tories or Whigs.

The 'country gentlemen' had controlled county politics in Yorkshire until 1727, when the newly organized supporters of Walpole fragmented them. That year the Ministerial Party came up with an excellent candidate – Cholmley Turner, a 'Home Born Bairn', as Sterne called him. Turner, the squire of Kirkleatham, an old-fashioned type who appealed to the northern squires, won in 1727. Encouraged, the Ministerial Party decided in 1734 that it could take the second shire seat too, but in this it failed despite a bitter campaign which used – as a later parliamentary investigation showed – every corrupt practice known to either side. Turner, however, kept his seat, demonstrating that he was his party's only real hope.

In that election of 1734 several local leaders emerged who would play a part in Sterne's life. On the side of the Country Interest was Dr John Burton, whom Sterne would immortalize in *Tristram Shandy* as Dr Slop. The physician led his party's campaign at Wakefield, where he then lived, and personally brought a caravan of rowdy Wakefield electors into York for the polling. There he guarded a polling booth, operated a spy network, and defended his people when they were set upon by rioters. In the intervening years Burton moved to York, where he continued his successful technique of trading medical care for votes from the poorer electors. He was also an indefatigable worker at his profession, and a remarkably successful practitioner for one who prescribed 'the fine Filings of a pewter Spoon' as a laxative to remove worms. He prospered so far as to be able to lease the new 'Red House' in Lop Lane, from which he could watch the comings and goings of the clergy through the south-west gate of the Minster Yard.[1]

Then Dr Burton conceived a new politico-medical scheme: he gathered

[1] Robert Davies, 'A memoir of John Burton', YAJ, II (1877–8), 403–40. The prescription: Burton to Mr Priestly, 27 November 1738, Minster Library: KK 28.

subscriptions to build a charity hospital. Because the hospital was badly needed, many of Burton's political opponents contributed. Still, the Country Interest made all the propaganda they could out of it. Richard Sterne made a contribution; Philip Harland of Sutton-on-the-Forest gave the land for the building; and both were on the first board of governors. The Honorable Lady Elizabeth Hastings then willed the Infirmary £500 and conveniently died before she was talked out of this rash move by Dr Jaques Sterne.[1]

The Infirmary opened in April 1740 and during its first year admitted 198 patients – a spectacular success and perfectly timed for the elections. Dr Burton was one of the original staff physicians. The two staff surgeons were passionate old-style Tories – Dr Francis Drake, the famous historian of York, and Dr John Fothergill (not to be confused with Sterne's friend Marmaduke Fothergill, squire of Bishop Field).[2]

What is more, Drs Burton and Drake had bought a large measure of control of the *York Courant*. No doubt its owner and editor, Caesar Ward, an admirably fair-minded and intelligent man, was sincerely committed to the Country Interest; but he was under the thumb of the rasher Dr Burton, who in 1738/9 had forced into bankruptcy the previous owner and put Ward in his place. Dr Drake also helped Ward financially, but not until a little later, in 1744, when he rescued Ward's printing business at the time that Ward's partner ran up heavy debts and committed suicide. Dr Drake, a widower, lodged in Caesar Ward's house, and it was understood locally that he did a good deal of anonymous writing for the paper.[3]

[1] *British Liberty Endanger'd*, 16. On Lady Elizabeth Hastings: M. G. Jones, *Church Quarterly Review*, CXXIX (1939), 71–90.

[2] *An Account of the Public Hospital*, 1743, at Minster Library: Hailstone B 8; numerous articles about the hospital in *York Courant*. Sterne scholars have confused Dr John Fothergill with Sterne's friend, Marmaduke Fothergill, Esq., an easy mistake since both men were active in the Country Interest. John Fothergill, the physician, can be identified from the correspondence of Sir Miles Stapylton with Lord Hardwicke and Lord Malton at BM: Add. MSS 35602, fols. 61–72. He was a quiet Roman Catholic, as the list of contributors at the Bar Convent reveals: shelf mark 3 B/10. (Not to be confused with the famous London physician of the same name, who came from Carr End, near Richmond in the North Riding, but who was a Quaker: DNB; Hartley Coleridge, *Worthies of Yorkshire and Lancashire*, 1836, p. 694ff.) Marmaduke Fothergill, styled 'Esq.', who was active in public affairs throughout Sterne's years in Yorkshire, was the son of the Reverend Marmaduke Fothergill, vicar of Skipworth and Pontefract. The son was heir to his cousin, the squire of Bishop Field: SKAIFE; George A. Auden, *Historical and Scientific Survey of York and District*, 1906, p. 231; obituary in *Gentleman's Magazine*, 1778, p. 392.

[3] YORK PRESS, 241–8; Thomas Gent, *Life of Thomas Gent*, ed. Joseph Hunter, 1832, pp. 191–2; *York Courant*, January and February 1738/9. On Dr Francis Drake:

From this distance it is impossible to demonstrate the details of the political activities and writings of these three Tory medical men, but there can be no doubt that they earned in the elections of 1734 and 1741-2 the implacable hatred of Jaques Sterne. Dr Fothergill, it appears, escaped the precentor's revenge, but both Burton and Drake would suffer heavily at his hands during the black days of the Jacobite rebellion of 1745.

On the Ministerial side, the leader was Sir Thomas Watson-Wentworth of Wentworth House, who for services in 1734 had been created Earl of Malton. Eventually he became the First Marquess of Rockingham. He was a high-handed man who alienated many of his party. Sterne seems never to have known him personally, although he became a friend of his son, the Second Marquess.

More important to Sterne's story was the witty, unscrupulous, eighty-two year old Lancelot Blackburn, 'the jolly old Archbishop of York', as Horace Walpole called him, 'who had all the manners of a man of quality, though he had been a Buccaneer and was a Clergyman; but he retained nothing of his first profession except the seraglio'. Many stories were circulated about his amorousness, inspired, in part at least, by a charge of adultery brought against him years before when he was sub-dean of Exeter. In point of fact, he was exonerated. The rumours were revived in 1743 and recorded in a poem, *Priestcraft and Lust; Or Lancelot to his Ladies, an Epistle from the Shades.* The tales of his buccaneering derived from an obscure period in the Leeward Islands, where he went after graduating from Oxford. He did not, as some said, steal a fiddle at Oxford and run away to sea; he was paid the customary bounty from the Crown to clergy going abroad. Whatever the details of his activities there, in later years he confessed to the Duke of Newcastle that he had once been a spy. One account, printed in the *Gentleman's Magazine*, makes him out a chaplain to a pirate ship and tells a tale of his fight with the ship's lieutenant. The two rowed ashore, says this writer, and Blackburn unfrocked himself to do battle. They placed themselves on the edge of a cliff and agreed that the victor would have the right to roll the vanquished over the precipice. 'The lieutenant went down and Blackburn started rolling him toward the cliff when the man came to and cried hold.'[1] Blackburn as prelate was not so vigorous, except in services to the king and Walpole. He neglected every clerical duty which required more than the

DNB; Robert Davies, 'A memoir of Francis Drake', YAS, III (1873-4), 33-54.   [1] *Gentleman's Magazine*, 1777, p. 376.

movement of a pen. Still, he was a clever political organizer and controlled a faction loyal, not so much to Malton, as to Walpole himself.[1]

Another important figure among the Whigs was a cousin of Sterne's by marriage, Thomas Pulleyn, squire of Burley Hall near Otley, Clerk of the Peace for the West Riding. Pulleyn, a widower, married in December 1739 Mary Sterne, a spinster of thirty-five, erstwhile hostess of Woodhouse during Sterne's boyhood.[2] Also working for the Ministerial Party were Sterne's later patron, Lord Fauconberg; his dean, Richard Osbaldeston; and the vast majority of the clergy.

Election activities of an official sort began on 23 July 1740, when the Country Interest called a nomination meeting at York. 'Many Gentlemen, Clergy, and Freeholders' were said to be there, though in fact they were mostly squires. Timothy and Richard Sterne were among them. The Earl of Carlisle, of Castle Howard, who heretofore had called himself a Whig, appeared and asserted his leadership by placing the names in nomination. His selection of Sir Miles Stapylton to retain his place as Knight of the Shire was a formality. The second nomination was their bid for the seat of Cholmley Turner: Carlisle nominated his twenty-two year old son, Charles Howard, Lord Morpeth. They were very confident. Three months later, on 27 October, their allies, the Freemen of York in the Country Interest, met at the Guildhall and made two nominations for the city election: Sir John Lister Kay to retain the seat he held, and Godfrey Wentworth to win the other.

The Ministerial Party should have met both challenges at once, but in fact they could not. They did make nominations for the city election – Edward Thompson, already in a secure seat, and Sir William Milner as his running mate. As to candidates for the Knights of the Shire, they were in trouble. Cholmley Turner, their only vote-getter among the squires, was a man of independent mind, not close to Malton. He was saying privately

[1] DNB; HERRING RETURNS, I, xxii; Norman Sykes, 'The buccaneer bishop: Lancelot Blackburn, 1658–1743', *Church Quarterly Review*, CXXX (1940), 81–100; Sykes, 'The cathedral chapter of Exeter and the general election of 1705', *English Historical Review*, XLV, 260–72; Horace Walpole, *Memoirs of the Reign of King George the Second*, 3 vols, 1846, I, 87.
[2] CLAY; MINSTER REGISTERS, YAJ, I, 308; III, 90; *York Courant*, 25 December 1739; Catharine Pullein, *The Pulleyns of Yorkshire*, Leeds, 1915; Cedric Collyer, 'Yorkshire elections of 1734', LPS, VII (1952–5), 53–82. See also at the York Public Library: MS *Assembly Rooms: Minutes Books*. Pulleyn was an antiquarian and so styled in the borrowers list of the Minster Library; at the BM is a chartulary of Fountains Abbey which he once owned: Add. MSS 3770.

that he would not run. His only child, a son, had recently died, and he was out of spirits and unwilling to face public life. Still, he kept his party dangling by refusing to make a public declaration.

Dr Jaques Sterne, furious with Turner as he probably was, held his peace and went quietly to work for the city contest. According to Dr Burton, the precentor was caught red-handed stealing the sacrament money from the minster, supposed to be given to the poor, and depositing it in the political fund of his party, but the story has never been confirmed.[1]

When the *York Gazetteer* appeared in March, the colophon, written by its founder, put the cards on the table: 'As this Paper is partly set on Foot, to correct the Weekly Poison of the York-Courant, 'tis hoped that the Well-Wishers to the Cause of *Liberty* and *Protestantism* will give it Encouragement.' Unfortunately for us, most issues of the *Gazetteer* have vanished, and no essay of Sterne's survives from earlier than June.[2]

The printer was John Jackson, a young man just setting up for himself after an apprenticeship to his father of the same name. He, like his father, was a strong supporter of Walpole. The *Gazetteer* was printed in Jackson's new shop in Petergate.

Poor Jackson soon learned how rough politics could be. The day before the paper was to appear, he was lured into an ale house and severely beaten. The instigator and possibly a participant in this attack was a well-known coal merchant of the city named John Garbutt, who had been active for the opposition in the previous city election. 'General Garbutt', as he was called locally, was a former sailor and the owner of coal ships. His past was shady, and he had failed to obey a sentence of transportation. Very likely the attack had been intended for Sterne as well as Jackson: the record of the Assize Court for that day shows that John Garbutt, mariner, was bound over by the justices of the peace to appear at the next assize for examination, and in the meantime 'to keep the peace toward John Jackson the Younger of the City of York printer and Lawrence Sterne of Sutton upon the Forrest in the

[1] Burton told the story in *British Liberty Endanger'd*, 17, adding that he sent an account of it to the *London Evening Post*, which printed it. I have searched in vain for it in the *Post* and other papers. He may have been slandering the precentor.

[2] For a detailed discussion of Sterne and the *Gazetteer*, see POLITICKS. The newspaper was successful enough to last until 1752. R. M. Wiles gives a technical description of it, listing the known issues and their locations in *Freshest Advices: Early Provincial Newspapers in England*, Columbus, Ohio, 1965, pp. 517-18. Since the appearance of Wiles's book, a run of the paper for 1742 was given to the Beverley Public Library – Nos. 45 (12 January 1742) to 96 (21, i.e. 28, December 1742), lacking No. 80 (14 September).

County of York Clerk & all other his Majesties Liege people'.[1] Jaques Sterne immediately set out to prosecute Garbutt.

The first issue of the *York Gazetteer* (now lost) appeared the next day, 10 March, despite the brawl, and Sterne had the thrill of seeing his prose in print for the first time. We can well imagine how he celebrated with John Hall-Stevenson, in the city to serve on the Grand Jury. Since Thomas Pulleyn and William Stainforth, a Stillington neighbour, were also on the Grand Jury, they probably had a gala evening.[2]

If this earliest essay is ever found, it will probably turn out to be an unexciting piece, competent, factual, persuasive, but neither ironic nor argumentative. Judging by what little we know of his political writing, Sterne began his campaign quietly. Cholmley Turner's continued silence would have precluded any discussion of county matters. Sterne would have aimed the essay at city electors and discussed the problems of the wool trade, which gave the York exporters much concern; or he would have found ways to suggest the wisdom of Edward Thompson and to assure the voters that his post as Commissioner of the Revenue for Ireland – for which the Country Interest repeatedly criticized him – was really an advantage to his constituents.

A month later, on 21 April, Cholmley Turner finally made a public resignation – a letter sent to both newspapers. With election day only three weeks away, the Ministerial Party could do nothing. Indeed, when it rolled around, the high sheriff declared that Viscount Morpeth and Sir Miles Stapylton were elected as Knights of the Shire because unopposed.

The city campaign meanwhile continued on its noisy way. On 5 May the candidates for the Country Interest made a traditional procession through the city, cheered by their followers and jeered by their opponents. A writer for the *Courant* complained that too many soldiers had appeared in the city, 'a sufficient Answer to any Man, who shall ask, Of what Use is a Standing Army in Great Britain?' The *London Evening Post* of 28 May printed a description of election day written by a certain H. W., who maintained that the York clergy had been joined in their support of Thompson by 'most of the Presbyterians and Quakers', that the Court Party had imported Freemen from all over the kingdom 'to outvote the resident Citizens', and that the

[1] PRO: Assizes. 41. 4; Kenneth Monkman, WINGED SKULL, p. 282, discloses the account of the beating. Two letters about the matter from Henry Masterman of the Crown Office to John Wilmer, a York attorney, dated 15 April and 6 May 1742, are in the papers of Acomb Manor.
[2] List of the Grand Jury in *York Courant*, 17 March 1740/1.

city was packed with sailors, soldiers, customs-house officers, and 'such a Glut of Time-serving Parsons, that made the Affair look more like a Visitation than an election'. The polling was begun on 13 May, and a few days later the papers announced that Edward Thompson would keep his seat; the other would go to Godfrey Wentworth of the Country Interest. In the city election, Sterne's party had just managed to hold the old balance.

Yet the loss of Turner's seat in the county election turned out to be serious. Walpole had lost supporters here and there all over England; he would have only the slimmest majority in the new Parliament.

But the election was not really over, as the leaders on both sides knew very well. Charles Howard, the twenty-three year old Viscount Morpeth, just chosen a Knight of the Shire, was dying of consumption. He had allowed himself to be nominated for his father's sake even though his disease had progressed steadily all spring. A by-election to fill his place seemed inevitable, and the friends of the ministry went quietly to work to prepare for a tough fight. On 3 June Sterne borrowed from the library of the dean and chapter a two-volume anthology of tracts edited by Bishop Edmund Gibson entitled *A Preservative Against Popery*.[1]

The earliest extant piece of writing by Laurence Sterne dates from this period of waiting for the death of Lord Morpeth. It is a broadside reprint of Sterne's article for the *Gazetteer* of 16 June 1741. (The practice of duplicating newspaper articles as broadsides was to become a major feature of this campaign, an attempt to reach voters who might not see the originals.) Sterne's piece attacks an account which had appeared in the *York Courant* of 9 June describing the launching of a new coal barge 'belonging to the Famous *John Garbut*, well known to this City by the Name of *General Garbut*', which was to be named *The Kaye and Wentworth*. One can imagine how that went down with Sterne after Garbutt's threats to him and his abuse of John Jackson, especially since the *Courant* story ended with an exhortation: 'it is hoped that all the *Honest* Citizens will ever remember both the Name of the Vessel, and the *great Services done to the Public by the Master of it*, at the last Election.' Sterne's answer begins by posing a set of four queries – a device he was to use again. He scolds the Country Interest for caressing and paying court 'to such a Fellow'. Garbutt had interfered with the freedom of election through his 'riotous, insulting Behavior', and Sterne asks 'Whether Those who can stoop to work with so low a Tool as *Garbut*, and when the Work is over can still stoop lower to Thank and Flatter him, have not let fall'n the

[1] BARR.

Mask of Patriotism and discovered under it, more of the Spirit of Slavery than Liberty?' The broadside which reprinted this article was itself printed off some time later, for it carried a news item dated 31 August, telling how Garbutt was arrested for returning from transportation and was committed to York Castle.[1] Uncle Jaques, it seems, was making trouble for the man, though in fact Garbutt did not remain in prison long.

Lord Morpeth died at Castle Howard on 9 August. Curiously, Morpeth's life was the third and last named on the Givendale prebendal deeds. Ironically, his passing brought Sterne a small fortune and at the same time set going a series of events which would all but destroy his chances for preferment.

The Country Interest was not ready to give in because their representative had died. On 30 August they held a nomination meeting, though an ominously small one. The man they nominated for the by-election was a stranger to most of them, George Fox, a vigorous man in his mid-forties. Fox was a hardworking politician who had already served as Member for Hindon, Wiltshire; but as a vote-getter, he had weaknesses: he was neither a country squire nor a Yorkshireman by birth. His family was Irish, his own inherited estates lay in that kingdom, and he had lived primarily in London. Only through his wife could he claim a Yorkshire connection: she brought him the estate of Bramham Park in the West Riding. Fox, who had a long and notable career in Parliament, is more often remembered as George Fox-Lane, for he changed his name a few years later. In 1762 he was created Lord Bingley.[2] Though a good candidate in many ways, he would not appeal to the squirearchy: Sterne's side had a chance against him.

The Ministerial Party got off with a jubilant nomination meeting at the George Inn. To the surprise and delight of the gathering, Lord Malton nominated Cholmley Turner himself. The old squire had discovered that he could not take the spectacle of a Tory Parliament. He plucked up his spirits and promised a vigorous campaign. Sterne and his uncle were there, of course.[3]

The Ministerial Party set about at once organizing a campaign which adumbrated many modern political techniques. The activities in each

[1] Discovered by Kenneth Monkman at the Leeds Central Library. A photograph of the broadside in WINGED SKULL, facing p. 108.
[2] On Fox: J. T. Ward, 'The saving of a Yorkshire estate: George Fox-Lane and

Bramham Park', YAJ, XLII (1967), 63–71.
[3] The meeting was held on 29 August: *London Evening Post*, 17 September 1741; Andrew Wilkinson to Newcastle, 31 August, BM: Add. MSS 32697, fol. 522.

Wapentake (subdivision of the Riding) were organized by a committee which reported to the central committee in York. The canvass, the propaganda, the financing, and – to be blunt – the bribes and threats, were smoothly co-ordinated. It was an unpleasant, dirty fight, but very strong. A canvass of the entire county was carefully laid out and executed. Probably Sterne helped in that, since he knew so many of the gentry. The major task was to contact personally every squire who controlled a block of votes, to try to bring him to Turner's side. Small freeholders voted so long as their property was worth 40s.; but most of the yeoman farmers, like those of Sutton, were also tenants of large landholders whom they dared not vote against. There was no such thing as a secret ballot, and poll books showing how everyone voted were published after each election. There was also a group of genuinely independent freeholders, such as the industrial workers in and about Halifax, who might support the party if given free transportation to York for the polling and all they wanted to drink when they got there. A secondary purpose of the canvass was to assess the party's chances of winning. Either party might pull out of the campaign whenever the leaders decided they would lose: campaigns were too expensive to throw away.

The canvasses were completed by November. The results were disconcerting to both parties, so many were the unexpected shifts of loyalty. John Stanhope of Horsforth, near Leeds, had been a staunch supporter of Walpole, but now he had gone to the other side – possibly won over by Dr Burton, an old neighbour with whom he shared an antiquarian interest. It was a serious loss to the Ministerial Party, for Stanhope, a prominent lawyer, orator and sportsman, ruled like a tyrant over a large area – his hunting domain – keeping the locals in line with lashes of his tongue or his riding whip, whichever served best.[1] Nevertheless, some leaders of the Country Interest were pessimistic. Sir Miles Stapylton and Edward Wortley, unable to convince the others to capitulate, walked out, taking their purses with them. But the struggle went on, and both sides settled into the serious business of persuading individual squires to switch sides or bribing them with promises of preferment for their families.

There were entertainments for the mob. On 12 November the Country Interest noisily celebrated the birthday of Admiral Vernon, their current hero, with the ringing of bells, the lighting of bonfires, and the shooting of

[1] For Stanhope, see A. M. W. Stirling, *Annals of a Yorkshire House*, 2 vols, 1911, I, 89–112 and *passim*. The connection with Burton: letters of Dr Burton to Andrew Ducarel and Richard Gaugh, ILLUSTRATIONS, IV, 589–92.

skyrockets from the top of the waterworks. 'General' Garbutt was arrested again; a certain Luke Coater tried to pull down the pales before Dr Burton's house and threatened to destroy the house itself.[1]

According to Dr Burton, Jaques Sterne chaired a committee which met regularly at the George Inn to comb through lists of electors looking for supporters of the Country Interest who were in debt to men of his own party. These unlucky folk were threatened with prosecution unless they came over to the Ministerial side. The charge is verified by one W—m H—p, in *A Remarkable Cause in a Note of Hand Try'd in the Court of Conscience* (1742), who described how he was hounded for debt because he would not vote for Turner. The committee compiled a 'black list' of tradesmen who supported Fox and started an embargo against them, Burton said; and Dr Sterne went so far as to threaten to demolish the church of Wheldrake unless the freeholders of the parish would defy their gentry and vote for Turner. Certainly all elections of that century were corrupt by modern standards, but this was shockingly so even to contemporaries. One need look no further for an explanation than to the characters of John Burton, Jaques Sterne and Lancelot Blackburn.

There is nothing to implicate Sterne in the more gross corruptions of the campaign, though what he wrote was not very high-minded. His essays of that autumn – the lost ones –were beginning to annoy the opposition in London. On 14 November *Common Sense* printed a letter which, in the course of attacking Whiggism in general, referred obliquely to Sterne as one of the 'Ministerial Hirelings' who surrounded Cholmley Turner and whose friendship did that gentleman no good. Caesar Ward readdressed the letter to his own readers and printed it on the 24th. Sterne's reply appeared in the London *Daily Gazetteer* of 2 December and in the *York Courant* of the 8th (lost), reprinted on the 15th (surviving). Calling the *Common Sense* letter 'a senseless Piece of raving and Abuse', Sterne, 'by way of caution', warns the reader that the author 'is a Zealous, Bigotted *Irish* Papist'.

> I know not what could tempt him to address himself to so great, so rich, so powerful a Body of Protestants as the Freeholders of this County, and in a Cause too, where their *true* Interest and his are inconsistent, unless we may imput it to the *Native* Assurance of his *Country* and the *Officious* Saint-Errantry of his Religion.[2]

In this period, when Roman Catholics had no right to vote or to hold public office, to brand a man a Papist was a serious matter. Nevertheless, this particular piece Sterne probably wrote with a clear conscience: Charles Molloy, chief essayist for *Common Sense*, was widely known to be an Irish Catholic.

Sterne had little respect for Catholicism during his early and middle years. In one sermon, he defined that religion as 'a system put together and contrived to operate upon men's weakness and passions – and thereby to pick their pockets' (II, 260). Yet late in his life he wrote the episode of the Monk in *A Sentimental Journey* where Yorick's prejudices are transcended by sympathy. His feelings about Catholicism, even in his younger years, probably were more moderate than his uncle's. Perhaps he balked at other similar assignments, thereby incurring his uncle's displeasure.

Sterne's work also had a light side, as shown by the *Gazetteer* of 15 December, for which he wrote three fillers. One is a humourless hit at Molloy. The other two contrast amusingly the entertainments offered to the voters by each party. To the great feast laid out in Pontefract by the Country Interest, no more than five voters came, while to that at York given by the 'Friends of Mr. Turner', the freeholders came almost to a man. 'Amongst many Loyal and honest Healths that were then toasted, they drank to Mr. Turner's good Success Prosperity to the County of York and to the Trade thereof, and that we may never want a HOME BORN BAIRN to *represent* the one and *protect* the other.'

Sterne was relaxing at Skelton Castle with Hall-Stevenson when the most persistent of his opponents made his first appearance in print – someone from Leeds who signed himself 'J. S.' Shortly before, on 8 August, the day Cholmley Turner was nominated, Sterne had written a letter extolling the virtues of this native son and deriding Fox's Irish background – a letter now lost. On 8 September, J. S.'s answering letter appeared in the *Courant*: 'I think it my Duty, as a Freeholder,' he wrote, 'to take off a *false Aspersion* cast on One of the Candidates, and industriously propagated in printed Hand Bills, that he is an Irishman.' He then laid out a reasonably accurate account of Fox's education, his Irish estates, his service in Parliament. 'Mr. *FOX* by Marriage to so considerable a Yorkshire Heiress, is possess'd of a great

Gazetteer of 19 January 1742, after the poll has been completed. The phrase, 'the Saint-Errantry of his Religion', was echoed by Sterne in his sermon, *The Abuses of Conscience*, 1750, which he used in *Tristram Shandy*. There the militant Roman Catholic is called a 'misguided saint-errant'.

Property in this County; and living in the Heart of it, in a noble and hospitable Manner, may be justly called a *Yorkshire-Man*.'

In a waggish mood, perhaps egged on by Hall-Stevenson, Sterne decided to place an answer in the pages of the *Courant* itself. So he wrote a letter which he signed 'J. Wainman' and posted it at the nearest post office, which was at Guisborough. But Ward was not fooled: on 29 September he published a testy notice:

> *When the Writer of a Letter sent Yesterday to the Printing Office, reflecting upon a worthy Clergyman in this County, and sign'd* J. Wainman, *thinks fit to subscribe* his own Name, *it will be soon enough to insert it; in the mean Time it may be proper to inform the* Vicar, *who penn'd it, that the Printer of this Paper is not to be impos'd upon by counterfeited* Letters *from* Guisbrough, *nor* fictitious Names *in* York.

Ward would be sorry he published that, for his opponents would soon cite his words as proof that J. S. was a clergyman and therefore identifiable.

But long before Ward's notice appeared, Jaques Sterne had decided who J. S. was. On 14 September he wrote to Lord Irwin, the Lord-Lieutenant of the East Riding, who managed the Ministerial campaign for that area,

> My Lord,
>   Your Lordship wou'd receive by the last post an Answer to Scott's Scurrilous Letter, wch is Jesuitical and neither Sense, Grammer, nor English; I think the answer wil hurt them very much; but if your Lordship wou'd have a serious one withal, one shal be given. I shal be always proud of your commands and am
>   Your Lordship's obedient servant,
>   Jaques Sterne[1]

This is the response of a psychotic man. J. S.'s letter had been quite grammatical, and contained nothing to suggest the Jesuit: it was a factually accurate, reasonable response to Sterne's original letter. Sterne's own reaction had been playful.

J. S., the precentor had concluded, was the Reverend James Scott, who lived at Leeds, where he was the curate of the Chapel of the Holy and Undivided Trinity. He had the living of nearby Bardsey. A native of Wakefield,

---

[1] Quoted by Cedric Collyer, 'Laurence Sterne and Yorkshire politics: some new evidence', LPS, VII (1952–5), 83–7. Lord Irwin, as he was always called locally, was Henry Ingram, Viscount Irvine (1691–1761), Lord-Lieutenant of the East Riding, 1736–61.

close to Leeds, he was a friend of Dr Burton's, a contributor to the Infirmary, and a supporter of the Country Interest in the elections of 1734.[1]

Since Sterne could not get his 'J. Wainman' letter accepted by the *Courant*, he printed a response in the *Gazetteer* on 29 September – probably. To that J. S. rejoined with his second letter, appearing in the *Courant* on 20 October. It was a flimsy thing, the substance of which was to blame Cholmley Turner for not staying out of politics. Nevertheless, it was reprinted in the *London Evening Post* of 12 November, and according to Dr Sterne the Country Interest was preparing to print 12,000 broadside copies.[2] Caesar Ward, to take the spotlight off the rival newspaper or, possibly, because he wanted to be fair, prefaced a note to J. S.'s letter with an invitation to print a reply from Turner's supporters, 'provided it is wrote with Decency and good Manners'.

The reply which Sterne produced has been called, with some exaggeration, 'Sterne's first book'. *Query upon Query* is a pamphlet which exists in three versions. Caesar Ward printed a cut version in the *York Courant* of 27 October. Uncle Jaques rewrote portions and published his version in the *Leeds Mercury* of 3 November and as a pamphlet – a move which must have annoyed Sterne. The original appeared in the London *Daily Gazetteer* on 28 October – apparently based upon a manuscript in Sterne's hand which he had sent to London at the time he gave copies to Ward and his uncle.[3]

Query upon Query opens with a description of J. S.'s letter, comic largely because it is just. 'Upon casting up the Contents of the three first Paragraphs', wrote Sterne,

> the *Sense Total* amounts just to this single Proposition. 'That last *April* Mr. *Turner* (as appears by Letter) had resigned all Thoughts of acting in a publick Station; But, that at the Solicitations of his Friends, upon Lord *Morpeth's* Death, He had alter'd his Intentions; which if He had not done, The County had been at Peace, and there had been no

[1] POLITICKS, 44–6; YORK PRESS, 288–90; HERRING RETURNS, I, 46; R. V. Taylor, *Biographia Leodiensis; or Biographical Sketches of the Worthies of Leeds and Neighbourhood*, 1864, pp. 254–9; ACT BOOK, 1755–68, fols. 49, 345.

[2] Jaques Sterne to Lord Irwin, 23 October, quoted by Collyer, 'Laurence Sterne and Yorkshire politics'.

[3] The variant versions were discovered by Collyer, 'Laurence Sterne and Yorkshire politics'. My quotations are taken from the *Daily Gazetteer* version. A MS in Jaques Sterne's hand, a fragment only, is among the Temple Newsam papers, Sheepscar Library, Leeds; the pamphlet is at the Minster Library. It was reproduced with minor variations only in the *Leeds Mercury* of 3 November.

contested Election. A most admirable and important Conclusion! You
have been pleased, Sir, to inform us, that before any Offer was made to
Mr. *Turner*, Every Person of Figure had given an absolute Refusal, and
if He had likewise refused – What then? Why, Every Body had refused; and unless *Two* Candidates had offer'd themselves, there could
have been no such Thing as a contested Election.

Sterne concludes by 'answering' the queries posed by J. S. with another set
of queries which, he maintains, will make further answers needless because
'a plain and honest Answer to each . . . will naturally direct you to the true
Solution of your own'. Flattering the reader's intelligence is an old trick of
the rhetor, but Sterne handled it deftly. *Query upon Query* seems to have had
an enormous popular appeal. It may have done more than anything else to
win the election.

From this point, in the duel with J. S., political issues became subordinate to the question of J. S.'s identity. It became a game of hide and seek,
entertaining to the Yorkshire electorate, else it would not have been continued, and possibly to the participants. Nevertheless, there were enough
potentially serious consequences to involve Sterne's honour. Since political
and civil liberties were then more perfectly enunciated than protected, J. S.
may well have wished to withhold his name. If Sterne should make a mistaken identification, he would injure an innocent man, thereby giving the
Country Party occasion to howl of injustice and persecution.

Sterne refrained from naming his antagonist in *Query upon Query*, but he
did identify him by implication: he spoke of him as 'a Teacher of Truth', i.e.,
a clergyman. Everyone knew there was only one clergyman in Leeds with
those initials – the Reverend James Scott. J. S. responded with a quick shot
from the bottom of a letter primarily about the wool trade. The letter, in the
Courant of 31 October, unsigned but dated from Leeds, concluded thus:

> As to the insinuation of J. S. being a Clergyman, it may be necessary
> to inform the Gentleman, that J. S. is not a Clergyman, but a Merchant
> in the Woollen-Trade . . . the four following Lines of Mr. Pope will
> stand for a sufficient Answer to all that the Author of the last Queries
> has writ, or can write, on this subject.
>> Let L—y *Scribble – what? that Thing of Silk,*
>> L—y *that mere white Curd of Ass's Milk?*
>> *Satire or Sense, alas! can* L—y *feel?*
>> *Who breaks a* Butterfly *upon a* Wheel?

Sterne replied in two letters, both of which appeared in the *Courant* of 10 November. In the first, he adopted a pose of anger: 'It is with some Difficulty, that I have prevailed with myself to take Pen in Hand to make a *serious* Reply to one of the most scurrilous and uncharitable Letters that ever appear'd in a civiliz'd and Christian Country.' He goes on to praise Turner as a 'tender affectionate Father', a '*real* patriot' who recruited, equipped and led a volunteer troop in the Jacobite rebellion of 1708 (true), and as a '*good* Man'.[1] It is not a very clever letter. One guesses that Sterne wrote according to the prescription of his uncle. The accompanying letter, of a vastly different sort, must have been Sterne's own idea of how to handle J. S. Caesar Ward printed it, though obviously he was shocked: above it he inserted a notice:

The following Letter is wrote by the same Gentleman that has wrote every Piece that has been inserted in this Paper in Vindication of Chomley Turner, *Esq.*

Sterne's purpose was to challenge J. S. in such a manner as to make him appear contemptible if he did not come forward and reveal himself:

To the PRINTER *of the* York Courant.
SIR,

As J. S. in your last Courant has shown some Marks of Fear and Penitence in denying his Name, and promising never to offend again, it would be almost an Act of Cruelty to pursue the Man any farther; however, since he has left the Field with ill Language in his Mouth, I shall send one Shot after him, which, I am confident, is too well founded to miss him.

A certain nasty Animal in *Egypt*, which, I think, *Herodotus* takes notice of, when he finds he cannot possibly defend himself, and prey any longer, partly out of Malice, partly out of Policy, he lets fly backward full against his Adversary, and thereby covers his Retreat with the Fumes of his own Filth and Excrement.

As this Creature is naturally very *impotent*, and its chief Safety depends on a plentiful Discharge on such Occasions, the Naturalists affirm, that Self-preservation directs it to a certain Vegitable on the Banks of the River *Nile*, which constantly arms it with a proper Habit of Body against all Emergencies. I am,
Yours, L. S.

[1] A broadside version dated 5 November discovered by Kenneth Monkman at the Sheepscar Library, Leeds: WINGED SKULL, 283.

Sterne then added injury to insult by an article in the *Gazetteer* the following week (as Curtis demonstrated, though the letter is lost) in which he exposed Scott by name and openly called him a Jacobite.

Scott could no longer remain silent: the following week, on the 24th, the *Courant* carried his letter addressed '*To* L. S. *at York*'. Over his own signature he emphatically denied that he was the J. S. of the letters and objected, with some justice, to the epithets which had been showered upon him – ignorant, scurrilous, uncharitable, proud. 'Is this acting consistently with the Spirit of Charity, which you observe indeed justly, but surely without having the least Claim to it yourself, should be the Characteristik of a *Teacher of Truth*?' He concluded by refusing to beg pardon, as he had been asked, but demanded that satisfaction from Sterne.

He was playing into Sterne's hand: Sterne could now bring forward his proof of Scott's identity, making him appear a liar and a coward. He did so in a letter for the *York Gazetteer*, probably in the lost issue of 1 December, and in broadside reproductions of the letter. One of these sheets was recently uncovered at the York Minster library, 'To the Rev. Mr. *James Scott* at *Leeds*'.[1] With ironic politeness he asks Mr Scott to suspend his pretentions until he hears Sterne out. 'When J. S.'s first Letter came out in Vindication of Mr. Fox's OWN good Sense and FAMILY Pedigree,' Sterne goes on, 'a Critical Review of it was offer'd to the Printer of the York Courant, but could not gain admittance' – i.e., the letter which Sterne (or Sterne *and* Hall-Stevenson) had posted from Guisborough. Referring to Ward's annoyed notice about that letter, which had appeared on 29 September, Sterne explains, quite accurately, '*He pleads the Benefit of the Clergy*, and justifys his Refusal of the Paper with saying it reflected upon a *Worthy Clergyman*. As this was near a Month before the *Query* upon *Query* appear'd, you see, Sir, a Chronological Argument. . . . That you are not indebted to *that* Paper for the Imputation.' It was a solid argument, despite the rhetoric, for no clergyman at Leeds had those initials but Mr Scott.

Caesar Ward was upset. The next week he printed a reply over his own name objecting to Sterne's chronological argument. Even *before* his notice referring to a clergyman, he explained, he had received an unsigned letter in Sterne's hand which concluded with the words 'I am Rev. Sir, Yours', showing that Sterne had identified J. S. even before he got a hint from Ward. The

---

[1] Discovered by Kenneth Monkman. A photograph in WINGED SKULL, facing p. 109.

argument was a poor one: whatever Sterne had thought about the identity of J. S. (who in fact had been identified by his uncle), he had said nothing publicly until after Ward provided the evidence. To this Ward added another *non sequitur*: when Sterne had come to the office of the *Courant* to make changes in the manuscript of *Query upon Query*, Ward had specifically assured him that J. S. was not a clergyman.

J. S. himself offered no rebuttal; instead, he published on the 15th another lampoon:

> *Mr* Pope *against* L. S. *once more.*
>
> A Wight, who reads not, and but scans and spells;
> A Word-Catcher that lives on Syllables.
> Who shames this Scribbler? break one Cobweb thro',
> He spins the slight self-pleasing Thread a-new:
> Destroy his Fib, or Sophistry, in vain,
> The Creature's at his dirty Work again,
> Thron'd in the Centre of his thin Designs,
> Proud of a vast Extent of flimzy Lines.
>
> *From his humble Servant,*
> J. S.

Sterne did not deign to reply – or rather, he did not wish to give the appearance of doing so. Probably he penned the letter published over the signature of the printer, Jackson, which appeared in the *Gazetteer* of 15 December (one of the issues extant). Ward's statement that he had received a letter in Sterne's hand, he or Jackson said, was a 'downright Falsehood'. Perhaps Sterne was on sure grounds here: the letter, which was, of course, that posted at Guisborough and signed 'J. Wainman', might have been in the hand of Hall-Stevenson. This letter had been put on display at the office of John Graves, attorney, and on the back of it was a certified oath to the effect that it was the very letter carried to Ward. Furthermore, Mr Graves and Emmanuel Gregson, who had gone together to take the manuscript of *Query upon Query* to Ward, were willing to attest upon oath that when Ward received it, he made a reflection 'that it was "*Vicar against Vicar*"'. Such evidence, though it might not close the case, certainly strengthened Sterne's contention. Most telling of all, Ward made no substantive reply. What he printed was a huff and a puff:

The Printer of this Paper will give himself no Concern about Letters printed in the last Gazetteer, *both the Author and Publisher of such a Jumble of False-hoods and Abuse being below his Notice.*[1]

Sterne had the stronger argument, beyond doubt, but it had a major weakness. It proved, not that J. S. *was* Mr Scott, but that Caesar Ward *thought* he was. Suppose Ward himself had been mistaken?

It may also give us pause that Sterne had not stopped the pen of J. S. Another of his letters appeared in the *Courant* shortly before the polling, repeating a number of his old arguments and attacking Sterne and his friends: 'the most abandon'd, profligate Set of Fellows, that ever put Pen to Paper'. On another page appeared 'A New Year's Gift *for* L—y', unsigned, but probably J. S.'s farewell to Sterne:

> Grave Legends tell, nor is it yet deny'd,
> That old St. Lawrence on a Grid-Iron fry'd;
> Our young St. Lawrence is so wond'rous dry,
> I'll wager, that he'd sooner *burn than fry*.
> And, try to *roast* him – he's so lean and *sallow*,
> 'Tis Ten to One he drops *more T—d than Tallow*.

Immediately above the poem was an announcement: 'There are now two vacant Prebend Stalls in the Cathedral; and there is no doubt that *dentur Dignissimis* will be strictly followed, as usual.' How Ward must have enjoyed making his announcement in that fashion. A few days before, Robert Hitch, prebendary of North Newbald, had 'over-heated himself at the strife about obtaining votes', fallen into a fever and died. Sterne promptly resigned the prebend of Givendale so that he could succeed to North Newbald. When the day for the induction ceremony rolled around, 8 January, he was so busy he could not attend. He was represented by proxies.[2]

Parties of voters from all over the county were soon streaming into York for the polling. Both sides provided nightly entertainments in the ale houses. Private homes were opened to visiting gentry. The streets were crowded with horsemen, carts, carriages. Flambeaux lit up the streets late into the night. Gentlemen gambled, and Christopher Oldfield, postmaster and

---

[1] In one of the variant issues for 22 December in the file of the *York Courant* at the Public Library of Hull, upon which I depend primarily. At least during some periods, Ward printed early and late editions of the paper.

[2] CHAPTER ACTS; INSTITUTIONS, fol. 59; ACT BOOK, 1710–62, fol. 106. The summons, schedule, induction and proxy papers at Minster Library: D 1.

proprietor of the George Inn, was authorized to place a bet of £1,000 against £10 that Turner would win. It was a momentous occasion to the small farmers, many of whom had never left their villages before. Despite the extreme cold they walked along the walls and stared at the great minster. Sterne must have spent much of his time in the coffee houses and taverns, laughing with his friends from the North Riding, renewing old acquaintances with gentlemen from Halifax or the area around Elvington and Catton, in whose eyes he now appeared a man of considerable importance. On 11 January Cholmley Turner made a spectacular entry into the city. He was met on the Great North Road by a party of mounted gentlemen; as they passed through Bootham Bar, he was cheered by a great multitude carrying party placards and wearing yellow cockades. The next day Fox made his entry through Monk Bar and was cheered by his own people. The polling began on the 13th and continued for nine days.

Cholmley Turner won. The election returns were announced on 21 January, and amid cheering throngs Turner was chaired through the streets. The next issue of the *Courant* carried Fox's polite congratulation to him. He had won by 40,062 votes to Fox's 33,859.[1]

If Dr Jaques Sterne turned through the leaves of the *Courant* that day, he felt no jubilation. Forces beyond his own vast energy were shaping his world. The issue of the following week told all of the story that we know:

> Last Tuesday died Mrs. Sterne, Wife of the Reverand Dr. Sterne, Precentor of the Cathedral, a Lady remarkable for Piety, Meekness, Charity, and every Qualification that can adorn her Sex; which has render'd her Death regretted by all who had the Pleasure of her Acquaintance.

As to Laurence Sterne – before his aunt's death, even before the polling was complete, his personal victory had turned to ashes. Someone had revealed that in exposing Scott, he had exposed the wrong man! He kept calm. Eventually he would make an apology, but not just yet. First he would deal with J. S., who, he was now convinced, was the sporting lawyer, John Stanhope of Horsforth. The following appeared in the *York Gazetteer* for 19 January:

[1] *York Courant*, 26 January. The poll books, BM: 810. K. 33; and 807. h. 20, contain no surprises. Timothy Sterne voted for Fox. I could not find an entry for Richard Sterne.

An EPITAPH.

On the Death of J—k St—n—pe

Since poor J. S. is dead and gone,
Let this be writ upon his Stone.
              Here lies J. S.
Devoid of Sense and eke of Strife,
Who in a Fox-Chace lost his Life,
That Tongue alas does now lie still,
That us'd the Strangest Things to tell;
So strange you'd swear 'twas all a Lye,
But for his KNOWN VERACITY.
– Whoo – Whup ye JACKS! ah weep full sore,
That he of Fox Chace says no more.[1]

Ironically, Walpole fell from power anyway. On 3 February, days after the returns were reported, he resigned as First Commissioner of the Treasury and Chancellor of the Exchequer. The news blew into York as rumour, then as letters, finally in the London newspapers. On Saturday the 6th, the church-bells of the city began to ring – not for any joy on the part of the parsons who ordered their ringing, but out of respect for the king. As one set of bells took up after another that morning until the whole countryside reverberated, the great bells of the minster were silent. Late in the afternoon, they began to sound.[2] Their tones were funereal to the sombre group gathered at the house of the dean. A few days completed the story: the Earl of Wilmington was forming a government, and Walpole would accept a seat in the Lords as Earl of Orford. True, the Country Interest did not take over at Whitehall, but for the first time since Sterne had come to England as a boy, the nation was being administered by someone other than Sir Robert Walpole. Many fearless writers began to attack the former minister in the newspapers. J. S. appeared again on the front page of the *Courant* of 23 February, chastising Walpole, but not taking any notice of L. S.

In mid-March Sterne resigned from the *York Gazetteer* – so one gathers from a pasquinade in the *Courant* of the 23rd:

L—y's *Reasons for writing no more* Gazetteers.

Presuming that to wear the Lawn
I had a just Pretence,

[1] Discovered by Kenneth Monkman and published by him in WINGED SKULL, 284.   [2] *York Courant*, 9 February.

I've scribbled now for one whole Year,
  To baffle Common Sense.

I've taken Pains by Logick Rules,
  To prove myself an Ass;
Not dreaming what a wond'rous Change
  Is like to come to pass.

But now my Pen I've splinter'd quite,
  And thrown away my Ink,
For 'till I see which Side will win,
  I'll neither write nor think.

What, Sterne must have wondered, was the use of politics? He might as well go back to his thatched cottage at Sutton and tend his garden. The Sutton registers testify that he did just that:

I laid out in the Garden, in ye year 1742

£   s.
The sum of 8: 15: 6
L. Sterne

He had not worked many weeks on that garden before another blow fell to his party. On 4 July Edward Thompson, the member for York whom Sterne had supported in the city election, suddenly died. The Ministerial Party had no replacement. The Country Interest made a nomination and filled the seat without opposition. The man they chose? George Fox of Bramham Park. Thus Cholmley Turner's opponent had a free ride to Parliament and took his place in the hall on the opposite side from the old squire of Kirkleatham.

The bells were still ringing in congratulation of Mr Fox when Sterne made up his mind that he was through with politics for good. He sat down and wrote a letter to the *Courant* which Caesar Ward was pleased to publish on 27 July:

To *the* Printer *of the* YORK COURANT

Sir,
I find by some late Preferments, that it may not be improper to change Sides; therefore I beg the Favour of you to inform the Publick, that I sincerely beg Pardon for the abusive Gazetteers I wrote during the late contested Election for the County of York, and that I heartily wish Mr. Fox Joy of his Election for the City.

Tempora Mutantur, & nos mutemur in illis.
I am, Sir, your Penitent Friend and Servant.
L. S.

The letter seems puzzling at first glance because the irony of the opening statement is not maintained. To wish Mr Fox joy of his election was hardly more than a courtesy. To beg pardon for abusive *Gazetteers* and to sign himself the 'Penitent Friend' of Caesar Ward amounted to an apology for his unfair journalism, especially his slandering of Scott. But another sort of explanation is required for that opening clause, 'I find by some late Preferments, that it may not be improper to change Sides.'

It must be said at once that Sterne did not change sides: he simply withdrew from politics. During the next contested election at York, that of 1758, he stayed in the country: 'The great Confusion of the Election, wch I hate . . . kept me here', he wrote to a friend. 'If you have 3 or 4 of the last York's Courants, pray Send 'em us, for We are as much Strangers to all that has pass'd amongst You, as if we were in a Mine in Siberia' (pp. 64–5). Had he really been a turncoat, he would have lost many of the friends with whom he worked in the campaign. But he seems to have alienated no one except his uncle. Consider the group who attended the meeting in which Cholmley Turner was nominated. Clergymen such as William Berdmore and Charles Cowper were later Sterne's allies in chapter quarrels. Archdeacon Francis Blackburne later tried to smooth over Sterne's difficulties with his uncle. Dean Osbaldeston remained a supporter and friend. Lord Fauconberg became his patron.

The statement was intended as an ironic confrontation of his uncle, and its motive was surely anger. No doubt it hurt the precentor, for it exposed his inability to lead his party subordinates, even his own nephew.

Probably the quarrel between Sterne and his uncle had been growing throughout the campaign. We can infer one cause from the history of Parson Yorick in *Tristram Shandy*. Yorick, though innocent of any malice, is persecuted for 'scattering his wit and his humour' (I, xi, 27). It is not hard to imagine Sterne's joking at his uncle's expense. John Croft gave another explanation, but not one which is acceptable. According to Croft, they 'fell out about a favourite Mistress of the Precentors, who proved with child by Laury . . . tho' at the time of their rupture, he gave out as a reason in the publick Coffee House, that it arose from that he wou'd not continue to write periodicall papers for his Uncle'. Sterne would have been less prone to a libertine life at this period than at any other. He was very much in the public eye and fully aware that his enemies would take advantage of any scandal they could uncover. Besides, he had just married. At a later time Jaques Sterne had a mistress, and a lampoon in the *Courant* implies that he had more than one; but there is no evidence of misbehaviour while his wife was still alive.[1] More likely, they quarrelled because Sterne was not tractable, because, as he said in the 'Memoirs', he was not a party man and refused to write certain essays. Love was not the area of Uncle Jaques's obsession. He might have understood a rivalry in love and forgiven it in time. But a betrayal in politics? Never.

Sterne himself probably did not feel much anger toward his uncle until his discovery that J. S. was not the Reverend James Scott. It was Jaques who had identified J. S. before Caesar Ward let slip any hint. No doubt he had urged Sterne to make the exposure. Sterne had done that, insulted Scott, slandered him, and accepted the onus put upon himself by Ward's announcement that he, L. S., was responsible for all the letters to the *Courant* in support of Turner. Then, when J. S. turned out to be John Stanhope, his uncle had left him holding the bag. Any decent man, finding that his error had compromised the honour of a subordinate, would have come forth to accept the responsibility. The precentor never did.

Disgusted, Sterne decided to resign from the *Gazetteer* as soon as he could. He was, of course, under an obligation to repay his uncle for the living and prebend. So he continued to write essays until the poll itself.[2] His work had been effective, especially *Query upon Query*, and the Ministerial Party had won. After Walpole's fall, Sterne probably thought he could resign with a

---

[1] The lampoons of 27 November and 4 December 1744, and 9 April 1745, are cited below in Chapter 8. CIRTIS, 29, suggests that another ballad copied into CURIOUS COLLECTION, about the foolish conduct of a wenching parson, alludes to Jaques Sterne, his mistress and his nephew. It begins

> Within the Walls of Ebor
> There liv'd a swagg'ring P[a]rs[o]n;
>   Who sigh'd for Bread,
>   And a soft Bed,
> To roll his reverend A[r]se on.

The parson might be Jaques, for there is reference to the man's interest in politics.

But the mistress is not Sarah Benson, Jaques's later mistress, but one 'Jo B--h--m'. To screen the fact that she has other lovers, Jo tells the parson a story about a 'dreadful Man of N[e]wb[a]ld' – perhaps an allusion to Laurence Sterne. However, the 'Man of Newbald' is not accused in the ballad; rather, the woman's story about him is her own invention, and 'none but Fools give Ear to 't'.

[2] Pat Rogers in 'Sterne and journalism', WINGED SKULL, 132–44, cites a letter in the *Gazetteer* of 12 January, during the week of the poll, which he believes was written by Sterne.

clear conscience. Very likely it was at this point that he promised his uncle to give him 'no further Trouble'.[1]

But Sterne had not yet discovered the full extent of his uncle's vindictiveness. That came during the late spring when the lease on North Newbald prebendal estate expired. When Sterne had made the exchange of prebends, his patron was not his uncle, but Archbishop Blackburn. Years later he told a friend that 'he owed his Preferment' to his work on the *Gazetteer,* 'so acceptable was it to the then Archbishop'.[2] The archbishop must have given him his choice of the two stalls which were then vacant. One infers so from the fact that the man who accepted the other stall, Hollis Pigott, was not politically active in Yorkshire. Sterne chose North Newbald because he knew that the current lease would soon expire. The last of the three lives named on it was that of an old woman at death's door. The estate was a considerable one – a large tract of land and a parsonage house at North Newbald village, and three houses in Stonegate, one of which was occupied by the printer, Thomas Gent, another by the prosperous bookseller, John Hildyard – the shop called The Sign of the Bible.[3] What Sterne did not know about was a reversionary lease which had been quietly signed some years back. The person responsible for this violation of the accepted ethics was not Sterne's predecessor in the stall, Robert Hitch, but *his* predecessor, George Bell. Bell had collected a fine in advance by giving a reversionary lease to Alderman John Read (Lord Mayor of York in 1719 and 1746), empowering Read to claim the entire estate upon the death of the old woman. Thomas Gent, the printer, had found out about it that autumn when Alderman Read informed him that he would be evicted. He had begged the assistance of Mr Hitch, but Hitch, of course, was powerless to help him.[4] One surmises that the story had not reached Sterne when he

---

[1] LETTERS, 34.

[2] ANONYMOUS LETTER.

[3] The three houses, still occupied, look from Stonegate like four. Today they are numbered 39, 37, 35 and 35A – this last, the double-fronted house, occupied successively in the eighteenth century by Francis Hildyard, John Hildyard, John Hinxman and the firm of John Todd and Henry Southeran. John Todd's sons, John and George W. Todd, had the shop from 1811, and Robert Sunter from 1837 to 1873. See P. T. Cooper, *The Sign of the Bible in Stonegate* (pamphlet of the Yorkshire Architectural Society), 1929. Mr John Harvey of the Historical Manuscripts Commission, York, kindly identified the houses from his files on local history. Although it has been said from time to time that Sterne once occupied one of these houses, that seems unlikely.

[4] The evidence for this account is in Thomas Gent's *Life,* ed. Joseph Hunter, 1832, pp. 194–6. 'Mr. Laurence Sterne,' wrote Gent, 'nephew to a doctor of divinity of that surname, having obtained his prebend, how he agreed with the alderman I cannot tell; but I found it was

exchanged the prebend of Givendale for that of North Newbald. But Jaques Sterne must have known it. It is impossible to imagine anything else. He was a crony of Hitch and worked with him during the campaign before the poor man 'overheated himself' and died. No one was so close to cathedral business as the precentor, who knew on other occasions the precise value of prebends.[1] He was well informed about the business of local printers. It looks very much as though he knew the truth about North Newbald prebend but kept quiet to spite his nephew. Sterne would have discovered it upon the death of the old woman that spring.

So Sterne wrote his letter to the *Courant* – at once an apology, which was due, and a revenge upon his uncle. It embarrassed the precentor in front of his political friends and affronted his dignity as head of the Sterne family. Dr Jaques Sterne would hate his nephew until the day he died.

Sterne's recantation was paid for dearly. With his uncle as his enemy, he would remain a 'lousy prebendary'.[2] He would retire to Sutton-on-the-Forest to take up parochial duties and to lead a life typical of the minor clergy. Still, he was his own man, free to make his mark in his own way when he should discover what that was. If Sterne sold his soul to his devilish uncle, he bought it back again.

---

in vain for me to make application to him, since Mr. Hitch could not relieve me. . . . God forgive the alderman!' Neither Hitch nor Sterne, of course, could do anything about the reversionary lease. I have searched in vain for this document in the files of the Church Commissioners, London, related to North Newbald estates: File 14,346; and at the Borthwick Inst., 'North Newbald prebendal estate papers: deeds 1676–1906'.

[1] See the two letters of J. Sterne to the Reverend Bradford, one undated, the other dated 19 March 1742/3 at BM: Add. MSS 32698, fol. 465; 32700, fol. 66.

[2] SENTIMENTAL JOURNEY, 105.

Vicar of Sutton
1741–1744

In the early autumn of 1741, Elizabeth told her relatives that she was expecting a baby. 'Does the world want odd people', wrote Elizabeth Robinson to her sister, 'or do we want strange cousins that the Sternes must increase and multiply? No folly ever becomes extinct, fools do so establish posterity.'[1] It was a cruel remark to come from a young lady who had not seen her cousin since they were girls and had never met her husband.

The autumn was a busy period for Sterne, into York for a conference with the printer and his annoying uncle, writing an answer to J. S., then hurrying back to Sutton to look after his bride. According to tradition, the couple lived at first in Church Farm – now Laurence House Farm. But the curate had left in the spring, and Sterne had taken possession of the 'large ruinous House' which was the parsonage. It was a long timber house with a thatched roof, three rooms below, as well as a 'back Kitchen adjoining', and four smaller rooms above. Sterne set to work repairing it, carefully noting his expenses in the parish registers – for a time:

	£	S	D
Laid out in Sashing the House	12: 0: 0 ADom: 1741		
In Stukoing and Bricking the Hall – – – –	4:	16:	0
In Building the Chair House – – – –	5:	0:	0
In Building the Parl^r Chimney – – – –	3:	0:	00
Little House – – – – – – –	2:	3:	0
Spent in Shapeing the Rooms, Plastering, underdrawing, & Jobbing – God knows what ——————————			

[1] CLIMENSON, I, 90. The comment can be dated September 1741 because in the same letter mention is made of the recent inoculation of Matthew Robinson, which took place on 13 September.

By the time they moved in, the house was finished with floorboards, plaster and, in some rooms, paper.[1]

These and other notations about the new garden Sterne entered into the registers for his wife's sake. If the value of the property were not maintained, his successor might sue Elizabeth for dilapidations. The ecclesiastical courts were not likely to absolve Sterne of responsibility because the dilapidations had come about while Mr Walker lived there or before: he would be expected to recover the damages in a suit against Mrs Walker. But how could he do that? The poor woman was now a neighbour trying to keep alive a large family of children and an ageing mother. Her husband's estate, counting two cows and one pig, had come to only £213.[2] So Sterne did the best he could to fix up the house himself. But it all came to naught in the end. In 1765, when he was living at Coxwold, a disgruntled curate at Sutton allowed the parsonage to burn to the ground. Sterne never replaced it, comforting himself, no doubt, with the thought that he had doubled the value of the living, as by then he had. After his death Elizabeth was rescued from a suit only through the powerful friends of her late husband.[3]

The couple could hardly afford to live in high style, but they were not poor. Sterne had the rectoral rights of Huby, that is, he had rights to all of the tithes in that village and to its 'glebe', as the arable lands belonging to the church were called. At Sutton he had vicaral rights – the small tithes only as well as a fixed emolument from the archbishop, augmented, fortunately, by the Crown. The value of the living was about £80.[4] The small

[1] Terrier of 18 May 1746, Borthwick Inst.: R. III. N. 7/LV.

[2] Will of John Walker, with inventory, at Borthwick Inst. On the legalities of dilapidations, William Cockburn, *The Clerk's Assistant; in the Practice of the Ecclesiastical Courts*, 3rd ed., Dublin, 1760, pp. 126–30.

[3] LETTERS, 433–9. Notes in the parish register by Sterne's successor, Andrew Cheap, reveal Cheap's fury at having to build a new parsonage at a cost of over £500.

[4] Two other terriers of 1749 and 1764 (in the hand of Sterne's curate, Marmaduke Callis) at the Borthwick Inst.: R. III. N. 5, 7, show that the fixed payments from the archbishop, the Crown and the 'moduses' (annual fees paid in lieu of

tithes) came to roughly £55. Other tithes and income from church lands may have added another £25. Thomas Beckwith surely overestimated the value of Sutton living when he said it came to £100: CURTIS, 43. Dr Goddard came closer when he estimated Sterne's *total* income, including, one supposes, that from his prebend, at £100: CLIMENSON, I, 73. Sterne himself said, speaking of 1741, that he had 'a bare hundred pounds a year', and he was probably including fees for substitute preaching: LETTER'S, 36. John Croft's remark that Sterne and his wife had £200 a year may refer to the period after Sterne got the Stillington living, and Croft probably included his notion of Elizabeth's income.

tithes, on any produce not grown in the arable fields, were paid in the chaotic manner fixed by ancient tradition. He received each year $2\frac{1}{2}d$. for every oxgang of cultivated pasture or garden; for every occupied house, 2*d.* at Easter.

> Item, a Funeral pays one Shilling, A Churching Sevenpence. A Marriage by Banns pays two Shillings & six pence. By Licence ten Shillings. Item, Every Communicant pays two Pence at Easter. Item, Every tenth Calf (one being due at six) by Custom of the Parish pays three Shillings & four Pence. Item, Every Cow pays One Penny, every Calf a Penny, every Foal a Penny, & a Swarm of Bees a Penny.[1]

Moreover, they had a modest income from other sources. At the time she married, Elizabeth's small fortune was paying her something in the neighbourhood of £50, and they had hardly moved into the vicarage when news arrived that it would be increased by £30. A distant cousin, an old woman whom Elizabeth had never known, died intestate, and Elizabeth with her sister fell heir to some houses at Leeds.[2] Sterne would try to set aside his wife's income. Although he said in the 'Memoirs' that his health was good at Sutton, he knew how high were the chances he might predecease her. The annual income from his prebend, aside from fines, was £10 or £12. He had collected a good fine in leasing the Givendale prebend to Lord Carlisle, and in 1743 he received some sort of fine for a new lease of the North Newbald estates. He seems to have found a way to put legal pressure upon Alderman Read, who held the reversionary lease: a year after Read took possession he signed a new lease with Sterne.[3] One guesses that he paid only a small fine since he had a previous claim which Sterne's predecessor had been unable to break. Sterne also began to augment his income by doing substitute preaching at the minster. The opportunities were good because most of the prebendaries did not live in York. The standard fee for a substitute preacher was £1.[4] For this amount, Sterne would spend perhaps half a day writing a sermon; then, after the morning service at Sutton, he would ride to York to preach, returning in time for evening service at the village. £1 was pretty important to Laurence Sterne. The

[1] Terrier for 1764.
[2] Lydia Botham to Elizabeth Robinson, 11 August 1741, MS at Huntington Library: MO 590. In his letter of 1751, Sterne said that £40 'would be nakedness to my Wife' (p. 41); he also spoke of her income as her 'future support' (p. 36).
[3] East Riding Deeds, R/177/416.
[4] LETTERS, 21–2, 25–31. On the substitute fee: CHAPTER ACTS, 1 March 1760.

couple's industry and thrift bespeak an ambition to live like rural gentry. Indeed, they were planning to invest in land.

Ironically, Sterne's new prosperity brought down upon him the most vexatious problem of his life. Exaggerated stories of Elizabeth's fortune reached Sterne's mother in Ireland, and she came unannounced to England. The couple had been living 'in perpetual Dread' of her 'thrusting herself' upon them, for they had heard about her 'Clamourous & rapacious Temper' from Jacob Costobadie, registrar of the dean and chapter, whom she had asked in 1731 to help settle her husband's estate. Sterne had not seen his mother since that year, when he was only eighteen. 'As during all that time I was not in a Condition to furnish her with Money, – I seldom heard from her.' Now, without any forewarning, she had shut up her embroidery shop and come to England hoping to live off the fortunes of her son's bride.

> The very Hour I received Notice of her Landing at Leverpool, I took Post to prevent her coming nearer Me, – stay'd three Days with her, – used all the Arguments I could fairly, to engage her to return to Ireland & end her Days with her Own Relations.
>
> I convinced her, that besides the Interest of my Wife's Fortune, I had then but a bare hundred pounds a year, out of Which my ill Health obliged me to keep a Curate, That we had moreover ourselves to keep, and in that Sort of Decency which left it not in our Powers to give her Much. (p. 36)

Sterne did not have a curate at this time, whatever he told his mother. He probably added the untruth when he wrote this letter, ten years later, in order to exonerate himself from the slander of his uncle. The other details which can be checked are accurate.

He pointed out how much cheaper it was to live in Ireland and that her pension, if drawn in England, would be discounted.

> I concluded with representing to her, the Inhumanity of a Mother *able* to Maintain herself, thus forcing herself as a Burden upon a Son who was scarce able to Support himself without breaking in upon the future Support of another Person whom she might imagine, was much dearer to me:
>
> In Short, I summ'd up all those Arguments with making her a present of Twenty Guineas, which with a Present of Cloaths &c – which I had given her the Day before, I doubted not, Would have the

Effect I wanted. But I was much Mistaken; for tho' she heard me With attention, Yet as Soon as she had got the Money into her Pocket, she told me with an Air of the utmost Insolence

'That as for going back to live in Ireland; She was determined to Shew me no such Sport – That she found, I had married a Wife who had brought me a Fortune – & she was resolved to enjoy her Share of it, & live the Rest of her Days at her ease either at York or Chester.'

(p. 36)

Sterne mustered up enough patience to say that he would not forget he was a son, 'Tho she had forgot she was a *Mother*'. Determined, Agnes moved to Chester, where for the next several years she lived with her daughter, Catherine. There they continued to raise 'perpetual Clamours' for money, living all the while on Agnes's pension of £20 and whatever Sterne sent them.

No doubt Sterne exaggerated his arguments to some degree, but he was right that living was cheap in Ireland. His mother would be happier there. Her outlook was Irish, and her unpolished manner would be less of a disadvantage there. Looking squarely at the social customs of that age, we must also allow his final point about his mother and wife: Agnes 'was neither born nor bred to the Expectation of a 4ᵗʰ part, of What the Government allowes her, & therefore has Reason to be contented with Such a Provision tho double the Summ would be nakedness to my Wife' (pp. 40–1).

But Agnes could not hear these arguments because she had been dreaming for years of the day when she would come to England and live in style. She had not drawn her pension in Ireland when it fell due, as Sterne thought, but had forgone it entirely for three years in order to have it payable in England.[1] She must have been intending ever since Sterne was a boy to come to England eventually.

'We were kind to her above our power & common Justice to ourselves. . . . We were supporting both her and my Sister in the Pleasures and Advantages of a Town Life, which for prudent Reasons we denied ourselves' (p. 37). The £20 Agnes took away upon this occasion represented a fifth of his income for the year. Thereafter, he sent her something around £10 a year, giving her a total of roughly £30, an income equal to that of a

[1] CURTIS, 43, describes a record of payments of Agnes's pension which he saw at the PRO. She drew £20 per annum from 1735/6 to 1758. The record has since been reshelved, and I have not been able to locate it.

curate. Agnes herself admitted the reasonableness of this support when she later said she was willing to accept a settlement of £8. Sterne was not guilty of abandoning her, as was later whispered, or of allowing her to take in washing for a living.[1] True, he did not take her into his house, but neither did she ask that. It may have been a mistake to support her at all, since she interpreted his assistance as a sign of weakness. When Sterne returned from Liverpool, the only comfort he could give Elizabeth was that at least his mother had decided to live at Chester, not at York as she had threatened.

The spring of 1742 was melancholy – Walpole's resignation, Agnes in Chester, the quarrel with Uncle Jaques. And then Elizabeth lost her baby.

> Memo That the Cherry Trees & Espalier Apple Hedge were planted in ye Garden October ye 9. 1742. The Nectarines and Peaches planted the same Day: The pails set up two Months before————

Village life was not always peaceful. So long as Archbishop Blackburn was alive, Sterne had an obligation to wrest some control from Squire Harland. Wilkinson, the curate, had let him down in that matter. He left an obsequious note in the registers about Harland's gift to the parish of 'fourteen elms springing Trees' planted in the vicarage garden and church-yard. Sterne was so irked that he inserted a little box into the middle of the curate's words in which he wrote, 'Faithfully recorded by R. Wilkinson!'

Village government was supposed to be in the hands of the vestry, over which Sterne presided, and theoretically all adult males who shared the communion had a vote. The vestry was empowered to levy the church rates, to modify the village laws, or 'pains',[2] to control the open-field farming, to maintain the petty schools at Huby and Sutton, and to pay the salary of the schoolmaster, John Dinsdale. They elected the churchwardens, the overseer of the poor, and other village officers. In actuality, Sutton had been run for years by an oligarchy of prosperous yeomen – Robert Sturdy, whose grandparents had been benefactors of the parish poor; William Thompson, who lived at New Park, an ancient royal hunting lodge at Huby; his relative, John Thompson, whose large farm was curiously named Bohemia; and others. They met informally at the local inn, where they carried on the real business of the town under the direction of William

[1] Letter of Daniel Watson, vicar of Leake, in *Monthly Repository of Theology and General Literature*, III (January 1808), 12.

[2] For discussions of parish government, see W. E. Tate, *The Parish Chest*, Cambridge, 1964; Sidney and Beatrice Webb, *The Parish and the County*, Vol. I of *English Local Government*, 5 vols, 1906, reissued, New York, 1963.

Bradshaw, the innkeeper, described as Philip Harland's estate agent and 'chief manager of yᵉ Town's Business in laying their Parish-Rates, &c.'¹ The squire, of course, had the effective power, not only because of his economic hold, but also because he was a justice of the peace.² What is more, he held the lease to the 'Rectory' of Sutton, that is, he was entitled to the 'great' tithes and the use of the glebe. If Sterne were to break the power of the squire and his myrmidons at the inn, he would have to induce the landless poor to use their vote in the vestry.

The only recorded episode in this struggle has to do with giving a 'settlement' in the parish to an outsider who wanted to open a new trade there. The story was told about Sterne by the servant, Greenwood: 'He was for many years at variance with the Harlands, the squires of his parish – it originated in his determination to give a settlement to a man who exercised a trade which required apprentices. Mr. Harland thought that thereby an expense might be brought on the parish.' The parish, of course, was responsible for its poor. 'Sterne was determined to carry his point', said Greenwood, '& let the man a farm of 10£ a year which gave him a settlement, & he never spoke to the Harlands after.'

The contest, however, petered out within five or six years, probably because Viscount Fauconberg did not want it. Sterne no longer felt any obligation to his uncle, and Archbishop Blackburn died in March 1743. His allegiance began to shift toward Lord Fauconberg, who, though he lived ten miles away at Coxwold, was lord of the manor of Sutton and owned half the land there. A number of the leading farmers leased land from him, and Philip Harland leased more of his estate from Fauconberg than he owned outright – though he was soon to purchase the freehold.³ One suspects that Fauconberg was planning the Sutton Enclosure Act a decade in advance of its enactment in 1756, and for that he needed the co-operation of both Harland and Sterne.

Certainly Greenwood overstated the case when he said in his simple way that Sterne stopped speaking to Harland. Their antagonism never reached the pitch of the quarrels between the Reverend Thomas Burton of Halifax and Squire Richard Sterne: Laurence continued to baptize and marry and bury members of the Harland family, and he never refused the squire

¹ James Borwick to Archdeacon Thomas Haytor, 7 February 1733/4, in Church Commissioners' file, Borthwick Inst.
² Undated draft of nominations to the Commission of the Peace, BM: Add. MSS 35602, fols. 62–4.
³ *Fauconberg Rentual, 1755–1771*, at Beinecke Library, Yale University.

communion or haled him into the spiritual courts. At the minster library is a copy of Sterne's sermon published in 1747, *The Case of Elijah and the Widow of Zerephath, consider'd*, inscribed in Sterne's hand, 'To Philip Harland, Es.' During the rebellion of 1745, when a subscription was raised for the defence of Yorkshire, the folk of Sutton and Huby made a contribution of £6. 9s. 6d., by no means an inconsequential sum.[1] A year later, as though in appreciation of their loyalty, Sterne permitted them as a parish to make a contribution to the public hospital, that opposition institution which had so plagued Sterne's own party: the list of contributors published in the *York Courant* on 13 January 1746/7 is made up entirely of individuals except for 'Parish of Sutton and Huby'. Then there is a letter of 1757 signed by Sterne, Harland and two gentlemen of Stillington threatening the overseers of the highways for Clifton with a court action if they do not keep the road to York passable. When the officials of Clifton declined to act, the four men took the case to court and won it.[2] Since the people of Sutton and Stillington depended upon that road to transport their crops to market, one can well imagine how they appreciated such prompt and forceful action by their squire and vicar. By 1760, Sterne was getting along so well with his old enemy that a group of local gentlemen trying to get the grumbling squire to co-operate in a new tax plan sent as their ambassador to him Parson Sterne.[3] These are *prima facie* evidences of developing harmony in Sutton parish.

Sterne seems to have had a special fondness for his more humble parishioners – the families of fifty or sixty labourers who owned no more than a cottage and a patch of garden, and the genuinely poor squatters who lived in makeshift hovels on the commons. From these arose the house servants whom he portrayed so lovingly as Susannah, Obadiah, Jonathan the coachman, and the fat foolish scullion. There were servants at the Hall, of course, and scattered among the prosperous farm families. Elizabeth and Laurence always had two or three. There were 'John Wood & Anne Slater Servants to me L. Sterne', who were married by banns on 1 April 1747. Elizabeth had a maid who once forgot to pack a guest's stockings – 'but she has a sweetheart in her head', Sterne wrote, 'wch puts all other things out'. When he worked for Sterne as a boy, Richard Greenwood lived in the vicarage. Stephen Jaques, the parish clerk, possibly a distant relative of Sterne's, would have doubled, by custom, as the gardener or footman. In 1758, Mr Jaques's

[1] *A List of the Voluntary Subscribers*, York, [1745], at BM: 1325. c. 22.
[2] LETTERS, 48–9.
[3] Richard Chapman to Lord Fauconberg, 6 July and 29 August 1760: NEWBURGH PAPERS.

successor was running errands for the parson: Sterne referred to him affectionately as 'my Sinful Amen'.[1]

Sterne's chief opportunity to influence these folk would have been through the Sunday services – a picture which has two distinct sides. Upon occasion, he lived up to the epithet given him by Bishop Warburton – a 'heteroclite parson'. Greenwood, telling about Sterne's debauches in York, added, 'He would frequently be absent many days together on these occasions, & should Sunday intervene did not return to perform the duties of the day – He did not attend well to the duties of his situation . . .'

The other side is revealed in a questionnaire which Sterne completed for Archbishop Herring's primary visitation of 1743.[2] He gave this account of Sutton parish: 'There is a Meeting House for Quakers, Liscens'd.' 'There is a small Benefaction for Bread, distributed faithfully every Sunday to the Poor who attend Morning & Evening Prayers, according to the Intention of the Founder.' 'Public Service is duly performed twice every Lord's Day.' 'The Sacrament is administered five Times every Year in my Church.' 'I have not refused the Sacrament to any one.' All who attend church are baptized 'Except one Quaker Woman whom I have prevailed with to come to Church, but have not been yet able to gain her consent to be Baptized.' One of Sterne's answers in the questionnaire, we are assured by the editors of the Herring *Returns*, is 'unique and stands alone' among those given by the entire clergy of Yorkshire and Nottinghamshire:

> I Catechise every Sunday in my Church during Lent, But explain our Religion to the Children and Servants of my Parishioners in my own House every Sunday Night during Lent, from six o'clock till nine. I mention the Length of Time as my Reason for not doing it in Church.

This statement, the truth of which cannot be doubted, shows Sterne 'sufficiently zealous to hold a three-hour instruction or confirmation class in his vicarage on the six Sunday evenings in Lent. . . . It shows that in 1743, whatever was the case later, Sterne took his work as a parish priest very seriously.'[3]

Sunday services, belonging to the common people, were always a major challenge to the parson who hoped to win the loyalty of his flock. No doubt

---

[1] LETTERS, 55, 64–5. Stephen Jaques was buried at Sutton on 6 October 1744.

[2] HERRING RETURNS, III, 92–3, reproduced in LETTERS, 21–2.

[3] Canon S. L. Ollard, 'Sterne as a young parish priest', TLS, 18 March 1926, p. 217. See also his note of 25 May 1933, p. 364, and self-correction of 1 June 1933, p. 380.

the squire boxed himself in in a comfortable pew, but once there, he had to listen to Mr Jaques reading psalms and canticles in a homely accent and tolerate the antics of the dog-whipper or knock-nobbler – an official charged with keeping the dogs under control, and in quiet moments keeping the congregation awake and attentive with his long wand. For hymns, the clerk probably pulled a pitch-pipe from under his cushion and whistled up a choir of local children, among whom were a few diehard basses. Small churches usually had no instrumental music unless the locals had got up their own orchestra of viols, flutes, clarinets, possibly with young Greenwood beating his drum.[1]

Sterne seems to have appreciated the tendency of his parishioners to reshape ritual as a folk art. At Stillington (a second parish which he would soon receive) during the cattle plague of 1749, he permitted the parish clerk to sing a psalm which the clerk himself had written:

I

O Lord We're fearfully distress'd
But thou can'st help us all
Thou can'st, if thou wilt do thy best
Let Men say what they will.

2

For this Distemperature full sad
Rages in Our Town.
It is enough to make one mad
The like was never known.

3

There's old John Crow, and Richard Pen
And likewise William Bland
With many more Upstantial Men
Now ruin'd out of hand.

4

And We shall all be quite undone
It is no boot to strive
And broke up every Mother's Son
As sure as We're alive.

[1] Peter H. Ditchfield, *The Parish Clerk*, New York, 1907, pp. 2–5.

5

No Christian Bull or Cow they say
But takes it *Sune* or *Syne*
And then its ten to one. I say
Good Lord take care of Mine.

6

For Lord thou know'st We are full poor
So help us if thou can
And we will put our trust no more
In any other Man.

7

The Doctor's tho they all have spoke
Like learned Gentlemen
And told us how the Entrails look
Of Cattle dead and gone

8

Yet they can nothing do at all
With all their learning store.
Then come away thyself Good Lord
And vex us not no more.

9

But come with scourge all in thine hand
O come without delay
And drive it forth from out the Land
For Ever and for Aye.[1]

Parson Sterne did not depend upon his parishioners to provide the whole show. He himself delivered a dramatic, extemporaneous sermon. What spontaneous gestures and inflexions he used can be imagined, especially in the light of his admiration for the pulpit theatricality of the Abbé Denis-Xavier Clément, whom he later heard in Paris.[2] Sterne projected this love of spontaneous oratory into *Tristram Shandy* – Walter Shandy's oration upon

---

[1] MS in the possession of Kenneth Monkman. A somewhat different version entitled 'A Psalm composed by the Clerk of Stillington & Sung by him at Divine Service on Sunday May 28th 1749' was discovered by L. P. Curtis in the MS commonplace book of Thomas Beckwith, Minster Library: MS Add. 40, fol. 3v; Curtis published it in 'Forged letters of Laurence Sterne', *PMLA*, L (1935), 1076–1106.

[2] LETTERS, 154–5.

death, Uncle Toby's apologetical oration on war, and, most especially, Trim's harangue to the servants in the kitchen, with look and tone and gestures graphically described and far more affecting than anything the corporal says. Greenwood had seen his master perform thus in the pulpit:

> . . . he never preached at Sutton but half the congregation were in tears . . . he used often to preach nearly extempore – He had engaged to preach at Fa[r]lington a few miles from Sutton, & when there found he had forgot his sermon – he only asked for a bible, & composed a most excellent sermon which he delivered from a scrap of paper no bigger than his hand.

Greenwood was recalling primarily the period 1743–5. As late as 1760, Sterne was using this style for rural congregations. A letter from Lord Fauconberg's steward, Richard Chapman, describes Sterne's successes during his first year as parson of Coxwold, his third living, presented to him in 1760. 'I gave Your Lordship's Service to Mr Sterne, whose doctrine, (tho Chiefly Extempory) takes so well amongs the Congregation that the Church can Scarce Contain the Number of People that appear every Sunday.'[1] One might note that Coxwold church holds about 300 people, and that there were only 158 families in Coxwold parish.[2] Sterne was bringing out virtually the entire village. Not many would have come from distant York only for the purpose of hearing the then famous author of *Tristram Shandy*.

Until recently, it has been thought that Sterne was a failure as a pulpit orator because of an unpleasant voice and manner. It has now been shown that illness robbed him of his voice in 1762. Unfortunately, the story of his poor preaching derives from the few sermons – possibly two only – which he preached after that time.[3] Strong evidence, to which we shall return in another chapter, indicates that he was one of the most popular preachers in York, though his sermons in the minster were probably somewhat quieter than in the country. The sermons he delivered to educated audiences he wrote out, saved, and some of them he eventually published. But these too, as he said, came 'more from the heart than the head'. He originally intended to publish them under the title, *The Dramatick Sermons of Mr. Yorick*.[4]

[1] Dated 20 July 1760: NEWBURGH PAPERS.
[2] Questionnaire completed by Sterne for Coxwold in DRUMMOND RETURNS.
[3] Arthur H. Cash, 'Voices sonorous and cracked', in *Quick Springs of Sense*, ed. Larry S. Champion, Athens, Georgia, 1974, pp. 197–209.
[4] Advertisement in *York Courant*, 4 March 1760; SERMONS, I, xlviii. Cf. TRISTRAM SHANDY, IV, xxvi, 317.

Considering all of this – his love of spontaneity, his admiration for dramatic oratory, his insistence that the heart, not the head, should speak – we can hardly doubt that Sterne's best sermons were those he ad-libbed for the country folk.

One of Sterne's more interesting duties was representing the parish at the colourful visitations of the archdeacon. Every spring the elderly apparator, William Coates, would ride into Sutton to deliver a 'process' for Sterne to read in church. In due time, the vicar, parish clerk, churchwardens, and any parishioners who were accused that year, would ride together fifteen miles to Thirsk, where they would join a large gathering in the parish church. Sutton belonged to the deanery of Bulmer, a subdivision of the archdeaconry of Cleveland (corresponding roughly to the North Riding). The visitations of the Archdeaconry Court of Cleveland consisted of three annual meetings, one for each deanery, a sort of circuit court which, despite its chaos, was the major device by which the larger church reviewed its parishes.[1]

It was the responsibility of the churchwardens to hand in a written 'presentment' of any parishioner who had violated the ecclesiastical law, but their duties were construed rather loosely. The vast majority of present-ments were for 'the crime of fornication'. Sometimes the accused were men, but more often unmarried mothers or expectant mothers. Hardly a year went by without some hapless girl or two, big with child, trailing along in the annual procession to Thirsk. To be sure, there were other charges, as the *Cleveland Court Books* reveal. William Avelock of Whitby parish was tried in 1740 for not bringing his child to be baptized in church, 'it being sus-pected that a Papish priest baptized it'. Poor Thomas Hart, the barber of Yarm, was excommunicated for practising his trade on a Sunday. Nothing so unusual happened at Sutton, though the parish had its share of quarrels over church rates. In 1752, Richard Mackley, a leading yeoman, was

---

[1] For a detailed discussion see Arthur H. Cash, 'Sterne as a judge in the spiritual courts', in *English Writers of the Eighteenth Century*, ed. John H. Middendorf, New York and London, 1971, pp. 17–36. CLEVELAND COURT records reveal that Sterne's attendance was good, not the best, but better than most wealthy clergy. From 1739, the year he first attended, to 1759, when he was writing *Tristram Shandy*, he missed eight visita-tions; seven of these absences were ex-cused. During his years of fame, Cleveland Archdeaconry Court met six times (one year it was inhibited by Drummond's primary visitation). Sterne, now repre-senting both Sutton and Coxwold, came twice. Once he was excused; three times, as the record states, he 'failed to appear'. In fact, he was abroad, and in each instance he was represented by a curate.

presented for not paying his rates. Two years later, John Bradshaw, one of Mackley's accusers, was presented for the same offence. But most of the 'crimes' of Sterne's parishioners were normal, that is, venereal.

The quiet town of Thirsk came dramatically to life on visitation days. Clergy, curates, churchwardens, clerks and accused persons from forty-two parishes converged upon the church. There were also many people in mourning, come to have the wills of their dead proved by the court; and there were masters of hospitals, physicians, midwives, schoolmasters, any-one 'exercising any Ecclesiastical function' who might have been asked to exhibit his credentials. The large church could accommodate the 400 or 500 people, especially since many waited on the steps or among the gravestones. But where, one wonders, did they put their horses?

The archdeacon, who was Dr Jaques Sterne, might be present. At other times the visitor (or judge) was his licensed official, or commissary, Dr William Ward, an elderly York lawyer. But Dr Ward was growing feeble, and usually he left the court to *his* surrogate, Dr Francis Topham. During Sterne's early years at Sutton, Dr Topham regularly presided, though sometimes he shared the bench with Uncle Jaques, who, being a lawyer, took a greater interest in the visitation than did most archdeacons.

Dr Topham would become in time the catalyst of Sterne's writing career, the central figure in his first extended fiction, *A Political Romance*. He was a Yorkshireman of Sterne's age, a graduate of Sidney Sussex, Cambridge, where Sterne might have first met him. In 1737/8, he was admitted advocate in the spiritual courts of York diocese and set to work on a brilliant career, eventually replacing Dr Ward as the leading church lawyer of the north.[1] He had a knack for church controversy and, with one exception, would remain in the good graces of all the archbishops who came to the see, for whom he performed numerous valuable services. He was competent and diligent. His major fault was ambition – if indeed that is a fault. It led him to indiscretions for which Sterne would one day pillory him.

The visitations must have been conducted at breakneck speed. Dr Topham, with the help of his registrar, had to prove any number of wills, examine the credentials of new clergy or other officials, swear in all the new churchwardens, review and refer to a later court session the more complex

[1] For his career, see VENN; ILLUSTRA-TIONS, III, 316–20, 693–701; Borthwick Inst.: *Consistory Court Book*, 26 January 1737/8; CHAPTER DEEDS, 25 April 1737; 31 January 1748; 8 June 1751; 1 August 1751; 8 September 1756; 22 February 1758.

problems. He would have made judgements upon some fifty simple cases, most of them terminating in an ordered penance or, if the accused were not there, an excommunication.

In the late afternoon the meetings broke up. The criminals took themselves homeward, the churchwardens retired to the ale houses for a friendly drink, and the clergy and lawyers walked to an inn for the visitation dinner. It is doubtful that Sterne alluded to Cleveland Court in the famous scene of the visitation dinner in *Tristram Shandy* (IV, xxv–xxix, 313–31). He depicts an unusually large gathering of dignitaries and lawyers, and the dinner is served at an inn of '★★★★' close to a printer's shop – an obvious indication of York. Sterne was suggesting a dinner following the primary visitation of an archbishop, a rare event which superseded the regular visitation. During his Sutton years, Sterne attended two primary visitations, that of Herring, when he appeared before His Grace in York on 5 July 1743, and that of Hutton, when he appeared at Thirsk on 20 June 1749.[1] Years of experience lie behind Sterne's scene, but probably it represents no particular historical event. Certainly he avoided drawing any figure which might be taken as an archbishop. With the exception of Dr Topham, who is recognizable in the pompous Didius, Sterne disguised the identity of other lawyers and judges behind the comic names of '*Agelastes*', '*Triptolemus*', '*Monopolus*, my politician . . . *Kysarcius*, my friend;——*Phutatorius*, my guide,——*Gastripheres*, the preserver of my life; *Somnolentius*, the balm and repose of it'.[2]

Whatever their original purpose, the spiritual courts of the eighteenth

---

[1] Borthwick Inst.: *Exhibition Book for Visitations of the Archbishops*, fols. 19–20. The credentials which Sterne exhibited in the spirituals are now at the BM: Add. Charters 16158–60, 16163–4, 16166. They bear the marks of court registrars for Cleveland archdeaconry visitations of 23 May 1739 (his first appearance for Sutton), 4 August 1750 (Archdeacon Blackburne's first appearance), 4 June 1761 (first appearance for Coxwold), and the primary visitations of Herring, 1743, Hutton, 1749, Drummond, 18 May 1764 (after the visitation dinner scene was written). For unknown reasons he failed to appear before Archbishop Gilbert at Thirsk on 11 September 1760, but later sent in his credentials to have them marked.

[2] TRISTRAM SHANDY, III, xx, 193–4.

James Aiken Work in his notes to the novel explains the meaning of the names thus: Agelastes, 'one who never laughs'; Triptolemus, 'probably taken from Triptolemus of Greek mythology . . . inventor of agriculture . . . giver of laws . . . a judge in the infernal regions'; Didius, 'an allusion to Julian Severus Didius who in A.D. 193 purchased the Roman Empire'; Kysarcius, 'a portmanteau-word, probably Sterne's translation of *Baise-cul*, a "great Lord" in Rabelais'; Phutatorius, 'copulator, lecher'; Gastripheres, 'another portmanteau-word, "Paunch-carrier," or "Big-belly"'; Somnolentius, 'one who sleeps'. On the identification of Didius as Dr Topham, below, Chapter 14.

century had lost most of their moral function and became almost exclusively a forum for settling financial grievances. Church rates, for instance, were a financial hazard to the churchwardens, who had to pay out of their own pockets any parish expenses not recovered through these taxes. Tithes were a large part, sometimes all, of the income of the parish priest, and if they were not paid he had no recourse except through ecclesiastical law. Sterne seems never to have had a tithe dispute; at least none ever reached the Cleveland Court. It is possible, of course, that he simply did not care to dispute these matters: he may have been like the parson of *Canterbury Tales*, 'ful looth . . . to cursen for his tithes'. Even the presentments for fornication were usually motivated by financial concern. A woman with an illegitimate child might end up homeless and a ward of the parish, to be supported out of the church rates. So the villagers of Sutton, if they acted in the typical manner, would have gone to some extremes to find a husband for such a woman, if at all possible the father of her child. The usual practice was to hold a kangaroo court, to force from the poor woman the name of her lover and, in turn, to compel them into a 'knobstock wedding' – named from the staves of office of local officials. It must have been hazardous to remain a bachelor in the country. A great many accused men and women 'absconded', as the record puts it, but occasionally the villagers managed to arrange a wedding. Then the couple would be charged in the spirituals with 'antenuptial fornication'. But there was a benefit in that since it precluded a charge in the temporal courts under the dread 'Bastardy Laws'.

The final act had to be played out in the parish church, where Sterne, as any parish priest of that age, had to supervise the penance ordered by the court or, that failing, the excommunication. The penance was a curious ritual, much of its meaning lost in the dim past. On an appointed Sunday, the girl or youth, or both, would appear at church bare-footed, bare-legged and bare-headed, wrapped in a white sheet and carrying a white wand. After prayers, Mr Sterne would summon her (in the case of a woman) to the front of the congregation and direct her to mount upon a chair. If she could read, he would hand her a printed penance. If not, which was more often the case, he would read it phrase by phrase, and she, with downcast eyes, would repeat after him,

WHEREAS, I good People forgetting my Duty to Almighty God have committed the Detestable Sin of Fornication with [name filled in] and thereby have justly provoked the heavy Wrath of God against me, to the great Danger of my own Soul, and evil Example of others, I do earnestly Repent, and am heartily sorry for the same, desiring Almighty God for the Merits of Jesus Christ, to forgive me both this and all other my Offences, and also ever hereafter, so to assist me with his Holy Spirit, that I never fall into the like Offence again, and for that End and Purpose, I desire you all here Present, to pray with me, and for me, saying,

OUR FATHER WHICH ART IN HEAVEN, AND SO FORTH.[1]

The prayer finished, Sterne pronounced an absolution, and the penitent, though still wrapped in the sheet, took her place once more among her neighbours. How many people of Sutton went through this torture by humiliation we cannot know because of the too brief records of Cleveland visitations, but all indications are that it was performed almost every year.

Although the vast majority of accused did penance, some few did not. What the ritual curse of excommunication was, we do not know, though it must have been a dread rite. The judge at the visitation pronounced a relatively innocuous 'lesser excommunication', cutting the offender off from the Eucharist and depriving him of a few legal rights. If, after a period of about six months, he did not repent, the parish priest was ordered to perform in church a 'denunciation'. After that, the offender was to be excluded from all 'commerce and conversation' with his neighbours. Few could take such punishment. Those who remained in the neighbourhood usually did the penance eventually. The original readers of *Tristram Shandy* must have heard tragic overtones in that comic scene of Dr Slop's ritual curse of Obadiah (III, xi, 170–9).

After 1742, Sterne began to see this entire drama from the opposite side of the spiritual bench. As prebendary of North Newbald, he became, in legal parlance, 'Dignitary of North Newbald Peculiar' – in more comprehensible language, the judge of a tiny spiritual court in that parish. A 'peculiar' court is any jurisdiction separated from the normal authority of the archdeacons. When prebendaryships were first established, many, though not all, included the spiritual jurisdiction over the parish wherein lay the

[1] Among the spiritual courts records at the Minster Library are hundreds of these printed penances. A part only of a printed penance is quoted.

prebendal estates, an obvious augmentation of the prebendary's power since he became lord of the spirit as well as lord of the manor. As the temporal powers dwindled, so too did the spiritual: in Sterne's time, conducting such a spiritual court was hardly more than another annoying duty. There was an elaborate network of such peculiars in York, most of them for a single parish, but a few, associated with the large estates of the cathedral officers, embraced a good many parishes. The largest was the Court of the Dean and Chapter, meeting at York, which served as an appeal court for the others.[1]

Sterne, though he probably found the duty troublesome, appears to have visited at North Newbald annually until 1760, when he turned the court over to a surrogate, the Reverend Anthony Almond of North Newbald.[2] No word of particular cases comes down to us, but most would have been for the recurrent crime of fornication. Nothing very complex arose, else it would have been referred to the Court of the Dean and Chapter. The lack of evidence in the full record of the higher court indicates one thing: that none of the accused parishioners at North Newbald contested Sterne's rulings. He must have been a lenient and fair judge.

Sterne was not overworked at Sutton, and he and Elizabeth had some social life. Elizabeth seems to have preferred the clerical circles of York. We find Sterne passing on his wife's greetings to the lady of Archdeacon Blackburne, and she had a friendship with the wife of Joseph Bridges, Sterne's Cambridge friend who was now vicar of St Martin's Coney Street and one of the vicars choral. Another of Elizabeth's friends was the wife of Charles Cowper, a canon residentiary. In the country, the couple went often to see the Croft family at Stillington.[3]

They probably saw Cousin Richard and his wife in their new home at Fulford on the south edge of York. But Richard died on 13 November 1744. 'As he was greatly beloved,' said the obituary notice in the *York Courant*, 'so he died as greatly lamented, being a sincere Friend and kind Relation.'

---

[1] Dean Osbaldeston's order in CHAP-TER ACTS, 12 November 1730. Records of this court are in the *Dean and Chapter Abstract Book* at the Borthwick Inst., and in loose papers at the Minster Library.

[2] The only records for North Newbald Peculiar are loose papers at the Minster Library: C 3 a. No wills were proved there. Nothing at all survives from the period in which Sterne visited personally, but we know he did so from indirect evidence: for the first four years after 1760, when Almond took charge, the churchwardens' presentments are addressed to Sterne, as though they were used to his presence and expected him to return.

[3] MEMOIRS; CROFT; LETTERS, 27, 51–2, 55, 59.

Cousin Timothy died two years later at the age of twenty-seven, so heavily in debt to his brothers-in-law as to leave his wife penniless.[1]

But in the village Elizabeth was lonely. There were no gentlewomen whom she could visit except Mrs Walker, the widow of the late vicar, and her ageing mother Mrs Simpson. She was hurt that her cousin, Elizabeth Robinson, did not look her up when she was in York for Race Week in August 1741, and it was an especially painful cut not to be invited to her cousin's wedding at the minister on 10 August 1742, one of the major social events of the year. Much later she complained to Elizabeth – now Mrs Montagu – of her 'indiferition'. 'Surely never poor Girl', she wrote, 'who had done no one thing to so merit such neglect – was ever so cast off by her Relations as I have been.'[2] Elizabeth helped with parish duties and left her name as witness in the marriage register. But the lot of a rural parson's wife was a trying one. The anecdote which Croft told of her suggests a determined thrift verging upon parsimony: 'A Flock of Geese assembled in the Church Yard at Sutton, when his Wife bawl'd out "Laurie, powl 'em," i.e. pluck the quills, on which they were ready to riot and mob Laurie.' Perhaps she would have been happier with a baby, but she was not to have one for six years.

Sterne's servant, Richard Greenwood, said that Elizabeth 'brought Sterne several children', but Greenwood, quite elderly when he told his recollections to Joseph Hunter, probably was recalling stillborn children. Not until 1745 did Elizabeth and Laurence baptize a child. There is no ready explanation for Greenwood's story of a son who 'lived 3 weeks', and as yet no way to confirm it. 'Sterne', said Greenwood, 'was inconsolable on his death, took to his chamber, & would not leave it of a week.' It is unthinkable that Laurence and Elizabeth would not have baptized this child, but no record of a baptism appears at Sutton, the surrounding villages or York. It is possible, of course, that Elizabeth, like Mrs Shandy, wanted to bear her child elsewhere, perhaps in the infirmary of some man-midwife.[3]

[1] Borthwick Inst.: administration papers for the goods of Timothy Sterne with accompanying document in which his widow renounces all claims upon the estate. Timothy was nominated as a justice of the peace late in 1746, but died before taking office: *York Journal*, 11 and 16 December 1746. A monument to his memory was raised in Bradford church.

[2] Undated MS letter at the Huntington Library: MO 5088; published in CLIM-ENSON, II, 176–7, and CURTIS, 136–7. Probably written in 1761.

[3] Since in the novel Elizabeth Shandy wanted to be delivered by the celebrated Dr Richard Manningham (p. 44), who historically speaking opened, in London, England's first lying-in ward, one might guess that Elizabeth Sterne went there to be delivered; but I have not located the baptism in any of the published registers for London.

Whether Greenwood's story is accurate or not, Sterne would have been disappointed not to have a son. His feelings may lie behind much of *Tristram Shandy*, the story of two brothers of doubtful potency whose overriding concern is to continue the family through a male heir.[1] Possibly Sterne blamed himself for the stillborn children. Some believe he suffered from syphilis.[2]

Elizabeth, lonely and without a child to love, gave rein to her quarrelsome disposition. By 1743 their marriage was in a downward spiral from which it never was rescued. To be sure, he never entirely lost his affection for Elizabeth and continued to protect her from the threats of the world even when he could no longer save her from his own weaknesses. But probably they ceased to think of themselves as happily married.

John Croft was ready with an explanation: 'Afterwards they did not live on the best terms and harmony together, chiefly owing to his infidelity to the Marriage Bed.' Sterne's own servant, at once more intimate with the situation and more respectful of the couple, saw the difficulties as more complex. He did not excuse or apologize for Sterne, but he did see that the quarrels between husband and wife were sometimes the cause of his master's infidelity. Greenwood began in Sterne's service in 1742 – only a year, or a year and a half, after the marriage, yet he recalled that 'During all the time he lived with them, they were upon very ill terms'. 'When any thing produced a difference between him & his wife, he would order Richard to bring out his horse, & they would go together to York, where he soon lost all his cares in the arms of some more blooming beauty.' There were other occasions, it must be added, when Sterne sought out women only because he was at York and for the moment free:

> He used to accompany his master whenever Sterne came to York, & when there he rarely spent a night without a girl or two which Richard used to procure for him – He promised Richard to reward him for keeping these private amours of his secret, particularly from Mrs Sterne – Richard says he was as good as his promise & that for his part he never mentioned these things concerning his master – Sterne too was continually after his female servants, & these things, &

[1] William Bowman Piper, 'Tristram Shandy's tragicomical testimony', *Criticism*, III (1961), 171–85.

[2] This opinion of George Saintsbury's in his introduction to the Everyman edition of *A Sentimental Journey*, 1926, is followed by Lodwick Hartley in *This Is Lorence*, Chapel Hill, 1943, reissued 1968 under the title, *Laurence Sterne: A Biographical Essay*.

sometimes his affairs at York, would come to the ears of Mrs Sterne, & as might be expected great quarrels ensued –

And so the spiral went on – a spat, a wild night in York, gossip, an unhappy wife who made him feel her fiery temper. Sterne began to let himself go in his personal habits. Elizabeth developed into a 'most eccentric woman'.[1]

Well might Tristram Shandy wonder 'that Nature, who makes every thing so well to answer its destination . . . should so eternally bungle it as she does, in making so simple a thing as a married man' (IX, xxi, 625). Sterne might have avoided much of his troubles had he known where his real talents lay, but in this period, he wrote, so far as we know, almost nothing – except sermons, which offered him no real challenge. Instead, he threw himself into parochial duties. He dissipated his wit in social conversation and his creative impulses in the arts of painting and fiddling. Before he discovered himself Sterne would be well into middle age.

[1] Daniel Watson. Sterne's slovenly dress: Dr James Atkinson as reported by Thomas Frognall Dibdin in *A Biographical, Antiquarian, and Picturesque Tour in the Northern Counties of England and Scotland*, 2 vols, 1838, I, 214.

7

Stillington
& the Tindal Farm
1744–1745

In the winter of 1743–4, the death of Sterne's neighbour, Richard Musgrave, vicar of Stillington, opened the possibility of a second living for Sterne. He began to step over to that village, two miles north of Sutton, to take the services: his hand first appears in the registers under the date of 16 February. On 14 March he was inducted into the living.

The 'Memoirs' contain a pleasant story about how Sterne got this living through his wife's influence. Alas, a critical view of the matter throws the fact in doubt. The story, as we have it, is less than perfect in its logic: 'By my wife's means I got the living of Stillington – a friend of her's in the south had promised her, that if she married a clergyman in Yorkshire, when the living became vacant, he would make her a compliment of it.' The story does not say that the promise was made upon condition that Elizabeth married Laurence Sterne, but rather 'a clergyman in Yorkshire'. The phrase, with its indefinite article, can only mean an unidentified person, possibly *any* clergyman in Yorkshire. If the account is correctly stated, one must conclude that Elizabeth did not yet know Laurence, or, at the least, that she had not identified him to her influential friend. Consequently, we are asked to believe that she was promised the compliment of a living which by *sheer chance* turned out to be adjacent to the living of the man she finally chose. Perhaps Lydia Sterne tampered with the passage when she edited the 'Memoirs'.[1]

[1] I would also reject the unlikely theory that Elizabeth's friend was Thomas, Sixth Baron Fairfax (1692–1782), the friend of Washington's, a theory advanced by Percy Fitzgerald in *Life of Laurence Sterne*, 2 vols, 1864, I, 220, and repeated by

On the other hand, there is circumstantial evidence that Sterne got the living on his own initiative. We know that he applied for another of Mr Musgrave's livings, that of Marton, just east of Stillington. He was turned down by the archbishop, who had instructions from his predecessor to combine Marton and yet another living in the area, Farlington Chapel, so the two could be given to a younger man named William Dawson.[1] Since Sterne took the initiative with Marton, it is likely he also applied for Stillington – not to the archbishop, in this case, but to Dean Osbaldeston. The official patron was the prebendary of Stillington, Richard Levett, but he lived in Buckinghamshire and probably left the matter in the hands of the dean. The presentation letter was an impersonal document, written according to the prescribed form by John Clough, assistant registrar to the dean and chapter, and sent to Mr Levett for his signature.[2]

The other formalities were equally impersonal, but they had their amusing side. Sterne had to produce testimony of his 'Good Life and Integrity of manners', and did so by soliciting the signatures of three prominent clergymen who had been his political allies in 1741–2, William Dodsworth, William Berdmore and Thomas Harrison. They signed a letter – also written out by the assistant registrar – attesting that Sterne had 'led his Life godly soberly and honestly' and 'applyed himself diligently to his Studies'.[3] On 27 February the dean and chapter determined to induct him as soon as he could get a dispensation to become a pluralist. For this purpose, Sterne had to acquire the empty title of 'Chaplain'. An ancient statute required all clergy holding more than one living either to have a degree in divinity (or civil law) or to be a chaplain. All noblemen had the right to a certain number of chaplains, but few wanted even one. So they gave the positions to the Archbishop of Canterbury, whose officers assigned them to anyone needing the qualification. Sterne became 'Chaplain to the Right

CROSS, 54. Lord Fairfax's connections with Yorkshire were severed in 1716, when his West Riding estates were sold to pay the debts of his late father.

[1] Dawson's letter to Archbishop Drummond, 4 September 1762, Borthwick Inst.: R. Bp. 20 B/61.

[2] Minster Library: D 1; dated 20 February 1743/4. Personal presentations were usually written out by the recipient and taken to the patron to be signed, as was done by Sterne when he received the

living of Coxwold. There was nothing unusual or Shandian in the procedure, as CURTIS thought.

[3] Dated 25 February, at Minster Library: D 1. Berdmore was vicar of Bishopthorpe, curate of Acaster Malbis, and prebendary of Bugthorpe; Dodsworth, curate of St Olave, rector of All Saints' in the Pavement, and prebendary of Givendale; and Harrison, rector of South Kilvington and rector of St Martin in Micklegate.

Honourable Charles, Earl of Aboyne'. This once set off speculations that Sterne had served as tutor to Charles Gordon, Fourth Earl of Aboyne, then eighteen, and had taken him about Europe. After all, Tristram Shandy had once promised to give 'a most delectable narrative' of his journey as governor of 'Mr. *Noddy*'s eldest son' (I, xi, 24–5).[1] Probably Sterne never laid eyes on the young Earl of Aboyne.

Sterne's new situation as a pluralist was unflattering in its normality. Half the clergy of the diocese held adjacent livings. Modern historians no longer deplore pluralism among the working clergy. Cases like Sterne's were, in fact, an answer to abuses such as selling livings. The truly shameful practice was the acquisition by high churchmen of numerous sinecures – unattended prebendal stalls, for instance, or wardenships of alms houses – not a matter of pluralism at all, technically speaking.[2]

It was not a rich living, having no augmentation from the Crown. As the prebendary's vicar, Sterne had the small tithes and some sort of fixed emolument paid by the prebendary out of whatever income he had from the great tithes. Sterne, who obviously disliked such a task, wrote only a sketchy 'terrier', or inventory, in 1749, in which he neglected to state the amount of this annual payment. Contemporary opinion set the value of the living at £50.[3] Again Sterne was trapped by customs which forced him to collect the rest of his income in trifling tithes for cows, calves, bees, gardens, apples and pigs. But he had the use of the quaint vicarage house. Mrs Musgrave vacated it a year later when she remarried, and presumably Sterne leased it. He may have wanted the living primarily for the 37 acres 2½ roods of farmland, which, added to the church lands at Huby and Sutton, brought under his control something like 120 acres.

Sterne now conducted morning services at Sutton and evensong at Stillington, reversing the order on the first Sunday of each month. His dispensation required him to 'exercise hospitality' at Stillington two months of the year, but Sterne had learned at Cambridge how to live with outworn statutes.

[1] J. M. Bullock, who made the suggestion in N&Q, Eleventh Series VIII (1913), 166, was answered correctly, but on weak evidence, by Edward Bensley, CL (1926), 65–6. The actual statutes and customs can be found in John Ecton, *Thesaurus Rerum Ecclesiasticarum*, 3rd ed., 1763, pp. 610–11. Sterne's dispensation document at BM: Add. Chart. 16162, dated 3 March.

[2] HERRING RETURNS, I, xii–xiv.
[3] CURTIS, 43. The terrier of 1749 at Borthwick Inst.: R. III. N. A terrier of 1778 at Minster Library: K. 2, shows a considerable improvement in the living. Kenneth Monkman has in his personal collection some twenty receipts in Sterne's hand for moduses received from Stephen Croft.

Probably he pursued his new duties diligently at first – they were not very heavy – slacking off in later years. 'Once . . . as he was going over the Fields on a sunday to preach at Stillington', said John Croft, 'it happened that his Pointer Dog sprung a Covey of Partridges, when he went directly home for his Gun and left his Flock that was waiting for him in the Church, in the lurch.'

The prebendary was, of course, the lord of the manor, and the entire parish lay within the Liberty of St Peter, that odd political entity governed by the dean and chapter.[1] In its externals, it must have differed little from Sutton. There were open fields and encroaching enclosures, 'substantial' yeoman farmers, the labouring cottagers, the poor. The church of St Nicholas was another damp old stone structure in bad repair. It has since been altered extensively.

There were fewer men who could vote at Stillington, and presumably the influence of Stephen Croft had brought some of them into the camp of the Ministerial Party. Nevertheless, Sterne was sometimes at odds with his Stillington neighbours, as with those at Sutton. John Croft told a memorable tragicomic story about this: 'Another time when he was skaiting on the Car at Stillington, the Ice broke in with him in the middle of the Pond, and none of the Parishioners wou'd assist to extricate him, as they were at variance.'

The village was governed, not by a vestry, but a 'jury', twelve men who, once elected, held their posts for life – a system left over from the old manorial courts. As vicar, Sterne was their president *ex officio*. These jury-men recorded all decisions in the quaint *Jury Book of Stillington Manor*, full of orders for cleaning the gripes and ditches, for the care of the poor, the division of labour in repairing bridges and gutters, the allotment of tasks in the open fields. There are many curious rules or 'pains'. 'We lay in pane y^t no person shall be allow^d to fetch ye Bull of ye common to any cow into any paster or Yard byt carry y^m to him, upon Forfeiture of [sixpence].' 'We of ye Juery do Lay apane y^t no person shall at any time Fetch ye common Bull of [?to] his hoose but drive there Cows to him Upon paine of being presented as ye Juery thinks proper.'[2]

Spiritual jurisdiction was invested in Stillington Prebendal Peculiar

---

[1] General information on the parish in LAWTON, 460; Thomas Gill, *Vallis Eboracensis*, 1852, pp. 414–15; *Victoria County History . . . North Riding*, II, 187–90; and the questionnaire completed by

Sterne's curate, Marmaduke Callis, in DRUMMOND RETURNS.

[2] CURTIS, 49. Yorkshire archivists are currently looking for the *Jury Book of Stillington Manor*, which has been lost from sight since Curtis examined it.

Court, another tiny ecclesiastical court, like that of North Newbald. There
are no records of Stillington visitations for the first six years of Sterne's
incumbency. The prebendary, Mr Levett, probably never came in person.
Then, for two years after Levett's death, the prebend was traded about
among wealthy churchmen. Later records suggest that during these years
Sterne and his neighbour, the Reverend Richard Mosley of Wigginton,
presided.[1] James Worsley, rector of Stonegrave, who became the prebendary
in 1750, was a man who took his clerical duties seriously. He usually visited
personally, and he faithfully turned in his records to the dean and chapter,
as he was supposed to do.[2] One is impressed with Worsley because, although he came from a powerful family, he seems never to have used the
church for selfish purposes.[3] The presentments were much like those we
have seen at Cleveland Court. During one of the years Sterne presided, 1755,
William Johnson and Jane Nelson were presented for 'the Crime of fornication together, they since being married'. Their penance is signed by Sterne.

One case is of particular interest, the trial of Jane Harbottle, a poor
woman, probably the village idiot.[4] We know something about her from the
parish registers. In 1744 Sterne baptized 'Tamar, the Bastard Child of Jane
Harbottle'. In 1749 it was 'Jonathan Bastard Child of Jane Harbottle & Th^s
Wood born – Feb. 23'. This ill-starred infant was buried in August 1751.
In 1752 was born 'Esther Bastard Child of Jane Harbottle'. The father of this
last child was alleged to be Robert Jepson, one of the leading yeoman farmers
of the village, married and the father of a considerable family. The situation
could no longer be tolerated, and the next year the churchwardens presented
both Jane and Jepson:

July ye 3 1753

No more presentments but thease as folous
We Hearby present Robert Jepson maried man for the Crime of

[1] Sterne presided in 1754–5, Mosley in
1751. Francis Wanley succeeded Levett
as prebendary, but soon resigned in a
trade with Hugh Thomas. A few months
later they traded back again. Then Wanley resigned a second time to accept a
better preferment.

[2] Minster Library: C 3 a. These loose
papers are the only record of the court.

[3] Eventually he married the daughter of
Sir James Pennyman, Bart., of Ormesley
Hall, where his descendants, who took the
name of Pennyman, continued until a few
years ago. His career: ACT BOOK,
1755–68, fols. 110, 113, 126, 282. He became Chaplain in Ordinary to George
III: obituary in *Gentleman's Magazine*,
1777, p. 459.

[4] First discovered by CURTIS, 47–8.
With the exception of the *Jury Book*, the
documents I have used are at the Minster
Library: BB 23, and the *Dean and Chapter
Abstract Book, 1739–1774*.

adultrey, by begetting a Basterd Childe upon *Jane Harbotle* and wee accordingly present the said Jane Harbotle for the Crime of Fornycation The Sade Jane Harbotle has Had three bastards and all by mared men

Jane pleaded guilty before Mr Worsley. She was sent to York to pay her fine and to pick up a printed penance. The sheet survives with Sterne's certification on it that Jane did her penance, bare-headed, bare-footed, white sheet, wand and all, on 8 September. 'Whereas I good People forgetting my Duty to Almighty God, have committed the Detestable Sin of Fornication with *Robert Jepson a Mary'd Man*', etc.

An entry in the *Jury Book* of the following spring shows that the parish set aside £5. 1s. 0d. for 'the use of Robert Jibson Childe by botil . . . per week 7 pence'. Obviously, the parish officers had not prevailed upon Jepson to support the child. He was cited specifically to appear at the next visitation. Sterne read the process in church on 21 July 1754; and Ben Camsell, a churchwarden, swore an affidavit, witnessed by Sterne, that he had personally served the citation on Jepson. Because Mr Worsley could not get to the visitation, held the next day, Sterne presided. Jepson failed to appear, and there was nothing to do but to excommunicate him. A full year was allowed to pass before Mr Worsley sent an order to complete the excommunication. Jepson was denounced in Stillington church, as Sterne's note attests, on 31 August 1755.

Someone, perhaps Sterne or Worsley or both, seems to have urged Jepson to make a defence, but he did nothing before his accuser died. Jane Harbottle, 'Spinster', died at Stillington in September 1758, leaving her two surviving children on the parish. On 14 February 1760, Jepson finally acted: his lawyer appeared before Mr Stables of the superior spiritual court of the dean and chapter and 'alleg'd that his client was not Guilty of the Crime of Adultery for which he stood presented in the said prebendal Court and desired him to be Dismiss'd & referred to Law which the Commissary Decreed'. Jepson was received back into the parish. Within two years he was elected overseer of the poor, and in 1769 he was elected to the jury. It is unthinkable that he could have won these honours without the support of the church. Probably it had become apparent to all that he was not guilty of fathering Jane Harbottle's bastard.

Jane herself had been treated kindly by the whole community. She had not been haled into the spiritual court until her third child. Once accused, she was given every consideration. On that day in 1753 when she walked into

York to get her penance, she carried in her pocket a note from Sterne to the
registrar:

> Mr *Clough*
>   The Bearer is the poor Woman who was presented at Stillington
> Visitation; and has left her Child to go & get these said Penances,
> wch I & Mr Mosely talked so much about. She is as poor as a Church
> Mouse & cannot absolutely raise a Shilling, to save her Life. So pray
> let her have the Penance – and so far as the Stamps, I will take care to
> discharge – If not above 3 or 4 Shillings –
>   Y^rs L *Sterne*
>
> *PS,*
> Pray dispatch her, That she may not have a 2^d Journey as she has a
> Child to leave——

The church could be merciful. At the bottom of the presentment is a note
in Mr Clough's hand: 'On Mr Sternes certifying her poverty she only paid
4^d for the penance, which was ret^d with a Certificate in due performance.'
The history of Jane Harbottle gives the lie to John Croft's pompous statement about Sterne, 'Am sorry to venture to pronounce . . . that he was
far from being a good man.'

At Stillington Sterne had two gentry families to consort with or to deal
with. There was William Stainforth, Esq., of obscure history, presumably
the brother and heir of a well-to-do widow, Frances Faceby.[1] Far more
important to Sterne was the squire, Stephen Croft. 'At Stillington the family
of the C[roft]s shewed us every kindness', he commented in the 'Memoirs'.
'"Twas most truly agreeable to be within a mile and a half of an amiable
family, who were ever cordial friends.' Stephen Croft had returned to his
estates only shortly before Sterne got the Stillington living. He had been
abroad learning the family wine-importing business, established a century
before. Sir Christopher Croft, the ancestor who had purchased the Stillington estate, Lord Mayor of York in 1618, 1629 and 1641, had been a contemporary of Sterne's ancestor, Sir Roger Jaques, and like Sir Roger he had

---

[1] Mrs Faceby is mentioned in LETTERS,
56, but was not identified by Curtis. She
is noticed in MINSTER REGISTERS,
YAJ, II, 356, as the widow of William
Faceby, who left her properties at Stillington. Upon her death they passed to her
brothers, George, who lived in London,
and William Stainforth. William was
active in the campaign of 1741–2 on the
side of the Ministerial Party, and he
served on the Grand Jury in 1740/1. He
signed the petition for the enclosure of
Stillington, and he helped Stephen Croft
change the course of the town road:
QUARTER SESSIONS, 292–3.

been knighted by Charles I. Stephen, from the age of twenty-one, was the sixth Croft squire at Stillington. Though not the lord of the manor, he and his ancestors had always held the lease of the prebendal estates and rectoral rights. He was, of course, a partner in the wine business.[1] Croft port is still marketed in England.

Although Stephen Croft is remembered today primarily as Sterne's friend, he was a man of affairs in his own time. Keenly interested in politics, he took an active part in Rockingham's later organization of northern Whigs and in the Yorkshire Association (for parliamentary reform) organized by the Reverend Christopher Wyville. His son-in-law, Nathaniel Cholmley, jokingly called him 'the Kings Walking Conversable Confidential Friend'.[2] His father, also Stephen, had been one of the founders of the York assembly rooms, and Stephen was elected a director in 1752, a post which later fell to his son, another Stephen.[3]

The Croft family emerges from the record as the highest sort of eighteenth-century landed gentry – people of taste, prudent, reserved, but kind and hospitable. Richard Spence, son of a Stillington blacksmith who became a printer in York and a well-known Methodist lay preacher, always spoke highly of the family, whom he had once served as a footman. In later years, when he would return to the village, he would pray outside the wall of the park, thanking God he had not been born on the other side where wealth and power might have tempted him away from religion, but he prayed 'with no intention to reflect upon any part of that highly respectable family, nor with any knowledge that their wealth had the same effect upon them'.[4] Stephen Croft's mother, who lived with him, was the daughter of Sir Edmund Anderson, Bart., of Broughton, Lincolnshire. Stephen's wife was Henrietta, daughter of Henry Thompson of Kirby Hall. During the years that Sterne was their neighbour, they completely rebuilt Stillington Hall, which stood

[1] SKAIFE; monument at Stillington church and the parish registers; Nicholas Carlisle, *Notices of the Ancient Family of Croft*, 1841. The genealogical chart by Joseph Hunter in *Familiae Minorum Gentium*, ed. John W. Clay (Harleian Soc. Pub., XXXVIII), 1895, is not to be trusted.
[2] Stephen Croft to Rockingham, 12 October 1779, in Wentworth-Woodhouse papers at Sheffield Central Library: R1-1209, 1858. On the association: Ian R. Christie, *Wilkes, Wyville and Reform*, 1962, pp. 74, 202–3 and *passim*. A Reynolds portrait of Stephen Croft was sold at Christie's, 13 May 1948. See photograph at the NPG: negative No. 5074. Etched in reverse by C. Carter and published in London, 1 October 1787.
[3] York Public Library: *Assembly Rooms: Minute Books*.
[4] [Richard Burdekin], *Memoir of the Life and Character of Mr. Robert Spence*, York, 1827, pp. 4–11, 52–3.

at the east edge of the village, looking down a gentle slope and across the Foss, turning it into one of the finest Georgian houses in the north, with many luxurious rooms finished with exquisite plasterwork. Late in the nineteenth century it passed out of the family and quickly fell victim to modern economic change. It stood a haunting ruin until 1967, when it was pulled down to make way for a housing development. This beautiful mansion was Sterne's delight for many years; 'he was a constant Guest at my brother's Table', reported John Croft.

Stephen Croft's young brother, John, became Sterne's chronicler and critic in that memoir written for Caleb Whitefoord. John Croft was not quite candid when he wrote, 'I was as it were brought up under him, as he was Vicar of Stillington, where I was born.' John was twelve when Sterne took charge of the parish, and he could hardly have known Sterne more than two years before then. He was Sterne's parishioner for three years, and then he was sent abroad to Oporto, where he remained for many years, returning to England only shortly before Sterne's death. 'My long absence abroad in Portugal', he admitted, and Sterne's 'being so much taken up in the gay World', at the time of his return, 'made a large gap in our Intimacy'. Croft was *never* 'intimate' with Sterne, despite his trying to suggest the contrary, though as a boy he had every opportunity to observe him closely.[1]

When Agnes Sterne, in Chester, heard of her son's second living, she began to consider ways of getting more money out of him. This time, instead of attacking directly, she sent her pretty daughter, Catherine, who could hardly have been more than twenty years old. Greenwood, the servant, recalling her visit in the summer of 1744, described her as 'one of the finest women ever seen'. Agnes also planned a new strategy: she sent Catherine first to York to win a powerful ally – Dr Jaques Sterne. The interview with the precentor was, in Sterne's opinion, the true reason for Catherine's trip, though the 'Pretence' was to make a month's visit with her brother. Sterne told the story in his letter to his uncle of 1751:

> In yᵉ Year 44. my Sister was sent from Chester by order of my Mother to York, That she might make her Complaints to You and engage You to Second them in these unreasonable Claims upon us.
>
> . . . As we were not able to give her a fortune, and were as little able to Maintain her as she expected – Therefore as the truest Mark of

[1] The DNB account of John Croft is not so enlightening as that in YORK PRESS, 307-10. See also SKAIFE.

our Friendship in Such a Situation, My Wife & self took no Small
Pains . . . to turn her Thoughts to some way of depending upon her
own Industry, In which we offer'd her all imaginable Assistance. 1ˢᵗ
By proposing to her, that if She would set herself to learn the Business
of a Mantua-Maker, as soon as she could get Insight enough into it, to
make a Gown & set up for herself, – *That* we would give her 30. pounds
to begin the World & Support her till Business fell in. – Or if she Would
go into a Milliners Shop in London, My Wife engaged not only to get
her into a Shop where she should have Ten pounds a Year Wages, But
to equip her with Cloaths &c: properly for the Place: or lastly if she
liked it better, As my Wife had then an Opportunity of recommending her to the family of one of the first of our Nobility – She undertook
to get her a creditable place in it where she would receive no less than
8 or 10 pᵈˢ a Year Wages with other Advantages. – My Sister shew'd
no seeming opposition to either of the two last proposals, till my Wife
had wrote & got a favourable Answer to the one – & an immediate
offer of the Other. – It will Astonish you, Sir, when I tell You, She
rejected them with the Utmost Scorn; – telling me, I might send my
own Children to Service when I had any But for her part, As she was
the Daughter of a Gentleman, *she would not Disgrace* herself, but would
Live as Such.   (pp. 37–8)

Finally, Sterne sent her back accompanied by Richard Greenwood, with
5 guineas of his money and 'a Six & thirty Piece which my Wife put into her
Hand as she took Horse'. Passing through York, Catherine stopped to talk
to Uncle Jaques, 'but for very strong Reasons, I believe She conceald from
you all that was necessary to Make a proper Handle of us Both'.

Sterne was so angry with the whole affair that thereafter he sent less
money, though 'we continued Sending What We could conveniently Spare'.
In one instance shortly after the visit, Sterne sent his mother £3 which she
said she did not receive. So he sent £3 more, and then went about tracing
down the first bill. When his mother saw what was happening, she admitted
to having cashed the first one also, 'But had *forgot it*'. Such treatment would
have been especially hard for Sterne to take in 1744. He and Elizabeth had
decided to go into debt to buy a farm.

On 1 November 1744 they purchased the Tindal Farm, at Sutton, which
bore the name of the man who originally had carved it out of the Forest of
Galtres. The seller was young William Dawson, now the curate of Marton

and Farlington Chapel. Lacking, perhaps, the complete price, or needing money for their new enterprise, Elizabeth and Laurence mortgaged the farm immediately to a certain William Shaw of York. A few days later, they purchased three more pieces from Richard Harland. One cannot identify the particular lands, so imperfect are the legal records, or know for certain how many acres they owned. We do know that their freeholds were now the fifth largest in Sutton. Possibly the Sternes had 200 acres of their own as well as the 120 acres of vicaral lands. In addition, they leased from Lord Fauconberg a 'fee farm' and a plot of 'hags and lunds' at Sutton, small tracts for which they paid a yearly fee.[1]

The venture was not so cheeky as it may seem. Farming was the major concern of most people, and Sterne could hardly have helped learning a good deal about it. He could count upon the co-operation and advice of neighbours such as Stephen Croft and Lord Fauconberg. His Lordship's steward, Richard Chapman, became a close and trusted friend.[2] As for the effort, he had been prepared by the hardships of his youth and the examples of industry and enterprise at Halifax.

Possibly the ownership of land was important to his self-esteem: the very idea of gentility implied rural property and farming. True, like most people, he and Elizabeth wanted a town house in York, but only a rural 'seat' could make urban life respectable. The clergy were encouraged to embrace this pattern, to improve the value of church lands, to acquire freeholds, to engage in all the activities typical of the country gentleman.[3] Mr Mosley had done that at Wigginton. He had bought land, rebuilt the vicarage, and was leading the life of a squire, staying in the country when it pleased him or in York, where he had two livings. In 1744 his son, Thomas, took over as curate of the parish and master of their temporal holdings, and yet another son would follow in these positions when Thomas's fortunes permitted him to leave. Here was living proof that a clergyman from modest beginnings could attain the romantic dream of his age.

For the next several years Sterne was engaged in developing a fully variegated farming enterprise in the yet under-exploited lowlands of the Vale of York. The sparse legal records suggest that he made use of pasture lands,

[1] *Fauconberg Rentual*; North Riding Deeds: N/296/343, N/297/344, N/441-2/531. For the relative size of holdings: 'One year Land Tax, 1759', and 'Sutton Land Tax Bill, 1759', documents in NEWBURGH PAPERS.

[2] Before he went abroad in 1765, Sterne gave Chapman legal control of his lands: North Riding Deeds, AM/553/741.
[3] BEST, 68.

'ings' along the Foss, and some of the higher common fields of the parish. Since some of his new property was 'brush and waste', we can surmise that he intended to try the new style of farming by enclosure. One thinks of the servant, Obadiah, of *Tristram Shandy*: 'We shall have a terrible piece of work of it in stubbing the ox-moor' (V, vii, 360). Curiously, there was a stretch of land north of Huby and west of Stillington called the Ox Moor.[1] Sterne would have employed many hands to clear and drain the fields, to fence them and to plant the first crops. He would have had to supervise the building of windmills, the clearing of ditches, the liming or manuring of fields. That first spring he may have managed to plant his first grain. If so, the outcome was probably disastrous: he wrote in the Sutton register,

> In May 1745
> A Dismal Storm of Hail fell upon this Town, & some other aj'acent ones wch did considerable Damage both to the Windows & Corn. Many of the Stones measured six Inches in Circumference.
> It broke almost all the South & West Windows both of this House & my Vicarage House at Stillington
>
> L. Sterne

Since rotation of crops was everywhere being urged or ordered by the local officials, Sterne was inevitably forced to plant the more risky high-labour crops of vegetables, beans and potatoes. Very probably he took up the tricky business of breeding and grazing Yorkshire black cattle. Since butter was a principal 'cash crop' of the North Riding, Sterne and Elizabeth eventually had a dairy of seven cows – surely not the quaint hobby which John Croft made it seem, but a vital part of a larger farm. Sterne would have kept a few oxen for pulling the wagons, and at least one team of those celebrated Yorkshire draft horses, so well trained that one ploughboy could handle both plough and horses without the need of a drover walking at the side.[2]

Harvesting, always a nerve-racking business, was extremely difficult since so many labourers were needed. Cereal crops, for instance, were cut by sickle. A 'sett' of three women and one man could cut and bind the sheaves from one acre in a day. Their pay? 10*d.* for each woman; 2*s.* for the man. A

[1] Ordnance Survey map of 1858.
[2] General information about farming from Arthur Young, *A Six-Months Tour through the North of England*, 4 vols, 1770–1; [William] Marshall, *The Rural Economy of Yorkshire*, 2 vols, 1788; Olga Wilkinson, *The Agricultural Revolution in the East Riding of Yorkshire* (East Yorkshire Local History Society, Local History Series V), 1956.

little later we find Sterne in 'the *crisis* of my affairs namely the getting down of my crop wch by the way is in danger of sprouting'. 'All hands are to be employed in cutting my barly wch is now shaking with this vile wind' (p. 54). Another time he had to ask his personal servants to take a wagonload of barley to the maltsman because no other help was available.

> – I have 4 Threshers every Day at Work, & they mortify me with declarations, That There is so much Barly they Cannot get thro' that species before X^mas Day – & God knows I have (I hope) near 80 Q^rs of Oats besides – how I shall manage Matters to get to You, as we wish for 3 Months, half distracts my Brain.   (pp. 65-6)

For all Sterne's effort, the farming venture did not work out well. There were setbacks: the hailstorm of 1745; the rebellion of that year, which took so many labourers away from the fields; the disastrous cattle plague which raged in England from 1744, reaching Stillington in 1749. The records of the Quarter Sessions Courts are full of orders to stop the sale and circulation of cattle and to destroy infected herds. Sterne was inspired with pessimism to write two sermons about God's wrathful vengeance upon his sinful people.[1]

Worst of all, he seems to have had little talent for farming. Croft said 'they allways sold their Butter cheaper than their Neighbours, as they had not the least idea of œconomy, [so] that they were allways behindhand and in arrears with Fortune.' His opinion is born out by the legal documents, which show that Sterne and Elizabeth never got out of debt. They did not pay off their first mortgage on the Tindal Farm until 3 June 1760, no doubt with the profits from *Tristram Shandy*. By then they had mortgaged it a second time to Stephen Croft and Dean John Fountayne, and that mortgage was not discharged until Lydia Sterne sold the farm after the death of her parents.[2]

In 1758, Sterne gave it all up. 'You are much to blame if you dig for marle, unless you are sure of it', he later wrote to a friend who was thinking of trying farming.

> I was once such a puppy myself, as to pare, and burn, and had my labour for my pains, and two hundred pounds out of pocket. – Curse on farming (said I) I will try if the pen will not succeed better than the spade. – The following up of that affair (I mean farming) made me lose

[1] SERMONS, II, 189, 376. The cattle plague was described vividly in the *York Courant* of 20 October 1747; 23 February 1747/8: it spread from Africa to Italy in 1735; raged across Switzerland, Poland, Germany and Holland; and jumped the Channel in 1744.

[2] North Riding Deeds, AF/492-3/690; BD/478-9/864. The original mortgage: X/45-6/67.

my temper, and a cart load of turneps was (I thought) very dear at two hundred pounds. –

In all your operations may your own good sense guide you – bought experience is the devil.   (pp. 394–5)

Nevertheless, Sterne would discover that the attempt had paid off in the long run. He and Elizabeth ended up holding a good deal of land, and the price of land was rising sharply in the North Riding. Aside from what they gained in the Enclosure Act, their freeholds had reached in 1761 a value of £1800.[1] Although he fell short of Richard Mosley's success, Sterne would be a landowner for the rest of his life, and land would be the mainstay of his widow.

From a modern perspective, it is not Sterne the entrepreneur who commands our greatest respect, but Sterne the rural parson. During his time at Sutton and Stillington the parishes flourished, the livings increased in value, and the Sunday services were popular – if irregular. Squire Harland and the local gentry came to respect him. But the villagers, as John Croft said, 'generally considered him as crazy, or crackbrained'. Croft may have exaggerated. Still, Sterne's portrait of himself in *Tristram Shandy* upon his 'lean, sorry, jack-ass of a horse', seems a cheerful admission that few villagers knew what to make of him:

> In the several sallies about his parish, and in the neighbouring visits to the gentry who lived around him, . . . the parson . . . would both hear and see enough to keep his philosophy from rusting. To speak the truth, he never could enter a village, but he caught the attention of both old and young.——Labour stood still as he pass'd,—— the bucket hung suspended in the middle of the well,——the spinning-wheel forgot its round,——even chuck-farthing and shuffle-cap themselves stood gaping till he had got out of sight; and as his movement was not of the quickest, he had generally time enough upon his hands to make his observations,——to hear the groans of the serious,—— and the laughter of the light-hearted;——all which he bore with excellent tranquility.   (I, x, 19)

[1] LETTERS, 147. On rising prices: Francis Topham to Andrew Ducarel, 29 May 1758, in ILLUSTRATIONS, III, 696. Archbishop Drummond's comment after Sterne's death, in LETTERS, 436, is somewhat unfair: 'The Inclosure was no merit of Sterne's, but it was a profit to him.' He probably did not know that Sterne and Elizabeth had purchased far more land than they acquired through the Enclosure Act. See below, Chapter 12.

8

The '45
1743–1747

Archbishop Thomas Herring, who came to the see of York in 1743, is sometimes called the last warrior bishop of England. During the Jacobite rebellion of 1745, he roused the county from its apathy, took the lead in organizing a small army, and rode in review of troops drawn up on Knavesmire. His supposed advice to the clergy to exchange a black cassock for a regimental coat earned him the sobriquet of 'Red Herring', though in fact the story was not true.

In peace his manner was reserved and dignified. In marked contrast to Archbishop Blackburn, he pursued his duties diligently. As Bishop of Bangor, he had conducted a celebrated primary visitation, travelling on horseback into remote areas of the Welsh mountains. At York, during the most thorough visitation the diocese had seen, he confirmed 30,000 people – a 'Godly work'. But Herring was as political as any prelate in England, and owed his rise largely to his devotion to Whiggism and his friendship with Lord Chancellor Hardwicke. He astonished York by speaking handsomely of his predecessor, and terrified many by dropping hints that Blackburn had left behind a set of 'characters' of the local clergy. He was the more unassailable because he had every qualification of a gentleman – except high birth – an intelligent, polished and well-read man. In Hogarth's striking portrait, he appears confident and gentle, with puckered lips suggesting something effeminate and eyes that do not match – one open and frank, the other rather sly.[1]

[1] DNB; VENN; GRAY; CURTIS, 22; introduction to HERRING RETURNS; SYKES, 75–81; Philip C. Yorke, *Life and Correspondence of . . . Hardwicke*, 3 vols, Cambridge and Chicago, 1913, *passim*; PYLE, 75–6, 88; *Letters from . . . Thomas Herring . . . to William Duncombe*, 1777; R. Garnett, 'Correspondence of Archbishop Herring and Lord Hardwicke during the rebellion of 1745', *English*

Laurence Sterne, not yet thirty years old, was signally honoured by the dean and chapter, who asked him to preach the sermon for the archbishop's enthronement at the minster on 11 June 1743. The *York Gazetteer* of the following Tuesday described how the prelate was 'sung up by the Choir . . . attended by the Chancellor, Advocates, Proctors and Officers of the Ecclesiastical Court in their Robes'. The 'excellent Sermon' (now lost) preached by Mr Sterne took as text Genesis 4: 7, 'If thou doest well, shalt thou not be accepted? And if thou doest not well, sin lieth at the door.'[1] This flippant allusion to Archbishop Blackburn's reputation may have told Herring at once that here was a parson who 'loved a jest in his heart'. So far as we know, Herring never, in succeeding years, showed any interest in Laurence Sterne.

A month later, Sterne published the most lugubrious piece he is known to have written, the funeral poem called 'The Unknown World: Verses Occasioned by hearing a Pass-Bell'. It was printed in the *Gentleman's Magazine* for July 1743 (p. 376), but it may have appeared first in some Yorkshire newspaper: the *Magazine* often picked up pieces from provincial papers. The poem, in octosyllabic couplets divided into stanzas by paragraph indentations, comments solemnly upon the mystery of death and the impossibility of knowing the nature of life beyond the grave, though it does not question the *existence* of an afterlife. It concludes on a pious note of acceptance. In the original manuscript,[2] quite different from the *Gentleman's Magazine* printing, Sterne had used symbols for four key words – ☉, *world*; Þ, *He*; ♅, *heaven*; and ♃, *soul*. Furthermore, the thorn, rendered as the letter 'y', is substituted for 'th' with a regularity far beyond conventional orthography, even to writing *they* as 'yy'. At the age of twenty-nine Sterne was already an experimenter in semiotics. The signs of 'The Unknown World' are the ancestors of the wiggly lines of *Tristram Shandy* and the little cross used to symbolize Dr Slop's crossing himself when frightened by the apparition of Obadiah on the great coach horse (II, ix, 106).

THE UNKNOWN ☉

Verses occasion'd by hearing a Pass-Bell,

By^e ye Rev^d M^r St—n.

Hark^e my gay Fr^d y^t solemn Toll

Historical Review, XIX (1904), 528–50, 719–42; John Ingamells, 'Hogarth's "Red" Herrings: a study in iconography', *Connoisseur*, January 1972.

[1] Discovered by Kenneth Monkman: WINGED SKULL, 285.
[2] For a century each curate of Coxwold passed the manuscript on to his successor.

Speaks ye departure of a soul;
'Tis gone, y^{ts} all we know – not where
Or how ye unbody'd soul do's fare.
　In y^t mysterious ☉ none knows,
But Þ alone to w^m it goes;
To whom departed souls return
To take y^{ir} Doom, to smile or mourn.
　Oh! by w^t glimm'ring light we view
The unknown ☉ we're hast'ning to!
God has lock'd up ye mystic Page,
And curtain'd darkness round ye stage!
　Wise ♅ to render search perplext,
Has drawn 'twixt y^s ☉ & ye next
A dark impenetrable screen
All behind wch is yet unseen!
　We talk of ♅ we talk of Hell;
But w^t yy. mean no tongue can tell!
Heaven is ye realm where angels are
And Hell ye chaos of despair.
　But w^t y^{ese} awful truths imply,
None of us know before we die!
Wheth^{er} we will or no, we must
Take ye succeeding ☉ on trust.
　This hour perhaps o^r Fr^d is well
Death-struck ye next he cries, Farewell!
I die! – & y^{et} for ought we see,
Ceases at once to breath & be.
　Thu^s launch'd f^m life's ambiguous shore
Ingulph'd in Death appears no more,
Then undirected to repair,
To distant ☉^s we know not where.
　Swift flies y^e ♃, perhaps 'tis gone,
A thousand leagues beyond ye sun;
Or 2^{ce} 10 thousand more 3^{ce} told,
Ere ye forsaken clay is cold!

It was finally lost, but not before it was
copied and printed by Thomas Gill in
Vallis Eboracensis, Easingwold, 1852, pp.
199–200.

And yet who knows if Fr^{nds} we lov'd
Tho' dead, may be so far remov'd;
Only ye vail of flesh between,
Perhaps yy. watch us though unseen.
　　Whilst we, y^{ir} loss lamenting, say,
They're out of hearing far away;
Guardians to us perhaps they're near
Conceal'd in Vehicles of air.
　　And yet no notices yy. give,
Nor tell us where, nor how yy. live;
Tho' conscious whilst with us below,
How much y^{ms} desired to know.
　　As if bound up by solemn Fate
To keep y^e secret of y^{ir} state,
To tell y^{ir} joys or pains to none,
That man might live by Faith alone.
　　Well, let my sovereign, if he please,
Lock up his marvellous decrees;
Why sh^d I wish him to reveal,
W^t he thinks proper to conceal?
　　It is enough y^t I believe
Heaven's $bright^r$ y^n I can conceive:
And he y^t makes it all his care
To serve God here shall see him there!
　　But oh! w^t $\odot^s$ shall I survey
The moment y^t I leave y^s clay?
How sudden y^e surprize, how new!
Let it, my God, be happy too.

The War of the Austrian Succession, which England had entered toward the end of Walpole's ministry, continued through the early forties. The York newspapers carried accounts of the fighting, but the war did not much affect life in Yorkshire. Not until 1743, when King George personally led his troops to victory in the Battle of Dettingen, did it seem real. That same year the Whig oligarchy shifted the ministry again: Henry Pelham became first minister, his brother, the Duke of Newcastle, playing a strong secondary role as Secretary of State. Life in the north stayed on an even keel. No one paid much attention to rumours in 1744 of an impending Jacobite invasion of

Britain, though in fact the danger was very real. Cardinal de Tencin, first minister to Louis XV, was plotting to foment troubles which would divert British troops from the continental war. Prince Charles Edward, son of the Pretender, actually went to Gravelines to take command of a small French invasion force, but he was disappointed when the fleet bringing his soldiers was scattered by a storm. The French ministry was never able to repeat the attempt, and the young Chevalier, as Charles Edward was often called, had to content himself with the prospect of a rebellion unsupported by France. In Scotland, about this time, John Murray of Broughton organized a secret Jacobite society to prepare for the coming of the prince.

What connection this rebel underground had with York, if any, is uncertain. The city corporation was predominantly Tory, and there were quiet Roman Catholics among them. They gave a warm reception to the Duke of Perth, a highlander and known Jacobite leader, when he came to York in 1744. In the spring of 1745, Sir Miles Stapylton, Knight of the Shire in the Country Interest and a silent Catholic, was suspiciously aggressive in urging that two 'violent party men', Bacon Morritt and Dr John Fothergill, be named to the Commission of the Peace.[1]

In July 1745 Prince Charles Edward launched that most daring of all English rebellions. He set sail with a few Scots soldiers and a handful of expatriate English Papists in two battered old ships, one of which had to turn back after it was damaged by a British man-of-war. On 24 July he landed at Eriskay in the Western Isles, and in the space of three weeks he had gathered an army, though still a tiny one of only 600 highlanders. On 19 August the little force raised its standard at Glenfinnan and proclaimed the Chevalier's father to be King James III and VIII; Prince Charles Edward himself they hailed as the prince regent.

In York no one seemed particularly worried. A proclamation was read on 5 September ordering all officials to take the Oaths of Allegiance and Supremacy, to seize the arms and horses of Roman Catholics, and to invoke the Five-Mile Act against them. But most justices hesitated to put into effect such harsh measures: the habit of quietly tolerating Catholics had become deep-rooted in Yorkshire. There were muddled accounts in the newspapers of Sir John Cope's muddled attempts to give battle, but there was

[1] Stapylton and Fothergill contributed to the building fund of the Bar Convent: convent muniments 3 B/10. For Stapylton's attempt to influence the commission: his correspondence with Malton and Hardwicke, May–June 1745, BM: Add. MSS 35602, fols. 61–72. On Fothergill, above, Chapter 5, p. 92, n. 2.

still not much alarm when Cope inadvertently opened a path for the prince to march into Edinburgh, where he arrived on 17 September with an army of highlanders 2,000 strong. On the 21st, they surprised and routed Cope's army at Prestonpans, and Charles Edward was in control of all Scotland.

Suddenly Yorkshire panicked. Now the rebels would surely come into England. Would it be by the eastern route through Newcastle? If so, they would come down through the shire and would surely attack York, which lay a few miles off the Great North Road. Or would they take the western route through Carlisle to Lancaster? The only cool head was the archbishop's. Herring had already begun to organize for defence. On the 11th he had called a meeting of county leaders at Byrom, the seat of Sir John Ramsden.[1]

On 24 September there was a convocation at York Castle of nobles, gentlemen, clergy, merchants, aldermen and city officials, 'the greatest Meeting of people of all Ranks and degrees that I believe was ever known upon any occasion', wrote Elizabeth Montagu's husband. At the archbishop's urging the leaders of the Ministerial Party appeared – Lord Malton, Lord Stafford, Cholmley Turner, Sir Conyers D'Arcy – and to the surprise of many, the leaders of the opposition party – Lord Carlisle, George Fox and Godfrey Wentworth. 'There was the utmost unanimity of spirit imaginable', wrote Edward Montagu.[2] His Grace made an impassioned speech upon the evils of foreign rule, playing down the religious issue and pleading for a united effort.[3] A subscription was set going to raise funds for the defence. Laurence Sterne was present. So was Dr John Burton.

The subscription was a great success. £20,000 was promised within a few days. The largest contribution came from Lord Malton, who gave £1,000. Lord Fauconberg signed for £200, Cholmley Turner for £100. There were a great many small donations, some for a single pound. Dr Topham gave £20, Richard Mosley £10, and Laurence Sterne £10. The list included many of Sterne's old political antagonists, John Stanhope of Horsforth, Philip Harland and Dr Burton. It must have contained the names of some Jacobites who were covering up, but very probably Herring had won over to the Hanoverian side many doubtful men who, without this show of unanimity and strength, might have supported the Stuarts.[4]

---

[1] General information on Yorkshire during the rebellion: Cedric Collyer, 'Yorkshire and the "Forty-five"', YAJ, XXXVIII (1952–5), 71–92.

[2] CLIMENSON, I, 209.

[3] *A Speech Made by His Grace* . . ., York, 1745. At the Minster Library is a list of those attending.

[4] *A List of the Voluntary Subscribers* . . ., Hull [1745], reissued from the original York ed., at BM: 1325. C. 22.

The county began to bustle. The York Blues were organized and equipped – four companies sponsored by the corporation; and the Independents – a troop of York gentlemen and their servants.[1] Many rural gentry raised troops on their own initiative and paid for their equipment. Individual towns organized brigades, and even villages began to drill their farmers, sometimes with brooms and 'scythes fixed on poles in the manner of pikes'.

Sutton and Stillington, north of the city, were particularly vulnerable because they lay on roads which the invaders would take if they came to York. Presumably the villages reacted in the way of so many others, organized themselves like military camps and laid plans to harass the enemy and to give intelligence to York. Sterne may have known more about military matters than anyone else in Sutton. Philip Harland, though a Tory, was surely no Jacobite, and he and Sterne probably worked closely together. From the villagers, they raised a contribution of £6. 9s. 6d to the defence. Stillington also made a contribution – £9. From the presses of York, there was a spate of sermons on the rebellion,[2] but Sterne's pulpit oratory from this period does not survive.

We have a glimpse of a militant parson in Greenwood's recollections. Like the servant, La Fleur, in *A Sentimental Journey*, young Greenwood could 'beat a drum, and play a march or two upon the fife', and like La Fleur he decided that 'the honour of beating a drum was likely to be its own reward' (pp. 124–5). He left Sterne's service, he said, in 1745, 'having had a few words with his master a short time before in consequence of his refusing to engage as drummer to Kingston's Light Horse, a regiment of cavalry raised in Yorkshire during the Rebellion'. The regiment was that organized in Nottinghamshire by the Duke of Kingston. Probably they recruited and trained for a while in York.

Sterne must have taken a keen interest also in another regiment of light horse, a group of North Riding foxhunters who transformed themselves into the 'Royal Hunters'. The man who was primarily responsible for organizing this colourful band, 'compos'd of Gentlemen and their Servants . . . to harrass the Rebels in their March, and give Intelligence of their Motions', was John Hall-Stevenson.[3]

[1] HARGROVE, I, 224.
[2] YORK PRESS, 250–2.
[3] SP 36/69, General James Oglethorpe to Newcastle with enclosed petition of the gentlemen. State papers at the PRO will be cited in this manner. No attempt is made to give folio numbers since the papers are loose and have been shuffled frequently. Dates will be given when possible since some bundles have been arranged chronologically.

Family matters kept Sterne close to home. On the first day of October, a week after the great meeting at York Castle, Elizabeth gave birth to her first child – a daughter. She was named Lydia after her maternal grandmother. Sterne's pride is apparent in the bold hand which appeared in the registers of both Sutton and Stillington: 'October ye 1st Born & Baptized Lydia the Daughter of the Reverend Mr Sterne Vicar of Sutton & of Elizabeth his Wife, Daughter of the Revd Mr Lumley late Rector of Bedale.' And then, among the burials of the next day, 'Lydia Daughter of Mr Sterne – Vicar of Sutton.' It would be two years before another child would be born alive to Elizabeth, and she too would be named Lydia. The sadness of the couple may have been somewhat relieved by a more cheerful family event. Ten days later, at Sutton, Mary Sterne, the widow of Cousin Richard, was married to Mr John Baird of Leith. Sterne must have pronounced the blessing with feeling, casting his eye upon the five year old boy who stood there – Richard, the family heir, the only child in Yorkshire who bore the name of Sterne. He would grow up to inherit Elvington, to sell it and to die childless, the last of the Sternes in Yorkshire.[1]

By mid-October, the county was as ready as it could be, considering the lack of trained soldiers and the shortage of arms. No one had illusions that these scattered, unpractised troops could meet the enemy head on. Stories flew about, how the highlanders ate children, how they fought in quick, short charges, bounding over the fields in great leaps, swinging their swords about their heads and uttering savage war cries. The Yorkshire militia planned only to harass and annoy the enemy. A decision was taken not to make a stand behind the medieval wall of the city, which would only crumble before the enemy cannon.

Brave, worried demonstrations of joy were made in York on 15 October, the anniversary of the king's coronation. The new troops paraded, volleys were fired, there were bonfires at night and a ball in the assembly rooms. Much of the celebration was repeated on the 30th, the king's birthday.

[1] CLAY. The 'Sterne family papers' at Halifax Library, shelf mark 2352-5, consist of legal documents, some dated 1761, relating to the guardianship of young Richard Sterne by his step-father, John Baird, at that time living at Brayton, near Selby. It appears that the boy inherited sizeable debts to Walter Palliser, Thomas Pulleyn and Jaques Sterne. Jaques sued the guardian in 1758. The boy's mother signed her name with the sign of 'X'. This Richard Sterne would marry, in 1765, Mary, daughter of Alderman Waine of Beverley, and like Walter Shandy in the novel would have difficulties with a marriage contract. The agreement required an Act of Parliament to break: *Journal of the House of Lords*, XXXIV, 43, 249.

Cholmley Turner rode into the city at the head of 100 men whom he had equipped at his own expense. An ox was roasted whole that night for the delight of the mob.

The worries of the county reached a crisis on 22 November, when the rebel army pulled out of Carlisle. That very day Dr John Burton went to the guildhall and explained to the recorder, Thomas Place, that he intended to go into the West Riding to collect £120 rent due on his two estates at Newby, near Clapham, which might lie in the path of the rebels should they take a western route. He then made inquiries about the city if anyone had letters or packages he might carry to Skipton, through which he would pass. Skipton, as everyone knew, was the centre of Papist activities in the West Riding. The next morning, Saturday 23 November, the city gates were opened before dawn, by special permission, and Dr Burton rode off in pouring rain accompanied by a servant who carried behind him a portmanteau.

The journey would precipitate woeful consequences for Dr Burton. For two years he would be hounded unmercifully for it – a story which reveals much about Dr Jaques Sterne. Although he would escape hanging, eventually his portrait as Dr Slop would be hung in *Tristram Shandy*.

Did Dr Burton make this journey to look after his business interests, as he was to maintain doggedly? Or did he go in search of Prince Charles Edward to take him money and to invite him to York, as Dr Jaques Sterne asserted? In 1749 Burton wrote a detailed account of his journey and its aftermath which he entitled *British Liberty Endanger'd; Demonstrated by the Following Narrative: Wherein Is Prov'd from Facts, that J. B. Has Hitherto Been a Better Friend to the English Constitution, in Church and State, than his Persecutors.* Heretofore, biographical studies of the physician have depended primarily upon this book for information about his adventure.[1] But there are extensive records of Burton's activities among the unpublished state papers at the Public Record Office. In the light of these, one readily sees how slanted was *British Liberty Endanger'd.* The doctor simply passed over his experiences among the rebels, writing instead an evasive narrative which gives a superficial appearance of accounting for his time away from York while it actually omits two full days.

Dr Burton and his servant reached Settle, about fifty miles from York, on Saturday evening, where the doctor met his estate agent, William

[1] Robert Davies, 'A memoir of John Burton', YAJ, II (1877–8), 403–40; Alban Doran, 'Burton ("Dr. Slop"): his forceps and his foes', *Journal of Obstetrics and Gynaecology of the British Empire*, XXIII (1913), 3–24, 65–86.

Hall.[1] While there, he heard that the rebel army had taken the road toward Lancaster, and knowing that such news would be received with joy in York, he sent a letter to the recorder. On Sunday morning, led by a guide named Richard Gelderd, whom Mr Hall had found for him, Dr Burton and his personal servant continued westward to Hornby, where they stopped at the inn of Leonard Johnson. Hornby is ten miles or so from the road down which the main body of rebels would come in their march from Kendal to Lancaster, but it lies on another north–south road which anyone would expect some portion of the army to use. The doctor gave no adequate reason, ever, why he should have gone so far west and so close to the enemy. In his book, he said he rode to Hornby on Saturday night (a small untruth) to seek lodgings. In his sworn statement, he said he went on Sunday out of curiosity and to get intelligence to send to York.[2] He was warned as he approached Hornby that there were parties of highlanders about – to which he responded by dismounting and unloading his pistols so that, as he explained, if he were taken the rebels would not think he came against them as an enemy.

Once at Mr Johnson's inn, he sent a letter up to Hornby Castle, where he had heard there was a party of highlanders. The letter, he maintained in his testimony, was addressed to the Duke of Perth, whom Burton had known slightly when the duke had visited York, and its import was only to request a pass so that he could return without fear that his horses would be confiscated. William Glover, a local Quaker, who carried the letter up, told how Lord Elcho came down from the castle, took and read the letter, called two highlanders, and told them to go and get the gentleman who had written it, 'but to be civil to him & not abuse him, but must bring him up'. The highlanders, in plaids and bonnets, went down to the inn and directly to Burton's room and 'captured' him as he was being shaved by the local barber. The barber and others said that the Scotsmen only invited Dr Burton to come with them and that he went without protest.[3]

An hour later Burton returned to the inn, paid his bill and asked the guide, Gelderd, to come with him to Lancaster, explaining that he could not be discharged here and would have to go with the rebel army to Lancaster

[1] SP 36/75, information of William Hall, dated 30 November 1745.

[2] SP 36/83, examination of John Burton before Andrew Stone, 7 May 1746; SP 36/75, examination of Richard Gelderd before William Dawson, 30 November 1745.

[3] SP 36/81, William Turner Carus to Rowland Winn, 10 February 1745/6; SP 36/76, information of William Glover, 1 December 1745; information of Dorothy Johnson, 1 December 1745.

where he would be given a pass. He set off with the guide and servant. They were met at the edge of the town by about fifty horsemen, said Gelderd, and rode two and two abreast to Lancaster, Burton talking intimately most of the time with a gentleman in a black wig (one Maxwell, as the doctor later explained, whom he had met when Maxwell came to York with the Duke of Perth). Close to Lancaster he parted from the soldiers. Two residents of Lancaster, John Parkinson and John Holland, testified that they saw Dr Burton and his servant and guide enter the town by themselves and that the rebel troop arrived half an hour later.[1]

Parkinson told a curious story, confirmed in part by two other witnesses.[2] He was watching the rebels enter the town from the inn of Jane Strangways at Bridge End. Dr Burton was in the room with several people, all watching from the window. The doctor talked excitedly, telling the people that he had been taken prisoner at Hornby but that he had no guard. He asked if anyone would carry a message to General Ligonier, who was marching up from London to confront the highlanders, and said that he would obtain a pass for the messenger. In his chatter he said 'treasonable' things about the strength of the rebels and how they would cut Ligonier to pieces. When the highland army began to come into town over the bridge, the doctor desired the people to stand back from the window lest they be taken for spies, but he himself leaned out of the window, 'gave several great Hem's, and asked wh^ch was the Prince'. Upon receiving an answer, the doctor left the room, joined the soldiers and went off with them.

Lancaster was soon swarming with highlanders. Dr Burton, on his parole of honour, he said, not to leave without permission, spent Sunday afternoon and all of Monday among them, coming and going from the inn of Isaac Rawlinson, where he and several rebel officers were lodged. Numerous people saw him about the town talking with various leaders of the forces, including the commander, Lord George Murray. Burton maintained to the last that he was gathering intelligence for the Crown and trying to locate the Duke of Perth. Eventually he did find the duke and obtained the pass, but not before he was taken to the house where Prince Charles Edward lodged. Here he was interviewed ('questioned' he said) by the Chevalier himself and his secretary.[3]

[1] SP 36/83, information of John Holland, 29 April 1746; SP 36/81, information of John Parkinson, 12 February 1745/6.
[2] SP 36/84, informations of Thomas Jackson, 14 June, and John Simpson, 8 June 1746.
[3] SP 36/81, informations of Isaac Rawlinson, 11 February, and R. G. Sawrey, 18 February 1745/6, and others. The actual pass was seen by Collyer.

The testimony which might well have hanged John Burton was given by the secretary, John Murray of Broughton, who has a secure place in history as the turncoat responsible for the deaths of Simon Fraser, Twelfth Lord Lovat, and numerous lesser figures among the rebels. In his statement before Andrew Stone in the Tower of London on 13 August 1746, Murray avowed this:

> This exam[t] being asked whether he recollects a Person called Doctor Burton, being with the Pretender's Army in Lancashire: He saith, he does remember a Person, who, he thinks was a Physician, but cannot recollect his Name: that, this Person came to them at Lancaster, and said that he had been at Hornby Castle: that, he desired this Exam[t] to introduce him to the Pretender, which he did accordingly: that, the said Person told the Pretender in this Exam[t]'s Presence, that He came from York: and that there were many Persons there, who would have joined him, if He had come that Way.[1]

Dr Burton returned to Settle on Tuesday, paid off his workmen and completed his business with Mr Hall. He went on to York on Wednesday. The news that he had been with the rebels in Lancaster had already reached York: one Birkbeck, postmaster of Settle, had written to the authorities. That evening the doctor gave an account of his adventures to the recorder, and the next morning to the archbishop and dean, including some details about the rebel strength and their plans. Archbishop Herring found it convenient to forget about this interview for many months. On Friday, Sir Rowland Winn wrote of his suspicions to the Duke of Newcastle.[2]

The man who 'left no Stone unturned' in his attempt to have Dr Burton arrested was the precentor and archdeacon, Dr Jaques Sterne. Dr Sterne was also a justice of the peace, and it was in this capacity that he went after Dr Burton, acting upon the statute which gave a justice almost as much power out of his own district as within, so long as he could find another justice to share responsibility. Burton, in *Civil Liberty Endanger'd*, described how the precentor went about finding an excuse for the arrest:

> A Relation of the Priest wrote a Letter to his Friend which arrived about Eleven o'Clock on *November* 30 [Saturday morning]. The Purport of this Letter, was to tell him, that 'the Rebels were got to *Rochdale*

---

[1] SP 36/86. The testimony was published by Robert Fitzroy Bell, ed., in *Memorials of John Murray of Broughton* (Scottish History Soc. Pub., XXVII), Edinburgh, 1898, p. 436.

[2] SP 36/75, dated 29 November 1745.

in *Lancashire*, and were coming to *York*,' and put a Query thus, as a Post-scrip, *viz*. Q. *If this is not owing to your beloved or popular* (which of these two Epithets he used I am not certain) *Dr. B[urto]ns Invitation*? This Letter one P[rie]st gave to another to run about with, and exclaim against me.   (pp. 31–2)

Dr Sterne and others came to the Guildhall and argued that the physician should be committed: the precentor 'perfectly foamed at the Mouth, especially when I laughed at him'. That afternoon Burton was arrested and committed to the castle of York by Jaques Sterne and the recorder, Mr Place.

It is not likely that Laurence Sterne was the relation of the precentor who wrote the letter, as has been suggested. It was almost certainly Thomas Pulleyn, who is twice mentioned in Dr Burton's book as one of his persecutors.[1]

Whitehall was soon suspicious of Dr Burton for other reasons. The rebels had levied a 'tax' upon the residents of Manchester which supposedly netted them £2,500. No one in the government could understand how they could raise such a sum by gross extortion; consequently, it was theorized that the device was a ruse to cover the fact that Charles Edward had received money from his English supporters. At least some interrogated prisoners believed that money had been contributed from York. So Newcastle was soon thanking Jaques Sterne for apprehending Dr Burton, and advising the justices of York to hold him on the chance that warrants might be sent to transport him to London.[2]

On the first day of December the rebels were at Macclesfield, but their way was blocked by the combined forces of Ligonier and the Duke of Cumberland, the king's warlike son. Lord George Murray in a brilliant piece of strategy divided his forces and sent one part toward Wales. Cumberland and Ligonier, fearful the rebels would be joined by the many Welsh Jacobites, moved to cut them off. Now no army stood between London and the prince, in charge of the other part of the rebel forces. He marched forward to Derby. Sir Charles Petrie, the historian of the Jacobite movement, argues that had Charles gone on he would have won the war, or at least would have won it had he at this juncture declared himself a Protestant (as indeed he was to do a few years later). The prince failed to make the declaration,

---

[1] Cf. POLITICKS, 18.
[2] BM: Add. MSS 33050, fols. 3–4; SP 36/76, Newcastle to Winn, 4 December, with reply of 6 December; SP/78, Newcastle to J. Sterne and Newcastle to Winn, 30 December; SP 36/95, information of Charles Stuart, 1 March 1746/7.

and no one rose to assist him. He may have received money, possibly from York; but no great families had declared themselves on his side, and no one had actually joined his army. The prince lost his nerve. On 6 December he ordered a retreat.[1]

The retreat precipitated a second crisis of panic in York. Would they come that way? Would they not be reckless and terrible in their destruction now that they were losing? In a secret, surprise move, Henry Ibbotson of Leeds, a justice, ordered the gates of the city to be closed and began search-ing the houses of reputed Papists for arms. The corporation was furious. 'The measure at this crisis was a right one,' wrote the archbishop, 'but they shut y[e] City gates & put the warrant in execution without acquainting a single soul of the Corporation. I doubt this will prove a disagreeable business: it has put y[e] Corporation into an huge ferment.' Jaques Sterne may have been the justice who acted with Ibbotson. He knew about the move the night before and wrote to Lord Irwin, 'This wil teach them for the future to do their own Duty.'[2]

The highland army did not come to York. They made their way back along the route they had used to invade England, and a sad retreat it was, with country people who had before let them pass now rising against them. They were harassed and tormented. The unwary were cut off from the main body, harrowed into barns and murdered by the farmers.

The fright had had a destructive effect on York, for it crumbled the spirit of unity which Archbishop Herring had so carefully fostered. The 'Bishop-thorpe truce' among political factions was broken by the most extreme among local politicians, and no one was more responsible for the new bitter-ness than Dr Jaques Sterne. To be sure, he was supported by many, includ-ing his nephew by marriage, Thomas Pulleyn; his close friend Sir Rowland Winn, deputy lieutenant and chief of the Ministerial Party in the West Riding; 'the little Earl', Lord Irwin, Lord Lieutenant of the East Riding; Justice Henry Ibbotson of Leeds; and Dr Samuel Baker, chancellor and residentiary canon. But, without doubt, Jaques Sterne was the most aggres-sive and insidious of his circle.[3]

'Ugly apprehension of an invasion hangs over the City', wrote Herring the day after Christmas, 'and the people's minds are perpetually harrassed

[1] Sir Charles Petrie, *The Jacobite Move-ment*, 1932, Chapter VII.

[2] Leeds City Library: Temple-Newsam Papers, PO/3C, 128, dated 7 December 1745; Herring to J. Hutton, 8 December, in Raine, 'Marske in Swaledale', YAJ, VI (1880-1), 255.

[3] Collyer.

STEPHEN CROFT
By Sir Joshua Reynolds, 1760

THE MARRIAGE OF MISS WHICHCOTE OF HARPSWELL WITH THE DEAN OF YORK
By Joseph Highmore, 1749

Thomas Whichcote of Harpswell, Lincolnshire, gives away his daughter Maria to John Fountayne, Dean of York. They are Van Dyck-ing

with real or false fears of publick mischief.'[1] In such an atmosphere it is no wonder that the innocent sometimes suffered. Lord Fauconberg, as everyone knew, had been reared a Catholic, but he had long conformed to the established church, freely taken the oaths, and loyally supported King George, Robert Walpole and the Pelhams. Yet His Lordship was deprived of his horses and forced to rely upon his friends to transport his fat, gouty person. But such orders were not the precentor's doing. His aim was not so bad as that.

Dr Sterne had long suspected a group of families of the gentry who wintered at York and had built town houses at the south edge of the city in or near Micklegate. It was an open secret that they were Papists, and that the centre of their religious life was a convent which stood inconspicuously outside Micklegate Bar. Here mass was said secretly by a Jesuit priest, Father Francis Mannock. 'The Nunnery', as it was called by Dr Sterne, tried to pass itself off as a girls' school, and indeed the nuns, disguised in the grey gowns and white caps of widows, did keep a school for the daughters of this quiet Roman Catholic community. Nevertheless, it was a true convent belonging to the Institute of the Blessed Virgin Mary, founded in 1642, which also supported a conventual house in Hammersmith – the only two convents in England at this time.[2] Acting upon the evidence of an affidavit charging a conspiracy to 'seduce' a young orphan girl from her religion, Jaques Sterne had the convent searched. 'I had a great deal of Talk with ye Lady Abbess &c to whom I gave good Advice if she wil follow it, telling her y^t I thought it woud be well for Themselves as well as this City if they woud leave it.'[3] Mother Mary Hodshon, the superior, refused to be intimidated. The convent had influential friends in the corporation, including some practical Protestants who valued the economic benefits of wealthy Catholic residents. Dr Sterne did not succeed in closing the convent, though he would harass it for the next decade.

Jaques Sterne hated the oligarchy of merchant aldermen who controlled the city, not only because they protected these families, but also because they had opposed Walpole and now opposed Henry Pelham. Naturally his suspicions fell upon their chief public servant, the lawyer Thomas Place,

[1] Letter to J. Hutton, in Raine, p. 256.
[2] CURTIS, 42; HERRING RETURNS, IV, 220; Henry James Coleridge, *St. Mary's Convent, Micklegate Bar, York*, 1887. The chapel of the Bar Convent, which was built later in the eighteenth century, demonstrates the difficulties under which

Catholic institutions operated: the beautiful little dome, built in imitation of St Peter's, is hidden beneath a slate roof, and there is a priest hole near the altar.
[3] SP 36/83, letter to [Henry Masterman], 24 May 1746.

who served as Recorder of York. Although Place had joined the precentor in the arrest of Dr Burton, he had dared to give the physician advice before he left the city and upon his return. Dr Sterne found an opportunity to attack Place in the aftermath of an incident of 11 December. That night, about 10 o'clock, a shot was fired from within the city close to Micklegate Bar. The soldiers guarding the gate, supposing themselves fired upon, ran to a house close by belonging to William Selby, Esq., a Catholic gentleman. They banged on his door. Selby, indisposed in the upper rooms, was slow in answering. It was later ascertained that two unidentified horsemen rode away in the dark, unchallenged in the confusion. Nevertheless, the soldiers searched Selby's house for arms. His arms had already been seized. The next morning Jaques Sterne demanded that Mr Place arrest and confine Selby. The recorder refused. Instead, Place set about collecting informations from a large number of witnesses, which the lord mayor reviewed and sent on to Whitehall. Within a few days an answer was returned by the Attorney-General: the evidence did not warrant a charge, and the guard placed at Selby's house should be removed. Dr Sterne was furious. 'O! Recorder! Recorder!' he exclaimed in a letter to Irwin. To the Duke of Newcastle he sent a complaint about 'The Great Tenderness and Delicacy shewn by the Recorder of this City in *refusing* to Commit Mr Selby, upon so remarkable an Occasion . . . I assure Your Grace, that he has acted all along as if he was *retained* by the Papists, and determin'd to *Protect* them.'[1] Uncle Jaques was beginning to look foolish even to his friends, and Archbishop Herring was constrained to offer an explanation to Newcastle:

> I would just intimate to y^r L^p that my good friend ye D^r is an honest man & means quite well, yet without seeing it himself, his Zeal & his Aversion now & then make him lay greater stress upon small matters than they will bear . . . tho ye Recorder is cautious, & in some instances, tender to ye Popish Gentlemen, I think him a perfect honest man, & one that ought by no means to be put out of humour at this Juncture.[2]

[1] SP 36/77, John Raper, Lord Mayor of York, to Newcastle; SP 36/78, Newcastle's reply, 23 December. See also the coverage in a newspaper which had come into being just three weeks before, the *York Journal: or, Weekly Advertiser* for 17 and 24 December. Whoever founded this newspaper, its policies were those of Jaques Sterne and his associates. On 25 March 1746, the name was changed to *York Journal: or, Protestant Courant*, and changed again on 12 December 1749 to the *Protestant York Courant*. For the known issues and their locations: R. M. Wiles, *Freshest Advices: Early Provincial Newspapers in England*, Columbus, Ohio, 1965, pp. 518–19.

[2] BM: Add. MSS 35598, fols. 146–7, dated 15 December.

As we might expect, Uncle Jaques also went after his old enemy Caesar Ward. He asked both Lord Irwin and Thomas Place to shut down the *York Courant*, but they refused. Sir Rowland Winn, whom he approached next, would probably have liked to break up the *Courant*, but he was fearful of the consequences. So the precentor never succeeded, though he kept trying. As late as June 1746, he was still attempting to bring an action against Ward.[1]

With Ward's friend and business associate, Dr Francis Drake, he did a little better. Drake would have been a special target, not only because he was a stalwart of the Country Interest, but because he was known to do much writing for the *Courant*. Moreover, he had saved Ward from bankruptcy only a few months before. But Jaques Sterne had an even better reason to hate the physician and historian: Dr Drake had lampooned him in the *Courant*. A letter of Stephen Thompson, a banker, dated 8 November 1745, told the story. Drake as city surgeon was required to take the oaths during the crisis. He refused. Thereupon, said Thompson, 'a virulent advertisement was handed about . . . which nobody doubts to father upon Parson Sterne, who was satirized a long time together in the York Courant, of which Drake has owned himself one of the authors.'[2] Thompson's phrase 'a long time together' seems a bit misleading. Probably he had reference to, first, a Latin epigram in the *Courant* of 27 November 1744, submitted by 'W. Charnley'. It was obligingly translated in the next issue by 'Thomas English':

> MOLLY he loves: But jealous *Sarah* growls;
> 'Tis hard for one to please two am'rous Souls.
> Ah Sarah! learn to look and not to see;
> Thy Husband long has known that Mystery.

To satisfy any doubt that the lines referred to Jaques Sterne and his mistress, Sarah Benson, Drake and his friends followed with this:

> An ANSWER *to the last Week's* Epigrammatist.
> YOUR *Epigram* is quite too keen,
>   To touch the Fair's Mistakes;
> For if it smells not all obscene,
>   I never smell'd a Jaques.

[1] Letters to Irwin and Winn of 2 November: Temple-Newsam Papers, PO/ 3C, 64–5; SP 36/84, information of Walter Pearson, 11 June 1746, with J. Sterne's accompanying letter to Newcastle of 14 June.

[2] Historical MSS Commission Report: *Lady du Cane*, p. 78.

Ward ran the entire series again, without comment, on 9 April 1745, all too short a time before the rebellion. We can hardly wonder that Dr Drake was arrested, as he was on 11 October, and bound over for £100 not to depart the city and to remain within five miles of his dwelling. In January he was dismissed from his post as city surgeon.[1]

Jaques Sterne's persecution of Dr John Burton (it merits no other description) was equally fruitless in the long run, but the run was long indeed during which Dr Burton suffered at the hands of the precentor. This is not to suggest that Dr Burton was innocent of treason: the evidence weighs heavily against him. Nor is it to say that he was an honest man: later years proved quite the opposite.[2] Still, whatever the physician's faults, Jaques Sterne's attempt to hang him was a travesty of justice so gross as to be self-defeating. A public trial of Dr Burton would have been embarrassing to the ministry, for it would have revealed that Burton was held incommunicado for many months, that his enemies tried to ruin him financially while he was a prisoner, that regular judicial proceedings were circumvented, that witnesses were bribed. To be sure, because the Habeas Corpus Act was suspended, no one in Burton's position could expect their rights to be fully recognized. Yet the government was surprisingly lenient toward suspected Jacobites, at least those who were English, far more lenient than almost any government in the twentieth century has been under similar circumstances. Dr Burton probably would have been freed after a few days had it not been for the machinations of his arch-enemy, the precentor. What were Uncle Jaques motives? Love of country, to be sure. Possibly a personal antipathy. But the main motive was political exigency. As Burton later put it, he was persecuted 'on an old Election Grudge': 'Dr. Sterne made no secret of publickly declaring, that it was determin'd to make a Victim of me in order to prevent any other from daring to oppose their Interest in any future Election.'[3]

---

[1] York Public Library: *Minutes of [Quarter] Sessions*, 1740–9; *York Journal: or, Weekly Advertiser*, 7 January 1745/6. On 14 March he was bound over by the lord mayor to appear at the next assize: SP 36/82, J. Sterne to [?Henry Masterman], 15 March 1745/6.

[2] Noël Denholm-Young, in 'Yorkshire monastic archives', *Bodleian Quarterly Record*, VIII (1935–7), 95–100, tells the story of Burton's dishonest acquisition of the monastic archives once stored in St Mary's Tower, York. They had come into the hands of a York physician, Dr William Roundel, who lent them to Dr Burton. When Roundel died, Burton refused to return them to the heirs; subsequently he sold them to William Constable of Burton Constable.

[3] SP 36/89, Burton to [?Andrew Stone], 1 November 1746.

Besides numerous short letters, Dr Burton wrote three elaborate accounts of his treatment at the hands of Jaques Sterne – a long letter of 1 November 1746, already cited, probably addressed to Andrew Stone, secretary to the Duke of Newcastle; a sworn petition to Attorney-General Ryder, dated 4 March 1746/7;[1] and his book, *British Liberty Endanger'd*. Although, as has been pointed out, his published account of his journey and his meeting with the rebels is slanted and sometimes false, his account of his arrest and imprisonment is accurate in every detail that can be checked. He had no need to falsify this portion of his experience.

Dr Burton had been arrested upon an order of Jaques Sterne and the recorder, Thomas Place. The keeper of the castle, however, required a detainer to hold him for more than a few days. Place was unwilling to join the precentor in signing such a document. So Uncle Jaques, to win support from some other justice, trumped up a false witness from among the prisoners in the castle. This was James Nesbitt, a Rotherham innkeeper and former soldier, who had been committed for saying treasonous things about the strength of the rebel army. To oblige the precentor, he now swore an information that Burton in the castle had said many treasonous things, and, moreover,

> the D[r] called for a Pint of wine & drank to the Downfall of the Guelps, after which the D[r] filled this Ex[t']s Glass who drank to the Downfall of whelps & Jacobites – who thereupon asked what this Ex[t] meant by that, who said the Popish Pretender, and Some time after that drinking again the D[r] drank to the Downfall of the Duke of Cumberland and Success to Prince Charles.[2]

In *British Liberty Endanger'd*, Burton tells us that the following day he was examined before nine justices, including Dr Sterne, the dean and the recorder. In such a situation, of course, Justice Sterne could not act with the concurrence of only one other justice, but only with that of the majority. Nesbitt was called to the hearing and made a fool of himself. The group broke up and most of them left for home, including the dean and recorder. But the precentor called back Mark Braithwaite and two others, who together signed an order to hold Dr Burton and not to admit him to bail. Although there is no evidence to corroborate the story, we can hardly put such manipulations past Jaques Sterne, especially since at this point he had

[1] SP 36/95.   [2] SP 36/77, examination of James Nesbitt at York Castle, 14 December 1745.

the approval of Archbishop Herring, who had already written to the Lord Chancellor that Dr Sterne had '*proof* that our Physician Dr. Burton, so far as his influence reaches, is a dangerous & barefaced traytor, as well as he is a bad man . . . a sort of Darling of the Party here, and had the Direction of a Printing Press'.[1]

Dr Burton, of course, maintained that Nesbitt himself had said the treasonous things which were attributed to him, Burton. Probably he was telling the truth. Burton asserted publicly and under oath that Nesbitt forswore himself, that Nesbitt confessed as much to Captain Cadogan, the officer in charge at the castle, and that he later admitted it before the lord chief justice. Burton asserted that the man had been threatened by the precentor with the loss of his military pension and coaxed with bribes. No counter assertions were made from the other side, and Burton was never prosecuted for his statements, though Jaques Sterne would surely have brought an action against him had he been able.

Nesbitt, having fulfilled Dr Sterne's initial purpose, was left to rot in prison. Perhaps he had forfeited his claim to protection by admitting his perjury. In a pitiful letter to the precentor, Nesbitt told how all the prisoners and even the guards had turned against him since his testimony: 'I dont doubt if sum of thire affedavids woud be taken ag^t me woud Swere my Life away, for God Sake Rev^d S^r I know its in your power to Relieve me from here . . . Committ me to the Care of the town Guard . . . I should think my Self Happy & be Content to lay upon the beare Stones rather then the best bead in this place.' Whether Nesbitt survived his gaol experience is doubtful. Some 100 prisoners had been brought to York Castle. The handsome prison, completed as recently as 1705 and considered the most modern and humane prison in Europe, simply could not hold such quantities of men. The last record of Nesbitt is his signature upon a petition from prisoners in the castle who are living in extreme poverty, dying of exposure and neglect.[2]

The winter of 1745–6 was unusually severe, with heavy snows lasting into March. Little provision was made for the prisoners. Archbishop Herring

[1] BM: Add. MSS 35598, fols. 146–7. The detainer itself, signed by J. Sterne, Mark Braithwaite, R. Oates and J. Stillington, is attached to Nesbitt's examination, cited above.

[2] Temple-Newsam Papers, PO/3C, 162, Nesbitt to J. Sterne, [?January 1745/6]; SP 36/91, 'Petition of the Prisoners', dated only 1746. In *British Liberty Endanger'd*, Burton said that Nesbitt appeared before the lord chief justice on 1 November 1747, but probably that is an error for 1746: few cases, if any, connected with the rebellion were carried over so long as into 1747. On York Castle: T. P. Cooper, *The History of the Castle of York*, 1911.

wrote in mid-February, 'The prisoners die and the Recorder told me yesterday, when the turnkey opens the cells in the morning, the steam and stench is intolerable and scarce credible. The very walls are covered with lice in the room over which the Grand Jury sit.'[1] Dr Burton, held in a private room, had his wants provided for by family and friends. But he was closely watched and repeatedly questioned by Captain Cadogan.

On 12 March Mr William Dick, a Crown messenger, arrived with orders to carry Dr Burton up to London. Dr Jaques Sterne thought that Burton should be transported in irons, but Mr Dick refused, saying that it was unnecessary and cruel: the doctor was suffering from gout in both feet and one hand. The hardest thing for Dr Burton, in all probability, was the resignation which he wrote out the day he was taken away: he resigned as staff physician from the public hospital which he had worked so hard to found. Then he left with the humane messenger, in whose house in London he would be confined for the next year.

Burton, always a clever financier, may have shared a secret laugh with Mr Dick as the coach passed through Micklegate Bar – a small bit of comfort in the midst of his woes. Most of the physician's debts were owed to men on the other side of the political fence. Since his arrest, these Whiggish creditors had been meeting in the George Inn trying to find ways of retrieving their money or, in Burton's view, ruining him. This removal to London foiled their plans: they could not bring an action against him while he was in the custody of the Crown. Justice Henry Ibbotson, now elevated to sheriff, began to write furious letters to Newcastle demanding the return of the doctor. Burton's enemies later said that he went broke for £5,000, discharged at 10s. in the £1, but the point is uncertain. He did have to sell the lease on his home, the Red House, and the theatre which stood on the same property, but he succeeded in protecting his wife's independent fortune.[2]

Jaques Sterne knew very well that James Nesbitt was too shaky a witness to provide evidence upon which Dr Burton might be hanged. For that service he turned to another prisoner in York Castle, an Irish soldier of

[1] Herring to Hardwicke, 14 February 1746, in Yorke, *Life of Hardwicke*, I, 501.
[2] The Red House and Theatre (much altered) still stand. Burton advertised the lease on them in *York Courant*, 8 April 1746. The bankruptcy: George Thompson, *An Account of What Passed between Mr. George Thompson . . . and Doctor John Burton*, 1756, p. 6. Meetings of creditors: *York Courant*, 17 December 1745; SP 36/82, Ibbotson to Newcastle, 20 March 1745/6; Burton to Ramsden, 27 March 1747; SP 36/83, Ibbotson to Newcastle, 12 May 1746; Burton to his wife, 15 April 1746; Ryder to Newcastle, 21 April 1746.

fortune named Richard Murth, who had been present upon that occasion when, according to Nesbitt, the physician had drunk those treasonable toasts. Consequently, Murth had a hold over Dr Burton, who counted upon him to testify to Nesbitt's perfidy. He was in a position to tease the doctor along and, as Jaques Sterne hoped, to get more information out of him.

The precentor understood the sort of man he was dealing with in Murth. The Irishman had first come to his attention through Nesbitt, who wrote to Dr Sterne that he recognized Murth as a former officer in the French service. At the time Burton was taken to London, one of the justices in York, un-identified, wrote about Murth to Whitehall: 'It is hard to say, how far a Fellow's information can be depended on, who stands committed in the Calendar of the Prisoners here, for a Notorious Cheat and a dangerous Im-poster.'[1] But none of this was apt to stop Jaques Sterne so long as he thought Murth could be useful. It might, in fact, have recommended him.

Murth was soon 'discharged by proclamation',[2] and sent to London as the precentor's own private spy. True, Dr Sterne generously offered the man's services to the government. He showed a letter of Murth's to the archbishop and to Henry Masterman, then in York, after which he wrote to Newcastle telling him that these men agreed 'that Murth being a very sensible man, & intirely trusted by the Jacobites, may be made an useful Agent for the Government, & do the Public great Service at this time, if properly encouraged'.[3] Newcastle did not warm to the idea. Nevertheless, Murth went to London, set himself up in Grosvenor Street, and began to play a sort of amateur double agent's game.

Uncle Jaques, it appears, believed that Dr Burton could 'make Discoveries' about the Jacobites of Yorkshire, and that Murth could turn the trick. 'If the D[r] has as yet disclosed nothing to your Grace of that nature,' he wrote to Newcastle, 'I do believe that Murth can bring him to it, & make Such Dis-coveries as will be of Use to the Public. If the Recorder and magistrates of this City had done their Duty, more things might have been brought to Light before this time.'[4] The precentor felt certain that Burton had 'some-thing also under Drake's Hand, which Drake wanted to have got from him, but I hope he has it with him'. And to whet the appetite of the ministry, Jaques Sterne did not hesitate to mention that the physician knew about

---

[1] SP 36/82, marked on the back, 'March 11th 1745. Extract of a letter relating to D[r] Burton committed at York of High Treason'.

[2] PRO: Assizes. 41. 4.

[3] SP 36/83, 12 April 1746.

[4] SP 36/83, letter to [Newcastle], 5 April 1746.

'Rhodes of Ripon, who has a good Estate'.[1] The estate of one convicted of high treason was forfeit to the Crown. But the precentor had become entangled in his own web. His deep conviction that Dr Burton could and would turn informant arose primarily from what he had been told by Captain Cadogan, the commander of the military detachment at York Castle, who had repeatedly questioned the doctor. Cadogan's ideas about the physician had been formed, not so much by his interviews with Dr Burton himself, as by conversations with Richard Murth. In point of fact, Jaques was now employing Murth to unravel the mysteries which Murth himself had ravelled.

Dr Burton, in turn, rose to Murth's bait naïvely. Burton probably was characterized correctly by that unidentified justice in York who wrote to Newcastle when the physician was taken to London: 'a very weak man, neither able to consider nor execute matters of great moment; of no address nor capacity in his profession; but very proper, for his Zeal, to carry on a bad Correspondence, to circulate Letters, convey money, and do other lower offices in such a wicked Conspiracy, as Treason'.[2] Burton trusted Murth to bring him money from York to London, and indeed had lent him money for Murth's own bail. (It is rather unlikely that in these dealings he was covertly bribing Murth; his letters do not suggest that at all.) Burton's first correspondence with the spy seems innocent enough, but it pleased Murth mightily. Burton wrote primarily about these money matters and sent instructions how Murth was to swear an affidavit about what really happened that night in York Castle when the doctor and Nesbitt had drunk together. But he made the mistake of saying that he could 'better contrive to send than receive letters' and of telling Murth to write under an assumed name and to burn his own letter. Murth, of course, sent the doctor's letter directly to Jaques Sterne, along with his renewed claim to be in on the councils of all the Jacobite party and a warning that if they knew what he was up to 'I should certainly be destroy'd by Sword or Poison'. It is hard to see how all this could have helped to uncover more: it resulted in the physician's being more closely confined and not allowed to be alone with anyone except his guard.[3]

Murth, unable to deliver the goods he had promised, began to bluster. He offered to reveal information about an 'infamous Black Dog Club' at

[1] SP 36/82, letter to unidentified person, 15 March 1745/6.

[2] SP 36/82, 11 March. Archbishop Herring described Burton as 'a silly fellow of no Mark or Likelihood': letter to Hard-wicke, 4 December 1745, at BM: Add. MSS 35598, fol. 145.

[3] SP 36/83, J. Sterne to Newcastle, 12 April, with enclosures of Murth to J. Sterne, 4 April, and Burton to Murth.

York, began to name more and more Jacobites, warned against the Recorder of York – 'beware of him' – and asserted that Dr Burton had been promised the post of physician extraordinary to the Pretender should the rebellion carry. He wrote to Archbishop Herring, offering to serve as a spy,[1] and finally declared he had evidence that the entire Country Interest was in on a great Jacobite plot. Of course he would like a little compensation, most especially 'if he could by any means be protected from the fear of Trouble, to which he is at present liable on account of laboring under some Debts'. That could be more easily arranged if he did some spying from abroad: 'Recommendations should not be wanting to make him known to the Queen of Spain's confessor.'[2]

The precentor continued throughout that spring to insist that Murth 'seems to me to be determined to act a right part, & I hope he will be properly encouraged',[3] but he was beginning to have doubts. When it came down to really serious business such as arguing Dr Burton's guilt to the authorities in London, he put no emphasis upon Murth's information. He must have come to the conclusion that the man was lying. We hear no more of the spy after May. Probably Murth took his cloak and dagger and absconded.

On 7 May Dr John Burton was formally examined, not before the Privy Council, as he said in his book, but before Newcastle's secretary, Andrew Stone. The doctor described his journey to Settle, Hornby and Lancaster, omitting no days and confirming many details gathered from other witnesses. He said nothing which would be grounds for a charge of treason, and described his interview with Prince Charles Edward as an interrogation. He insisted that he was taken to Lancaster and into the prince's house as a prisoner, and that he talked to people only to gather intelligence for the government. After the examination, he was allowed to receive visitors. But Attorney-General Ryder decided there was not enough evidence to convict the doctor; he should be held while more was gathered.[4] The physician would have to remain in prison for another nine months while Jaques Sterne's agents scoured the West Riding seeking witnesses. The creditors were furious again.

In April the rebel army was wiped out in the bloody battle of Culloden,

[1] BM: Add. MSS 32706, fol. 372, undated.

[2] SP 36/83, statement sworn by Murth before J. Waite, 17 May 1746.

[3] SP 36/83, J. Sterne to [Henry Masterman], 24 May.

[4] SP 36/83, Ryder to Newcastle, 30 May; examination of Burton at Whitehall, dated 7 May, with an addition of 8 May.

and there followed that terrible slaughter of soldiers and highland citizens which for ever broke the power of the clans and blackened the name of the Duke of Cumberland. A few days after the celebrations in York, the *York Journal: or, Protestant Courant* of 29 April ran an article denying the 'malicious' report that Thomas Pulleyn had encouraged a mob to attack the nunnery or that Dr Jaques Sterne had inspired them to break the windows of Mr Place's house.

More and more Jacobite soldiers were brought into the prisons. The number in York grew to 200. Henry Masterman came down from London to examine them. Most of the accused could speak no English, and Gaelic interpreters who were not themselves prisoners were almost impossible to come by. Many prisoners were ill, and Masterman's personal servant caught gaol fever and died. Frightened for his own life, Masterman limited his interrogations to those who were healthy and completed his work in twelve days. The others would be examined, he wrote to Newcastle, by Drs Sterne and Baker, 'whose zeal . . . for the Service of the Governm^t is too well known, (in these parts) to want any further mention of it'.[1]

On 23 July the Duke of Cumberland, returning from Scotland in a great progress, stopped at York. With pomp and ceremony, he was received by the archbishop, dean, and clergy (including Laurence Sterne?), the lord mayor, aldermen, sheriffs of the city, judges of the assize, and high sheriff in the Great House in the Minster Yard, which now belonged to Dr Sterne.[2] It must have been one of Uncle Jaques's finest hours.

The trials of the prisoners got under way in August and went on for two months. The night of 8 October, a rhyme was tacked up on the door of the minster:

> What means these Vile and Idle pranks
> To Murder men and then give thanks
> Stop preacher Stop and go no further
> God never Accepts of Thanks for Murder.[3]

[1] SP 36/83, 9 April 1746.

[2] *York Courant* and *York Journal: or, Protestant Courant*, 29 July 1746; letter from York, dated 23 July, in the *London Evening Post*, 2 August 1746.

[3] Temple-Newsam Papers, PO/3. 11, enclosed with a copy of a letter from Mr Elsley to Lord Irwin. Under Canon Law, the clergy were prohibited from any secular jurisdiction, 'especially in Cases of Blood': Edmund Gibson, *Codex Juris Ecclesiastici Anglicani*, 2 vols with continuous pagination, 1713, p. 1031. Nevertheless, it had long been the practice to name clergy to the Commission of the Peace, in which capacity many served with distinction: Sidney and Beatrice Webb, *The Parish and the County*, Vol. I of *English Local Government*, 5 vols, 1906, reissued, New York, 1963, pp. 350–60.

A writer for the *York Journal: or, Protestant Courant* of the following week asserted that it was written 'by some Biggotted Papist, or perhaps . . . proceeded from the envenom'd Stomach of a *Duck* or a *Drake* (Animals remarkable for *Dabbling* in *Puddle* and *Nastiness*)'. Dr Drake had appeared before a judge in the Guildhall in July, but had been released after 'a most severe Reprimand'.[1]

The treason trials were concluded in mid-October. Fifty-three were condemned to death. On the 28th a hangman was hired, William Stout of Hexham. His price: 20 guineas and all the clothes. At the last minute, thirty-nine were reprieved.[2] The other fourteen were executed on 4 November on Knavesmire. According to the *London Evening Post* of the 8th, they were hanged slowly for ten minutes, then stripped naked upon a stage built for the purpose, and their hearts cut out. The hangman held the heart up to the crowd, crying 'Gentlemen, behold the heart of a traitor'. Loud huzzas. The legs were scored, the heads cut off. The heads of William Connolly and James Mayne were placed on spikes over Micklegate Bar.[3] 'The whole', according to the *Post*, 'was conducted throughout with the utmost Decency and good Order.'

Nothing more convincingly demonstrates the madness of Jaques Sterne than his next move. A month after the executions, he tried to buy for himself the freedom of the city – that is, a membership in the corporation which would allow him to take part directly in city elections – for 200 guineas and a portrait of the Duke of Cumberland. His letter was read at a meeting of the corporation, 'but', wrote Caesar Ward, 'no Member present offering any Thing in Behalf of this Generous and Disinterested Proposal, it was Unanimously drop'd'.[4]

Dr Burton lingered in prison, writing melancholy letters to his wife and trying to pass the time in antiquarian studies. He was allowed for a while to do research on the records of the Tower of London.[5] Though he begged

[1] *York Journal: or, Protestant Courant*, 22 July 1746.

[2] SP 36/89, list of condemned prisoners, each name marked 'to be reprieved' or 'to suffer'.

[3] HARGROVE, I, 226.

[4] *York Courant.* 16 December 1746. J. Sterne's letter in CURTIS, 425.

[5] SP 36/84, Burton to Andrew Stone, 23 June 1746. Davies saw the notes: 'Memoir of John Burton'. Burton also became interested in the accounts of Prince Charles Edward given by his fellow prisoners, and after his release went to Scotland to collect more information; eventually he published *A Genuine and True Journal of the Most Miraculous Escape of the Young Chevalier*, 1749. On his researches in Scotland, see Robert Forbes, *The Lyon in Mourning*, ed. Henry Paton (Scottish History Soc. Pub., XX), 1895, pp. 281–313.

repeatedly for a trial, he was never formally charged. He was simply held until the suspension of the Habeas Corpus Act ran out.

Murray of Broughton gave his evidence against the doctor in August – evidence sufficient to convict Burton of high treason. Why then was he not tried in the autumn with other suspected Jacobites? For one thing, national political developments worked in his favour. Lord Chancellor Hardwicke and the Pelhams had decided on a policy of tolerance: unity on major issues could be purchased by winking at minor ones. The ministry stayed in power, not by polarizing the voters along party lines, but by give and take with people of divergent views. They were no longer interested in the question of Popery, since English Catholics had clearly demonstrated their loyalty to George II. Jaques Sterne held the opposite view: destroy Burton, he argued, and they would destroy the Tory faction in York: 'I wil venture to prophecy y^t there is an end to the Tory Interest in this place, if the Jacobites have their Deserts at this Juncture', he wrote. 'We have the Game in our Hands, if we have the Skill & Honesty to play it well, & not Suffer ourselves to be Dupes to the Torys.'[1] His plea fell on deaf ears.

The leaders of the Country Interest, sensing how the wind blew, decided they could get Burton released – as Jaques was well aware. To his letter, pleading for the destruction of Burton, he added a postscript: 'I just now hear that Fox [George Fox of Bramham Park] has writ to our Jacobite Printer [Caesar Ward], to let him know that they have managed so well for our friend Dr. Burton that he might shortly expect to see him.'[2]

The political influence of Dr Burton's friends probably helped to release him, though his discharge was owing in some measure to justice, long overdue. In December, the physician asked for and received leave to visit Archbishop Herring, then in London. He did see Herring, and followed up the visit with a long letter to His Grace summarizing his arguments for his innocence and pleading the injustice of a long detention without charge or trial.[3] The archbishop sent the doctor's letter to Newcastle with one of his own, in which he declared:

[1] SP 36/83, J. Sterne to [Henry Masterman], 24 May 1746. On the policies of the ministry: Cedric Collyer, 'The Rockinghams and Yorkshire politics, 1742–1761', *Publications of the Thoresby Society*, XLI (1946–53), 352–82; SYKES, 36.

[2] SP 36/83, a cover for a letter, addressed to Henry Masterman, with the note written on it in J. Sterne's hand, no doubt the cover for J. Sterne's letter of 24 May 1746, though separated from it in the bundle.

[3] SP 36/90, Burton to Herring, 26 December; Burton to [?Masterman], 20 December; *British Liberty Endanger'd*, 63–5.

He desir'd of me, that I would testify to your Grace, That, at his return from Hornby Castle to York, he inform'd me, That the Design of the Rebels was, to fight Ligonier, or march into Wales or to London, & that he gave me this information voluntarily. Upon recollection I remember this, & could not refuse him y[e] Justice of doing as he desir'd me.[1]

There is no ready explanation why the archbishop had not remembered this at the time of Dr Burton's arrest.

If belated justice helped the physician, so too did past injustice. It may have been the grossness of Jaques Sterne's persecution which ultimately saved him. On 20 February 1747, the Habeas Corpus Act was reinstated. On 12 March, Attorney-General Ryder sent to Newcastle his opinion that Burton should be released on bail.[2] On the 25th, he was freed. He had been confined at Mr Dick's house exactly a year, and it had been sixteen months since his arrest. But the case was not yet over: the bail had bound him to appear at the York assizes when next they met. He did so appear the following July. No one came forward to accuse him, and the case was dismissed. Who, one wonders, had convinced Dr Sterne that a public trial would cost him dear?

There is no evidence that Laurence Sterne joined his uncle in this persecution, but his attitudes were much the same. He approved of the precentor's endeavours, suspected the Catholics of York, and cared not at all to be fair to Dr John Burton.

During most of the winter of 1745–6, Sterne remained at Sutton-on-the-Forest and Stillington. His only known appearance at York suggests that the war between the Houses of Stuart and Hanover had evoked a truce in the war between the reverend Sternes. On 18 January, some weeks after the rebels had fled northward, Sterne attended a chapter meeting, the first since he had been inducted into the prebend of North Newbald. The business of the day was simple, but of some moment: the group collated to the prebend of Warthill Dr William Herring, LLD, first cousin to the archbishop, a man destined to become diocesan chancellor. Presumably Sterne was invited for some practical purpose, probably because they might lack a quorum. He may have been sitting in for his uncle, who was absent. The others, Samuel Baker, Thomas Lamplugh and the dean, had been helping Jaques examine the prisoners at the castle. They would hardly have asked anyone to join them who was opposed to their policies.

[1] SP 36/90, dated 29 December 1746.   [2] SP 36/95.

Then Sterne appeared again in the newspaper columns. It has long been speculated that he took up his pen in defence of the Crown during the '45. Kenneth Monkman has identified at least one article by Sterne, published after Culloden but before the York assizes. It appeared on 1 July, in the *York Journal: or, Protestant Courant* (renamed in 1749 the *Protestant York Courant*).[1]

In the essay, Sterne attacks the Roman Catholic gentry who winter in York and the oligarchy of merchants who encourage them – a matter which had infuriated his uncle. He complains bitterly that certain citizens 'caress' and 'take within our Bosoms some of those very People, whose Principles, whose Religion and Riches, have been the Means of forming this unnatural Rebellion'. He described how 'every Success obtained by our Arms cast a Damp and Sullenness upon them', how 'at Cope's unfortunate Defeat they *exulted*'. And now, at the highlanders' defeat, 'they are quite Chop-fallen. Where be their Gibes? their Gambols? their Songs? Their Flashes of Merriment? Not one now to mock their own Grinning.' He concludes with an exhortation: 'instead of wishing them to live amongst us, let us earnestly wish them to retire from us.' Sterne is more tolerant of rural Catholics than his uncle would have been: he carefully excludes from his attack 'our own neighbouring Gentry (from whom is our natural Support)' – thinking, no doubt, of Lord Fauconberg. Otherwise, he expresses the view of Jaques Sterne.

Finally, in the long run, it was Laurence, not Jaques, who most severely punished Dr Burton. The precentor tormented the doctor for two years, but failed to destroy him: Burton bounded back, took his place again in York society, prospered, and again became active in politics. Sterne, who had learned in the election of 1741/2 not to involve himself in 'dirty work', did not attack the physician through legal or political means. He bided his time for fourteen more years until he had forged a weapon infinitely more effective and cruel: he turned Dr Burton into Dr Slop of *Tristram Shandy* and damaged him for eternity. True, Sterne's satire was directed primarily against Burton as a man-midwife – a satire he richly deserved.[2] But in two respects Sterne was distinctly unfair to him, and neither of these was essential to the medical satire.

First, Sterne made Dr Slop a Catholic. Burton was surely a Protestant.

[1] On the newspaper, above, p. 166, n. 1. Information about the article and quotations taken from STERNE, HAMLET, AND YORICK.

[2] Arthur H. Cash, 'The birth of Tristram Shandy: Sterne and Dr. Burton', in *Studies in the Eighteenth Century*, ed. R. F. Brissenden, Canberra, 1968, pp. 133–54.

He was the son of an Anglican clergyman, he regularly attended services, and he never failed of his obligations to the established church. He appears on none of the lists of Catholics drawn up in Yorkshire, and he was never accused of Papism by Jaques Sterne. On the knotty moral issue faced by all obstetricians, whether the child or the mother should be saved first, he took the position regularly taken by Protestant physicians: that his first responsibility was to save the mother. That stand was never taken publicly by eighteenth-century physicians who admitted to Catholicism.[1] Finally, when Dr Burton died in 1771, a monument to his and his wife's memory was placed in the chancel of the church of the Holy Trinity, Micklegate.

The second and even more cruel cut which Sterne gave to Dr Burton was highly personal. Among the papers at the Public Record Office is the testimony of a witness who saw Dr Burton in a Lancaster street wearing a white cockade.[2] Jaques Sterne had long been searching for such a statement: a white cockade in the hat, the symbol of the rebels, would be particularly damning evidence in his view.[3] The witness was a man of some standing in the community – Cuthbert Davis, collector of the excise for Lancaster. His statement was sworn before a lawyer and justice whom Jaques Sterne trusted implicitly, and the document was examined by the precentor himself before it was sent to London.[4] It gives particulars, notably details of Dr Burton's physical appearance.[5] The statement, we can be certain, contains nothing which would give it away as erroneous or false. So one would expect Cuthbert Davis to have described the physician in terms like those Sterne used in describing Dr Slop: 'a little, squat, uncourtly figure of a Doctor *Slop*, of about four feet and a half perpendicular height, with a breadth of back, and a sesquipedality of belly, which might have done honour to a serjeant in the horse-guards' (II, ix, 104). This figure was not what the witness saw in Lancaster:

Cuthbert Davis of Lancaster
    Says that on Sunday Evening Novr 24th he saw a tall Well sett Gentlem^n in a light Colored Coat in Boots with a Whip under his Arm . . . who he says was called Dr Burton of York.

[1] Burton, *Essay towards a Complete New System of Midwifry*, 1751, p. 208. Cf. John Glaister, *Dr. William Smellie and His Contemporaries*, Glasgow, 1894, p. 263.
[2] SP 36/83, information of Cuthbert Davis, sworn before James Fenton, LLD, 18 April 1746.
[3] SP 36/83, J. Sterne to Newcastle, 12 April 1746; J. Sterne to [Henry Masterman], 24 May 1746.
[4] SP 36/83, J. Sterne to Newcastle, 17 May 1746.
[5] No portrait of Dr John Burton is known today.

Crazy Castle

THERE is a Castle in the North,
   Seated upon a swampy clay,
At present but of little worth,
   In former times it had its day.

    . . . . .

In this retreat, whilom so sweet,
   Once TRISTRAM and his Cousin dwelt,
They talk of CRAZY when they meet,
   As if their tender hearts would melt.

John Hall-Stevenson's poeticisms from *Crazy Tales* (1762) look back over the years when Sterne visited his 'cousin' at Skelton Castle. Curiously, we lack documentary evidence for specific visits between 1741 and 1761. Still, as the poem and later letters suggest, Sterne often escaped from the worries of Sutton-on-the-Forest to the more exhilarating life at Skelton.

Skelton Castle, in the far north of Yorkshire, close to Saltburn-by-the-Sea, had been a baronial castle of the Bruce family. A ruinous pile, much of it uninhabitable, it could be spooky, gloomy, romantically beautiful, or amusing – depending on one's mood. It stood insecurely upon a platform of earth held in place by sheer stone walls rising out of a moat.

If many a buttress did not reach,
   A kind, and salutary hand,
Did not encourage, and beseech,
   The terrace and the house to stand,
Left to themselves and at a loss,
They'd tumble down, into the foss.

Over the Castle hangs a tow'r,
Threatning destruction ev'ry hour,

> Where owls, and bats, and the jackdaw,
> Their Vespers and their Sabbath keep . . .

The square keep was indeed half tumbled into the moat, but another, larger Norman tower was still strong. A round tower, said to antedate the Conquest, rose out of the water itself. In the centre was a massive Norman hall connected to the towers by lighter buildings.[1] There must have been a portcullis, dungeons, empty rooms and mysterious passageways. Unfortunately for us, the castle no longer has this character. Hall-Stevenson's grandson, John, who took the name of Wharton, allowed it to stand empty for a decade, during which its destruction was all but final. He eventually took possession of it and began a massive reconstruction along neo-gothic lines, completely changing its appearance. Only the larger of the square towers stands to remind us of 'Crazy Castle', as Hall liked to call the old fortress.

John Hall-Stevenson had developed into an erratic man, sometimes gay and gregarious, sometimes morose and withdrawn. In public, he was urbane in dress and bearing.[2] He passed his winters in a London town house and was keenly interested in the London political scene. At a later period he idolized John Wilkes, and his best accomplishments as a poet were the satires he wrote in support of Wilkes.[3] In the country, his interests were good company and foxhunting. Thomas Gilbert, who had given up his fellowship at Peterhouse to become the poetic squire of Skinningrave, not far from Skelton, wrote in 1741,

> On *Monday* morning, every vassal
> Cries whip and spur for *Skelton-Castle*,
> Where bounty, wit, and mirth appear,
> And pleasure crowns each smiling year.[4]

But there was the other, morose side to Hall. He declined to accept public offices in Yorkshire, grew slovenly in his dress, and, by his own description, slothful, anti-clerical, and solitary.[5] A hypochondriac, he would refuse to get

[1] The plate of Skelton Castle used as frontispiece to *Crazy Tales* coincides in most details with that in J. W. Ord, *History and Antiquities of Cleveland*, 1846, p. 253, made from a sketch provided by a local clergyman.

[2] Alexander Carlyle, *Autobiography*, 3rd ed., 1861, p. 454.

[3] My comments upon Hall-Stevenson as a writer derive primarily from Lodwick Hartley, 'Sterne's Eugenius as indiscreet author: the literary career of John Hall-Stevenson', *PMLA*, LXXXVI (1971), 428–45.

[4] *Poems on Several Occasions*, 1747, p. 216. The poem is dated 16 March 1740/1.

[5] 'Epitaph upon a Living Subject', *Works*, 3 vols, 1795, II, 196–203. On his eccentricity: Richard Brinsley Peake, *Memoirs of the Colman Family*, 2 vols, 1841,

out of bed if the weathercock on the castle turret indicated a 'pestiferous' north-east wind. One such day, according to a popular story, Sterne employed a boy to climb the tower and tie the weathercock so as to indicate a westerly wind, whereupon Hall-Stevenson rose from his bed full of good spirits. When the string broke and the arrow reversed itself, Hall went back to bed.[1] No doubt his troubles can be attributed in part to an unhappy marriage. As an old man, he complained to his grandson that his opportunity to accomplish something of worth was 'blasted by premature marriage'.[2] Probably he was irked by his father-in-law. He had taken his wife's surname to win her fortune: she and her sister were to be co-heiresses of their father. But after the two girls were married, Ambrose Stevenson fell into pecuniary straits and moved into Skelton Castle as a dependant.[3] Hall-Stevenson thereafter tried to drop the 'Stevenson' from his name – without much success. He thought of himself as poor, but there are poverties and poverties. Hall may have complained to his grandson that he was forced to 'vegetate in ye country', but in fact he never gave up his London house or curtailed his entertainments at Skelton. When he had to pay off a £2,000 mortgage on the castle, he complained that the demand would 'clip my wings and hinder my flight to town this year'.

During the rebellion, it was a different story. In the dark autumn months of 1745, Hall bustled about to organize the foxhunting squires of Yorkshire into a troop of light horse. Twenty-eight gentlemen, including such prominent men as Dr John Dealtry of York and Edwin Lascelles of Harewood, petitioned the Lords-Lieutenant to accept their support under the name of the Royal Hunters.[4] General Oglethorpe, a Yorkshire squire himself, took personal command. He was pleased with their spirit and liked the idea of hard-riding hunters, accompanied by their grooms and gamekeepers, turning their skills toward pursuing the rebels. Some thought it was all too flashy:

I, 375–6. The last public office Hall-Stevenson is known to have held was membership on the Grand Jury for the Lent assizes of 1746, after he returned from the battlefield: *York Journal: or, Weekly Advertiser*, 11 March 1745/6. He had previously served on the Grand Jury in 1740/1: *York Courant*, 17 March 1741. He was once suggested for the Commission of the Peace, but I do not know if he served: list in the Thomas Beckwith *Commonplace Book*, Minster Library: MSS Add. 40.

[1] CURTIS, 141; cf. LETTERS, 139.
[2] SEVEN LETTERS, 17–18.
[3] GRAY. I do not know the source Gray had for this story.
[4] PRO: SP 36/69; Cedric Collyer, 'Yorkshire and the "Forty-five"', YAJ, XXXVIII (1952–5), 71–95.

'The bucks', wrote Stephen Thompson, '. . . have listed under a mad general – Oglethorpe . . . they are to act as a flying squadron, to harass the enemy in their march, and to give intelligence. They make more noise here than they deserve, their numbers being much magnified.'[1] Others were enthusiastic. Thomas Gilbert, though he did not join them, celebrated them in verse:

> See *Britain*'s youth, unus'd to war's alarms,
> Forsake their downy rest, and beauty's charms;
> All the soft sweets of luxury decline,
> With firm united hearts in battle join;
> And, under *Oglethorpe*'s auspicious care,
> Endure the toils of a rough winter's war;
> Whose great example will their bosoms fire
> To conquer, or in freedom's cause expire.[2]

The Royal Hunters did endure a rough winter's war, and they did prove their worth. They were in the field earlier than most volunteer troops. In November they played a part in a battle which left 200 enemy dead. A month later, in a skirmish, they lost two officers. The Duke of Cumberland thanked them personally.[3]

Whatever hardships he may have suffered, Hall was exhilarated by his war experience. He returned to Skelton Castle with renewed determination to enjoy life, and thereafter surrounded himself with amusing companions, most of them sportsmen or military men. Several were veterans of the Royal Hunters. His hospitality became proverbial and is talked about by all the antiquarians of Cleveland. 'When a man keeps an hospitable table', wrote William Hutton,

> there are people enough who can smell out his roast meat; he need not send into the highways and hedges for people to eat it. A late proprietor of this beautiful castle (the grandest building I ever saw), was of this generous class. He kept a full-spread board, and wore down the steps of his cellar. His open heart filled his dining-room with choice com-

[1] Historical Manuscripts Commission Report, *Lady du Cane*, p. 77.
[2] *Poems on Several Occasions*, 251–4.
[3] *York Journal; or, Weekly Advertiser*, 7 January 1745/6. The battlefield activities:
Henry Fielding's *The True Patriot*, 19 November, in the edition of Miriam Austin Locke, Tuscaloosa, Alabama, 1964, p. 55; *London Evening Post*, 2 January 1745/6.

pany; one of which was that celebrated divine, Lawrence Sterne, of facetious memory.[1]

Hall brought home from the Royal Hunters one of his fellow soldiers, Robert Lascelles, who became his court jester. Lascelles was a most amusing man, an accomplished sportsman, a raconteur and something of a poet. Sterne seldom failed, in his letters to Hall-Stevenson, to send affectionate greetings to 'Panty', as Lascelles came to be called after Rabelais's character Pantagruel. Although Lascelles spent most of the next thirty years at Skelton Castle, he did not come cap-in-hand: he was comfortably wealthy. For several generations his family had been the squires of Mount Grace, close to Northallerton, an estate to which he fell heir in his middle years. Mount Grace had once been a Carthusian priory. After living with Hall at Crazy Castle, Panty may have had enough of stone ruins: he promptly sold Mount Grace.[2] In 1752 he took holy orders with the intention of becoming an army chaplain and was serving in that capacity in 1761. But his priestly status did not prevent his accepting an appointment as Hall's gamekeeper in 1755. He declined a living proffered him by Archbishop Drummond in 1762, explaining that he wanted to live in Cleveland. Not until 1777 did he get a suitable place: Hall-Stevenson presented him to the vicarage of Gilling West, near Richmond, where he lived until his death in 1801, pursuing his responsibilities as a parish priest, and his sports to the very end. His little book was published posthumously in 1815 – *Angling, Shooting, and Coursing*.[3] An excellent painting of Panty, by Singleton, a pupil of Romney, hangs at Skelton Castle – the likeable, puckish face of a man in his middle sixties.

It seems likely that Hall and Lascelles together formed the convivial club which we now call the Demoniacs. Unfortunately, we know little about it, not even its official name. No membership list or book of rules survives, though it appears that Sterne was among the original members.[4]

---

[1] Quoted by Ord, p. 256.
[2] Miss Ursula Lascelles of Slingsby generously provided information about Mount Grace and that branch of her family. Probably Robert Lascelles was the son of William, of Mount Grace, and his wife Alice, née Woodman.
[3] CURTIS, 125; SEVEN LETTERS; 'Epitaph upon a Rector', Hall-Stevenson's *Works*, II, 178–83.

[4] The major source of information is William Durrant Cooper's article for N&Q, Second Series VII (1859), 15, and his edition of SEVEN LETTERS found at Skelton Castle. The Cooper papers, consisting of twenty-four letters and other manuscripts which had remained in Cooper's hands, were recently acquired by the Beinecke Library, Yale University. I presume Zachary Moore's early member-

Another was Zachary Harmage Moore, the ne'er-do-well squire of North and South Loftus. An inveterate sportsman,[1] Moore had served in the Royal Hunters. Charles Turner as a youth looked upon John Hall-Stevenson and Zachary Moore as two 'Apollos of Mind Wit Learning Spirit and Debauchery'. Moore is remembered for the manner in which he fell from high estate. One account says that he was cheated out of a fortune of £25,000 a year by the chicanery of a steward, but most tell how he squandered away his wealth. 'There is a tradition at Lofthouse, that during his travels on the continent his horse's shoes were made of silver; and that so careless was he of money, that he would not turn his horse's head if they got loose or fell off, but replaced them with new ones.'[2] When his fortune failed, so did most of his friends, and Moore ended as an ensign of foot stationed at Gibraltar. As late as 1767 he was still abroad, serving in Minorca as Commissioner of Must on a salary of £182.[3]

Another of the original group was Andrew Irvine, described as 'sinecure master of Kirkleatham School'. His house near Skelton Castle was celebrated in the ballad of 'Trout Hall', written, no doubt, by members of the group.

> Ye Fishers and Shooters and Foxhunters all,
> And Racers and Cockers attend to my call,
> While I sing forth the praises of famous trout hall;
> Sing Tantarara, trout hall, trout hall,
> Sing Tantarara trout hall.

ship in the group from his known association with John Hall-Stevenson in the forties and fifties. Other early members of the club, Sterne, Hall-Stevenson, Robert Lascelles and Andrew Irvine, were listed in a minute book of a convivial club seen by Cooper at Skelton Castle. It is no longer there. In fact, few manuscripts of historic value, if any, remain at the castle. Cooper was also invited to look at the Turner family papers at Kirkleatham, and there he saw a manuscript for which Sterne scholars have since looked in vain – a copy in the hand, not of Sterne, but of some amanuensis, of the first seventeen chapters of the fourth volume of *Tristram Shandy* – the only manuscript of the novel of which there is any record at all. It contained, said Cooper, two emendations in Sterne's hand. The Turner house at Kirkleatham has now been pulled down and the library dispersed.

[1] A certain Guy Herbert, who was appointed Moore's gamekeeper in 1738, became Hall-Stevenson's gamekeeper in 1742: QUARTER SESSIONS, 222, 239.

[2] Ord, 257; cf. *European Magazine*, April 1785, p. 253. Turner's remark, in his letter to Hall-Stevenson, 20 September 1772, Cooper papers, No. 9.

[3] *Royal Kalendar; or Correct Annual Register for 1767*, 7th ed., 1767, p. 118: at BM, P. P. 2506. g. Moore was dead by the time of Turner's letter, 1772.

Panty Lascelles, who described Irvine as 'a dealer in guttle', i.e., a gourmand, nicknamed him 'Paddy Andrew' for his florid Irish face.[1]

Sports seem to have been their main concern. Sterne, so far as we know, did not hunt; but in the 'Memoirs' he said he enjoyed shooting. John Croft reported that Sterne became a good shot. Laurence Sterne the sportsman. It is not the picture which usually comes to mind, but is of a piece with our vision of him as a rural gentleman. No doubt he spent many happy days shooting and angling under the guidance of Panty Lascelles.

Hall-Stevenson's rather bad lines on the club indicate other pastimes.

> Some fell to fiddling, some to fluting,
> Some to shooting, some to fishing.
> Others to pishing and disputing,
> Or to computing by wishing.

Tradition says that they often discussed classical literature, though Ord, the antiquarian, overpainted the picture of their 'noctes ambrosianae', their 'Attic grace and Roman vivacity, sentiment and humour, pathos and ridicule'. But Hall-Stevenson was a good Latinist, and he and Panty wrote Latin verses at each other.[2]

Certain members of the Crazy Castle set can be identified through Sterne's letters or Hall's assignment to them of a story in *Crazy Tales*. The ribald stories are hung together on the scheme of the *Canterbury Tales*: each is supposed to be told by a member of the group. No doubt the club had changed considerably by 1762, when *Crazy Tales* appeared, but whether the men whom Sterne met through his friend were actually enrolled in the club is not very material.

Thomas Scrope was a familiar of Hall's. Though he was the scion of an ancient family at Cockerington, Lincolnshire, he lived upon the fine estate of Coleby, near the city of Lincoln, which he had inherited. Hall assigned to him 'Thomas of Coleby's Tale – Portia, or Passion overacted'. Indeed Scrope, a militia officer, too often overacted his passions. He was

[1] Cooper's N&Q article; SEVEN LETTERS, 20. The ballad, a broadside, among the Cooper papers, No. 3. I am sceptical of Cross's opinion that Irvine was a Cambridge Doctor of Theology since there is no such degree and I can find no university record of him.

[2] Cooper papers, Nos. 1, 5–7; SEVEN LETTERS, 11–12. Ord's description is taken from the editor's introduction to the posthumous *Works* of Hall-Stevenson, 1795, I, x–xl. The editor of the *Works* has not been identified. A letter in the Cooper papers, No. 14, from Sir F. Norton to Edward May, 24 December 1789, suggests that May may have been the editor.

accused, at various times, of killing a highwayman who had attacked him, of drawing his sword in the House of Commons, of being mad, and of causing a riot when he drew his sword to head off a mob of voters during the Lincoln election of 1761. Later he was a henchman of John Wilkes, and in 1768 bought his way into Parliament by paying off his supporters in Lincoln while disguised as a Cherokee chief. Among the Demoniacs, he was known as Cardinal Scrope.[1]

We know less about Nathaniel Garland, traditionally included in the club probably because of Sterne's and Hall's brief allusions to him in their letters.[2]

Charles Turner, the eccentric nephew and heir of old Cholmley Turner, the Whig leader, was a regular member. He lived with his uncle at nearby Kirkleatham and became the squire in effect long before his uncle died in 1757. He entertained Sterne there at least once, probably many times. Although he was celebrated as a master farmer, his passion was hunting, and he usually dressed like a gamekeeper.[3]

There was also a politician among them, the figure behind Hall's 'Privy-Counsellor's Tale'. The allusion to the Privy Council must have been no more than a private joke, probably about some Yorkshire politician.[4] Could it have been the prominent Edwin Lascelles of Harewood, whom Sterne and Hall had known since their Cambridge days? Lascelles had become the representative of Scarborough as early as 1744, and he had served in the Royal Hunters. In the late fifties he was courting his future wife, Anne Chaloner, in the neighbouring village of Guisborough.

In 1755 we find Hall-Stevenson writing to Lascelles on behalf of a new friend, an architect who hoped to draw the designs for Lascelles's projected house at Harewood. This unknown architect, distantly related to Charles

[1] Francis Hill, *Georgian Lincoln*, Cambridge, 1966, pp. 90–3; Hall-Stevenson, *Works*, II, 39–40, 172–3; LETTERS, 248, 270; CURTIS, 249; obituaries in *European Magazine*, XXI (1792), 408; *Gentleman's Magazine*, LXII (January–June 1792), 480.
[2] LETTERS, 270; CURTIS, 270; SEVEN LETTERS, 1–2, 7. Garland subscribed to Sterne's *Sermons* of 1760 and 1769. In 1762, Jean-Baptiste Tollet, writing to Hall-Stevenson from Paris, sent greetings to Lascelles, Garland and Gilbert: Cooper papers, No. 22.

[3] LETTERS, 379; CURTIS, 382; Cooper papers, No. 9. For an account of his reversionary politics, see Cedric Collyer, 'The Rockingham connection and country opinion in the early years of George III', LPS, VII (1952–5), 251–75.
[4] Hartley points out that neither Sir Francis Dashwood nor George Bubb-Dodington, the men usually suggested for Hall-Stevenson's 'Privy Counsellor', is a likely candidate for the role because at the time of the poem Hall-Stevenson was opposed to their political faction.

Turner, would soon have a meteoric rise to fame as Sir William Chambers, Surveyor-General and Comptroller for George III, founder and Treasurer of the Royal Academy, and designer of numerous celebrated buildings, among them Somerset House. Chambers found his earliest patron in Hall-Stevenson and his earliest supporters among the Crazy Castle group. Although his designs for Harewood House were never used, he did, in gratitude to Hall-Stevenson, make designs for an altered Skelton Castle – also never put to use. He made alterations in Charles Turner's London house and built a Temple of Romulus and Remus for Scrope which still stands at Coleby. Chambers, no doubt, is the architect of Hall-Stevenson's 'Don Pringello's Tale'.[1] The tale is prefaced with a jesting explanation that the architect was a Spaniard of benevolent temper who built at his own expense public and private castles in Spain and along the Garonne in France. In fact Chambers was a Scot born in Sweden, educated in Ripon in the North Riding, and a student of architecture in France. Don Pringello came to England on purpose, goes Hall's fiction, to rebuild Crazy Castle, 'but, struck with its venerable remains, he could only be prevailed upon to add a few ornaments, suitable to the stile and taste of the age it was built in'. Probably Hall-Stevenson could not afford more than a few ornaments. Sterne picked up the joke in *Tristram Shandy* where, at one point, he says he is writing from 'a handsome pavillion built by *Pringello*, upon the banks of the *Garonne*' (VII, xxviii, 516). In a second waggish reference, he calls it '*Perdrillo's* pavillion' (VII, xliii, 538).

A good many of the Skelton group were military men. Colonel, later General, John Hale, of Tocketts, not far from Skelton, was probably one of their number. He married Mary, the second Chaloner sister of Guisborough. Tradition holds that another member of the club was Charles Lee, the ugly, quarrelsome army officer who became an American, served as Washington's second-in-command, and was court-martialled for his misconduct in the battle near Monmouth courthouse. 'Savage' Lee was a friend of Hall-Stevenson's,[2] but it is not at all clear that Sterne met him at Skelton Castle, if ever. In a letter of 1761, Sterne sent greetings to two colonels, one of whom

[1] The identification has been convincingly argued by Lodwick Hartley in 'The Don Pringello of Sterne and Hall-Stevenson', N&Q, in press, upon new documentary evidence and new information which came to light in John Harris, *Sir William Chambers: Knight of the Polar Star*, 1970. See in Harris, pp. 3 and n. 3, 40, 144 n. 5, 290; and the catalogue of Chambers's designs and works, Nos. 18, 52, 70, 73, 109 and 127.

[2] Carlyle, *Autobiography*, 453–6; Hall-Stevenson, *Works*, II, 188–95; Hartley.

is usually taken to be Lee, though in fact Lee had not been made a colonel by that date. More likely Sterne's greetings were intended for Hall-Stevenson's two younger brothers, George Lawson Hall and Thomas Hall. Both men were career officers, Thomas rising eventually to the rank of general.[1]

The most interesting soldier, or former soldier, whom Sterne met at Skelton was William Hewett of Stretton, Leicestershire, colonel of the Leicestershire Volunteers. Hall-Stevenson may have assigned to him the cleanest of all the *Crazy Tales*, 'Arsinoe: or Passion Overstrained'. 'Old Hewett', as he was called, spent most of his time travelling for pleasure. He became intimate with Voltaire and Tobias Smollett, and was known for his way of maintaining among strange peoples the manners of a perfect Englishman. Smollett left a memorable account of him in *Humphry Clinker*: 'one of the most original characters upon earth'. He was known in Italy as Cavallo Bianco, for his pale horse and death-like appearance. In Turkey he was called 'Demonstrator', some said for his ability in debate, others for his agility in love. In 1767 at Florence, convinced that he was suffering from an incurable disease, Old Hewett decided to imitate Pomponius Atticus by starving himself to death; and 'this resolution he executed like an ancient Roman', seeing company, entertaining his guests with music, joking and laughing until he died.[2]

It is easy to understand how happy Sterne was among all these old soldiers and misfit squires. They must have fostered his love of eccentrics, of 'humorists', as they were popularly called, encouraging those attitudes which allowed him to create Uncle Toby, a good-natured military eccentric, and Walter Shandy, who might be a compound of all the oddities of human conduct which Sterne observed at Skelton Castle.

The link between the Demoniacs and Sterne's humorous characters seems all the more likely when we consider Sterne's earliest known use of this sort of character. If Hall and Lascelles organized their club after the disbandment of the Royal Hunters, the group would have met for the first time late in 1746 or early in 1747. On 3 November 1747 Sterne published a

---

[1] LETTERS, 140. CURTIS, 141, gives an account of Hall-Stevenson's middle brother, George Lawson Hall. The youngest brother, General Thomas Hall, was baptized on 16 April 1727, admitted to Jesus College on 2 January 1741, but took no degree. He married a Miss Carter of Cambridge and eventually made his home at Weston Colville, Cambridge: GRAY; Robert Surtees, *History and Antiquities of Durham*, 4 vols, 1816–40, II, 291.

[2] *Humphry Clinker*, 1771, II, Matthew Bramble's letter of 4 July. See also CURTIS, 202–3; SEVEN LETTERS, 4.

piece signed 'Hamlet' in the *York Journal: or, Protestant Courant* – the last political essay he is known to have written. It has a tone different from the pieces written during the by-election. The occasion was the humiliating defeat of the Allies at Bergen-op-Zoom in the Low Countries. The purpose was to exclaim against the 'ambitious Tyrant', Louis XV, who, 'contrary to the Laws of Nations', is now 'invading a free and happy People'.[1] Certain of Sterne's techniques in this essay adumbrate *Tristram Shandy*: the narrator presents himself by telling us a few realistic details about his peculiarities, and he makes the writing itself part of the essay. This narrator is older than Tristram, but he is a bachelor – as we suspect Tristram is, but never know for certain. He is a man of firm Protestant principles; but like Yorick in *A Sentimental Journey* he is tolerant enough to pity a Papist – 'when I consider him as nurs'd up in Bigotry and Nonsense'. His foibles suggest both Walter Shandy and Tristram. In fact, some of the sentences would be taken as echoes of *Tristram Shandy* had they not appeared a dozen years before:

> . . . I have some Oddities, which I believe are common enough to those who have not known the Discipline of a married State.—— However, my Friends allow them to be very pardonable, as in my most violent Moods I never go beyond the Snapping of a Pipe [cf. TRISTRAM SHANDY, p. 101], or the skimming my Hat and Wig across the Room [cf. p. 362].
>
> As I have a warm Affection for my Country, I never hear any ill News from Abroad, but it costs me a Pipe or two, and the storming of *Bergen-op-Zoom*, cost me no less than three Glasses and a China Cup, which were unluckily overturn'd by my Hat which I had tossed from me in my Wrath.
>
> I imagine I make a queer Figure enough, as I march and counter-march hastily across my Room, make a sudden Halt, and perhaps stand in a musing Posture for some Time, and at last begin . . . [cf. pp. 540, 616].

The old bachelor half promises to write again – upon religion, politics, love of poetry, 'or any Thing', but in fact, nothing else from his pen appeared.

As to the *craft* of writing, Sterne, already an accomplished essayist, had nothing to learn at Skelton Castle. The poets in the group, Hall-Stevenson, Panty Lascelles and Thomas Gilbert, were hardly more than poetasters.

[1] The entire letter in STERNE, HAMLET, AND YORICK.

Hall's verses of the fifties were trifles.[1] The fables, epistles and personal satires of the early sixties, all in poor, some in execrable taste, made their way into the world riding on the coat-tails of *Tristram Shandy*. Hall's friendship became something of a burden to Sterne when he was the toast of London in 1760. Soon after the novel appeared, Hall published his pornographic and scatological *Two Lyric Epistles: One to my Cousin Shandy, On His Coming to Town; and the Other to the Grown Gentlewomen, the Misses of ****. Two years later, in *Crazy Tales*, he assigned to Sterne an indecent story called 'My Cousin's Tale'. Sterne found it prudent to disavow the friendship to Bishop Warburton,[2] though in fact he did not reproach Hall, much less cut him off. Besides, Hall could be so comical in his remorse for literary misdeeds. On another occasion when he had cast aspersions on Bishop Warburton's wife and consequently was racked by the reviewers, Sterne wrote to him,

> Thou has so tender a conscience my dear Cosin Antonio, and takest on so sadly for thy sins, that thou wast certainly meant and intended to have gone to heaven – if ever Wit went there – but of that, I have some slight mistrusts, inasmuch as we have all of us (accounting myself, thou siest, as one) had, if not our good things, at least our good sayings in this life; & the Devil thou knowest, who is made up of spight, will not let them pass for nothing.   (p. 280)[3]

Sterne usually enjoyed a bawdy joke, though in some moods he could complain about the coarseness of the 'Dissipation' at Skelton: 'What a stupid, selfish, unsentimental set of Beings are the Bulk of our Sex!' he would later write to Eliza Draper (pp. 364–5). But he always returned for more. It was Hall-Stevenson, however, who gave their revels a demonic cast. His verse is heavy with gothic imagery, and the characters in many of his porno-

[1] *Hymn to Miss Lawrence in the Pump-Room at Bath*, 1753; 'Vacation', 1758, but unpublished until the *Works*.

[2] LETTERS, 115.

[3] One of Hall-Stevenson's publications after Sterne's death is hard to account for, an obscene piece offered as a continuation of *Tristram Shandy*, Vol. XIII (Sterne, of course, wrote only nine volumes), called *A Sentimental Dialogue between Two Souls in the Palpable Bodies of an English Lady of Quality and an Irish Gentleman*. In charity, we may suppose he had arranged publica-tion before Sterne's death. At least he has now been absolved of the responsibility for the scurrilous *Yorick's Sentimental Journey Continued*, 1769, by 'Eugenius'. The argument, initiated by Karl F. Thompson, 'The authorship of "Yorick's Sentimental Journey Continued"', N&Q, CXCV (1950), 318–19, has been completed by Lodwick Hartley in '"Yorick's Sentimental Journey Continued": a reconsideration of the authorship', *South Atlantic Quarterly*, LXX (1971), 180–90.

graphic fables are monks and nuns. Probably he was influenced by Sir Francis Dashwood, with whom he had a friendship at least as early as the fifties. The Demoniacs Club may have been modelled to a degree upon Dashwood's Hell-Fire Club at West Wycombe, Buckinghamshire, sometimes called the Rabelaisian Monks of Medmenham Abbey. But if Dashwood's group was actually as impious and scandalous as some believe, the Skelton club could have been only a pale reflection of it. It is hardly likely that the black rite was performed at Skelton Castle. True, William Hewett and Hall-Stevenson himself paraded a secularism, but no evidence has arisen to cast doubt upon the faith of the other members. The most rakish of them, Zachary Moore, founded a Sunday school at Loftus. But the affectation of impiety had a certain vogue among mid-century rakes. Hall may have visited the Medmenham group, and Moore was a friend of 'Jemmy' Worsdale of the Dublin Hell-Fire Club.[1]

Sterne himself found it easy to speak in metaphors from diabolism. The name by which we know the club is taken from his letter of 1761, in which he asks Hall to greet 'what few remain of the Demoniacs' (p. 140). At another time, he sends his services to 'the household of faith' (p. 270). When Sterne, writing to Hall at Harrogate in 1761, described a quarrel with some unknown visitor to Skelton Castle over a question of learning and taste, he cast the account in an elaborate image of the black rite, possibly because the other man, whoever he was, had been associated with the Medmenham brotherhood:

> Panty is mistaken, I quarrel with no one. – There was that coxcomb of
> —— in the house, who lost temper with me for no reason upon earth
> but that I could not fall down and worship a brazen image of learning
> and eloquence, which he set up to the persecution of all true believers
> – I sat down upon *his altar*, and whistled in the time of his divine
> service – and broke down his carved work, and kicked his incense pot
> to the D[evil], so he retreated, *sed non sine felle in corde suo*.   (p. 142)

Since Dashwood's club had given François Rabelais a status parallel to that of a patron saint, one surmises that the cult of Rabelais flourished at Skelton. Panty Lascelles's nickname is evidence. The club may be responsible in part for the Rabelaisian influence in *Tristram Shandy*.[2] Parson Yorick

[1] Louis C. Jones, *Clubs of the Georgian Rakes*, New York, 1942, pp. 155–65.
[2] Huntington Brown, *Rabelais in English Literature*, Cambridge, Mass., 1933, pp.

188–206 and *passim*; John M. Stedmond, *The Comic Art of Laurence Sterne*, Toronto, 1967.

carries in his pocket a translation of *Gargantua and Pantagruel*, from which he reads aloud the marvellously funny encounter of Gymnast with Tripot (V, xxix, 387–9). The Demoniacs may also have introduced Sterne to later Rabelaisians – Béroalde, Scarron and Bruscambille. *Le Moyen de parvenir* of François Béroalde de Verville (1599), which Sterne laughingly called 'a vile, – but Witty book',[1] was named by John Croft as one of the works most read by Sterne. Béroalde openly imitates the bawdy humour of Rabelais, and his loose narrative, supposed to be stories exchanged by a group of friends, bears analogies to both Hall-Stevenson's *Crazy Tales* and the comic symposia of *Tristram Shandy*. Sterne also knew Scarron's *Roman comique* (1651), probably in the translation by Tom Brown.[2] Sieur Deslauriers was another Rabelaisian, who wrote under his stage name, Bruscambille. His *Prologues tant sérieux que facécieux* (1610), a madcap jumble of paradoxes and essays, including a treatise on long and short noses, is the very book upon which Walter Shandy laid greedy hands in a London bookseller's. 'There are not three *Bruscambilles* in *Christendom*,——said the stall-man, except what are chain'd up in the libraries of the curious. My father flung down the money as quick as lightening,——took *Bruscambille* into his bosom,——hyed home . . . as he would have hyed home with a treasure' (III, xxxv, 225).

Sterne probably found much of the odd lore that went into *Tristram Shandy* at Skelton Castle, but the point is difficult to demonstrate. The idea was first suggested by Dr John Ferriar in that early study of Sterne's sources.[3] Ferriar had difficulty locating a copy of the *Serées, or Evening Conferences* of Guillaume Bouchet (1584), one of the authoritative studies on noses consulted by Walter Shandy. About the copy which he finally located, Ferriar commented, 'I have great reason to believe that it was in the SKELTON library some years ago, where I suspect Sterne found most of the authors of this class; for Mr Hall's poetry shews that he knew and read them much.' It is a good hypothesis, but no documentary evidence has been discovered to strengthen it, and for good reason: at the time Ferriar was writing, the

---

[1] LETTERS, 416. Dr John Ferriar knew of a copy which Sterne seems to have picked up in Paris at a later date, inscribed with his name and bearing 'evident marks of its having been frequently turned over': CURTIS, 417.

[2] William A. Eddy, 'Tom Brown and *Tristram Shandy*', *Modern Language Notes*, XLIV (1929), 379–81.

[3] 'Comments on Sterne', in the *Manchester Philosophical and Literary Transactions*, 1793, reprinted in the *Annual Register*, 1793, pp. 379–98, expanded and published as *Illustrations of Sterne*, 1798, and expanded again as a two-volume edition, 1812. I cite the 1798 edition, pp. 41–2.

wind was whistling through the broken windows and swinging doors of derelict Skelton Castle, and Hall-Stevenson's books had been dispersed.

Nevertheless, it is not hard to imagine Sterne and the Demoniacs laughing over Bouchet and other facetiae. Perhaps it was at the castle that Sterne ran across the curious story of Francis I of France, which he tells us in *Tristram Shandy* (IV, xxi) he took from the *Menagiana,* a curious collection of opinions compiled by Gilles Ménage, a French philologist. Perhaps he saw there Obadiah Walker's *Of Education, Especially of Young Gentlemen* (1673), which inspired the 'Tristrapaedia', that nonsensical tome which Walter Shandy writes as a guide for the education of his son.[1]

In the final analysis, the Demoniacs gave Sterne something far more valuable than literary influence: they gave him friendship. Though men of sound education and lively wit, most of them did not fit easily into the more conventional circles of the polite world. They had created their own congenial society, in which heteroclite parsons like Panty Lascelles and Lorry Sterne could feel at home. Hall-Stevenson and the Demoniacs probably renewed Sterne's good spirits again and again during his years of poor health, marital difficulties and floundering career – the years in which he was searching for his personal and artistic centre of gravity.

[1] John M. Turnbull, 'The prototype of Walter Shandy's *Tristrapædia*', *Review of* *English Studies,* II (1926), 212–15; C. J. Rawson, N&Q, CCII (1957), 255–6.

Hobby Horses

According to Tristram Shandy, there is no instrument more fit to draw a man's character with than his hobby horse.

> A man and his HOBBY-HORSE, tho' I cannot say that they act and re-act exactly after the same manner in which the soul and body do upon each other; Yet doubtless there is a communication between them of some kind, and my opinion rather is, that there is something in it more of the manner of electrified bodies,——and that by means of the heated parts of the rider, which come immediately into contact with the back of the HOBBY-HORSE. – By long journies and much friction, it so happens that the body of the rider is at length fill'd as full of HOBBY-HORSICAL matter as it can hold;——so that if you are able to give but a clear description of the nature of the one, you may form a pretty exact notion of the genius and character of the other. (I, xxiv, 77)

James Boswell at the age of nineteen read the first two volumes of *Tristram Shandy* and grasped the principle at once. He met Sterne in London in 1760 and read him some verses. Sterne, he said, 'capered', patted him on the shoulder, and told him he was a second Matt Prior. Boswell went home and began 'A Poetical Epistle to Doctor Sterne, Parson Yorick, and Tristram Shandy'. One part of the unfinished poem attempts to sketch Sterne's character through his hobbies:

> He had of Books a chosen few,
> He read as Humour bid him do;
> If Metaphisics seem'd too dark,
> Shifted to Gay from Dr Clark;
> If in the least it hurt his eyes,
> He instantaneously would rise,
> Take up his violin and play –

JOHN HALL-STEVENSON
By Philippe Mercier, 1740

THE REVEREND ROBERT LASCELLES
By Henry Singleton

His Pencil next, then sketch away.
Here goes a flow'r! extreamly neat.
Let me attempt Sue's count'nance sweet,
The little Gipsey drest in blue,
Who to the Pulpit sits next Pew,
Whose tender-smiling, starlike eyes
Make mine half wander from the skies.
   Sometimes our Priest with limbs so taper
Before his glass would cut a caper,
Indulging each suggestion airy,
Each whim and innocent vagary.
The heliconian stream he'd quaff
And by himself transported laugh.
In short, without the help of Sherry,
He ever Hearty was and merry.

Boswell, with his knack for interviewing celebrities, may have elicited these details from Sterne.[1] In some small degree Sterne verified them in *Tristram Shandy*, when he had Tristram describe himself as 'both fiddler and painter, according as the fly stings' (p. 14). In the 'Memoirs' he said, speaking of his years at Sutton, 'Books, painting, fiddling, and shooting were my amusements.'

It seems natural to seize upon 'books' as the most significant item on the list. In *Tristram Shandy*, Sterne alludes to hundreds of authors, ancient and modern, satirical, philosophical, scientific, historical, obstetrical, or merely hobby-horsical. One comes away with the impression that he had spent years ranging freely over the whole of literature, reading Locke's *Essay* over and over again, to be sure, but avoiding the pitfalls of obsession. Tristram's hobby, which is the story of his life, is not a 'vicious beast' like the hobbies which tyrannized Walter Shandy, but 'a sporting little filly-folly' (VIII, xxxi, 584).

The purpose of this biography is to throw light upon Sterne's work by the study of his life, not the other way around. It would be inappropriate to attempt a detailed or all-inclusive commentary upon the literary allusions in *Tristram Shandy* and *A Sentimental Journey*, much less to slip into a study of literary influences. Still, the references to other authors in Sterne's novels, especially when similar references occur in the letters, give us some notion

[1] Frederick A. Pottle, 'Bozzy and Yorick', *Blackwood's Magazine*, CCCXIII (1925), 297–313.

of how and what Sterne read during the earlier years. To exclude any consideration of them would distort the picture of the historic man.[1]

Sterne shared the literary tastes and interests of most gentlemen of his time and station. He must have been reading the Augustans from his college years. He alluded to Dennis's criticism and was familiar with the writings of Tom Brown.[2] Steele's *Spectator*, No. 260, may have planted the idea for a comic treatise on noses, and both Addison and Steele sketched hobby-horsical soldiers suggestive of Uncle Toby.[3] He was fond of Pope, mentioning or quoting him in letters, and paraphrasing the *Essay on Man* in his dedication of the last volume of *Tristram Shandy*. He liked Swift even more. Swift's influence upon *A Political Romance* is strong and direct, that on *Tristram Shandy* somewhat obscured.[4] In the final volume of the novel, Tristram asks, 'what has this book done more than [Warburton's] Legation of Moses, or [Swift's] Tale of a Tub, that it may not swim down the gutter of Time along with them?' (IX, viii, 610). One of the few books from Sterne's personal library which survives, possibly the only one, is a scrapbook of Irish ballads, broadsides and newspaper clippings from the period of about 1713–35, now in the Cambridge University Library; it contains many items on Swift and probably was treasured for that reason.[5] He certainly read that famous joint work of the Scriblerus Club, the *Memoirs of Martinus Scriblerus*, when it came out in 1741 in the second volume of Pope's *Works*. This rambling story of a 'humorist' father determined to beget and rear a son in

[1] My discussion has been assisted by the three major studies of Sterne's sources: CROSS, Chapter VI; James A. Work, *The Indebtedness of 'Tristram Shandy' to Certain English Authors, 1670–1740*, unpublished PhD dissertation, Yale, 1934; and John M. Stedmond, *The Comic Art of Laurence Sterne*, Toronto, 1967. Stedmond includes an appendix listing the known direct plagiarisms in the novels. Numerous shorter studies of the sources are listed by Lodwick Hartley, *Laurence Sterne in the Twentieth Century*, Chapel Hill, North Carolina, 1966. Other information in notes to LETTERS, TRISTRAM SHANDY and SENTIMENTAL JOURNEY. Expanded notes are being prepared for the University of Florida scholarly *Works of Laurence Sterne* under the general editorship of Melvyn New.

[2] TRISTRAM SHANDY, II, xii, III; William A. Eddy, 'Tom Brown and *Tristram Shandy*', *Modern Language Notes*, XLIV (1929), 379–81.

[3] Addison's *Spectators*, Nos. 105, 371; Steele's *Tatlers*, Nos. 51, 202.

[4] Gerald Wayne Donnelly, introduction to *A Critical Edition of Laurence Sterne's 'A Political Romance'*, unpublished MA thesis, Florida, 1970; Work, *Indebtedness of 'Tristram Shandy'*.

[5] Cambridge University Library: HIB. 3. 730. I. It is possible, of course, that Sterne kept it for sentimental reasons, because his father or some Irish friend had collected it. In the margin next to a manuscript poem in the book, 'The Ballyspallan Ballad', is a note in Sterne's hand, 'This was made by a Footman'.

accordance with his favourite scientific and philosophic theories probably inspired the main plan of *Tristram Shandy*. He also may have known Matthew Prior's 'Alma' (1718), a comic dialogue on similar problems. Little wonder Sterne was thrilled when, after *Tristram Shandy* appeared, old Lord Bathurst, who had been a friend to Swift and Pope, told him he was worthy of the great Augustans.[1]

To be sure, Sterne enjoyed the literature of his own generation. The plan of *Tristram Shandy* was surely influenced to some degree by a little book which appeared in 1756, *The Life and Memoirs of Ephraim Tristram Bates*, containing many details from the life of a British soldier – and much use of asterisks.[2] In 1759, when he first tried to sell his book to Robert Dodsley, he suggested the format used by Andrew Millar for Jane Collier's comic work of 1753, *An Essay on the Art of Ingeniously Tormenting*. Five months later, when proposing his scheme for printing *Tristram Shandy* in York, he switched to Johnson's *Rasselas*, which had just appeared, as the model for his format. Curiously, there is no certain evidence of his reading the novels of Richardson, Fielding or Smollett, though we can hardly doubt he did so. He knew *Les Égaremens du cœur et de l'esprit* of Crébillon *fils* long before he made the acquaintance of its author.[3] He was much amused by Colley Cibber, who may have influenced the style of *Tristram Shandy*. Sterne once possessed a volume in which was bound Bishop Berkeley's *Querist* (1750) and Cibber's *Letter . . . to Mr. Pope* (1742). When he had finished reading it, he sent the volume to his friend Marmaduke Fothergill, first writing on the fly-leaf,

> L. S. To Mr. Fothergil greetings – with Cibber's 2ᵈ Letter to Pope. have been doing Penance at the rate of 4 Quarts of Tar Water a Day [Berkeley's famous panacea], for the Pleasure – committed of sitting up till 3 in the Morning. – Dean Swift used to say to the Irish – 'Burn everything yᵗ comes from England but yᵉ coals.'[4]

Sterne's dictum, 'I wrote not [to] be *fed*, but to be *famous*', inverts what Cibber had written to Pope.

Sterne had a special fondness for the great writers of the Renaissance, not

[1] LETTERS, 305.
[2] Helen Sard Hughes, 'A precursor of *Tristram Shandy*', *Journal of English and Germanic Philology*, XVII (1918), 227–51; Edward Bensley, 'An alleged source of "Tristram Shandy"', N&Q, CLIX (1930), 27, 84.

[3] LETTERS, 88, 162.
[4] CURTIS, 85. The library at Gray's Court, where Curtis saw this volume, has been dispersed, and I have not been able to find the book. Sterne's phrase: LETTERS, 90; TRISTRAM SHANDY, V, xvi, 373.

only Rabelais, to whom he was exposed, as we have speculated, at Skelton Castle, but also Erasmus, Shakespeare and Cervantes.

Critics have found in *The Praise of Folly* a strong influence upon Sterne's clowning narrator, though Erasmus is alluded to only once in the novel (III, xxxvii, 229) and paraphrased only once in the letters (p. 93).

Sterne's delight in Shakespeare is obvious. He knew the history plays well and could recite from memory Hotspur's description of the aftermath of battle in *1 Henry IV*.[1] The comedies perhaps meant less to him. He paraphrased *As You Like It*, but that was the famous passage, 'All the world's a stage'.[2] It was the tragedies which Sterne most often read. He refers to tragedies in both novels and letters, especially to *Romeo and Juliet*, *Othello* and *Hamlet*. There are at least eight paraphrases of Hamlet in *Tristram Shandy* and two in *A Sentimental Journey*,[3] as well as that amusing scene where Yorick, having identified himself to the Comte de Bissy as Shakespeare's Yorick, receives a passport issued to 'the King's jester'. As we have seen, Sterne wrote under the pseudonym 'Hamlet' in 1747, a dozen years before he appropriated the name of 'Yorick' for his rural parson.

It is not really a paradox that Sterne should create a fiction which partakes at once of gay and bawdy Rabelaisian wit and the Shakespearian tragic sense of life: the Renaissance provided Sterne with an inspiring model for tragicomedy – not 'my dear *Rabelais*', but 'dearer *Cervantes*'. Well might Sterne leave to Swift the title of 'the English Rabelais', for Sterne's satire is far less deadly. When Sterne spoke of one satirical device, 'describing silly and trifling Events, with the Circumstantial Pomp of great Ones', he did not call it Rabelaisian or Swiftian, but a 'Cervantic humour'. To Cervantes Sterne often refers in letters and novels. It is the spirit of Cervantes that he invokes as he approaches those sweet, amusing scenes with Maria of Moulins, which occur in both novels – Sterne's sentimental comedy at its best.[4]

The most visible literary source for *Tristram Shandy* is Robert Burton's *Anatomy of Melancholy*, first published in 1621, but reaching a final version,

[1] LETTERS, 27.

[2] TRISTRAM SHANDY, II, xix, 145.

[3] SENTIMENTAL JOURNEY, 156, 187, 222–8; TRISTRAM SHANDY, 23–4, 31–3, 107, 151, 191, 196, 324.

[4] TRISTRAM SHANDY, 191, 628; SENTIMENTAL JOURNEY, 270; LETTERS, 77. See Stout's introduction to SENTIMENTAL JOURNEY and his articles, 'Some borrowings in Sterne from Rabelais and Cervantes', *English Language Notes*, III (1965), 111–18; 'Yorick's *Sentimental Journey*: a comic "Pilgrim's Progress" for the man of feeling', *ELH*, XXX (1963), 395–412.

which Sterne probably used, in 1652. Sterne's plagiarisms of Burton have annoyed his critics since they were first pointed out by Dr John Ferriar late in the eighteenth century. Sterne indeed took numerous passages from Burton and used his book as a handy source for quotations from the ancients; but Ferriar, in calling the *Anatomy* the 'grand magazine' for *Tristram Shandy*, put an onus of plagiarism on Sterne somewhat heavier than he ought to bear. As has been demonstrated recently, Sterne, 'far from being the lazy and unscrupulous plagiarist of nineteenth-century tradition, in fact went to far more trouble in finding and arranging his borrowings than would have been needed to write something completely original'.[1] He always tips off the reader to what he is doing, presuming that he understands the traditional Renaissance comedy of plagiarism. The joke is epitomized by a famous passage in *Tristram Shandy* – 'Tell me, ye learned, shall we for ever be adding so much to the *bulk*——so little to the *stock*?' and so forth (V, i, 342–3) – a disavowal of plagiarism which itself is taken from Burton, who had in turn plagiarized parts of the passage from still earlier sources.

One of the major traditions behind *Tristram Shandy* is that joyous erudition which we call 'learned wit' or 'Menippean satire', a style which requires a narrator who reads or seems to read with abandon.[2] Part of Sterne's game is to draw his reader along by easily recognized allusions until Tristram can finally prove him an ass. No one, he finally learns, can have read so much as Tristram:

> ——And pray [asks the reader] who was *Tickletoby*'s mare?——tis just as discreditable and unscholar-like a question, Sir, as to have asked what year (*ab urb.con.*) the second Punic War broke out.——Who was Tickletoby's mare!——Read, read, read, read, my unlearned reader! read,——or by the knowledge of the great saint *Paraleipomenon* ——I tell you before-hand, you had better throw down the book at once.   (III, xxxvi, 226)

Was Laurence Sterne such a reader as his narrator? It is doubtful. When he was writing *Tristram Shandy*, at least the early volumes, he kept beside him, not only Burton's *Anatomy*, but also a useful encyclopedia and the best recent history of modern England. From Ephraim Chambers's *Cyclopaedia: or, an Universal Dictionary of Arts and Sciences*, the second edition of 1738, he helped himself to information in the articles on 'Fortifications', 'Code',

[1] Graham Petrie, 'A rhetorical topic in "Tristram Shandy"', *Modern Language Review*, LXV (1970), 261–6.

[2] D. W. Jefferson, '*Tristram Shandy* and the tradition of learned wit', *Essays in Criticism*, I (1951), 225–48.

'Soul', 'Sensory', 'Caesarean Section', 'Stoics' and 'Bridge'.[1] From Nicholas Tindal's two-volume *Continuation of Mr. Rapin de Thoyras's History of England, from the Revolution to the Accession of King George II* (1744–5), Sterne took the historical data for his story of the Shandy family. The narrative is founded upon a remarkably accurate historiography established by numerous references to political and military history as told by Tindal.[2] Probably in the course of writing his novel, Sterne consulted other books with which he had no familiarity. It seems unlikely, for instance, that he had a personal interest in the old-fashioned social and political views of Sir Robert Filmer.[3] He probably cast about for a theory which would lend credence to his fictional squire. At other times, when he could not find authorities to suit his needs, he simply invented them – as those writers on noses, 'Prignitz' and 'Scroderus' (III, xxxv, 225). Sterne read widely, to be sure, but one must be wary of identifying him with Tristram.

The reading which Sterne incorporated into *Tristram Shandy* was not always pursued for pleasure. The devastating satire of Dr John Burton's obstetrical practice is a case in point. Sterne may have begun to read books on obstetrics as early as 1747, when Elizabeth's condition indicated the need for a man-midwife. A physician would not have been called in casually. In that age their services in childbearing were never sought unless a woman's condition was dangerous. Sterne surely returned to the topic in 1751, the year that Elizabeth was delivered of a dead child.[4] That same year, Dr Burton published his *Essay toward a Complete New System of Midwifry*. It was followed two years later by his *Letter to William Smellie, M. D.* Sterne took virtually all the obstetrical materials of *Tristram Shandy* from these two books, putting into Dr Slop's bag the instruments Burton had invented, and into the mouths of both Slop and Walter Shandy the theories Burton advocated – including Walter's notion that when a child is delivered by the feet, 'instead of the cerebrum being propell'd towards the cerebellum, the cerebellum, on the contrary, was propell'd simply towards the cerebrum where it could do

[1] Edward Bensley, 'A debt of Sterne's', TLS, 1 November 1928, p. 806; Bernard L. Greenberg, 'Laurence Sterne and Chambers' *Cyclopaedia*', *Modern Language Notes*, LXIX (1954), 560–2; W. G. Day, 'A note on Sterne's "Des Eaux" ', N&Q, CCXV (1970), 303.

[2] Theodore Baird, 'The time-scheme in *Tristram Shandy* and a source', *PMLA*, LI (1936), 803–20. TINDAL was advertised in the *York Courant*, 6 November 1744, for sale at the Sign of the Bible.

[3] Wilfred Watson, 'The fifth commandment: some allusions to Sir Robert Filmer's writing in *Tristram Shandy*', *Modern Language Notes*, LXIII (1947), 234–40.

[4] LETTERS, 39–40, 44–6.

no manner of hurt' (II, xix, 151). Black humour indeed – hilarious in the novel, but deadly serious in Sutton parsonage.[1]

Not much is known about Sterne's library at the parsonage.[2] The only books which have been identified as belonging to it are that scrapbook of Irish clippings and the volume binding together those unlikely companions, Berkeley and Cibber. The only contemporary comment about it is in Boswell's poem: 'He had of books a chosen few.' He probably could not have afforded more than a small library.

Scholars have sometimes been misled by the so-called *Unique Catalogue of Laurence Sterne's Library*, which appeared in 1930 – the reprint of a York sale catalogue listing 2,505 items.[3] The original was issued shortly after Sterne's death by J. Todd and H. Sotheran, who had become the proprietors of the Sign of the Bible. The books on sale included, not only Sterne's library, but also the collections of other people: the title specifies that Sterne's books are 'among' them. There is no way to tell which were Sterne's. One would suppose that the file of the *York Journal: or Weekly Advertiser* had belonged to him, but not so: it had originally been delivered to the Reverend George Goundrill, vicar of Sproatley, who died within a few weeks of Sterne.[4] Even if we could distinguish Sterne's books, we would still be left with the puzzle of which he had *read*. In a letter of July 1761, he told of buying 700 books 'dog cheap' (p. 142). Knowing how hard he worked during the few remaining years, how much he travelled and how often he was ill, it is difficult to imagine his reading many of them.

Other evidence of Sterne's reading is contained in the borrowers' list for the library of the dean and chapter, though this too must be approached with caution: the prebendaries did not expect to take home many books. Most of the time, it appears, they did their reading in the library itself – a convenient place to browse and to write their sermons. We know that Sterne read there: he left a note in a book which he had not taken out.[5]

[1] Arthur H. Cash, 'The birth of Tristram Shandy: Sterne and Dr Burton', in *Studies in the Eighteenth Century*, ed. R. F. Brissenden, Canberra, 1968, pp. 133–54.

[2] For his library of sermons and moral philosophy, below, Chapter 11.

[3] *A Facsimile Reproduction of a Unique Catalogue of Laurence Sterne's Library*, preface by Charles Whibley, London and New York, 1930.

[4] STERNE, HAMLET, AND YORICK.

[5] Minster Library: pamphlets of Robert Whatley bound under the title, *Whatley vs. Walpole*, primarily Whatley's complaints against Walpole for not rewarding his services. Sterne's note: 'The Event, which Mr. Whatley has not told, was, he was presented with a living in Lincolnshire & became a Prebendary of York.' Whatley was made prebendary of Bilton on 12 July 1729.

Sterne borrowed only a few books from the library. During the period of 1741–3 he took out nine, one of which was on the topic of Popery – material for his political pamphlets, no doubt.[1] He carried away nothing else until June 1751; then over the next three and a half years, he borrowed fourteen books, plus one for a friend, including three musical works. As historical data, the list is meagre.

In his novel, Sterne tried to avoid any suggestion that he (or Tristram) could be caught up in a passion for particular subjects: 'When a man gives himself up to the government of a ruling passion,——or, in other words, when his HOBBY-HORSE grows head-strong,——farewell cool reason and fair discretion!' (II, v, 93). The borrowers' list suggests that he learned this lesson the hard way. In 1742 and 1743, he was reading sixteenth- and seventeenth-century history: *Histoire du Concile de Trent* (translated from the Italian of Fra Paola Sarpi to the French of Pierre François le Courayer, two volumes, 1736); the *State Papers* of John Thurloe, a secretary to Oliver Cromwell (ed. Thomas Birch, seven volumes, 1742); *The Negotiations of Sir Thomas Roe . . . 1621–1628*, which included his correspondence with the Queen of Bohemia (1740). Perhaps his interest in Adolf van den Boom's *Nouvelle description des Pays-Bas* (Cologne, 1669) was somehow related to this historical study.

In the period 1751–4, he shifted to antiquarian studies: John Speed's *Historie of Great Britaine under the Conquests of the Romans, Saxons, Danes, and Normans*, the third edition of 1632 (first published 1611); Ralph Thoresby, *Ducatus Leondiensis: or, the Topography of . . . Leeds* (1715); the *Monasticon Anglicanum* of Roger Dodsworth and William Dugdale (three volumes, 1655–73); and that justly celebrated book of his old political enemy Dr Francis Drake, *Eboracum: or the History and Antiquities of the City of York* (1736). Sterne may have dismounted from his antiquarian hobby horse before long, but he remained fascinated by relics of the past. In his last years, at Coxwold, he often walked among the lovely, haunting ruins of Byland Abbey. Giving himself over to a romantic imagination, he peopled the old Cistercian abbey with ghostly inhabitants, including a sympathetic nun, Cordelia. But that was the Sterne of the *Journal to Eliza*, who was self-consciously relaxing discipline. In the historical part of his mind, he knew very well that nuns did not live in abbeys.

[1] *A Preservative against Popery*, ed. Edmund Gibson, 3 vols, 1738; Sterne borrowed Vol. II on 3 June 1741. For bibliographical descriptions and the dates of Sterne's borrowings, I depend upon BARR. For a more general description of the borrowers' list: Elizabeth Brunskill, *Eighteenth-Century Reading* (York Georgian Soc., Occasional Paper VI), York, 1950.

For a time, Sterne pursued systematically another topic, for which the eighteenth century had no name: we would call it cultural anthropology. In 1743 he read Monsigneur le Duc du Mayne, *Lettre . . . sur les cérémonies de la Chine* (1700), and another work, the identity of which is uncertain: Thomas Taylor, the keeper of the library,[1] recorded it as 'Lettre sur les Superstitions Chinoises'. A decade later he borrowed the translation of an anthology, originally in French, edited by Jean Frédério Bernard, the English version of which was called *The Religious Ceremonies and Customs of the Several Nations of the Known World* (1731). He did not take home John Spencer's religious history, *De legibus Hebræorum ritualibus (Concerning the Ritual Laws of the Hebrews)* (1685), though he may have read it at the library. Spencer is the source of those comforting precedents which Walter Shandy found after his son was accidentally circumcised by a falling window sash (V, xxvii, 384).

Sterne's attitude toward factual accuracy can be seen in his habit of using encyclopedias. As early as 1752, he borrowed from the chapter library three of the five volumes of Peter Bayle's *Dictionary Historical and Critical* (second English edition, 1734–8), and a few months later he again took out the first two volumes. Bayle may have given him his idea for the fragment on whiskers in *Tristram Shandy* and for the name of the servant La Fleur in *A Sentimental Journey*. One passage he used as a footnote to 'Slawkenbergius's Tale'.[2]

In short, Sterne was something more than a Swiftian 'ancient', ranging over the vast meadows of literature gathering sweetness and light. One side of him was distinctly 'modern' and scholarly. He probably kept notes on his reading. He could concentrate upon particular topics and was quite willing to do whatever work was required to understand them. He had a high respect for historical and scientific fact and felt the obligation to state facts accurately, whatever use he made of them.

The book which Sterne studied most carefully, which he read and reread all of his life, the book which informed all of his work, sermons and novels, was John Locke's *Essay Concerning Human Understanding*. Certainly he knew Locke's other books too: in sermons he borrowed from *The Reasonableness of Christianity* and *Some Thoughts Concerning Education*.[3] But the book he really loved was the great *Essay*, 'a history-book', as Tristram says, 'of what passes

---

[1] Appointed 11 March 1750/1: CHAPTER ACTS.

[2] TRISTRAM SHANDY, 261. The influence of Bayle on Sterne was first suggested in 1798 by William Jackson in *The Four Ages*.

[3] HAMMOND, 82–3, 138–41.

in a man's own mind' (II, ii, 85). Today scholars find the influence of Locke on every page of *Tristram Shandy*, as indeed Sterne predicted they would.[1]

Upon the foundation of Lockian thought, Sterne placed a thin overlay of other philosophical concepts. Some, like the moral and theological doctrines of Tillotson and Clarke, the great Latitudinarians from whom he borrowed most freely in the sermons, meshed well with certain points of Locke's philosophy.[2] But other philosophic writers, such as La Rochefoucauld, whom he paraphrased in *Tristram Shandy* (I, xii, 26), or Francis Bacon,[3] he appreciated for incisive commentary made at a commonsense level more than for philosophic thought. Sterne was especially fond of Bishop Joseph Hall, the seventeenth-century divine, plagiarizing from him in his sermons, paraphrasing him in *A Sentimental Journey*, and disagreeing with him in *Tristram Shandy*;[4] but what he enjoyed was the bishop's writing style, not his ethics or theology. Montaigne is another case. One of Sterne's contemporaries, thinking he saw the effects of the French essayist, questioned Sterne on the point. Sterne readily admitted the influence, but he wanted to make clear that Montaigne's philosophy *as such* had not been important: '"for my conning Montaigne as much as my pray'r book" – there you are right again, – but mark, a 2ᵈ time, I have not said I admire him as much.' Montaigne probably influenced Sterne's narrative method.[5] When it came to philosophy, nothing really interested Sterne but Locke.

Late in his life, in France, Sterne was asked by Jean-Baptiste Suard if he would not try to explain his own genius. The answer, though left to us only in the words of Suard's biographer, Dominique-Joseph Garat, reveals how Locke, as Sterne interpreted him, pervaded Sterne's thought. His 'originality', he explained, derived from an organization of personality in which predominated the principle of creativity, which Sterne labelled 'sacred' – an

---

[1] The complex body of scholarship on Sterne and Locke is summarized by Lodwick Hartley in *Sterne in the Twentieth Century*, pp. 23–8. Other comments have appeared since, notably those of Jean-Jacques Mayoux, Denis Donoghue and Helene Moglen in WINGED SKULL.

[2] Melvyn New, *Laurence Sterne as Satirist*, Gainesville, Florida, 1969, pp. 11–13 and *passim*.

[3] The only genuine plagiarism in Vol. I is from Bacon's editor, Archbishop Thomas Tenison: Stedmond's appendix;

C. M. Tenison, N&Q, Eighth Series VI (1894), 6; Gwin J. Kolb, N&Q, CXCVI (1951), 226–7.

[4] HAMMOND, 81–2, 125–32; Gardner D. Stout, Jr, 'Sterne's borrowings from Bishop Joseph Hall's *Quo Vadis?*', *English Language Notes*, II (1965), 196–200.

[5] LETTERS,   122;   TRISTRAM SHANDY, 7, 291, 316. Wayne C. Booth, in *The Rhetoric of Fiction*, Chicago, 1961, pp. 221–40, 430–2, discusses the relationship of Sterne to Montaigne and others in his tradition.

'immortal flame which nourishes and devours life, which exalts and varies surprisingly the sensations'. The word *sensations* tips us off that he was thinking of Locke's epistemology. Sterne did not mean to compliment himself in the remark; he simply understood from Locke that sensations and the principles which operated upon them were sacred; therefore, genius, his or anyone's genius, was also sacred. This principle, he went on, 'is called *imagination* or *sensibility*, depending on whether it shows itself in the pen of the writer, in painting, or in the passions of men'. Secondly, Sterne attributed his originality to 'the daily reading of the Old and New Testaments, books to his taste and suited to his position'. Thirdly, he gave credit to the study of Locke, 'taken up in his youth and continued all of his life'. Locke was, in his opinion, 'religious', in fact, 'too religious to undertake any explanation of the miracle of sensation, much less to expect God to account for it'. Locke, founding his philosophy upon this miracle of sensation, had been able to explain 'all the secrets of understanding and the ways to avoid error, arriving at those truths which are accessible – a holy philosophy, without which there will never be on earth either a true universal religion or a true morality or a true power of man over nature'.[1]

Sterne had other hobbies, about which we have scattered information. He appears to have studied French on his own – and very poor French it turned out to be. Richard Phelps, Sterne's travelling companion in 1762, wrote from Paris to Henry Egerton,

> Tristram is so well recover'd as to talk more bad French in one day, than would serve a reasonable man a whole Month. He talks à tort et à travers to whoever sits next to him wherever he happens to be. . . . They know however that Tristram is a great Genius in his own Country, and he would very probably be so in this, if he would but learn to speak before he attempts talking.[2]

One suspects that Sterne took part in amateur theatricals in York. We find him in 1762, with the English colony at Toulouse, organizing a Christmas holiday production of Mrs Centlivre's *Busy Body* (1709), and another play by Cibber and Vanbrugh, *The Provok'd Husband; or, A Journey to London* (1728); the latter Sterne may have rewritten as 'A Journey to Toulouse'.[3] He seems to have had fine-honed views on the natural 'grammar' of posture,

[1] *Mémoires Historiques sur la Vie de M. Suard*, 2 vols, Paris, 1820, II, 148–9; translation and paraphrase, mine.

[2] EGERTON LETTERS, AH 2238.

[3] LETTERS, 190–1. In 1760, Sterne hinted to Garrick that he would be willing to write a 'Cervantic Comedy' upon the materials of *Tristram Shandy*: LETTERS, 87.

movement and facial expression, picked up, in part at least, from popular eighteenth-century literature on acting. He spoke of the theory in both of his novels, as well as in the 'dramatic' sermons, to which it applied with equal validity: 'Nature', he said, 'has assigned a different look, tone of voice, and gesture, peculiar to every passion and affection.'[1] In *Tristram Shandy*, especially, the narrator repeatedly lifts and drops an imaginary curtain upon his scene, describing in minute detail the looks and gestures of his actors. But whether or not Sterne ever put himself into a dramatic production as an actor, we do not know.

Readers of *Tristram Shandy* readily assume that Sterne knew a great deal about music, so common are the musical images. In the 'Memoirs' he said he enjoyed 'fiddling'. Boswell said he played the violin, and one neighbour in York told an anecdote in which he represented Sterne as first violinist for a chamber music society. When Sterne died, he left behind a bass viol.[2] Perhaps he played several stringed instruments. In 1752 he borrowed from the library of the dean and chapter the sonatas of three composers, Henrick Albicastro, Antonio Vivaldi and Carlo Martini. From *Tristram Shandy* we learn little about Sterne the practising musician, except, of course, how familiar he was with the art. The musical images are usually comic – descriptions of bodily attitudes (IV, vi, 276–7), vocal modulations (IV, xxvii, 318), or of his own 'rhapsodical work' (I, xiii, 35): 'To write a book is for all the world like humming a song——be but in tune with yourself, madam, 'tis no matter how high or how low you take it' (IV, xxv, 315). One passage, purporting to be a musical prologue to the next act of Tristram's farce, becomes comic onomatopoeia:

> Ptr..r..r..ing——twing——twang——prut——trut——'tis a curs-
> ed bad fiddle.——Do you know whether my fiddle's in tune or no?
> ——trut..prut..——They should be *fifths*.——'Tis wickedly strung
> ——tr...a.e.i.o.u.-twang.——The bridge is a mile too high, and the
> sound-post absolutely down,——else——trut . . prut——hark! 'tis
> not so bad a tone.——Diddle diddle, diddle diddle, diddle diddle, dum.
>
> (V, xv, 371)

[1] SERMONS, II, 344. Cf. TRISTRAM SHANDY, 293, 361, 414–15; SENTIMENTAL JOURNEY, 162, 171–2. For a full discussion, see William V. Holtz, *Image and Immortality: A Study of 'Tristram Shandy'*, Providence, Rhode Island, 1970, pp. 11–15, 55–9. Richard A. Davies, in his yet unpublished article, 'Tristram Shandy, eccentric orator', has pointed to the similarities between Tristram's comic oratory and the popular comic orators of Sterne's time – John Henley, Christopher Smart, Charles Macklin, Samuel Foote and others.

[2] LETTERS, 441.

To us Sterne seems remarkably modern in his association of artistic impulses with the libido, especially when he draws analogies between the visual arts and writing:

> Just heaven! how does the *Poco più* and the *Poco meno* of the *Italian* artists;——the insensible MORE OR LESS, determine the precise line of beauty in the sentence, as well as in the statue! How do the slight touches of the chisel, the pencil, the pen, the fiddle-stick, *et cætera*, ——give the true swell, which gives the true pleasure!   (II, vi, 100)

But we may be seeing here, not a psychological insight, but a direct expression of Sterne's personality. It was reported at York that he 'was fond of drawing; and of drawing, as well as of writing, what he ought *not* to have drawn and written'.[1]

Sterne was drawing when a child. That schoolboy exercise book, already described, was covered with sketches of his schoolmates, of owls, cocks, hens, of ladies and gentlemen, a drummer and many soldiers. He was still pursuing the hobby during his final illness, making plans to continue the drawing lessons he had been giving to Mrs James. He also worked with colour media, 'painting', he said in the 'Memoirs'. A striking passage of *A Sentimental Journey* develops a contrast between Yorick's 'dusty black' clerical garb, symbolizing a death-like withdrawal from life, and the vital world of pleasure 'in yellow, blue, and green'.[2]

In the early years, Sterne esteemed William Hogarth above all other artists – at least that is suggested by *Tristram Shandy*. The first instalment of the novel contained that detailed description of Corporal Trim reading the sermon, which is given in precise Hogarthian terms (II, xvii, 122-3). He was especially mindful of Hogarth's comments about the art of the quick sketch:

> Such were the out-lines of Dr. *Slop*'s figure, which,——if you have read
> *Hogarth*'s analysis of beauty, and if you have not, I wish you would:

[1] Thomas Frognall Dibdin, *Bibliographical, Antiquarian, and Picturesque Tour in the Northern Counties of England and in Scotland*, 1838, I, 213, note, from Dibdin's conversation with Dr James Atkinson of York. I am doubtful of Dibdin's report that Sterne illustrated a copy of *A Sentimental Journey* with indecent pictures since Sterne was quite ill during most of the three weeks he lived after the appearance of that book. CROSS, p. 118, speculated that Sterne may have designed the vignette of the two fighting game cocks which appeared in Sterne's *Political Romance*, but CURTIS, 69, points out correctly that it was no more than a printer's device belonging to Caesar Ward.

[2] SENTIMENTAL JOURNEY, 156. A similar use of colour symbolism on p. 197.

——you must know, may as certainly be caricatur'd, and convey'd to the mind by three strokes as three hundred.   (II, ix, 104–5)

How thrilled Sterne must have been when Hogarth returned the compliment by presenting him with a drawing of the sermon-reading scene. Engraved by Ravenet, it appeared as the frontispiece to the second, the London, edition of Volumes I–II. Hogarth's drawing of the baptism scene, which appeared a year later as frontispiece to Volumes III–IV, may not have been a gift.[1]

Probably Sterne's accomplishments as draughtsman and painter were not high. The fullest account comes from John Croft:

> He was not steady at his Pastimes, or Recreations. At one time he wou'd take up the Gun and follow shooting till he became a good shott, then he wou'd take up the Pencil and paint Pictures. He chiefly copied Portraits. He had a good Idea of Drawing, but not the least of mixing his colours.

Croft was probably right. We know Sterne liked to do portraits: in 1759 he intended to paint his new inamorata, Catherine Fourmantel.[2] And we know that he sometimes copied the work of other artists – the story which lies behind the one surviving piece of his work as a painter.

In the forties, probably, Sterne and a friend, Thomas Bridges, painted each other on a single canvas in the costumes of mountebanks. The painting itself is now lost, but we have an engraving of it which appeared in Thomas Frognall Dibdin's *Bibliographical, Antiquarian, and Picturesque Tour in the Northern Counties of England and in Scotland* (1838). Dibdin saw the picture at the home of Dr James Atkinson, a York surgeon and bibliophile whose father had known Sterne. Sterne seems to have liked this canvas better than any other he worked on. It is the only one he valued enough to consider part of his legacy: in the memorandum he left his wife in 1761, when he feared he might die abroad, he told Elizabeth how she must get back the painting from a lady who had 'most cavallierly' taken possession of it (p. 148). For all Sterne's pride, the painting was not very original – at least not Sterne's part of it. The two figures stand on a platform, with behind them a conventional, stylized representation of a town. The chief mountebank, a bearded figure

---

[1] Sterne's friendships with Hogarth and Reynolds: Holtz, *Image and Immortality*. The original Hogarth drawings are in the Berg Collection of the New York Public Library. Kenneth Monkman discusses the variant engravings and changes made by Hogarth, 'The bibliography of the early editions of *Tristram Shandy*', *The Library*, Fifth Series XXV (1970), 11–39.

[2] LETTERS, 81.

who represents Sterne's friend, very earnestly offers his medicines to the
crowd. Sterne appears as a lively and amused harlequin, hat in hand, making
a slight bow to the audience – the portion painted by Bridges – a delightfully
appropriate image for the author of *Tristram Shandy*. Judging from Sterne's
later portraits by Reynolds and Nollekens, one concludes that Bridges
produced a fair likeness, though the nose seems too hooked. But Sterne's own
work, the portrait of Bridges, is primarily a copy. His model was a copper-
plate broadside on which appear a comic poem and picture, called 'The
Infallible Mountebank, or Quack Doctor'.[1] In Sterne's painting of Bridges,
the costume, the pose and even the bearded face are strikingly similar to the
broadside. Bridges, on the other hand, did not depend upon the macaroni
who appears in the plate: his painting of Sterne is original.

The mountebank picture implies a great deal about Sterne's pastimes
during the middle years of the century. Thomas Bridges – whose name we
know from the print in Dibdin's *Tour* – is almost certainly Thomas Bridges
of Hull, a businessman and humorist. Sterne might have known him at
Cambridge, where he attended St John's College. Another possibility is that
he met him through the Croft family, for Bridges was a partner in the wine-
importing firm of Sell, Bridges and Blunt. He voted Whig in the Yorkshire
by-election of 1741/2 and subscribed to the defences of the county during
the rebellion. When the wine business failed in 1759, Bridges went to
London where he became a minor Grub Street writer, author of an amusing
travesty of Homer, a piece called 'The Adventures of a Bank-note', some
poems, a comic opera and a musical entertainment.[2] It is certainly interesting to discover Sterne intimate with another humorist – a man of his own
age, of like education and political views, who moved in the same circle of
York gentlemen. Especially interesting is their switching to writing careers
in the same year.

Whatever John Croft meant by his odd remark, 'There are severall
Pictures of his [Sterne's] painting at York, such as they are', nothing else
from Sterne's brush has been identified. Other drawings have been wrongly

[1] Discovered by Kenneth Monkman in a guard book at BM: C. 121. g. 9. fol. 211. See Appendix, Plates I–II.
[2] DNB; David Erskine Baker, *Biographia Dramatica*, 1782, I, 44. In the *List of the Voluntary Subscribers*, Hull [1745], 'Thomas Bridges, Junior, of Hull' subscribed £20. In the poll book for the election of 1741/2 at the BM: 810. K. 33, 'Thomas Bridges, Gent., of Silkston, Hull' voted for Turner. The topic of mountebanks and macaronis was popular: the *York Courant*, 8 January 1745, ran a story on the famous charlatan, Joshua Ward, who also made a broadside mocking himself.

attributed to Sterne – the designs which appeared in a volume of poems by Michael Woodhull, published in Italy in 1772, and a sketch mistakenly said to be of Elizabeth Sterne.[1] But the mountebank picture is the only genuine work from his brush of which we have any visible remains.

Cut off from the London scene, Sterne probably longed for the company of accomplished painters. He took a keen interest in Christopher Steele, the portrait painter, who set up a studio in York in 1756. Richard Cumberland later circulated a story that Sterne had patronized Steele's talented young apprentice, none other than George Romney; but Romney denied it, saying that he knew Sterne only slightly, that Sterne had treated him with the civility that a good-natured man would naturally show to a promising pupil.[2] During the single year when 'Count' Steele – as he was called for his flashy dress – kept a studio in York, he painted a portrait of Sterne, now lost.[3]

Sterne may not have been an accomplished painter, but he was sensitive to spatial and chromatic arrangements and had a highly developed visual imagination. His habit of apprehending experience in visual terms was deeply ingrained. His fictional world, whether Walter Shandy on his bed of pain or Paris as seen from the window of an inn, was not always passed from his imagination to ours through the medium of language alone. Sterne often

[1] The designs for the Woodhull volume, signed 'L. Stern', were attributed to Sterne by the editors of his *Works*, 1780. In N&Q, Third Series VII (1865), 53–4, Sir P. Stafford Carey pointed out that they were more probably the work of Lewis Stern, 1708–77, who lived in Rome and painted primarily game birds, flowers, fruit and scriptural scenes. In N&Q, Second Series XII (1861), 369, Carey had described the sketch, supposed to be of Elizabeth Sterne, 'the most unprepossessing piece of femininity I ever saw portrayed'. The sketch, in Carey's possession, was signed 'Pigrich' and endorsed in an eighteenth-century hand, 'Mrs. Sterne, wife of Sterne'. Carey did not suggest that Sterne had drawn it; on the contrary, he expressed a hope that the artist could be identified, suggesting the unlikely possibility of Hogarth. Neither did Paul Stapfer suggest that Sterne had drawn it when he first published the cartoon in *Laurence Sterne: étude biographique et littéraire*, Paris, 1870, reissued the same year under the more familiar title *Laurence Sterne – sa personne et ses ouvrages*. I have found no evidence to corroborate CROSS, Holtz, and others in their opinion that Sterne was the artist. I do not think that this drawing of a woman aged about seventy or seventy-five can possibly represent Elizabeth Sterne, who died at the age of fifty-eight, much less that it could be drawn by her husband who died when she was aged fifty-three.

[2] Richard Cumberland, 'Memoirs of Mr. George Romney', *European Magazine*, XLIII (January–June 1803), 417–23; Arthur R. Chamberlain, *George Romney*, 1910, p. 239; Darley Dale, '"Count" Steele', *Northern Notes and Queries*, I (1906–7), 70–8; DNB.

[3] William Hayley, *Life of George Romney*, Chichester, 1809, pp. 26–7.

interposed his visual apprehension before the verbal, translating his primarily imagined situations and characters into secondarily imagined paintings, precisely drafted and detailed, or into imagined sketches, often comic, always charged with symbolic meaning. These, in turn, he communicated by means of words. Thus, in some episodes, though not all, the artistic shaping of the raw materials is doubled. This device, or habit of mind, opened Sterne's novels to a wide range of innovative effects – a variable aesthetic distance, initial impressions which can be played off against the artistic or historiographic demands of his storytelling art, emotion against intellect, the comforting timelessness of the static tableau against the inexorable forward march of days and years.[1]

Sterne's artistic ideal was naturalness, whether in fiction or in painting. To him 'canting critics' such as René le Bossu (III, xii, 180–2) or Roger de Piles,[2] who insisted upon measurable regularity, were a threat, not only to art but to life itself. In a memorable serio-comic passage upon Montreuil, Tristram draws a contrast between architectural beauty and the beauty of a woman. The church of Montreuil represents balance, regularity and formality: it suggests the Platonic Forms, ideal, eternal, beautiful and sterile. Janatone, the innkeeper's daughter, is the creature only of a day, but her vital beauty is what Tristram chooses to draw – and of course the image becomes sexual – 'with as determin'd a pencil, as if I had her in the wettest drapery'.

——But your worships chuse rather that I give you the length, breadth, and perpendicular height of the great parish church, or a drawing of the façade of the abbey of Saint *Austreberte* which . . .

---

[1] Detailed discussions of the relationships between Sterne's fiction and the visual arts in Ernest A. Baker, *History of the English Novel*, 10 vols, 1924–39, IV, 263–5; Rudolph Maack, *Laurence Sterne im Lichte seiner Zeit*, Hamburg, 1936; Peter Quennell, *Four Portraits*, 1945; Wylie Sypher, *Four Stages of Renaissance Style*, Garden City, 1955; Henri Fluchère, *Laurence Sterne*, Paris, 1961; Martin Price, *To the Palace of Wisdom*, Garden City, 1964; Ronald Paulson, *Hogarth: His Life, Art, and Times*, 2 vols, New Haven, 1971, II, 302–6; Holtz, *Image and Immortality*; R. F. Brissenden, 'Sterne and painting', in *Of Books and Humankind*, ed. John Butt, 1964, pp. 93–108; William V. Holtz, 'Typography, *Tristram Shandy*, the Aposiopesis, etc.', in WINGED SKULL, 247–56; and Peter Ford, 'No Gross Daubing': *Tristram Shandy and the visual arts*, unpublished MA thesis, 1970, State University of New York, New Paltz College.

[2] The passage in which Tristram gives a numerical value to every aspect of his story, p. 16, is a satire of Roger de Piles, *Cours de peinture par principes*, Paris, 1708, translated into English, 1743, as *Principles of Painting*.

will be so these fifty years to come——so your worships and reverences, may all measure them at your leisures——but he who measures thee, *Janatone*, must do it now——thou carriest the principles of change within thy frame; and considering the chances of a transitory life, I would not answer for thee a moment; e'er twice twelve months are pass'd and gone, thou mayest grow out like a pumkin, and lose thy shapes——or, thou mayest go off like a flower, and lose thy beauty—— nay, thou mayest go off like a hussy——and lose thyself. (VII, ix, 490)

Tristram never finishes his portrait of Janatone. He is interrupted by a thought about Aunt Dinah, who ran off with the coachman, and then a thought about Sir Joshua Reynolds, after which he finds it impossible to continue the drawing. 'So you must e'en be content with the original.' Ultimate naturalness, of course, is no art, but 'the original'.

Prebendary of York
1747–1751

To the south of York Minster stands a light gothic church with a delicate lantern tower, St Michael le Belfry, parish church for the Minster Yard. Here every year a charity sermon was preached to raise funds for the Blue Coat School for poor boys and the Grey Coat School for girls. The preacher invited in 1747 was Laurence Sterne. For the occasion he wrote *The Case of Elijah and the Widow of Zarephath, consider'd*. One April morning he mounted the pulpit of St Michael's and turned to look over an audience as fashionable as York could provide. The lord mayor, aldermen and sheriffs were there with their ladies, as well as a large number of clergy. He spoke to them, not so much about the divine miracle worked by the prophet, as about the human exchanges of kindness and sympathy, 'that friendly softness' which God has woven into our natures 'to be a check upon too great a propensity towards self-love' (I, 73). At the climax of the story, he passed quickly over the central incident, Elijah's bringing back to life the son of the kind widow, lingering instead over its aftermath. Unobtrusively flattering the benevolence of the ladies and gentlemen, he invited them to imagine the scene as a painting:

> It would be a pleasure to a good mind to stop here a moment, and figure to itself the picture of so joyful an event. – To behold on one hand the raptures of the parent. . . . To conceive on the other side of the *piece*, the holy man approaching with the child in his arms———full of honest triumph in his looks, but sweetened with all the kind sympathy which a gentle nature could overflow with upon so happy an event. (I, 79)

When, as he calculated, the audience was close to tears, he began an impassioned plea for the poor children of York. The collection of £64. 11s. 8d. was noted as far away as London. 'Is it that we are like iron', Sterne once asked, 'and must first be heated before we can be wrought upon?'¹

That summer, *The Case of Elijah* was published – the first work by Sterne to appear under separate cover. It was printed by Caesar Ward, advertised in the *Gentleman's Magazine* for July 1747 (p. 348), and sold by John Hildyard at the Sign of the Bible in Stonegate. Sterne dedicated it to Dean Richard Osbaldeston, soon to be elevated to the see of Carlisle, referring gracefully to 'the Sense of many Favours and Civilities which I have received from you'.

Why should this prebendary of North Newbald be asked to preach a charity sermon? The previous year it had been Archbishop Thomas Herring. The next year it would be the archbishop's cousin, William Herring, now the powerful chancellor of the diocese as well as a canon residentiary. There were only three reasons to invite an eighteenth-century clergyman to preach a charity sermon – because he was influential, because he was famous or because he was a good preacher. The archbishop was all three; what is more, he preached for the Blue and Grey Coat Schools during the height of the rebellion. Little wonder that the collection was the largest ever taken – £94. His cousin was a man of influence – no doubt a great many of the ladies and gentlemen in the audience were obliged to the chancellor or ambitious for his support – but his collection came to only £63, a smaller sum than Sterne raised.² Sterne, certainly no popular hero, was poor and had no patronage. He would have been asked only because he was an excellent preacher. His delivery was dramatic, his voice in these years was strong and sonorous, and he could be counted upon to deliver, as he later put it, 'a theologic flap upon the heart'.³

Consider also his other occasional sermons: in 1741 Sterne had been invited to preach the fast sermon at the minster following the declaration of war; in 1743 he had preached the enthronement sermon for Archbishop Herring. On two other unexplained occasions he preached at the request of the chapter,⁴ and three years hence he would be asked to do the assize sermon in the minster – always an important occasion since it signalled the beginning of Race Week. Moreover, he seems to have preached more sub-

¹ SERMONS, I, 319; *York Journal; or, Protestant Courant*, 21 April 1747; *General Advertiser*, 25 April, cited by Cross in SERMONS, I, xviii.

² *York Courant*, 25 March and 1 April 1746; 12 April 1748.

³ LETTERS, 134. On Sterne's voice and delivery, above, Chapter 7.

⁴ Minster Library: *St. Peter's Accountbook*, 1720–69, 2 January 1752/3; 29 September 1753.

stitute sermons at York Minster than anyone else. During one year, as he told Archdeacon Francis Blackburne, he picked up an extra £20 this way. Since the fee was £1, he had done twenty sermons, besides the two he was required to provide as prebendary of North Newbald – a quarter of the eighty-eight regular sermons delivered annually at the minster.[1] No doubt he was helped to these small jobs by Dean Osbaldeston and his successor, Dean Fountayne, both of whom were friends.[2] But the deans could hardly have allowed him to appear so often had he not been the effective pulpit orator described by his servant: 'the Minster was crowded whenever it was known that he was to preach.' Indeed, all the evidence indicates that Laurence Sterne was one of the best preachers in York.

Probably most of his surviving sermons were written for delivery at the minster or before some assembly of ladies and gentlemen who had invited him to preach. It seems likely that most of the sermons he ad-libbed to his rural flocks were never committed to paper. The point, however, is uncertain: 'Asa: A Thanksgiving Sermon', delivered at Coxwold during the celebration of the coronation of George II, on 22 September 1761, was 'Preached Extempory', according to one witness, yet it appeared among the posthumously published sermons.[3]

When Sterne did compose sermons on paper, he worked at home, not in the library of the dean and chapter, as he might have done. His servant, Greenwood, retained a picture of his master at this task: 'In person tall & thin – when composing would often pull down his wig over one eye, & remove it from side to side.' John Croft said that Elizabeth sometimes helped him to write his sermons. It would seem that Sterne owned a small library of theology, ethics and sermons, probably collected by some older clergyman. In any event, the traceable sources he used were all in print before 1733, with the exception of Swift's sermons, published in 1744,[4] presumably one of the few books Sterne added to this collection.

[1] LETTERS, 31. Sterne would not have exaggerated to any great degree when writing to so knowledgeable a man as Blackburne. For the schedule of regular sermons, see at Minster Library, Thomas Ellway, *Anthems: For Two, Three, Four, Five, Six, Seven, and Eight Voices*, 2nd ed., 1753.

[2] Probably his acknowledgement of Osbaldeston's favours in the dedication to *The Case of Elijah* refers to these appointments. Osbaldeston, after he became Bishop of Carlisle, visited Sterne at Coxwold: LETTERS, 116. He was translated to the see of London in 1762, but had no opportunity to befriend Sterne in the capital: he died in the spring of 1764 shortly before Sterne returned from abroad.

[3] SERMONS, II, 299–312; CURTIS, 145–6.

[4] HAMMOND, 56. Had Sterne worked

Borrowed passages in the sermons suggest that some of these works Sterne read carefully, from cover to cover – William Wollaston's *Religion of Nature Delineated* (1724), or Richard Steele's *Christian Hero* (1701). But his interest in a book did not often lead him to seek out others by the same author. He was familiar with Bishop Joseph Butler's *Fifteen Sermons preached at the Rolls Chapel* (1726), but never made use – in existing sermons – of the more famous *Analogy of Religion*. The seventeenth-century Bishop Joseph Hall is another case in point: Sterne borrowed from the bishop's relatively obscure *Contemplations on the Historical Passages of the Old and New Testaments* (1662), but not the better-known *Characters*, the *Satires* or the *Epistles*. Probably the only sermonists whom he read extensively were John Tillotson and Samuel Clarke. True, neither became his models for organization or style, but from both he took many doctrines, examples and specific passages.[1] Nothing was unusual about Sterne's admiration for these divines: during the eighteenth century, no sermon writer was more widely admired and imitated than Tillotson, the great Latitudinarian; and Clarke was considered by many of his contemporaries to be the greatest philosopher of his time.

Sterne seems to have kept a commonplace book into which he copied passages from his reading, possibly arranging them thematically rather than by authors. As he wrote his sermons, he would frequently turn to these notes, sometimes weaving together with great skill passages from several disparate sources. When he was in a hurry, he shamelessly rifled obscure works – Walter Leightonhouse's *Twelve Sermons* (1697), Thomas Wise's *Fourteen Discourses* (1717), or the seldom-read *Sermons on Several Occasions* (1702), by Dr Edward Young, father of the poet.

For his plagiarisms, Sterne was roasted by critics, but not until he was long dead. One suspects that they were more incensed by his general reputation than by the plagiarisms themselves. From the Elizabethan age onwards, plagiarism in sermons had been condoned by the church and even encouraged. Still, the question is difficult since attitudes were shifting in the middle and late years of the eighteenth century. Benjamin Franklin's friends were disgusted to discover that a preacher had borrowed a passage from Dr James Foster, while Franklin himself 'rather approved his giving us good sermons compos'd by others, than bad ones of his own manufacture'.[2] In *Tristram*

---

much at the library, he probably would have borrowed some passages from more recent books.

[1] HAMMOND, 71–2, 81–2, 86 and *passim.*
[2] Quoted by HAMMOND, 78; see also 1–16, 74–89.

Shandy, Sterne seems to condemn his own plagiarisms, though laughingly: Parson Yorick writes on the back of one of his homilies:

> ——*For this sermon I shall be hanged,*——*for I have stolen the greatest part of it. Doctor* Paidagunes *found me out.* ☞ *Set a thief to catch a thief.*
> ——
> (VI, xi, 427)

In another passage he mocks, in the figure of Homenas, the clergyman who plagiarizes ineptly (IV, xxv, 315–16). A more extensive and ribald satire of Homenas appears in Sterne's 'Fragment in the Manner of Rabelais', probably rejected from the first version of *Tristram Shandy*. There we find the plagiarist in the library, before him a volume of Clarke's sermons from which he has clapped into his own sermon 'Five whole Pages, nine round Paragraphs, and a Dozen and a half of good Thoughts all of a Row'. But then he begins to imagine what will happen when he is found out:

> There will be the Deuce & all to pay. – *Why are the Bells ringing backwards*; You Lad! – *What's all that Crowd about, honest Man!* Homenas *was got upon Dr Clark's back, Sir*——*and what of that, my Lad? Why Sir, He has broke his Neck, and fractured his Skull and beshit himself into the Bargain, by a fall from the Pulpit two Stories high.* Alass poor *Homenas!* . . . 'twill be all over with me before G-d, – I may as well shite as shoot.——[1]

These satirical fragments seem to be written by a man who took some pride in plagiarizing skilfully, but who knew he should not be doing it at all. True he occasionally acknowledged his indebtedness, but all too seldom.[2] Only five of Sterne's forty-five known sermons are free from borrowings – so far as anyone has been able to show.[3] Sterne may have been a good sermonist, but he was certainly a lazy one.

It must also be said that his attitude was different towards published

[1] Quoted from Melvyn New's edition, 'Sterne's Rabelaisian fragment: a text from the holograph manuscript', *PMLA*, LXXXII (1972), 1083–92. The MS is now at the Pierpont Morgan Library in New York City.

[2] SERMONS, I, 132, 172, 185, 205; II, 236. In Sermon XLIV, 'The Ways of Providence Justified to Man', he borrowed certain key passages verbatim from Wollaston (HAMMOND, 178–80) to which he referred in a note on the manuscript: 'I have borrowed most of the Reflections upon the Characters from Wollaston, or at least have enlarged from his hints, though the Sermon is truly mine such as it is.' The manuscript, seen and described by Isaac Reed, is now lost: CROSS, 242–3.

[3] Sermon IX, 'The Character of Herod'; XXX, 'Description of the World'; XXXII, 'Thirtieth of January'; XLII, 'Search the Scriptures'; and XLV, 'The Ingratitude of Israel'.

sermons than towards those he intended to preach and forget. He may have been embarrassed, when asked to publish *The Case of Elijah*, because it contained short passages lifted from Hall, Tillotson and Wollaston.[1] His dedication to the dean contains an ambiguous statement about 'the Novelty of his Vehicle': 'there can be little left to be said upon the Subject . . . which has not been often thought, and much better express'd by many who have gone before.' The most flagrant plagiarisms, as Hammond points out, are among the sermons which Sterne did not prepare for publication – the posthumous *Sermons by the Late Rev. Mr. Sterne* (3 volumes, 1769). These 'sweepings of the Author's study' are the least worked-over and possibly the earliest written. In *The Sermons of Mr. Yorick* (4 volumes, 1760–6), which Sterne himself saw through the press, the plagiarisms are comparatively few and the acknowledgements of sources more frequent. He may have lost track of where other borrowings had come from, as he said, uneasily, in the preface to Volume I.

Nevertheless, one must finally conclude that Sterne's practice was blameable, though a venial sin. Much as he enjoyed delivering sermons, he was probably bored by the task of writing them. So he compiled and used that commonplace book. The case is not parallel to the novels, where his plagiarism purposely followed a literary tradition and demanded some effort. In the sermons, plagiarism was the easy way out. Most important, Sterne himself felt that he should not do it.

As time passed and Sterne collected more and more sermons, he tended to re-use older ones, sometimes revising them. Manuscripts survive for 'Temporal Advantages of Religion' and 'Penances', both of which show rewriting.[2] The alterations in 'Penances' he made at two different times, but not for purpose of publication, it seems, since the sermon was not printed during his lifetime.

Dating the sermons is all but impossible. Probably few, if any, date from the early period of Sterne's ministry; it is more likely that most were composed during the decade after he settled in Sutton, 1742–51. But one can never be absolutely certain when Sterne wrote or revised a particular sermon, not even those he is known to have preached on specific occasions: they

[1] HAMMOND, 127–8, 168, 180. On p. 145, Hammond cites what he believes to be a borrowing from Clarke, and others from Tillotson and Wollaston on pp. 161, 183, which I would not interpret as plagiarisms. His study is weak in this respect: many of the 'borrowings' listed in the appendix resemble their putative sources in content, but not in wording.

[2] The MS of 'Temporal Advantages of Religion' (No. XXVIII) at the Huntington Library; that of 'Penances' (XXXVII) at the Pierpont Morgan Library.

might so easily have been selected from his existing stock.¹ One can hazard
a guess that one small group, the sermons attacking Methodism, were
written for York audiences after 1747.² That was the year that John Wesley
set on foot a plan to organize a Methodist Society in the city. For a few
years they met in the Bedern, directly behind the minster; then for a short
period, 1752–4, they held their meetings virtually in the walls of the
cathedral itself: they took over 'The Hole in the Wall', the ruin of an ancient
chapel attached to the minster and communicating by a door with the north
aisle of the nave. An anonymous satire of the period plays upon the irony of
the situation:

> Good people repair to Lord Irving's Square
> Which lies in the bounds of St. Peter's;
> From the 'Hole in the Wall' you've an absolute call,
> To hear the new Methodist preachers.
> Come leave your vocations, never mind your relations,
> Let children go beg or cease eating;
> Don't mind your affairs, come abandon your cares,
> Come, come to the Methodist meeting.
> Of preachers they've store, I think I know four, –
> All men of profound sense and learning;
> Our orthodox priests, who mere rhetoric teach,
> Can't compete with their skill in discerning.
> A stonecutter leads, a barber succeeds,
> The third is a clergyman's servant,
> The fourth beats the drum, and his call is come, come,
> And he makes better pay than his serjeant.³

¹ HAMMOND offers a tenuous argument that all of the sermons were written before 1751 (except 'National Mercies Considered', written for the inauguration of George III). I do not find his argument convincing. Especially weak is the dating of Sermon XXV, 'Humility': he dates it 1743 on the ground that Sterne reported the presence of Quakers in his parish that year (HERRING RETURNS) and the sermon mentions Quakers. But Sterne was exposed to Quakers all his life. Hammond's general points are more convincing: that most of the posthumous sermons (XXVIII–XLV) were written earlier than the others; that as Sterne developed a stock of sermons, he began to rewrite his favourites.

² Sermons XIV, 'Self-Examination'; XXV, 'Humility'; XXXVII, 'Penances'; and XXXVIII, 'On Enthusiasm'.

³ Quoted by John Lyth in *Glimpses of Early Methodism in York*, York and London, 1885, pp. 74–80. Lyth identified the lay preachers as John Nelson, the stonecutter and a celebrated Methodist, a man who was viciously stoned by a mob at Acomb, outside York, in 1747; William Shent, a

Often as Sterne appeared in the high pulpit of York Minster, he took little part in chapter affairs during the tenure of Dean Osbaldeston. The dean, who managed to remain friendly with both Sterne and his uncle, probably discouraged his participation in order to keep the peace. But when Osbaldeston was elevated to the bishopric of Carlisle in 1747, he was succeeded by an old Cambridge friend of Sterne's, John Fountayne. Thereafter Sterne was drawn into chapter affairs – with woeful consequences.

John Fountayne was no stranger to York. Born and reared at Melton in the East Riding, he had succeeded to the estate of Melton Hall at the death of his older brother.[1] He loved the life of a rural squire and spent a great deal of time at Melton. His appointment to the deanery was the result of family connections with the prelacy. His mother was a cousin to Osbaldeston; his sister was a daughter-in-law of Stephen Weston, Bishop of Exeter. Most lucky of all, his childless aunt was married to Thomas Sherlock, Bishop of London, whom Henry Pelham and the Duke of Newcastle jokingly called their 'Pope'. Sherlock, who nominated the ministry's appointments in the church, had far more political influence than did the Archbishop of Canterbury. In fact he twice turned down that post, preferring the greater power of the London see. Sherlock made a pet of his wife's nephew, obtained for him a wealthy canonry of Salisbury only weeks after Fountayne was ordained in 1739, and got him an additional rich prebend at Windsor in 1741. He even went so far as to try to get his nephew a bishopric, but Newcastle balked at that because Fountayne was so young. Now, in 1747, Sherlock wrote to Newcastle, explaining that the younger man should not be raised at the expense of Osbaldeston, who had been a faithful supporter of the ministry, but the deanery of York would do very well 'to support the credit, wch he and his family before him have had in his country, and wch has at all times, invariably been applyed to promote the true Interest of the Government'.[2]

---

barber of Leeds; John Maskew of Dainhead, the clergyman's servant; and John Johnson, or 'Drummer Johnson', a soldier and leader of the movement in York. In 1745, the society moved to Pump Yard, and in 1759 they built a chapel in Peasholme Green. Although the movement was never so strong in the North Riding as elsewhere in Yorkshire, there was a meeting house in Stillington by 1764 (DRUMMOND RETURNS), probably established shortly after Sterne moved to Coxwold.

[1] For his family and career: DNB; VENN; Joseph Foster, *Pedigrees of the County Families of Yorkshire*, 4 vols, 1874–5, II, 'Fountayne of Melton', and III, 'Fountayne-Wilson of Leeds'; Joseph Hunter, *South Yorkshire*, 2 vols, 1828–31, I, 367–9.

[2] BM: Add. MSS 32712, fols. 93–4; Edward Carpenter, *Thomas Sherlock*, 1936.

Thus Sherlock vetoed the other candidate for the deanery, who had been nominated by Archbishop Herring – Jaques Sterne.[1] Uncle Jaques must have been bitterly disappointed, though he managed to say the polite thing and to promise support of the ministry anyway. Herring, who had the task of breaking the bad news to Jaques, wrote to Newcastle: 'upon my conscience, I think he would perform [his promise], for he knows no use of Money, but to spend it, & spares no Cost or Pains for the service of the King's Government: If it could be had, a Prebend in one of the three Great Churches would be acceptable to him.'[2] But Sherlock seems to have known that Dr Sterne's rash conduct had become a liability to his friends. The precentor would have to wait several years for his reward, growing more and more unhappy with the ministry, Dean Fountayne and Fountayne's friends in York.

His nephew was one of those friends, not for political so much as personal reasons. Fountayne and Sterne had in common their youthful days at Cambridge. They laughed easily together, and indeed opened themselves to criticism by their way of falling into the rowdy talk of undergraduates. Their enemies accused them of an 'undistinguished' manner, using coarse language, and sometimes acting like 'warm and violent men'.[3] But Fountayne was more prudent than his friend: he would never publish anything remotely similar to Sterne's description in *Tristram Shandy* of the dean and chapter of Strasburg, 'assembled in the morning to consider the case of butter'd buns' – a cant term for harlot (pp. 254–5). The new dean may have had great need for Lorry Sterne's fund of good cheer. He was downcast, his wife having recently died when she was close to childbirth.

At a serious level, Sterne and Fountayne shared common attitudes toward the church. The dean's only published works, a sermon *On the Lisbon Earthquake* (1755), and another of the following year, *A Fast Sermon*, were written in the tradition which predominates in Sterne's sermons – Latitudinarianism modified by Locke. Both eschewed the legalistic, authoritarian approach to church government so common among high churchmen of the previous generation – including both Thomas Sherlock and Jaques Sterne.

In politics too John Fountayne could swing with the times, though Sterne probably tried to stand clear of his friend's political involvements. In his capacity as squire of Melton, Fountayne had been active in old Lord

---

[1] Undated memorandum among the Newcastle papers, BM: Add. MSS 32933, fol. 411.
[2] Dated 25 July 1747, BM: Add. MSS 32712, fols. 225–6.
[3] LETTER TO THE DEAN, 2; REPLY, 7, 47–8.

Rockingham's party, and he was one of the first to join the revamped party organized by the Second Lord Rockingham and Sir George Savile. As late as 1780 he was active in the reform movement headed by Christopher Wyvill.[1]

As might be expected, Sterne appeared at the chapter meeting of 24 October 1747, when the new dean was installed. Fountayne, like any politician of that time, set about placing his friends in such minor positions in the power structure as he could control. He insisted upon his rights as custos rotulorum for the Liberty of St Peter[2] and promptly nominated a new Commission of the Peace. Although no list of his nominees survives, Sterne was surely on it. A little later, in 1753, we catch a glimpse of Justices Fountayne and Sterne sitting in session and promulgating an order to close all shops and stalls within the Liberty on Sundays.[3] Sterne's major obligation as a justice of the peace would have been to serve the parish of Stillington, included in the Liberty, a jurisdiction he would have shared with Stephen Croft, also a justice.[4] Their duties in such a small community would have been light. Perhaps two or three times a year they tried some local citizen for a minor crime or, in more serious cases, bound the accused over for trial at the quarter sessions or assizes. Richard Greenwood, recollecting Sterne the justice, said that he 'would often espouse a cause which he was sure of bringing thro' at the Quarter Sessions, he could talk down the Lawyers so – this he delighted in'. Sterne continued as a justice of the Liberty until he turned author.[5]

Theoretically, appointments to the commission were not political, and Sterne may have thought that his acceptance would not involve him in politics again. But his uncle could hardly be expected to take it in this light. Incensed that Sterne had joined the faction of his competitor, Jaques found a way to break the truce which he and Laurence had established during the rebellion. Sterne's mother provided the opportunity. Perhaps she had heard

---

[1] Rockingham to Newcastle, 12 December 1746, BM: Add. MSS 35602, fol. 245; Ian R. Christie, *Wilkes, Wyville and Reform*, 1962, pp. 74, 202–3; Cedric Collyer, 'The Rockinghams and Yorkshire politics, 1742–1761', *Publications of the Thoresby Society*, XLI (1946–53), 352–82.

[2] Fountayne to Newcastle, 7 December 1747, BM: Add. MSS 35602, fol. 334.

[3] The printed order, dated 14 July 1753, is now framed and hanging in the chapter clerk's office.

[4] At a later date Stephen Croft and the Reverend Andrew Cheap, Sterne's successor at Sutton, were both justices for the Liberty: *A List of the Noblemen and Gentlemen for the Commission of the Peace for the Liberty of St. Peter*, York, 1789, at Minster Library.

[5] See the footnote in ANSWER, 17, presumably the evidence upon which Davies made his assertion that Sterne was a justice: YORK PRESS, 257.

about Fountayne's arrival and in her simple-minded way supposed that her son would be made rich through some preferment from the dean. She appeared at Sutton and again played out the old scene of blusters and threats. The timing was hard on Elizabeth, who was in the late stages of pregnancy, and, as her husband said, 'under an apparent Necessity of a Man Mid-wife to attend her'.[1] Nevertheless, Sterne agreed to give his mother £8 a year while he lived. She accepted, and their ancient quarrel would seem to have been at an end. Furthermore, he sent her off with 10 guineas even though the gift left him short of funds.

Because Agnes had used her brother-in-law's name in these parleys, Sterne asked her to stop in York, on her way back to Chester, to tell his uncle about the agreement. Agnes did that, but neglected to tell him about the 10 guineas in her pocket – 'I suppose', Sterne later wrote to him, 'to make a Penny of us both'. Jaques Sterne, when he heard about the £8 settlement, was keenly interested. Here was an opportunity to harass his nephew too tempting to resist. He advised his sister-in-law not to accept the settlement – not until she had won a further guarantee that in case of her son's death the allowance would be payable out of Elizabeth's fortune.

Sterne, when he heard the story, was at first incredulous and then furious. How could he burden Elizabeth, if she were widowed, with the responsibility of caring for this grasping mother-in-law? Although he had the power in law to entail her fortune, as he later wrote to his uncle,

I feel I have *no Power* in Equity or in Conscience to do so; & I will add in her behalf, considering how much she has merited at my hands, as the best of Wives, That was I capable of being worried into so cruel a Measure as to give away hers & her Child's Bread upon the clamour which you and my Mother have raised – That I should not only be the Weakest, But the *Worst Man* that ever Woman trusted with all She had.' (p. 39)

He talked the situation over with his wife, and they decided that Elizabeth should be the one to go to Dr Sterne, to explain their position, and to ask him to change his advice. The uncle declined the interview, sending word that his nephew might 'appear before' him. Since a confrontation 'was likely to produce nothing but an angry Expostulation (which could do no good, but might do Hurt) – I beg'd in *my Turn* to be excused' (p. 33). Sterne supposed that his uncle would let the matter drop – which he did, for a time.

[1] LETTERS, 39.

Sterne's conscience was clear, as he said, and he needed no advice. He informed his mother that he would not comply with her new demand.[1] Agnes returned to Chester, but possibly she had so alienated her son that she received no support during the next three years.

A daughter was born to Elizabeth on 1 December 1747. If a man-midwife were called in at the birth, as Sterne predicted, we have no record of it. No doubt there were troubles enough:

> We shall have a rare month of it, said my father, turning his head from *Obadiah*, and looking wistfully in my uncle *Toby*'s face for some time——we shall have a devilish month of it, brother *Toby*, said my father, setting his arms a-kimbo, and shaking his head; fire, water, women, wind——brother *Toby*!——'Tis some misfortune, quoth my uncle *Toby*——That it is, cried my father,——to have so many jarring elements breaking loose, and riding triumph in every corner of a gentleman's house——Little boots it to the peace of a family, brother *Toby*, that you and I possess ourselves, and sit here silent and unmoved,—— whilst such a storm is whistling over our heads.   (IV, xvi, 291–2)

This child lived. Like her older sister who had died, she was named Lydia after her maternal grandmother. She would grow up to be the delight of her father, the nurse of her mother, and the worry of her godmother, Mrs Elizabeth Montagu.

In York, things had barely settled down after the change of deans when a new archbishop was appointed – Dr Matthew Hutton. The old Archbishop of Canterbury, John Potter, had died in the autumn of 1747. The Pelhams and Lord Chancellor Hardwicke wanted Thomas Herring to succeed him. Herring was reluctant. He wrote three refusals, but threw each into the fire. Hardwicke was insistent. Among the advantages, he explained, Herring would be delivered 'from being implicated in the disagreeable *embarras* of elections, and from the invidious suggestions of people who fancy themselves not sufficiently supported. The circumstances of *York* bring more trouble of this kind upon an archbishop than any other see in England.'[2] Herring finally gave in.

On 5 January Dr Jaques Sterne acted as proxy in the enthronement cere-

---

[1] Sterne, writing at a later time, said that all this happened in December, but it must have been November since it preceded the birth of his daughter.

[2] Philip C. Yorke, *Life and Correspondence of Philip Yorke, Earl of Hardwicke*, 3 vols, Cambridge and Chicago, 1913, II, 80–4.

monies for the new Archbishop of York, who was, like Herring, an old friend of the precentor's from their days at Jesus College. Although Matthew Hutton succeeded Herring first at Bangor, now at York, and eventually at Canterbury, he was a very different man, a hard-line legalist in the church and an old-fashioned Walpolian in matters of state. He still considered Catholics and Jacobites the greatest threat to the nation, and political bribery its strongest cement. He was himself unabashedly ambitious. According to Edmund Pyle, he left an estate of £50,000 when he died, 'which he had saved out of the Church in twelve years, and not one penny to any good use or public charity'.[1]

Thus the stage was set for a contest between the new dean and the new Archbishop of York. The dean's faction was close to the Pelham ministry, and they shared the spirit of conciliation adopted by the government during the late years of the War of the Austrian Succession. Such a man was the dean's chief ally, Dr William Herring, recently preferred as residentiary and chancellor of the diocese. He was a lawyer by profession, a proctor, who had first come to York as secretary to his cousin, the archbishop. Holding the degree of Doctor of Laws, he had quickly moved up to the post of notary public and joint-registrar of the archbishop's courts. Finally, his cousin made him vicar-general and chancellor – that is, chief legalist and judge in the spiritual courts, not only for the see, but for the Northern Province. He was a generation older than Fountayne, and he suffered from palsy, which caused him, as Sterne put it, to 'flap' pitifully. Sterne complimented him in *A Political Romance* as the 'grave, knowing old man'.[2]

[1] PYLE, 76, 307–8. Hutton's career: DNB; VENN; Canon Raine, 'Marske in Swaledale', YAJ, VI (1880–1), 172–261.

[2] His palsy is evident, not only from Sterne's image in LETTERS, 26, but also from his handwriting. Heretofore, Sterne scholars have been under the mistaken impression that Dr William Herring (1691–1762) was chancellor of the minster. He held the more powerful post of diocesan chancellor (also called vicar-general of spirituals) and official principal (judge) of the Consistory Court of York, from 2 April 1747. See at Borthwick Inst.: *Chancery Court Book, 1728–33*. Although chief judiciary of the archbishops, he was also canon residentiary at the minster from 25 July 1747. For details of his career:

CHAPTER DEEDS, 1727–47, fols. 551–3, 549, 562ᵛ; ACT BOOK, 1733–44, fol. 207; CHAPTER ACTS, 13 March 1743; 14 May 1746; 25 July 1747. VENN calls him a brother to Archbishop Thomas Herring, but CURTIS, 30, correctly says that he was a cousin. See Walter Rye, *Norfolk Families*, Norwich, 1913, p. 329, and *Thoroton Society Record Series*, XX (1961), p. 33. Obituaries in *Gentleman's Magazine*, 1762, p. 46, and *York Courant*, 12 January 1762. The DNB confuses him with his son, also named William (1718–74), rector of Bolton-Percy, prebendary of Apesthorpe at York Minster from 1744, dean of St Asaph from 1751, and precentor of Salisbury from 1756, but *not* chancellor of York diocese.

The new archbishop's chief men were Dr Jaques Sterne and Dr Francis Topham. Their regressive views on ecclesiastical law and their more rigid politics inevitably moved them toward opposition to the ministry, though how far they had gone in that direction in 1747 is not known. By 1753 their stand was clear to everyone. That year Fountayne wrote to Rockingham about the Whig dissidents of York, 'Here are yet workings amongst some who love to Fish in troubled Waters; & dayly meetings held at Sterne's, Topham's &c, but let them please themselves with their Imaginations wch will prove as vain as they are evil.'[1] Jaques, it seems, yearned to be accepted into the celebrated Leicester House faction led by Frederick, Prince of Wales.[2]

Jaques Sterne was the first to throw down the gauntlet. The arena he chose was the spiritual courts; the champion he challenged was William Herring. He opened an attack upon the convent of St Mary, which he had let alone since the rebellion. Now he ordered the nuns to quit their house, an order which was ignored since it had no legal basis. He then brought a charge against Mother Mary Hodshon and Sister Elizabeth Stanfield in the ecclesiastical courts: they were running a school even though they had not taken the sacrament in their parish church. For his action, Jaques was scolded in broadsides and in the pages of the *York Courant*,[3] but he had the support of Archbishop Hutton, who defended 'poor Dr Sterne, whom every impertinent Gossip, every Papist & Enemy to the Government in York are ready to load with Calumnys'.[4] The case was quickly appealed to the highest spiritual, the Chancery Court, over which Dr Herring presided. It met to consider the case twenty times between 5 May 1748 and 23 November 1749, though the principals themselves were seldom present: they were represented by their proctors.[5] On 27 September *The York Journal: or, Protestant Courant*, friendly to the precentor, perhaps even owned by him,

[1] Dated 12 December 1753, at Sheffield Central Public Library: F. 35. a. Newcastle had little respect for Archbishop Hutton: SYKES, 38–40.

[2] A bas-relief portrait of Princess Augusta, wife of Prince Frederick, is to be found on the mantel of the fireplace which Jaques added to the Great House.

[3] *The Case of the Mistresses or Governesses of a Boarding-School at York*, a broadside at Minster Library: B 6; letter signed 'Spectator' in *York Courant*, 17 January 1748/9, both probably written by Dr Francis Drake.

[4] HUTTON-FOUNTAYNE LETTERS, fol. 46.

[5] Borthwick Inst.: *Chancery Court Book, 1742–65*. A file at the Bar Convent identifies Mother Hodshon as the daughter of Ralph Hodshon of Lintz, Durham, mother superior from 1746 until her death in 1760. Elizabeth Stanfield was daughter and heiress of Francis Stanfield of Holderness.

announced gleefully that the ladies had been fined £4. 7s. 0d. 'In all Probability', the writer added, 'the Poor of the Parish are in a fair Way of being
well supported.' But the tables were turned the following March when the
judge ordered Dr Sterne to appear in person to answer certain allegations
about his mistreatment of the defendants. Finally, Herring decreed that
Mother Hodshon 'be admonished to repair and resort to her parish Church
for the future and to behave herself decently and orderly there'. She was
ordered to pay 'moderate Expenses for the Commonwealth', and the case
would seem to have been closed. But Jaques Sterne insisted that he be
reimbursed for *his* expenses, and upon that point the case dragged on until
it was inhibited by a decree from the High Court of Delegates in London.[1]

Jaques had only hurt himself by forcing the case to London and under
the nose of Newcastle. When Dr Thomas Hayter, Archdeacon of the West
Riding, died in October, Jaques wrote off to Newcastle asking to succeed
Hayter in his prebend at Westminster,[2] but he was passed over.

The king's peace was declared in York on 7 February 1748/9,[3] but the
smaller war within the church went on. The second stage followed the
death in November 1749 of Dr Samuel Baker, residentiary and friend of
Jaques Sterne's. Archbishop Hutton, anticipating a vacancy at the cathedral,
had decided that the new residentiary would be his relative and chaplain,
Dr Francis Wanley. His choice was seconded, perhaps even initiated, by
Dr Sterne, for Wanley was married to a niece of Jaques's late wife. Wanley
was currently the chancellor of the minster (a relatively minor post, not to
be confused with the diocesan chancellorship held by William Herring),
but he seldom showed his face in York. He was one of those fine gentlemen
of the church whose family connections brought so many offers of preferment
that his chief problem was deciding which to accept.[4] The dean's candidate

---

[1] *The York Journal; or, Protestant Courant*
of 3 October 1749 stated the outcome in
terms similar to those of the court record,
but the *York Courant* of the same date said,
'the famous Cause . . . between a certain
Pious Doctor and two Religious Ladies
. . . was not finally determin'd; but will
come under the Cognizance of a Superior
Court.'

[2] BM: Add. MSS 32719, fols. 251–2.

[3] *York Journal; or, Protestant Courant*, 14
February.

[4] HUTTON-FOUNTAYNE LETTERS,
45–6. A few months before, he had been

preferred to the prebend of Stillington, but
he had resigned it to accept that of
Laughton and the chancellorship of the
minster. When things did not work out
to his liking, he resigned both in August
1750, and took back Stillington. He kept
it only a few days, resigning to accept the
prebend of Weighton, which he could
hold simultaneously with the deanery of
the collegiate church of Ripon – a wealthy
preferment because of two sinecure
masterships of hospitals annexed to it.
See VENN; ACT BOOK, 1744–55, fols.
228, 256–7, 272–4, 279–82; J. T. Fowler,

was of a different cut. Fountayne wanted the popular William Berdmore, vicar of Bishopthorpe and two York churches, a man who satisfied York's notion of a working clergyman. Berdmore was also married to Chancellor Herring's daughter.[1]

The dean settled the matter in his own way – with a *coup*. It was rumoured that Dr Herring kept a man posted at Settrington, where old Dr Baker lay, to bring instant news of his death so that a chapter meeting could be called at once. The dean denied it. Nevertheless, Mr Berdmore 'protested residence' in a meeting the morning after Dr Baker died. The archbishop, who did not get around to making his nomination of Wanley until the following day, was told that the position had been filled. Furious, he wrote to Archbishop Herring at Canterbury, 'I have been treated as if I was unconcern'd in what happen'd in ye Church!' Fountayne only asserted blandly that Dr Wanley was 'a perfect Stranger to me', and, having heard that he would soon become Dean of Ripon, had no expectation he would want to reside at York. Not in the least satisfied with this answer, the archbishop accused the dean's side of being 'aggressors'. Nevertheless, Hutton did not want this relatively minor affair to get out of hand. He asked Dr Topham to act as his envoy in settling their differences. 'I would willingly live in Peace & Friendship with all the Members of the Church & you in particular', he wrote to Fountayne, though so far, he added, all of his proposals had been rejected as 'incompatible with your Ideas of Decanal Power'.[2] Fountayne agreed to treat with this ambassador, but distrusting Dr Topham he began to gather evidences for a showdown: he started a volume of letters, copies of the correspondence which had passed among the principals in the quarrel. In this task he was assisted by Laurence Sterne, who copied many of the letters.[3] Although Sterne played no public role in the *coup*, it looks as though he was advising the dean.

The next round was fired by the precentor, but the shot had been loaded by Dr Topham. They aimed at the powers of the dean. Because Dr Wanley was seldom in York, Fountayne had been appointing substitute preachers for

---

Memorials of the Church of SS Peter and Wilfred, Ripon (Surtees Soc. Pub., LXXVIII), 1884, pp. 273–4; and *Ripon Millenar: A Record of the Festival*, 1892, p. 114.
  [1] DEALTARY LETTERS, fol. 131^v; LETTERS, 25. For his career: HERRING RETURNS, I, 6–7, 45–6; ACT BOOK, 1744–55, fol. 177; MINSTER REGISTERS, YAJ, I, 305; III, 118.
  [2] HUTTON-FOUNTAYNE LETTERS, 5–8, 18–19, 32.
  [3] Approximately a quarter of the HUTTON-FOUNTAYNE LETTERS are in Sterne's hand, another quarter in the dean's, and the rest in various hands.

him whenever his turn to preach came around. But in January of 1750/1, to everyone's surprise, Dr Sterne raised an objection to this practice. He and Dr Topham had discovered some ancient cathedral statutes which gave the authority for appointing substitutes not to the dean, but to the chancellor – Dr Wanley himself. To drive the point home, the precentor, a few weeks later, arranged a substitute for one of his own turns, but pointedly informed, not the dean, but Dr Wanley.

The deans at York Minster had been in control of substitute preaching for a century. Fountayne was not about to stand aside while his powers were stripped away. Hearing that Wanley would again be absent when his turn came up, he took it upon himself to appoint the substitute, choosing more- over a young man who was particularly disagreeable to Jaques Sterne, the Reverend William Williamson. Fountayne had recently preferred Mr Williamson to a new living and had supported his election as a vicar choral, both over the protests of Dr Sterne. The morning of the day Williamson was to preach, the dean, to make all secure, gave orders to the verger to admit no one to the pulpit except Mr Williamson and to lock the pulpit door behind him. Of course the inevitable happened. Wanley showed up at the minster just before the service began, a sermon in his hand. In front of the entire congregation he shoved and rattled the locked door of the pulpit in which Mr Williamson was standing. After the service the clergy retired to the vestry where Wanley furiously berated the dean. Then he and Jaques Sterne marched out to seek their friend Topham, and the three men wrote a joint letter of protest to Archbishop Hutton, then in London. Soon there- after, Hutton approached Archbishop Herring in the House of Lords, 'his hands trembling in a violent rage', and stammered out, 'My Lord, I am made a Cypher of in the Church of York!'[1]

The archbishop probably meant well, but in this case he was duped by Francis Topham, supposed to be his peacemaker. Whatever ancient statutes were on the books, the dean had long been the officer who authorized substitutions. He was the only logical person for that task, the only one whose duties were confined to the minster. Half the sermons were delivered by substitutes. Wanley, who lived away, could not possibly keep track of them. Yet Topham, instead of explaining this to the archbishop, was poison- ing him against the dean and his friends, 'a Set of *Strange People*' with whom it would be difficult to live on good terms.[2]

[1] HUTTON-FOUNTAYNE LETTERS,   [2] ANSWER, 18–19.
43ᵛ.

Topham's responsibility for fomenting the quarrel is evident in the correspondence, and Sterne said as much in *A Political Romance*. The satire, not written until 1759, looks back nearly a decade to this episode. The general scheme of the *Romance* is to represent the high clergy of York as the petty officers of a rural parish. Archbishop Hutton is seen as one of the parsons, the dean is John the parish clerk, and Topham is Trim the sexton. (Curious that Sterne should re-use the name 'Trim' in *Tristram Shandy* for a very different sort of character.) The dean's powers are represented as the clerk's desk, which angers the parson after Trim points out that it is almost as high as the parson's desk (p. 16).

However insidious Topham's handling of the archbishop, Hutton declared himself convinced of the lawyer's arguments. Besides, he wrote, no one had the right to lock a prebendary out of the pulpit to preserve it for an outsider, most especially 'an inferior Sing-Song Officer of the Church, who has nothing to do with the Pulpit but by mere favor & Indulgence'.[1]

Tempers died down, and the opponents began a long discussion of two old statutes concerning residentiaries. At this point Laurence Sterne came forward and began to take part publicly: he attended seven of the eleven meetings between 1 February and 21 May 1750. He may have done so only to help a friend whose personal life had again taken a sad turn. Fountayne had remarried shortly after coming to York, and now this second wife was seriously ill during her first pregnancy. He was frequently absent, and Sterne may have been sitting in for him. (Mrs Fountayne did die in childbirth, as the *Courant* of 28 August reported, leaving behind an infant daughter 'happy in her Ignorance of the Want of such a Mother'.) The statutes were eventually annulled, but no solution was found to the problem of authority in appointing substitute preachers.[2] The dean simply continued his former practices.

Sterne was personally concerned with the question of substitutes since he himself preached so many of those sermons. He even took his uncle's turn during the month of May in both 1749 and 1750. But both engagements had been arranged through an agent, and Uncle Jaques might not have known who was representing him.[3]

Jaques was busy again with the convent. In the spring of 1750 he sent

---

[1] HUTTON-FOUNTAYNE LETTERS, 36.

[2] The dean also settled to his satisfaction another disagreement with the archbishop, not represented in the *Romance* – a contest over the rights to lease certain properties at Battersea.

[3] LETTERS, 25.

three emissaries to the nuns to order them to dismiss their priest, to desist from housing pensioners and to cut back on the number of pupils. Their patron, Viscount Fairfax, of Gilling Castle, advised them to abandon the house temporarily, but the courageous ladies refused. They did hasten to pay the fine levied the year before,[1] but that was not enough to placate Jaques. The precentor was then in London, where he opened a cause against the sisters in the High Court of Delegates. The delegates finally decided to order Dr Herring to reopen Jaques's cause in the York court. Herring complied, but not until 18 April of the following year. He again admonished the women to attend their parish church and presented them with another bill of costs.[2]

But Jaques had begun to despair of pleasing Newcastle and winning a rich sinecure. He decided to accept a lesser preferment, the best that Hutton could offer. On 13 April 1750, when he was still in London, he resigned the archdeaconry of Cleveland and was inducted by proxy into the archdeaconry of the East Riding. 'No one, I am persuaded,' he told the clergy of the East Riding at the first visitation, 'will suspect that a Difference in the Income was any Motive with me to the Exchange.' The only reason, he explained, was the pleasure of working among his old neighbours of the East Riding where his own parishes lay.[3] Hutton was able to do much better by Dr Topham. In August 1751 he preferred the lawyer to the richest post in the spiritual courts, the commissaryship of the Exchequer and Prerogative Court of York. Jaques Sterne probably had no hopes for this position, which by tradition was given only to laymen. He and Topham continued good friends.

Sterne attended the chapter meeting of 8 April when the decision was taken to induct his uncle into the new archdeaconry. That afternoon he preached at the minster. His sermon was 'Penances', and on the manuscript he wrote, 'Present, Dr. Herring, Dr. Wanley, and Dr. Berdmore'. As he looked down at Wanley, the irony of what he was saying must have struck him: 'God's commandments are not grievous . . . he has proposed peace and plenty, joy and victory, as the encouragement and portion of his servants' (II, 256). The temporal rewards to God's servants were destined for others that spring. Wanley had resigned the vicarage of Aldborough in favour of

[1] Henry James Coleridge, *St Mary's Convent, Micklegate Bar, York*, 1887, pp. 167–8, reports that they paid a fine of £32. 23s. 6d. on 10 May.
[2] According to Coleridge, they paid another fine of £15. 10s. 0d. See also LETTERS, 427–8, and *Chancery Court Book*.
[3] *A Charge Delivered to the Clergy of the Archdeaconry . . . 1751*, York, 1752.

his brother-in-law so that he could accept the richer rectory of Stokesley. The deal had been made with the indulgence of Uncle Jaques, who was the patron of Aldborough. Jaques was happy to go along because this brother-in-law of Wanley's, the Reverend Henry Goodricke, was Jaques's nephew by marriage.[1] Sterne probably wished Mr Goodricke well, but his uncle's passing him by when he was eligible for a third living must have galled him, especially since this uncle had goaded his mother into greater demands for money.

On the heels of disappointment came a flattering compliment. Sterne was invited to preach the annual assize sermon at the minster. On Sunday, 29 July 1750 he preached the sermon which he came to regard as his favourite, *The Abuses of Conscience*. Voltaire much admired this sermon, remarking in his article on conscience in the *Dictionnaire philosophique* that it was 'the best thing perhaps that was ever said' upon the important subject of a deceitful conscience. Sterne gave the sermon a handicap when he introduced it into *Tristram Shandy*, where it pales in the light of the brilliant comedy. It is the finest fruit of his experience as preacher and moral theorist, embodying the major concepts of his ethical thought,[2] but adapting them cleverly to the occasion. The sermon of a clergyman who is also a justice of the peace, it is written for an assembly of judges, yet it comments upon the inadequacy of human laws and the obligations to obey the higher, unwritten laws of reason and religion. Sterne must have been aware that he implied a criticism of his uncle's legalistic position. The Honourable Mr Baron Clive, the Honourable Mr Baron Smythe, Sir William Pennyman, Bart (the high sheriff) and the members of the Grand Jury were not displeased. They unanimously requested that the sermon be sent to the press – or so the dedication says. Caesar Ward printed it, and John Hildyard put it on sale.[3] True, the honour was somewhat dimmed by the advertisement in the *Courant* of 7 August, which gave notice that copies of Sterne's previous sermon, *The Case of Elijah*, were still available.

Not every sermon was so successful. Three months later, Sterne wrote

---

[1] LETTERS, 426; ACT BOOK, 1744–55, fol. 263; J. Sterne to Newcastle, 13 May 1750, and Andrew Wilkinson to Newcastle, 18 May 1750, at BM: Add. MSS 32720, fols. 319, 333. Curiously, Goodricke married the daughter of Philip Harland and retired to Sutton in his old age. The plaque to his memory is the only legible monument in Sutton church to one who was not born a Harland.

[2] Arthur H. Cash, 'The sermon in *Tristram Shandy*', *ELH*, XXXI (1964), 395–417.

[3] Sterne alluded to these events in TRISTRAM SHANDY, II, xvii, 142.

on the manuscript of 'Our Conversation in Heaven', 'Made for All Saints and preach'd on that Day 1750 for the Dean.——Present: one Bellows Blower, three Singing Men, one Vicar and one Residentiary.——Memorandum: Dined with Duke Humphrey.'[1]

The very day Sterne preached 'Our Conversation in Heaven', he discovered that his uncle was tightening the screws on him. After the service, he stepped over to Hildyard's shop to leave word that he would be glad to take a forthcoming turn of Archdeacon Blackburne's. Hildyard, whose trade depended heavily upon the clergy, often served as agent in locating substitute preachers. The bookseller beckoned him into an inner room, as Sterne later described it, 'with the aweful Solemnity of a Premier who held a Lettre de Cachêt'.

> Sir – My Friend the A. Deacon of Cleveland [Blackburne] not caring to preach his Turn, as I conjectured, Has left me to provide a Preacher, – But before I can take any Steps in it with Regard to You – I want first to know, Sir, upon what Footing You and Dr Sterne are? – upon what Footing! – Yes Sir, How your Quarel Stands? – Whats that to you? – How our Quarel stands! Whats that to You, you Puppy? But Sir, Mr Blackburn would know – What's that to Him? – But Sir, dont be angry, I only want to know of You, whether Dr Sterne will be displeased in Case You should preach – Go Look; Ive just now been preaching and You could not have fitter Opportunity to be satisfyed. – I hope, Mr Sterne, You are not Angry. Yes I am; But much more astonished at Your *Impudence*.   (p. 26)

Palsied Dr Herring's 'flapping' in at that moment interrupted the dialogue, and to the chancellor poor Hildyard turned for help. In a moment he returned and beseeched Sterne to let the matter pass and to please preach the turn. 'I was forced', wrote Sterne, 'to tell him in plain Prose tho' somewhat elevated – That I would not preach, & that he might get a Parson whe[rever he cou]ld find one.' But Dr Herring kept the conversation going, and Sterne finally decided that Hildyard's 'Impertinance' had issued 'not so much from his Heart, as from his Head, The Defects of which no One in Reason is Accountable for'. At length he agreed to take the turn, and they parted friends. Feeling that the situation boded troubles with his uncle, he sat down and wrote Blackburne a minute account of all that had passed.

[1] The manuscript, now lost, was seen by Isaac Reed, who made a note of Sterne's comment: CROSS, 242–3.

Francis Blackburne, the new Archdeacon of Cleveland, had indeed sent a 'Cautious Hint' to the bookseller that the precentor disapproved of Sterne's numerous appearances in the minster pulpit. A few weeks before, he had offered to mediate Sterne's disagreement with his uncle, but nothing had come of it. He hoped now to avoid a quarrel himself. But when he discovered how Hildyard had bungled the matter, he replied to Sterne's letter with warm expressions of confidence and begged him to continue as his substitute. Sterne, relieved and gratified, tried in turn to declare 'the sense I have of the Obligation wch so much Civility and Gentleness have laid me under' (p. 30). He would continue preaching for Blackburne, and would consider it a favour. 'I say a *Favor*, For, by the by, my Daughter will be Twenty Pounds a Better Fortune by the Favors I've rec^d of this kind from the Dean & Residentiaries this Year . . . You who are a Father will easily guess & as easily excuse my Motive' (p. 31).

Blackburne, an open man, wrote to Jaques Sterne, begging his pardon but telling him that he could not honour his request. Uncle Jaques responded icily:

Good Mr Archdeacon,
    I wil beg Leave to rely upon Your Pardon for taking the Liberty I do with you in relation to your Turns of preaching in the Minster. What occasions it is, Mr Hildyard's employing the last time the Only person unacceptable to me in the whole Church, an ungrateful & unworthy nephew of my Own, the Vicar of Sutton; and I should be much obligd to you, if you woud please either to appoint any person Yourself, or leave it to Your Register to appoint One when you are not here. If any of my turns woud Suit you better than Your Own, I woud change with you.[1]

Blackburne stood firm. Sterne preached the turn for him, which fell on 26 December.

For this defiance, probably, Dr Jaques Sterne revenged himself upon his nephew by a Machiavellian move which blackened Sterne's reputation for the rest of his life. Sterne's mother had recently come to York. Somehow, the uncle manipulated her into a York gaol. She may have been gaoled for debt. At the least, her brother-in-law put her into a situation which looked like that to the world.

Although details are not clear, the major events were these, or something

[1] LETTERS, 427.

like them: Agnes, nearing the age of sixty, had been living in Chester. Some time before, her daughter Catherine had married a publican and gone to London.[1] Agnes, alone and unhappy, perhaps hounded for debts, sold what she had and came to York. She saw her son, but alienated him anew.[2] She then found some sort of lodging and with Jaques Sterne's help began to send up a 'clamour' of complaint about Sterne. Things stood thus when Sterne came to a chapter meeting on 25 January 1750/1. Dean Fountayne then tried to intercede on Sterne's behalf, but Jaques put them off with the excuse that he was busy with his 'Nunnery cause'.[3] In March, Agnes's funds ran out or, possibly, her creditors began to press her. She threw herself upon the mercy of her brother-in-law. His mercy was to convince her she should lodge in a gaol.

'Shall I tell you what York scandal says?' wrote Sterne's acquaintance, the Reverend Mr Daniel Watson, vicar of Leake, in 1776: 'Sterne, when possessed of preferment of 300l. a year, would not pay 10l. to release his mother out of Ousebridge prison, when poverty was her only fault, and her character so good that two of her neighbours clubbed to set her at liberty, to gain a livelihood, as she had been accustomed to do, by taking in washing.'[4] This was the gossip after Sterne's death, a story known also to Watson's correspondent, another acquaintance of Sterne's – George Whately. 'Nothing is more true than the story about his mother', Whately replied. A decade later the same essential account was repeated by John Croft (who was abroad at the time of the event) and by Horace Walpole (who picked it up in London).[5] We have only one contemporary comment made without a judgement upon Sterne – the remark of the servant, Greenwood (who had left Sterne's service five years before): 'Richard', wrote his interviewer, '. . . thinks he has heard that his mother was in great distress at York, & that his master would have relieved her, but was prevented by his wife.' Probably Greenwood had heard that the quarrel was about Elizabeth's fortune, which it certainly was to some extent.

[1] CROFT. In 1767, Sterne spoke of his sister as 'still living, but most unhappily estranged from me by my uncle's wickedness, and her own folly': MEMOIRS.

[2] Writing in 1751, Sterne spoke of the 'Double Game' Agnes had played with her son and brother-in-law 'Since she came to York': LETTERS, 37.

[3] LETTERS, 34, 427. Coleridge saw a record of the nuns' last fine, paid on 6 March.

[4] *Monthly Repository of Theology and General Literature*, III (1808), 12.

[5] 'A dead ass', said Walpole, 'was more important to him than a living mother': *Walpoliana*, ed. John Pinkerton, 2 vols, 1799, I, 133–4.

On the basis of this slim evidence, one must agree with Professor Cross's hypothesis that Agnes was indeed lodged in some gaol through the machinations of her brother-in-law.[1] The gaol could hardly have been the Castle of York, as Philip Thickeness had it,[2] for no one but offenders against the Crown were kept there, and debtors never. Although Ousebridge Prison did house debtors, it was under the control of Jaques Sterne's old enemies, the corporation. But there was a prison very much under the precentor's control, that which served the Liberty of St Peter. It occupied the two lower floors of the Hall of Pleas, just inside Peter Gate, the west gate to the Minster Yard. The sessions before the justices of the Liberty were held on the upper floor. The keeper of the prison, who lived in an attached house, was, of course, the servant of these justices. Although Sterne himself was one of their number, his uncle was far more active and influential in that capacity. We can hardly doubt that Agnes Sterne was put up in Peter Prison, not in the barred cells of the lowest floors, but in one of the unlocked rooms on the middle floor where derelicts and minor offenders were housed.[3]

Agnes, poor woman, having lived so much of her life in poverty, probably resigned herself to an arrangement she thought was inevitable. Jaques would have had to do no more: the story would have spread like wildfire. No doubt Agnes was naïve and foolish, but she had a right to concerned advice from a brother-in-law: Jaques did not help her to get out of prison, but to get in. Sterne had a right to fair treatment from his uncle, but the precentor had not the decency to inform him what had happened. He was at Sutton when he heard about it in April. He wrote to his uncle immediately.[4] He had resolved to remain silent about his mother, despite the gossip he knew was circulating,

> But being told of late by some of My Friends, That this Clamour has been kept up against me, & by as Singular a Stroke of Ill-Design as could be levell'd against a Defenceless Man Who Lives retired in the

[1] CROSS, 100, 109–10.

[2] 'During the time Mr. S[tern]e was wallowing in the luxuries of life, and expences of THE TOWN, His mother, was a prisoner, for a small debt in the Castle of York!': *Sketches and Characters of the Most Eminent and Most Singular Persons Now Living*, 2 vols, Bristol, 1770, I, 217–19.

[3] HARGROVE, II, 192–7, 130–1. The order of the justices of St Peter issued by Fountayne, Sterne and Cowper, cited above, was dated from the Hall of Pleas.

[4] This letter, dated 5 April 1751, is our major evidence of what happened. The holograph is lost; the transcript made by Diana Bosville of Gunthwaite, Yorkshire, from which Curtis took his text, is now at the Beinecke Library, Yale.

Country & has few Opportunities of Disabusing the World, That my Mother has moreover been fix'd in that Very place where a hard report might do me (as a Clergyman) the most real Disservice, – I was roused by the advice of my Friends to think of some way of defending myself.

(p. 33)

No doubt he copied the letter and showed it to his friends.

Sterne, one surmises, soon found another lodging for his mother. Agnes did settle in York and, so far as is known, she did not become an object of charity.[1] She was eventually reconciled to her son, though possibly not for several more years. Her financial plight had certainly caught Sterne unprepared – he told his uncle that it might hurt him to lay open 'the Nakedness of my Circumstances'. He had been kept poor by debts he explained – lamely – incurred through his schooling, the university and the fees he paid when coming into his preferments. One suspects that the debts were connected with his farming venture: during the previous four years he and Elizabeth had been heavily taxed by the farms and the cost of getting them under way. Only two years later they were forced to give a second mortgage on Tindal Farm as security for a loan from John Fountayne and Stephen Croft.[2] He may have feared to reveal the truth to his uncle, recalling the tricks played on debtors during the 1741/2 election campaign. He was frank, of course, when he spoke of his 'want of good Health for many Years' and 'the Want of all that good Management in beginning the World, with wch I hope to end it'. The situation would have worried a healthy man. 'Was I, Sir, to Dye this Night I have not more than the very Income of 20 p^{ds} a Year (which my Mother enjoys [from her pension]) to divide equally betwixt my Wife, a helpless Child, & perhaps a third unhappy Sharer, that Might come into the World some Months after its Fathers Death, to claim its Part.' He did not mean that his current income was only £20. It was more like £200. He meant that after his death, his estate (exclusive of his wife's small fortune) would return an income of only £20. The estimate was probably accurate in 1751. He did not say that he would never help his mother, but he insisted that his first obligation was to his wife and child. 'I *think* I *have no Right* to apply one Shilling of My income to any Other Purpose but that of laying by a Provision for my Wife & Child; and That

---

[1] Various churchwardens' account books for Belfrey parish which record the money given to the poor, now at the Minster Library, make no mention of Agnes.

[2] North Riding Deeds, X/45–6/67, dated 5–6 April 1753.

it will be time enough (if then) to add somewhat to my Mother's Pension of 20 p^ds a Year.' He refused once more to entail his wife's fortune to his mother:

> . . . she, Whose Bread I am thus defending, was the Person, who brought it into the Family, & Whose Birth & Education would ill enable her to Strugle in the World Without it . . . the Other Person, who now claims it from her, & has raised us so much Sorrow upon that score, – brought not one Sixpense into the Family – & tho' it would give me Pain enough to report it upon any Other Occasion . . . She was the Daughter of no Other than a poor Suttler who followed the Camp in Flanders – was neither born nor bred to the Expectation of a 4th part, of What the Goverment allowes her, & therefore has Reason to be contented with Such a Provision tho double the Summ would be nakedness to my Wife.¹   (pp. 40–1)

There is one very strong evidence that Sterne exaggerated little in this letter of self-vindication – the support given him by friends. John Fountayne, no doubt, was as ambitious as the next dean. He could not have afforded to stand by a man with a reputation like Sterne's unless his position were defensible. Three months later, on 12 July 1751, he preferred Sterne to the commissaryship of the Peculiar Court of the Dean (Pickering and Pockling-ton). Probably Sterne was happy to accept it, not for the income, which was small, but for its symbolic value. Fountayne, who had succeeded in keeping his right to appoint substitute preachers, continued to engage Sterne in that capacity. Sterne, in his turn, stood by his friend, writing a *clerum* for him to deliver at Cambridge so that he could obtain his doctor's degree, and supporting him in the final resolution of the old problem of substitutions.

At this juncture, Uncle Jaques suddenly did an about-face with the nunnery. In London there had been a hearing on the case in Doctors Commons, and Jaques had been publicly teased by Dr George Lee, a celebrated lawyer and judge of the Prerogative Court of Canterbury. He was sorry, said Dr Lee in court, that the York clergy should have recourse to 'such rough methods of making Converts of the Ladies . . . the Laws for establishing the Reformation were now grown obsolete & out of date, & the present age too polite & refind to mind or submit to such old unfashionable

---

¹ CURTIS, 5–6, upon information sup- plied by Thomas Sadlier, Ulster King of Arms, concluded that Sterne slurred his mother's birth in this passage. In STERNE'S MOTHER, I have argued that he did not.

proceedings'.¹ The criticism must have had a special cutting edge, coming from Dr Lee, who was an active member of the Leicester House faction to which Jaques aspired.² The precentor defended himself to Archdeacon Blackburne, but one supposes he saw the writing on the wall. He was getting old and his health was beginning to fail.³ It might be wise to court the ministry again. Whatever his reasons, Jaques unexpectedly embraced the Herring-Hardwicke philosophy of tolerance and conciliation. He let it be known that he would like to talk to the nuns. A few weeks later, Mother Hodshon and Sister Stanfield waited upon him and found themselves received 'graciously'. 'Without the shadow of any compromise of principle on their part', says the convent historian, Dr Sterne promised to be their friend and to forget the past. The ladies returned to the convent, and 'the Community at once repaired to the Chapel to recite the *Te Deum*'.⁴ Jaques proved as good as his word. Five years later when Sister Stanfield was drawn into a tithe dispute in connection with her family estate, Jaques went to considerable trouble to help her out, even wielding his influence in the chapter to buy off the young clergyman who had challenged her tithe payments.⁵

But he was too late to win many friends in Yorkshire, where he now had the general reputation of a 'vicious man' who lived openly with his house-keeper. The Reverend Richard Warneford, one of the vicars choral, is remembered for his temerity in twitting the precentor on that score. Asked by Dr Sterne to explain his absence from the service, Warneford replied, 'Why, Mr. Precentor, I went to Acomb where my wife was very ill, my *own* wife, Mr. Precentor.'⁶

In 1752 Jaques politely begged of Newcastle a stall at Canterbury, but

¹ Jaques Sterne to Francis Blackburne, 6 December 1750, in LETTERS, 427.
² Introduction to *Political Journals* of George Bubb-Dodington, ed. John Carswell and Lewis Arnold Dralle, Oxford, 1965, p. xx; Basil Williams, *Life of William Pitt*, 2 vols, 1914, II, 59.
³ The dean and chapter gave him leave to spend the winter of 1752–3 at Bath.
⁴ Coleridge, p. 167. The account is verified by court records in so far as they show no further action against the nuns after the spring of 1751.
⁵ The tithes were claimed by the Reverend Matthew Topham (no known

relation to the lawyer) on the estate inherited by Sister Stanfield. Jaques induced him to drop the charges by obtaining for him a 'small thing' in the gift of the dean and chapter – the curacy of Mappleton: letters of J. Sterne to Sister Stanfield and Mother Hodshon, 13 November to 21 [?December] 1755, in LETTERS, 431–2, and Bar Convent muniments, 3 B/5–9.
⁶ William Gray, owner of the Great House from 1788, to Canon Dixon, 14 November 1840, quoted by Mrs Edwin Gray in *Papers and Diaries of a York Family*, 1927, pp. 6–7.

again he was passed over.[1] He scaled down the request: a prebend at Durham would suit very well, 'but I submit it intirely to Your Grace's Judgment & Pleasure, only begging Leave to hope that as I have spent now upwards of Thirty five Years in a faithful Service of the Crown, at an Expence that I believe No Clergyman else has done, that I shall . . . receive a Mark of the King's Favour'.[2] Upon the duke's asking about the value of his preferments, Jaques sent a list – a prebend at Southwell with 'a Corpse belonging to it . . . of about 200£ a year', his livings at Rise and Hornsea-cum-Riston, and 'nothing else but the Arch-Deaconry . . . and a Residen-tiaryship & Precentorship of York'.[3] His annual income from these benefices amounted to about £900.

At last, in 1755, Jaques got the stall at Durham. It added to his income £550, in exchange for which he resigned the archdeaconry of the East Riding, worth £60. Discovering that the income of the Durham stall during the period it had been vacant had been divided among the residentiaries, he at once petitioned the Bishop of Durham to decide between their and his own claims. When the bishop, understandably, declined to interfere, Jaques, with the help of Dr Topham, commenced a suit, not for the sake of the money, as he protested, but for the sake of the church. The ancient prece-dents for episcopal authority must be upheld.[4] Yet he maintained a suave ex-terior at Durham, as his fellow prebendary, William Warburton, reported after they first met – 'Dr. Stearne, a divine . . . what the French call a *bon vivan*'.[5]

By the time he got the preferment, Jaques was frequently confined to bed with the gout.[6] By March 1758 he had retired to his rectory at Rise. 'Preaching . . . in our large Church at York made the old Complaint in my Lungs return . . . I find the Duty now too hard for me.'[7] He had his mistress to take care of him and was ready for a rest. His revenge upon his nephew had been sweet enough to satisfy. Never again – at least during his lifetime – did Uncle Jaques give Laurence any trouble.

[1] Herring to Newcastle, 22 April 1752, BM: Add. MSS 32726, fol. 470. The *Victoria County History . . . York*, III, 71, mistakenly says that Herring suggested the name of Laurence Sterne for the Canterbury prebend.

[2] Dated 19 September 1752: LETTERS, 428.

[3] Dated 24 November 1752: LETTERS, 429.

[4] Papers relating to this petition and suit, including eight letters by Jaques Sterne and one by Francis Topham, were discovered by Kenneth Monkman at the Bowes Museum, Durham.

[5] CURTIS, 428–9.

[6] J. Sterne to Newcastle, 21 May 1755: LETTERS, 431.

[7] J. Sterne to the Bishop of Durham, 5 March 1758, among the papers at the Bowes Museum.

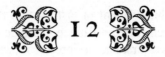

12

Commissary of the Peculiar Courts
1750–1756

To qualify as a commissary, or commissioned judge in the spiritual courts, according to Canon Law 127, the candidate should be 'well affected and zealously bent to *religion*', a man 'touching whose life and *manners* no evil example is had'.[1] Sterne would have qualified for the first part, but hardly the second. His ministry at Sutton and Stillington and his sermons at York were appreciated; but those furtive meetings with women of the town must have been known. However, the York clergy were complacent about sins of the flesh among their own members. They had never challenged Dr Jaques Sterne. No objections were raised when Lord Fauconberg preferred Sterne as commissary of the Peculiar Court of Alne and Tollerton in 1750, or when the next year John Fountayne made him commissary to the dean in charge of the large Peculiar Court of Pickering and Pocklington.

The Alne and Tollerton appointment caused not a ripple in York and raised the envy of no one – not even Dr Topham. It was a small neighbourhood affair, close to Sutton, no different from the Peculiar Courts of North Newbald and Stillington except that it covered three parishes – Alne and Tollerton (combined), Wigginton, and Skelton (the village north of York, not Hall-Stevenson's seat). Originally the court had been associated with the prebend of the minster treasurer, but that office had been abolished by Henry VIII, who granted the estate and rights to his chaplain, Anthony Belasyse. Subsequently, they passed down in the Belasyse family to Lord

[1] BURN, I, 419. The spiritual courts, including the peculiar courts, are dis-   cussed above in Chapter 6.

Fauconberg, who by this accident of history was the hereditary judge[1] – even though he had been reared a Roman Catholic.[2] But he had long conformed and, like his ancestors, had no interest in actually presiding.

It was a little unusual that Lord Fauconberg appointed a clergyman to a post usually held by lawyers. Perhaps he was trying to extend his influence over the parish priests of the neighbourhood. The enclosures were in the offing, and it was almost impossible to induce Parliament to pass an enclosure act which was opposed by local clergy. Sterne too may have been thinking of what he might gain that way. There were precious few other profits from this insignificant preferment. His fees came to £1 or £2 a year.[3]

Sterne was sworn in as Lord Fauconberg's commissary on 29 December 1750,[4] during the lull between the settlement of the Hutton-Fountayne dispute and the gaoling of Agnes Sterne. He presided for the first time on 12 June 1751, in the beautiful little Norman church at Alne, where the visitation was always convened. One wonders if he wore the costume of an ecclesiastical dignitary sometimes mentioned in the newspapers.[5] Did the sight of Lorry Sterne in judicial robes move his neighbours to laughter?

Pickering and Pocklington was a different sort of appointment and a more impressive court. It was the prebendal jurisdiction of the dean – more properly called the 'Deanery Court' – the second largest peculiar at York, embracing nineteen parishes and chapelries.[6] The visitation was always divided into two sessions meeting on successive days in the towns of

[1] In his oath of office, Sterne promised 'to act do and dispatch all & Singular such Acts and things which . . . the Right Honorable Thomas Lord Viscount Fauconberg Baron . . . could by law act do and dispose like if [*sic*] he was personally present': *Alne and Tollerton Subscription Book*. On a later occasion, Fauconberg sharply rebuked the dean and chapter for illegally granting a marriage licence 'into my said Peculiar': letter dated 15 December 1779, at Minster Library: BB 25. The records of the court at the Borthwick Inst. are remarkably complete, including the *Subscription Book*, an *Exhibition Book*, a *Court Book* and numerous loose papers: R. VI. C.

[2] Although Fauconberg conformed, he remained close to the Catholic leaders of the North Riding. During the rebellion he offered to stand surety for the loyalty of his neighbour, Lord Fairfax of Gilling Castle: Herring to Hardwicke, 15 September 1745, in R. Garnett, 'Correspondence of Archbishop Herring and Lord Hardwicke during the rebellion of 1745', *English Historical Review*, XIX (1904), 528–50, 719–42.

[3] See the record of fees from 1765 made by the registrar, Richard Mackley, among the court papers at the Borthwick Inst.

[4] *Subscription Book.*

[5] *York Gazetteer*, 1 June 1743, quoted in WINGED SKULL, 285.

[6] A good set of records survives for the Deanery Court. At the Borthwick Inst. is the *Court Book*: R. As. 87; at the Minster Library, the *Exhibition Book*: S 3 [5]. d; and loose papers: C 3 a.

Pickering and Pocklington. Sterne, in the allegory of *A Political Romance*, represented it as a pair of worn plush breeches – one leg, we suppose, for Pickering, the other for Pocklington.

On 12 July 1751, Sterne was sworn in as the dean's 'Substitute or Surrogate', a temporary title. On the process published in advance of the visitation for 15–16 August, he was styled in the regular manner, 'Commissary or Official'. Since he never registered a patent for his new office, one presumes he took out a less secure but inexpensive unregistered patent, which cost him 10*s*. instead of £10.[1]

Fountayne had good practical reasons for choosing Sterne. He trusted him. They had sat together as justices for the Liberty, where Sterne had shown a zest and talent for judicial work. The new office would burnish his friend's image, which had become rather tarnished, in part through Sterne's support of the dean.

It has been suggested that Fountayne was repaying Sterne for ghost-writing a Latin sermon.[2] True, the dean needed the sermon to take his doctor's degree *'per saltum'* – a device whereby wealthy clergy could bypass most of the requirements for an earned degree. He had to preach a Latin *'clerum'* at Great St Mary's. In fact, he was at Cambridge when the Pickering and Pocklington commissaryship was voided by the death of old Dr Ward.[3] But Sterne himself did not consider that he had been repaid for the sermon, which he had composed entirely, not just translated. In the memorandum he left Elizabeth before going abroad, he spoke of 'My *Conscio ad Clerum* in Latin wch I made for Fountayne, to preach before the University . . . He got Honour by it – What Got I?' (p. 147). Ought we to suppose that Sterne was forgetting the favour of Pickering and Pocklington? He might have been doing the favour for Fountayne. The dean needed someone for the post who was not afraid of Dr Francis Topham. The lawyer wanted it for himself, and he was certain to raise a row when he did not get it. True, the preferment raised Sterne in the esteem of the community, and he needed that. But it certainly did not make him rich. It paid about £4 or £5 a year.[4]

---

[1] The device is discussed by Francis Topham in REPLY, 22–3.

[2] CROSS, 99.

[3] *York Courant*, 2 July 1751; REPLY, 30–2. On the DD degree *per saltum*: WINSTANLEY, 71–4; Adam Wall, *Account of the Different Ceremonies . . . Cambridge*, Cambridge, 1798, p. 3.

[4] The notary, John Blanchard, attested that it was worth £6 or £7: REPLY, 54; but a note in Sterne's hand on the call sheet for Pickering (alone), in 1752, indicates that he had received only £2 for this first half of the visitation.

Fountayne had ample reason to distrust Topham, whom he accused of playing a 'double and insidious Part . . . in the Dispute between Archbishop *Hutton* and the Dean, relating to the Residentiaryship'.[1] But there were other, more idealistic reasons for wanting to check his rise. During the past three decades, Dr William Ward had won most of the commissaryships in the spirituals, and Topham had openly declared an ambition to succeed to all these preferments. In the dean's view, to allow Ward's empire to pass whole to Topham would be a backward step.

The lawyer represented an old-fashioned view of the church as a structure of laws with little or no relation to Christian morality as such. Indeed, in the established church every visible duty was defined by law; the bishops could command nothing of the clergy, the clergy nothing of the laity, except what was prescribed in law.[2] The strict construction of ecclesiastical law had its philosophical exponents, notably, in the eighteenth century, Bishop Edmund Gibson in the introduction to his celebrated *Codex juris ecclesiastici Anglicani: or, the Statutes, Constitutions, Canons, Rubricks and Articles of the Church of England* (2 volumes, 1713). In York, the adherents to this philosophy were Archbishop Hutton, Dr Jaques Sterne[3] and Dr Francis Topham.

In opposition to them stood Dean Fountayne, Sterne and most of their friends at the minster, who were late Latitudinarians. They believed that Natural Law superseded any man-made statute. Archdeacon Blackburne differed in that he was a fundamentalist, but in his opposition to legalism he was more extreme and more open. He had already begun a series of pamphlets protesting the imposition upon the clergy of the Thirty-Nine Articles of Religion. His *Confessional* (1766) would eventually spark off a national debate – the Feather's-Tavern Petition controversy of 1771.[4] The attitude of these men had been expressed philosophically by Benjamin Hoadly in the famous Bangorian controversy begun in 1717. Hoadly denied that Christ had delegated to the church any authority to make laws or to

[1] ANSWER, 8.
[2] BEST, 37–9; Ronald A. Marchant, *The Puritans and the Church Courts in the Diocese of York, 1560–1642, passim.*
[3] See Jaques Sterne's charge to the clergy of Cleveland archdeaconry in 1746, *The Danger Arising to our Civil and Religious Liberties . . .*, York, 1747.
[4] WINSTANLEY, 303–16; SYKES, 381–6. Not until 12 February 1969 did the Church Assembly, meeting in London,

vote to recommend doing away with the requirement that clergy subscribe to the Thirty-Nine Articles of Religion, though to date their recommendation has not passed into law. On Blackburne's career: DNB; VENN; CURTIS, 28, 30; YORK PRESS, 301–2; ANECDOTES, III, 10–23; ILLUSTRATIONS, III, 715–20. The archdeacon's portrait is at St Catharine's College, Cambridge.

judge its fellow men. The church, argued Hoadly, should teach an obligation to morality, but morality itself derived only from individual conscience.[1]

Seen in this light, Sterne and Topham as candidates for ecclesiastical jurisdiction were diametrically opposed. Topham's great skill lay in casuistry. He was a genius with the letter of the law, but cared nothing for its spirit. Time and again he tried to manipulate church decisions by digging out ancient statutes and holding them up as precedents. Sterne's position, as expressed in his sermons, was moderate. On the one hand, he castigated the Methodists for supplanting objective standards with subjective feelings. On the other, he was contemptuous of Catholics for handing over their conscience to be judged by rules set down by 'the Pope's commissary and the notaries of his ecclesiastic court' (I, 233). True moral judgement could be made only in the conscience, but made 'with a view to scripture, which is the rule in this case——and to reason, which is the applier of this rule in all cases' (I, 237). Sterne understood that one man is sometimes required to judge another, but he must do so in all humility, remembering that every individual has his own 'different views and different senses of things', that some may have 'complexional defects' which lead them to acts 'wrong in themselves' though they may not be so in the eyes of God (II, 361).[2]

Fountayne was also impressed by the lawyer William Stables. In his youth, Stables had gone to school to Mr Sharpe at Hipperholme, but ten years before Sterne.[3] He had long been Dr Ward's surrogate in the largest and most important of the peculiars, the Court of the Dean and Chapter. This jurisdiction, controlled by the chapter as a collective body, served a large number of parishes close to or within the walls of York but belonging to the Liberty of St Peter; and it accepted appeals from the smaller peculiars. Sterne represented it in *A Political Romance* as a pulpit cloth and velvet cushion, 'not in *John*'s Gift, but in the Church-Wardens''. They were given to 'William Doe' – Mr Stables. On 12 July, the same day that Sterne was sworn in for Pickering and Pocklington, Stables was elected by the chapter to the Dean and Chapter Court.

The remainder of Ward's preferments were presented by Archbishop

[1] SYKES, 290–6.
[2] The passage is paraphrased from William Wollaston's *Religion of Nature Delineated*: HAMMOND, 178–9. In the published sermons Sterne did not comment specifically upon the Anglican spiritual courts. His moral views about judging oneself and others are expressed in Sermons XIV, 'Self-Examination'; XXV, 'Humility'; XXVII, 'The Abuses of Conscience'; XXXVII, 'Penances'; and XXXVIII, 'On Enthusiasm'.
[3] VENN.

Hutton to Dr Topham.[1] Chief among them was the commissaryship of the Exchequer and Prerogative Court, a post which had once enriched the Sterne family when it was held by Archbishop Sterne's eldest son. The 'Keeper General', as the commissary was often called, did nothing but prove wills or, when there was no will, issue papers of administration. The law was so set up that wills and administrations for virtually all wealthy clergy, gentry and nobility had to be handled here.[2] The fees were high and numerous. Sterne and Fountayne were amused by the haste with which Dr Topham snatched the post when Hutton offered it,[3] but what cared Dr Topham? A year later he was able to purchase from Jaques Sterne that portion of the Great House which once had been the Treasurer's House, one of the finest residences in York. Sterne, who represented the Exchequer and Prerogative Court in *A Political Romance* as a great, warm watch-coat, called it 'the Most Comfortable Part of the Place'.

Nevertheless, Dr Topham was bitterly disappointed when he received neither the Court of the Dean and Chapter nor Pickering and Pocklington. It was a question of prestige, not money, as he readily admitted: 'Matters of Jurisdiction, let the Profits attending them be ever so small, are always considered in an honorary View.'[4] The commotion he raised in 1751 was hushed up within a few weeks, but the entire matter was brought into the open nearly a decade later when he and Fountayne publicly aired their quarrel in a series of pamphlets – an affair which led Sterne to write *A Political Romance*.

Topham's bitterness arose from a promise of support which John Fountayne had naïvely given him when Fountayne first came to York. The lawyer maintained in his later pamphlets that the dean had promised the commissaryship of the Dean and Chapter Court. Fountayne denied it, pointing out that he could hardly have promised a post which was not in his gift but that of the chapter as a body. Topham hysterically accused him of stacking the meeting, and asserted that he brought a patent made out for Stables which he kept hidden under his coat until he saw that he could swing the vote. But the meeting when Stables was elected was quite

[1] A partial record of Topham's preferments can be found in CHAPTER DEEDS, 1728–47, fol. 564ᵛ; 1747–68, fol. 16.

[2] It handled all cases involving *bona notabilia*, the goods of deceased persons who had owned property outside their own diocese, had died outside it, or (in the case of clergy) had more than one living.

[3] HUTTON-FOUNTAYNE LETTERS, 47ᵛ.

[4] REPLY, 25.

regular, attended by Fountayne, Dr William Herring and Mr William Berd-more – men who always voted together, to be sure; but they were the residentiaries regularly in charge of minster business during this period. Sterne was also at this meeting, having come to town to be sworn into his new commissaryship; but one cannot imagine his vote having any effect.

The dean's past promise to support Topham had also included Pickering and Pocklington Court – altogether a different matter since this gift was entirely in Fountayne's hands. Perhaps Fountayne would have kept the promise, reluctantly, had not chance events released him from it. The release was brought about by a pathetic old lawyer who had become desperate over his failing health and poverty – Dr Mark Braithwaite. Summoning an unwonted courage,[1] old 'Mark Slender', as Sterne named him in the *Romance*, went to the equally decrepit but wealthy Dr Ward and begged him to resign Pickering and Pocklington in his favour. His friend was happy to comply, provided, of course, that Braithwaite got the approval of the dean – and Dr Topham, who had the promise of the post. Fountayne gave his consent readily, but Topham was hesitant. At length, after much talk, Topham released Pickering and Pocklington to the old man. Then poor Braithwaite discovered that he could not afford the patent. So he and Dr Ward put their heads together again and came up with another plan. Instead of resigning the commissaryship, Dr Ward would allow Dr Braith-waite to act as his surrogate and to keep the entire profit. In April 1749 the old man took charge of the court, but he was able to continue for only three months before his health broke. Confined to bed, he struggled for life for another year, but died in August 1750.[2]

That left Dr Ward still the commissary; but when he died a year later, Topham expected to get the position. In his view, Dr Braithwaite had not taken out a patent; therefore, he had not accepted the preferment; therefore, the promise still belonged to Topham. That was not the way Dean Foun-tayne reasoned it: he had given the post to Dr Braithwaite; the lawyer had been free to take out a patent; his decision not to do so was immaterial. 'Surely', said the dean, 'giving the Place to Dr. *Topham*'s Friend, *at his Request*, was the same as if the Dean had given it to Dr. *Topham himself*; for all that was promised, or pretended to be so, was the Gift of *one Turn only*.'[3] Consequently Fountayne felt free to bestow the commissaryship where he

[1] His timid nature is revealed in a letter to Newcastle of 6 January 1745/6. PRO: SP 36/80.

[2] *York Courant*, 21 August 1750; *Court Book*.

[3] ANSWER, 7.

pleased. Moreover, in recent years Topham had lost the dean's trust. Once Fountayne had written to the lawyer, 'to acquaint him with the Suspicion of his betraying the Interest of the Deanery to the Archbishop'. Topham had replied that his circumstances were 'easy and affluent', and that he did not need the dean's support. 'When the Doctor had thus thrown the Dean's Favours at his Head, he saw no Reason to lay them again at his Feet.'[1]

A close reading of the two men's arguments in their later pamphlets leaves no doubt: the dean did not break faith with Topham. The lawyer had resigned his pretensions to Pickering and Pocklington, and Fountayne had kept the letter in which he did so.[2] His confused jumble of arguments fails to convince. The dean's arguments are more coherent, but then Laurence Sterne probably wrote many of them. Dr Topham called the dean's *Answer to a Letter* 'the Child and Offspring of many Parents'.

In the summer of 1751 Dr Topham seems to have known that he could not win a public debate about his claims to Pickering and Pocklington: he let that matter rest for several years. But he complained loudly to his friends about the Dean and Chapter Court. In the dean's (or Sterne's) words, he 'clapp'd a Promise upon the Dean's Back about giving him the Patent of the COMMISSARYSHIP of the DEAN and CHAPTER, which Promise he never made'.[3] Fountayne finally put a stop to Topham's gossip: that autumn, after a public dinner for the judges of the quarter sessions, he challenged the lawyer. Flanked by his little army of Dr Herring, Mr Berdmore and Mr Sterne, he asked Dr Topham before the assembled company to do him justice. According to an affidavit later sworn by Fountayne's friends, Dr Topham at first maintained that he had never circulated a story about the dean's breaking a promise to him; 'but being pressed by Mr. Sterne . . . with an undeniable Proof, That he, Dr. *Topham*, did propagate the said Story, Dr. *Topham*, did at last acknowledge it.'[4] He was under the impression, said Topham, that the dean had promised the Dean and Chapter commissaryship in a letter. Could he produce the letter? asked the dean.

---

[1] ANSWER, 8-9.
[2] Dated 21 May 1750: ANSWER, 5-6. Fountayne, however, was guilty of one small lie: he said that the Pickering and Pocklington post had remained open for two months during which time Topham never came forward to claim it: ANSWER, 7. He may have felt free to stretch the

point because Sterne did not sign the *Subscription Book* until 1 September; nevertheless, in the 'process' of 1 August, Sterne is styled 'Commissary . . . lawfully authorized'.
[3] ANSWER, 18.
[4] Testimony of Sterne, Berdmore and William Herring: ANSWER, 14-16.

No. Then Fountayne drew from his pocket two letters. One was from Topham, a request for Fountayne's support. The other was Fountayne's reply, 'in which the Dean took no Notice of the Request at all in Dr. Topham's Letter'.[1] The lawyer had the wisdom to see that he was beaten. He retired to his study and held his peace.

The dean and residentiaries could so easily have handled this matter without Sterne's assistance. One wonders why he should have joined in this public humiliation of Topham. In the allegory of *A Political Romance*, there is a mysterious allusion to some personal disservice which Topham had done Sterne. There we find Lorry Slim thanking Trim (Topham) and treating him to a supper 'for turning John Lund's Cows and Horses out of my Hard-Corn Close'. But then Lorry is told by two neighbours, who will take an oath on it, that Trim himself had set the gate open (p. 29). The timing of events suggests that Sterne was alluding to some sort of interference by Topham in the affairs of Sterne's mother. The two men had made peace, it seems, after the quarrel about residentiaries. In December, when Sterne was sworn in as commissary of Alne and Tollerton, he went through the regular practice of authorizing several men to act as his surrogates. He named Dr Topham among them. When he repeated the process for Pickering and Pocklington Court six months later, he skipped over the lawyer's name. The intervening months were those in which Agnes Sterne fell into difficulties and was 'lodged' in gaol. Could Dr Topham have advised his friend Jaques Sterne how to handle Agnes, only to pretend to Laurence that he was trying to help him? If that were the case, Sterne got his revenge in the *Romance* when he described Trim as 'a little, dirty, pimping, pettifogging, ambidextrous Fellow, – who neither cared what he did or said of any, provided he could get a Penny by it' (p. 9).

Sterne now went to work as a commissary. He was reasonably well prepared, having received some instruction in law at Cambridge and having behind him the experience of presiding at North Newbald and occasionally at Stillington. Nevertheless, he felt some need of brushing up his knowledge: on 13 November he borrowed, from the library of the dean and chapter, Bishop Gibson's *Codex*.[2] He must have read other legal works and talked about law with his associates. One amusing result would be his use in *Tristram Shandy* of Henry Swinburne's *Treatise of Testaments and Last Wills*, wherein occurs the curious argument, debated hilariously in the scene of

---

[1] A portion of Topham's letter and the dean's reply in full in ANSWER, 10.   [2] BARR.

the visitation dinner, that a mother is not of kin with her child.[1] He also could seek the expert advice of Jacob Costobadie, the registrar for the Dean and Chapter Court and most of the peculiars.[2] Mr Costobadie, too old to travel much, usually sent substitutes to the courts – John Blanchard, John Clough or Richard Mackley, all experienced proctors and notaries, in whose hands Sterne could leave the technical details. Sterne soon authorized Samuel Harding, vicar of Pickering, to prove wills for the Deanery Court, thereby freeing himself of the most time-consuming work.[3]

There was also the helpful division of the spirituals into a 'visitation', where only summary trials were conducted, and a 'court' for the formal, plenary trials. Sterne presided only at visitations. Unlike the smaller peculiars, such as North Newbald, the difficult or technical cases were not sent to Mr Stables's Dean and Chapter Court. Both Pickering and Pocklington, and Alne and Tollerton held a special 'court' separately. These sessions no longer convened behind the wooden partitions erected for that purpose in the nave of the minster, one of which, near the chapter house door, 'served often in the Evening for very indecent purposes'.[4] During this period they met in the chambers of lawyers. Invariably Sterne delegated his authority in the 'court' to one or another of the trained lawyers among his surrogates. Only once did he preside at these special, formal trials, probably because the lawyer he had appointed could not attend.[5]

In short, the institution of the spiritual courts had evolved in such a way as to require of the commissary no special training. The cases which Sterne adjudicated may have been humanly complex, but they were legally simple.

Sterne's experience as the dean's commissary must have been pleasantly exciting. Pocklington church, built in the early perpendicular style, is locally called 'the Cathedral of the Wolds'. The Pickering meeting was held in a large, beautiful Norman church. Both towns were cultural and economic centres for areas somewhat remote from York. The arrival of the commis-

[1] TRISTRAM SHANDY, IV, xxix, 328. Sir Robert Brook, whom Sterne also cites, he found in Swinburne.

[2] For a sketch of his life: *The Parish Register of Wensley*, ed. Hartley Thwaite (Yorkshire Archaeological Soc. Parish Register Sec., CXXX), 1967, pp. 221–2.

[3] The bond of Samuel Harding, dated 1752, is among the court papers.

[4] Thomas Beckwith, in his MS *History of York*, at the Minster Library, tells about their being pulled down in 1776, adding, 'It were greatly to be wished that the Inquisition were abolished.'

[5] In the court of Pickering and Pocklington on 14 December 1753, Sterne heard the continuation of a case involving creditors' claims upon the estate of Mary Walker. By a curious coincidence, that day he proved the will of George Atkinson, which is now at the North Riding Record Office: ZE*. 17.

sary was always announced in advance by a 'Process' written in the elegant scribal hand of Jacob Costobadie, in which Sterne was described as 'Clerk Master of Arts Commissary or Official of the Peculiar and Spiritual Jurisdiction of the Deanery of the Cathedral and Metropolitical Church of Saint Peter of York lawfully authorized'. He sent to 'all and singular Clerks and Literate Persons whomsoever and wheresoever within the said Jurisdiction Greetings' and, referring to himself in the first person plural, continued:

> We charge you and every of you that you or one of you peremptorily cite all and singular Rectors Vicars Curates and Wardens of the Parishes and Chapelrys . . . that they and every of them appear before Us . . . humbly to undergo such our Visitation in this behalf to be exercised and celebrated and also to hear do and receive what shall be then and there expounded and administered to them and further to do and receive what the Nature and Quality of our said Visitation require of them . . .

No doubt there was ceremony appropriate to the pomp of this epistle, though the details are lost. Sterne may have opened each visitation with a sermon. In the evening he would have been honoured at the traditional visitation dinner, where the visitor was expected to make informal inquiries into the state of the parishes and to give his unofficial advice and guidance. Was he ever served hot roasted chestnuts?

There is a good record of the trials held before Commissary Mr Laurence Sterne, but they differ little from those at the spiritual courts of Cleveland, North Newbald or Stillington. The citation at the bottom of the process for 1753 tells the essentials:

> Cite Robert Atkinson and his wife of Pocklington for
> the Crime of Antenuptial Fornication
> Cite Mary Barnard of the same place for the Crime of
> Fornication she having born a Bastard Child
> Cite Timothy Sowersby of Givendale for neglecting to
> make up his Church Wardens Accounts
> Cite Ann Haxby of Kilham for the Crime of Fornication
> with Thomas Creaser (since absconded) she
> having born a Bastard Child.

As judicial decisions, they were cut and dried, and Sterne hurried over their unpleasant aspects. Elizabeth Cook of Barnby Moor, presented at Pocklington in 1758 for the crime of fornication, appeared, confessed and did her penance by 4 o'clock of the day she was presented. Unfortunately the accused sometimes failed to defend themselves. The call, or roll, for the Pickering visitation of 1761 (the last time Sterne appeared there) tells us that three women cited for fornication

> were thrice publicly and openly called . . . and in no wise appearing or excusing their Contumacy, the said Commissary pronounced them and every of them to be Contumacious and in penalty of such their Contumacy he Decreed the Lay persons to be Excommunicated and did Excommunicate such Lay persons within the said Jurisdiction.

Sterne seems to have been gratified by the role of commissary. During the eight years between his appointments and the period when he turned writer, he never failed to appear either at the Alne and Tollerton or the Pickering and Pocklington visitations. Even after he became the celebrated author of *Tristram Shandy*, he continued to preside when he could. He was at Alne in 1761 and 1765, at Pickering (though not Pocklington) in 1761.[1]

The deference must have flattered his ego; the human drama must have fascinated him; and he may have taken pride in performing well a practical task. He had opportunities to redress the grievances of abused parishioners as well as to protect the rights of clergy and parish officers. The numerous trials for fornication were as pragmatic as anything else – a device, deeply ingrained in the folkways of rural England, for curtailing bastardy and checking poverty. Who knows? He may have shared Dr Samuel Johnson's reasons for thinking that public penance was justified when a woman was convicted of fornication: 'Consider', said Johnson, 'of what importance to society the chastity of women is. Upon that all the property in the world depends.'[2]

Sterne was never a harsh judge. This is the inference from his *Court Books* – the records of the plenary trials held in the 'court', as distinct from the 'visitation'. Virtually none of those cases involved moral matters. Rather, they hinged upon technical points of law – contested wills, problems of responsibility for church repair, questions of tithes or rates – cases which were deferred for plenary trial so that they could be settled by trained lawyers. There are only two possible exceptions, trials of women, both in

[1] There is no ready explanation for his missing the visitation of 1766. But in 1762–3 he was abroad; in 1764 the court was inhibited by a primary visitation; and in 1767 Sterne was seriously ill.

[2] Boswell's *Life of Johnson*, ed. George Birkbeck Hill, revised L. F. Powell, 6 vols, Oxford, 2nd ed., 1964, V, 208–9.

1753, upon charges not recorded – possibly fornication. The record is too sparse to tell the full story, but it *may* be that these two trials were deferred because the women protested against Sterne's ruling. So we can conclude this much: of the sixty or so people tried for sexual offences before Sterne, all, except possibly two, accepted his decision without contest. Obviously he was fair and lenient – the same Mr Sterne who had been kind to Jane Harbottle of Stillington. No doubt he had his weaknesses, but one of them was not the sin of pride. When he judged his fellow men, he did so to maintain the social order, knowing very well that he was not pronouncing upon sin: that judgement could be made only by God.

During the years between the Topham–Fountayne quarrel over the spiritual courts in 1751, and Sterne's allegory of it in the *Romance* (1759), he was involved in no church controversies. He occasionally attended chapter meetings, but not often. Once, over the opposition of the Honourable Mary, Dowager Marchioness of Nottingham, the dean and chapter sold off the 3,486 trees of Langwith Wood for a price of £150.[1] In *Tristram Shandy*, Walter and Toby Shandy once rode out 'to save if possible a beautiful wood, which the dean and chapter were hewing down to give to the poor' – to which sentence Sterne added a footnote: 'Mr. *Shandy* must mean the poor in spirit; inasmuch as they divided the money amongst themselves' (VIII, xxvi, 579–80).

Sterne's public life after 1751 was uneventful, though he must have attended that year the coming-of-age party for the Second Lord Rockingham, which was also a coming-to-politics party. On 13 May the youthful marquis entertained 1,845 people, setting up tables all over the great Wentworth House – for 383 in the Grand Hall, for 412 in 'Bedlam and Tower', etc. The servants prepared, among other things, four roasted oxen, fifteen sheep, nine calves, fifteen lambs, twelve hundred pigeons, and 'a horse load of crabs and lobsters'.[2]

Within that 'very small machine',[3] his own family, his daughter was fast becoming the 'child and darling of my heart'.[4] But there were sad times. Elizabeth was pregnant again in the spring of 1751. Probably this is the period of Sterne's pitiful letters to Theophilus Garencieres, the York

[1] CHAPTER ACTS, 1 March, 1 May 1752.
[2] 'An Account of the Preparation and Entertainment given by the Rt. Honourable Charles Marquess of Rockingham', MS at Minster Library: BB 53. Considering Sterne's past activities, it is unthinkable that Rockingham would have failed to invite him, though there is no specific evidence that he attended.
[3] LETTERS, 160; cf. TRISTRAM SHANDY, V, vi, 358.
[4] LETTERS, 307.

apothecary. He sends for medicines to help Elizabeth in her labour, 'wch is expected every Hour'. In another he writes, 'Mrs Sterne was last Night deliverd of a dead Child; She is very weak & I think wants some comforting Liquid or other' (pp. 44–6). Elizabeth was destined to bear no children alive after Lydia – not, at least, to our certain knowledge.

To add to her troubles, Elizabeth was lonely. Early in 1753 her sister became seriously ill. Likeable, scatterbrained Lydia Botham had long since fallen from the high estate in which she had begun her married life. The Reverend John Botham, luckless and imprudent, had spent their small fortune in high living, and they had been reduced to poverty.[1] Elizabeth Sterne first heard about the illness from her cousin, Elizabeth Montagu, who had remained a faithful friend and correspondent of Lydia Botham's. Elizabeth's reply reveals all too clearly her unhappy state of mind. She profusely thanks Mrs Montagu for her letter, 'which had I received in a more happy Hour, wou'd have made me almost Frantick with Joy; For being thus Cruelly Seperated from all my Friends, the l[e]ast mark of their kindness towards me, or Remembrance of me, gives me unspeakable Delight'. In one strange passage, Elizabeth assures her cousin,

> I spare no pains to improve every little Accident that – recalls you to my Remembrance . . . about three weeks ago, I took a long Ride Thro' very bad weather, & worse Roads, merely for the Satisfaction of enjoying a Conversation with a Gentleman who though unknown to You, had conceiv'd the – highest Opinion of you from the perusal of several of your Letters.

Her protest showing through this overwrought compliment bespeaks a growing neurosis.[2]

Lydia Botham died in March. Mrs Montagu made Lydia's eldest daughter her protégée and took charge of her education, but she did not come to see Elizabeth or maintain their correspondence.

Sterne during this period often must have felt discouraged and depressed – though no letters come down to attest his mood. It had been nine years since he got Stillington, but he had made no other advance in his career, except the commissaryships with their meagre income of £5 or £6. Next door at Wigginton he watched the progress of the Mosley family. True, his friend Richard Mosley was fifteen years his senior, but he had made an im-

---

[1] CLIMENSON, I, 55, 180–1, 230–1.   [2] LETTERS, 430–1.

pressive success of his life. He had two livings at York and extensive lands at Wigginton. One son was already in holy orders with one living at York and another at Skelton, adjacent to Wigginton. Yet another son was preparing to enter the priesthood.[1] Thomas, the elder brother, preferred to live at Wigginton, where he had grown up and where the family estates lay; so he was serving there as his father's curate. He had brought a bride to that village in 1752, Frances Pulleyn, daughter of the Whig politico and stepdaughter of Sterne's cousin, Mary. Since Frances was Pulleyn's only child, the extensive Pulleyn estates were destined to come into the Mosley family.[2] In the spring of 1754 Richard Mosley resigned Wigginton in his son's favour, and on 2 April Sterne inducted young Thomas into the living[3] – his third.

Sterne's own hopes for a third living had been dashed in the previous autumn. He had continued to assist Lord Fauconberg whenever he could, probably with an eye to the curacy of Coxwold, in Fauconberg's gift. The Reverend Henry Thompson of Coxwold was in poor health. How disappointing that Fauconberg should give the living to, of all people, Sterne's former curate, Richard Wilkinson. It speaks well for Wilkinson that during the period when he worked for Sterne at Sutton he was granted priest's orders, even though he had no university degree. But Sterne had little respect for him because he had neglected the parish registers.[4] Wilkinson had become the curate at Kilburn, the next village to Coxwold, and earned the gratitude of Lord Fauconberg by frequently preaching at Coxwold when Mr Thompson was ill. So Fauconberg gave him in 1744 'a small thing', the curacy of Birdforth Chapel, and now in 1753 the more lucrative curacy of Coxwold.[5] (Sterne eventually got the Coxwold living, but not until Wilkinson's death in 1760.)

Sterne would have attended Richard Mosley's funeral in June 1754.[6] He

[1] For the brothers' careers: VENN; Robert Forsyth Scott, *Admissions to . . . St. John . . . Cambridge*, III, 505; HERRING RETURNS, III, 39–40, 141–2, 210–11; ACT BOOK, 1744–45, fols. 61, 123; 1755–68, fols. 268, 374; *York Courant*, 26 May 1767.
[2] They were eventually inherited by the son of this couple, Thomas Pulleyn Mosley: MINSTER REGISTERS, YAJ, I, 308–9.
[3] *Alne and Tollerton Exhibition Book*.
[4] A note in Sterne's hand in the baptismal

register for 1741 reads, 'N. B. I fear the Register for this year is defective By the Negligence of the Gentleman who was Curate.'
[5] Fauconberg to Herring, 25 November 1744, at Borthwick Inst.: R. Bp. 5/236. Wilkinson's career: HERRING RETURNS, II, 122; ACT BOOK, 1710–62, fol. 98ᵛ; 1744–55, fols. 12, 382; Archbishop Hutton's *Court Book*, 1748–9, Borthwick Inst.: R. VI. B. 11, 13 June 1749.
[6] *York Courant*, 18 June 1754.

must have wondered, as he stood by the grave of his old friend, how he had accomplished so much in fifty-six years. He himself could hardly expect to live so long. Indeed he would not: he would die at fifty-four.

Is it going too far to suggest this picture of Sterne, who had a reputation for gaiety and high spirits, standing like Hamlet by the grave, meditating on life and death? Probably not. One of his miscellaneous pieces, though undated, reveals a melancholic Sterne – the 'Fragment inédit', addressed to an unidentified Mr Cook.[1] The speaker is a contemplative man walking among the plum trees of his garden, meditating upon the possibility of vast numbers of macrocosmic worlds among the stars overhead and myriads of imperceptible microcosms about him. 'We are situate', he says, 'on a kind of isthmus, wch separates two Infinitys.' He retires to bed and in his sleep dreams that he is an experimental philosopher. He makes a terrifying discovery that his world is being drawn toward some astronomical holocaust. Awakening in a fright, the dreamer rushes into the garden, where he realizes that the vast planet upon which he had lived in the dream now appears only as a small plum shaking in the wind. 'But thus it is: *Plums* fall, and *Planets* shall perish. . . . The time will come when ye powers of heaven shall be shaken, and ye stars shall fall like ye fruit of a tree, when it is shaken by a mighty wind.'

The 'Fragment inédit' follows a long tradition of speculation upon multiple worlds – Fontenelle's *Entretiens sur la pluralité des mondes*, Malebranche's *Recherche de la vérité*, Pascal's *Pensées* – but it is also a product of its own time, almost a compendium of eighteenth-century thought about the telescope and microscope. Sterne took his concept of relative duration from Addison's *Spectator*, No. 94, in which Addison expands Locke's definition of duration. But Sterne's vision goes further. Not only are there microcosms, macrocosms and relative time, but the 'thinking principle' can be shared by

---

[1] First published by Paul Stapfer in *Laurence Sterne – sa personne et ses ouvrages*, Paris, 1870. The manuscript was obtained for him, Stapfer explained, by the Reverend John Oates of Elizabeth College in the island of Guernsey. Mr Oates can be identified as John Oates, MA, graduate of Lincoln College, Oxford, Vice-Principal of Elizabeth College from 1860, Principal from 1868. The owner of the manuscript, an unidentified lady of York, allowed Mr Oates to take the manuscript to Stapfer, who copied and returned it. Meanwhile the lady had fallen ill and was unable to answer questions about it. The story would invite suspicion were it not that Mr Oates would necessarily have had to be privy to any deception. Stapfer may have withheld the lady's name upon her request. There remains a possibility that Stapfer made an honest error in assigning the piece to Sterne, but that cannot be tested without the manuscript. Until it is recovered, we must accept his judgement. Stapfer's point that the style is similar to Sterne's seems strained, but it is not very material since Sterne could write in such a variety of styles.

the smallest as well as the greatest beings.[1] With its suggestions of Brob-dingnag and Lilliput, the 'Fragment' may be taken as a neo-classical satire on human pride, but it lacks the bitterness of Swift. The lesson in humility is directed primarily at the speaker, who is left contemplating gloomily a world which seems unstable in its relativity.

Sterne's depressed state is also suggested by the stories of his unkempt appearance. One of these is an anecdote – containing no hint of a date. According to Dr James Atkinson, whose father had known Sterne in York, 'so slovenly was his dress, and strange his gait, the little boys used to flock around him, and walk by his side'.[2] It is doubtful that he dressed like this in his more sociable later years. James Boswell was amused by the stories he had heard of Sterne's eccentric dress, possibly from Sterne himself. In his poem of 1760 he tried to sketch Sterne's appearance, not the celebrated author in London, but Sterne in the country, where, of course, Boswell had never actually seen him.

> . . . with Ecclesiastic Gown
> Of Colour dubious, black or brown,
> And wig centauric, form'd with care
> From human and equestrian hair,
> Thro' shades of which appear'd the caul;
> Nay, some affirm his pate and all . . .

He also pictured the parson in his study:

> A threadbare Coat with sleeves full wide
> A formal nightgown's place supply'd.
> He wore, his new ones not t'abuse,
> A pair of ancient, downheel'd shoes;
> He roll'd his stockings 'bove his knees,
> And was as *dégagé*'s you please.[3]

Sterne's business affairs took a turn for the better with the Sutton En-closure Act of 1756. This enclosure of 3,000 acres was the largest in York-shire during the eighteenth century, though small compared to some which

[1] Stapfer's note, pp. l–lii; Melvyn New, 'Laurence Sterne and Henry Baker's *The Microscope Made Easy*', *Studies in English Literature*, X (1970), 591–604. See also, Jean-Claude Sallé, 'A source of Sterne's conception of time', *Review of English Studies*, New Series VI (1955), 180–2.

[2] Told by Thomas Frognall Dibdin in *Biographical, Antiquarian, and Picturesque Tour in the Northern Counties of England and Scotland*, 2 vols, 1838, I, 213–14.

[3] Quoted by Frederick A. Pottle, 'Bozzy and Yorick', *Blackwood's Magazine*, CCCXIII (1925), 297–313.

---

followed in the nineteenth.[1] Sterne received only a small portion; Sutton vicarage received another; and the bulk was divided between Fauconberg and Harland.

The enclosure movement was an answer, though an imperfect one, to the ancient problem of whether productive resources could best be managed in public or private hands. In theory, the common fields were granted to the gentry or nobility only when the yeomen, who had controlled them through their vestries, had depleted them of nutrients and left them useless. To restore such lands to production required a capital expenditure which the small farmers would not or could not provide. Hence the justice, it was argued, of granting the lands to men of wealth. No doubt the practice sometimes was abused. The powerful men who received these grants could easily silence most opposition. Often, especially in other parts of England, they converted the enclosed lands to sheep pasture, a practice which little benefited the community: sheep pasture required none of the labour which the farmers had to sell and produced none of the food they needed to buy. In Yorkshire, however, such abuses were rare, and most enclosed lands were made ready for food production. By 1788 an agricultural expert was estimating that food production in the county had tripled since the enclosures.[2] On the other hand, the enclosure movement increased the numbers of the rootless poor. It forced many of the smaller yeomen to sell their holdings, and it drove the peasants off the commons where they had built their humble dwellings, kept their kitchen gardens and gathered their fuel. Exactly what were the results of the enclosure at Sutton-on-the-Forest the record does not show, but if Fauconberg, Harland or Sterne abused their privileges, no objections were raised in the hearings. And the three seem to have kept their popularity in the village.

Sterne and Harland would have been busy in the autumn and winter of 1755 with numerous meetings about the enclosure. With Lord Fauconberg, they had to decide how the land was to be divided, Sterne representing both his own and the church's interests. They had to locate gentlemen from outside willing to be named commissioners and to win the co-operation of local people. They petitioned the bill to the House of Lords on 23 January 1756; it received royal assent on 9 March.[3] The commissioners appeared for hear-

[1] Gilbert Slater, *English Peasantry and the Enclosure of Common Fields*, 1907, Appendix B.
[2] [William] Marshall, *The Rural Economy of Yorkshire*, 1788, p. 291.
[3] *Journal of the House of Lords*, XXVIII, 461, 472–7; *Journal of the House of Commons*, XXVII, 500, 519. On the process of enclosure: Roland Edward Prothero, First Baron Ernle, *English Farming Past and Present*, 1927, pp. 248–51 and *passim*.

ings and, after listening to proposals and arguments, made the awards. A survey then had to be made, and the process dragged on. Sterne did not get legal possession of his portion until 7 December 1762, long after he had moved away from Sutton.

He was assigned two fields of 30 acres each, a small piece of 32 perches next to the churchyard, and a garden plot by the vicarage. If he began to fence and improve them before he actually owned them – a common practice – he probably put more money in than he took out. The greatest immediate advantage was the improvement in the living. The vicarage received three small plots, great tithes were simplified, small tithes were extinguished and replaced by a fixed emolument of £24. In lieu of tithes on their new lands, Harland and Lord Fauconberg were to pay a compensation of £76.[1] The Enclosure Act must have nearly doubled the value of the living.[2] Eventually, there would be even greater rewards in Lord Fauconberg's patronage. When Sterne received the Coxwold living in 1760, he commented to a friend, 'I hope I have been of some service to his Lordship, and he has sufficiently requited me' (p. 143).

By 1756, Sterne's professional and business affairs were on a sound footing. His mother, though still in York, was living quietly. Uncle Jaques was too old and ill to wield much power. With friends like Dean Fountayne and Lord Fauconberg, Sterne had good prospects of a third living. Although still in debt, he owned considerable property and his parishes were returning a good income. Had he waited patiently, he might have ended his life as a prosperous Yorkshire clergyman, perhaps as prosperous as Richard Mosley had been. But his life with Elizabeth was unhappy, and he had no son to inherit a fortune. Besides, he was restless by nature. 'To stand still, or get on but slowly,' says Tristram Shandy, 'is death and the devil' (VII, xiii, 493).

[1] North Riding Deeds, AL/91–142/33 and 'Certificate of the Apportionment of Annual Rents, No. 34'.

[2] BEST, 67, points out that clergy usually favoured enclosures because they improved the value of livings. Although Sterne signed the petition for the later enclosure at Stillington, he was not active in making the arrangements, which were completed while he was living at Coxwold. The Stillington enclosure of 1,400 acres had some local opposition, but not much. Most of the land went to Stephen Croft, though some to William Stainforth and some to the prebendaries of Stillington. The living was much improved: 18 acres were granted in exchange for small tithes. The grants were made final in February 1768, a few weeks before Sterne died: CHAPTER ACTS, 10 March 1766; North Riding Deeds, AH/167–214/38; *Private Acts of Parliament*, 6 Geo. III. C. 16; *Journal of the House of Lords*, XXXI, 289, 309, 315; *Journal of the House of Commons*, 3 March 1766.

A Political Romance
1757–1759

The Treaty of Aix-la-Chapelle in 1748 had not brought to a close the struggle for power between France and England, as everyone knew. *Bête comme la Paix* was the expression in Paris.[1] In 1751, Robert Clive captured the French fort at Arcot, in the Indian Carnatic. In 1754 George Washington clashed with French troops moving outward from Fort Duquesne. This long global struggle, which came to be called the Seven Years War, broke out in Europe in 1756 when Frederick II of Prussia, learning that a formidable alliance against him was being shaped by France, Austria and Russia, stole a march and captured Dresden. Britain hesitated – until she had lost Minorca. The Lord Mayor of York marched in procession on 21 May to read His Majesty's declaration of war from the steps of the Guildhall and then the south steps of the minster.[2]

Frederick's campaign went badly. Invasion panic swept England, and food prices soared. Newcastle, first minister since the death of Pelham, was no strategist and lacked popular support. The public called for William Pitt, who had faithfully represented the interests of the common man, and whose patriotism was unquestioned. By the summer of 1757 the two leaders had settled on a coalition cabinet, with Newcastle in charge of domestic and Pitt of foreign affairs.

The general tension erupted in riots over the high cost of provisions, and Dean Fountayne, with other clergy and gentry, organized a subscription for the purpose of lowering the price of corn.[3] Pitt, yielding to popular demand, sent back to Germany the Hanoverian and Hessian troops stationed in England, but in return insisted upon a change in the militia laws so that the nation could protect itself. The disfranchised poor, finding themselves

[1] Basil Williams, *The Whig Supremacy, 1714–1760*, 2nd ed., revised by C. H. Stuart, Oxford, 1962, p. 265.

[2] *York Courant*, 25 May 1756.

[3] Broadside, dated 12 December 1757, at Minster Library: D. 1.

subject to the new draft, rose in protest. In Yorkshire, the militia riots began in Bulmer Wapentake, and many of Sterne's parishioners must have been involved. The mob vented its wrath against local justices, and it is not unlikely they threatened Sterne. At Settrington, in the East Riding, rioters attacked the house of Sterne's friend, the Reverend Henry Egerton, but he managed to buy them off. The several mobs converged upon York. At Bootham, outside the walls, they levelled the Cockpit and pulled down the dwelling of an attorney and justice, William Bower. Dr Francis Topham barely escaped losing his fine house in the Minster Yard. The lord mayor finally shut the city gates, read the Riot Act, and ordered the citizens to stand to arms. Several rioters were shot and others arrested before the York mob was dispersed.[1]

Sterne remembered the anxieties of these labouring poor, and in *A Political Romance* he described one such man who believed he was past his fifty-second year and ought to be excused from service in the militia. He had come with a groat in his hand, to ask permission to search the parish registers for his birthday. 'The Parson bid the poor Fellow put the Groat into his Pocket, and go into the Kitchen'; he would be glad to search for him (p. 6). Perhaps all this increased concern about the ages of the poor was somehow connected with the temporary loss of the Sutton parish registers from 1757 to 1760. Sterne kept the records on notes during this period and had them copied into the book later.[2]

In the spring of 1757 John Gilbert, Bishop of Salisbury, was elevated to the see of York. Hutton had succeeded to Canterbury upon the death of Archbishop Herring. Newcastle would never have made these promotions, but he was temporarily out of office. Gilbert, a handsome, affable man of Epicurean tastes, was something of a courtier: he was Chancellor of the Order of the Garter. Horace Walpole's account of how he won the clergy of

---

[1] Thomas Beckwith's MS *History of York* at Minster Library; HARGROVE, I, 234–6; information sworn by Henry Egerton, 16 December 1757 in EGERTON LETTERS, AH 2161 C; Francis Topham to Andrew Ducarel, 3 October 1757, ILLUSTRATIONS, III, 318–19; Cedric Collyer, 'The Rockinghams and Yorkshire politics, 1742–1761', *Publications of the Thoresby Society*, XLI (1946–53), 352–82.

[2] The baptismal record is in an unidentified hand between 25 February 1757 (Sterne's last entry) and 3 June 1760 (the first entry of his new curate, William Raper). The same hand made the burial record between 3 March 1756 (Sterne's last) and 17 January 1760 (Raper's first). Yet the marriage register, in a separate book, is all in Sterne's hand for this period. We know Sterne was keeping the full record in some form because he sent signed copies to the archbishop, as required, for the years 1756–8; Raper sent them for 1759: at Borthwick Inst.

York is nonsense, but amusing: 'they rung the bells at York backwards, in detestation of him. He opened a great table there, and in six months they thought him the most Christian Prelate that had ever sat in that see.' But Gilbert was sickly; it was said that he 'rather languished, than lived' through his pontificate.[1] Consequently, he was glad to have Dr Topham represent him in the traditional quarrels with the dean and chapter.[2] On one occasion, the dean and chapter refused to allow Dr Topham to rush them into a hasty induction of the archbishop's brother to his new prebend. Gilbert was seriously ill at the time, and feared he might die before his brother was secure in his stall.[3] Sterne alluded to the incident in *A Political Romance* – the allegory of the close stool.

Sterne, though not involved in these new quarrels, was having troubles enough in his own village. In the spring of 1758 his name was dragged into a scandal. A story was spread about Sutton that Mrs Catherine Sturdy, wife of a leading yeoman, was having an affair with a gentleman, someone well known locally, though he is unidentified today. Poor Robert Sturdy,[4] who was ill and in low spirits, tended to believe the story. The whisper had been started by a certain Mr Young, an agent of Lord Fauconberg's. Young, when challenged, said he got his information from the parson. Sterne, concerned for his parishioners' and his own honour, called Young to account before Fauconberg's chief steward, Richard Chapman, and William Thompson of New Park, one of the substantial farmers of Sutton. Young admitted that the story was false. The tale had been 'invented & spread ab^t by a Company of idle Dykers', said Sterne, 'wthout any Hint or Foundation from him. or me. This He solemn[l]y declares with all the Asserverations a Man can make; How far he deserves Credit with regard to his *own* Innocence in the Affair, is not my Business to determine, – all that concerns me, is my own Innocence & Honor, wch he has fully vindicated in a paper signed by him'.[5] Sterne then quieted

[1] W. Dickinson Rastall, *History of Southwell*, London, 1787, p. 329; Walpole, *Memoirs of the Reign of George the Second*, 3 vols, 1847, II, 375. On Gilbert's sumptuous entertainments: CLIMENSON, II, 190–1; his health and character: Stephen Hyde Cassan, *Lives of the Bishops of Sherborne and Salisbury*, Salisbury, 1824, p. 268ff.

[2] Topham's letters to Ducarel of 1758 in ILLUSTRATIONS, III, 693–701.

[3] LETTER TO THE DEAN, 19; ANSWER, 28–9.

[4] Probably the descendant of John Sturdy, who established in 1711 a rent charge of 5s. for the benefit of the poor: LAWTON, 463. He married (1) Alice Taylor, 1745, and (2) Catherine Groves, 1755. He served as churchwarden in 1741, 1750, 1755 and 1766: CLEVELAND COURT.

[5] The letter, dated 14 March 1758, was recently discovered in Queens' College Library, Cambridge. Published by Kenneth Monkman and James Diggle in

the Sturdys with assurance of his high regard for Mrs Sturdy's virtue. Next, he wrote off to the man accused of debauching her, protesting his esteem and his trust that his correspondent would not 'suppose me capable of acting worse than an Assassin (wch such a Report would make me)'. Young's accusation of Sterne was surely false. Nothing in his life suggests the gossipmonger.

But even worse was being said of Sterne in the village, as he explained in this letter: 'That In consideration of a favor shown by me in procuring a Farm for an poor Farmer here, – I had lay'[d with] his Wife, wth Circumstances of time & [place].' The woman's husband brushed the story aside, and Elizabeth laughed at it, said Sterne. We, having no other evidence to go on, must let the matter go at that. The story probably hurt not only Sterne's reputation, but Elizabeth's stability. It may have brought to mind other, more solidly grounded suspicions. Elizabeth was close to breaking point.

When the tide of war was turning in 1758, when Frederick's ally, Prince Ferdinand of Brunswick, was driving the French back across the Rhine and Pitt was dispatching his fleets and youthful commanders to North America and India, Sterne's life was occupied with frustratingly unheroic tasks and pastimes. 'To Morrow We are indispensably obliged to be at Newborough (L^d F[auconber]gs.) – on Friday my Wife has engaged herself in the Afternoon at Cowper's – & I had both set my heart upon going to the Concert, & sent to engage Mr. Fothergil to meet me there a little after three' (LETTERS, 52).

During the latter half of that year, both Laurence and Elizabeth were involved in a variety of business and personal dealings with the Reverend John Blake, a somewhat younger man who had been friendly to both Sternes since 1746, when he had served as curate at Wigginton. Blake was the son of Sterne's friend, the Reverend Zachariah Blake, late curate of Fulford and master of the Royal Grammar School of St Peter. The younger Blake had recently become rector of Catton, the parish where Sterne had once been curate, and had succeeded his father as master of the school.[1]

Sterne's letters to Blake are puzzling because he seems to be talking about

'Yorick and his flock: a new Sterne letter', TLS, 14 March 1968, p. 276.

[1] Sterne named the elder Blake among his surrogates for Pickering and Pocklington Court. The younger Blake was also serving currently as chaplain to the county hospital, and he would soon be preferred to the living of Scrayingham. See Angelo Raine, *History of St Peter's School: York*, 1926; CURTIS, 51; ACT BOOK, 1744–55, fols. 100, 123, 252; 1755–68, fol. 2; *York Courant*, 13 January 1746/7. Blake, who subscribed to Sterne's *Sermons*, 1760, and *A Sentimental Journey*, died in 1784. His licence to marry Ann Place is now in the possession of Kenneth Monkman. Of the sixteen letters Sterne wrote to him which were known a

several things at once. On 17 December 1758 he wrote to Blake that when he would arrive at York, 'I have 4 Personages I equally want to see, The Dean, Jack Taylor, yʳself, & my Mother – & I have much to say to each' (p. 65). Probably he was referring to four separate matters.

Of Agnes Sterne, there is only one other mention in the Blake letters, a brief comment in September: 'I hope my mothers Affair is by this Time ended, to ᵒᵘʳ/my Comfort & I trust her's' (p. 61). Lacking other information, one supposes that Sterne was speaking of Agnes's debts which had caused so much trouble seven years before.

Elizabeth figures importantly in the Blake letters. She took a keen interest in Blake's romance with Margaret Ash, a girl who was under the thumb of a suspicious, grasping mother. Blake valued Elizabeth's advice, and she responded generously with suggestions, encouragement and such gifts as were at her disposal:

> My Wife sends you & Mʳˢ Ash a Couple of Stubble Geese – one for each, She would have sent You a Couple, but thinks tis better to keep yᵉ other Goose in our Bean Stubble till another Week – all We can say in their behalf is, That they are, (if not very fat) at least in good health & in perfect *freedome*, for they have never been confind a moment. (p. 60)

Probably Blake considered Laurence something of an expert in the legalities of marriage because of his experience as a commissary. But there was a difficulty in that: among the several estates owned by the young lady's mother, a widow, one lay in Tollerton, where Sterne had the spiritual jurisdiction, and another in Allerthorpe, a parish reporting to Pickering and Pocklington Court. In fact, Mrs Ash had once been presented for neglecting her obligation to repair Allerthorpe church.[1] Sterne, consequently, tried to keep his advising of Blake a secret. Mrs Ash's counsellor was the lawyer, John Stanhope of Horsforth – old J. S. of the election campaign.

---

century ago, Curtis was able to recover fourteen entire and a fragment of a fifteenth: LETTERS, 50–67, 73–4. The complete MS of Letter No. 29, only a fragment in Curtis's edition, has since been acquired by the Huntington Library: HM 81. A single, final page of the missing letter was recently donated to the Laurence Sterne Trust and is at Shandy Hall. The holograph of No. 22, which Curtis published from a transcript by Percy Fitzgerald, is now at the Houghton Library, Harvard: it differs from the published version only in minor details. One holograph manuscript, that of No. 30, has been relocated: it is in the Berg Collection of the New York Public Library.

[1] CURTIS, 53; the original presentment is at the Minster Library: C3.

Among the several problems the young couple faced, the most critical was a marriage contract. The mother wanted Blake to settle all his fortune upon his bride and any children he might have by her. But Sterne pointed out that if she should die leaving children behind, Blake would have nothing to give a second wife or *her* children.¹ The demands of the Ash family Sterne described as 'a Contexture of Plots ag^st y^r Fortune & Person, Grand Mama standing first in the Dramatis Personæ, the Lôup Garôu or raw head & Bloody bones to frighten Master Jacky into silence & make him go to bed with Missy, *supperless* and in Peace' (p. 58). But Blake was not long left 'STANDHOPEING', as Sterne put it – adding, 'was there ever so vile a Conundrum?' (p. 60).² Miss shortly married someone else. Blake remained single for another decade, but finally married Ann Place, daughter of the late recorder of York.

Although Laurence and Elizabeth were in harmony when it came to advising their friend, they were wary of each other in the mystifying transactions which Sterne called 'my Bristol Affair'. Whatever this might be, it involved another friend besides Blake, a certain Jack Taylor, probably John Taylor, Esq., of Fulford, who was publicly active during this period.³ Sterne appears to have taken some financial risk which hinged upon his receiving a message by express, presumably from Bristol, which would arrive at the shop of a York apothecary and be forwarded according to a prearranged plan. 'I think', wrote Sterne, 'I have put the whole into such a train that I cannot miscarry.' Blake was posting letters, paying out money for Sterne, and fretting about keeping the account up to date. Both were anxious for news about the demise or recovery of an unidentified man who lay ill at some remote place (pp. 50, 57). At first, Sterne tried to keep the business secret from Elizabeth. 'I tore off the Bottom of y^rs', he wrote to Blake, 'before I let my Wife see it, to save a Lye – However She has since observed the Curtaildment and seem'd very desirous of knowing what it Containd, wch I conceal'

¹ The Huntington Library holograph of Letter No. 29, datable from internal evidence as early October 1758.

² According to an anecdote told by Dr James Atkinson of York in *Medical Bibliography*, York, 1833, '"You are always letting puns," an old clergyman said to Sterne, "it deserves punishment,"–"that," replied Sterne, "is – as the pun is meant".'

³ Born 1699; married Elizabeth, daughter of Anthony Elcock: SKAIFE.

He subscribed to the defences in 1745 and was among those who started the subscription to lower corn prices in 1756. Served on the Grand Jury of 1750 for whom Sterne wrote *The Abuses of Conscience*. Subscribed to the Marine Society: CURTIS, 59. Taylor lived in Fulford, where he leased from the dean and chapter certain herbage: CHAPTER DEEDS, 1728–47, fol. 507; 1747–68, fol. 20; *Account Book of the Dean and Chapter*, 1743–82, fol. 27.

(p. 54). Unbeknown to Sterne, Elizabeth was writing to Blake about this matter, upon which she thought her own happiness depended. Perhaps Sterne was gambling with her fortune. If so, he probably lost some of it, though not the loyalty of his wife. In her letter to Blake, she asked that Taylor should not press her husband because he was doing all he could to mend things. His repentance, she said, was 'extravagant'.[1] Probably we shall never know the full story.

The Bristol affair may have been connected with the fourth and most important matter alluded to in the Blake letters. Sterne was moving to York in expectation of advancement in the church. He was planning to lay claim to the next residentiaryship at the minster, probably at the death of his uncle, whose health was failing.[2] He could have counted upon the votes of Fountayne, Berdmore and a less active residentiary, Charles Cowper, though not Dr Herring, who had ambitions of putting his son in the post. The legalities would require the candidate himself to take the initiative: he would be expected to appear at a chapter meeting and 'protest residence' – announce that he was actually residing at the minster. To do so, Sterne would have to be living in the Minster Yard, where in fact he was soon to move. He was in and out of York frequently. He appeared in the minster pulpit early in October and again on 28 December to preach 'The Character of Herod' on Innocents' Day. But he attended no chapter meetings. Perhaps he and the dean were planning a *coup* like that which had brought in Berdmore ten years before.

By 17 December, as he wrote to Blake, he had settled most of his business affairs. 'I . . . shall clear my hands & head of all country Entanglements.' He had found a promising tenant for the farms, one Thomas Wright, who had also agreed to collect most of the tithes in exchange for a percentage. 'This will bring me & mine into a narrow Compass – & make us, I hope both rich & happy' (p. 66). Sterne's daughter later complained that the contract with Wright was disadvantageous.[3]

Sterne did change the pattern of his life in the next few months. He with-

[1] Unpublished letter of Elizabeth Sterne to Blake, recently donated to the Laurence Sterne Trust, Shandy Hall.

[2] The evidence for Sterne's plan is to be found in his letter of 1761 to Mrs Montagu in which he speaks about his break with Dr Herring. The chancellor, said Sterne, had tried to bring about a separation be-

tween himself and Fountayne, 'not out of Zeal for the Dean's Character, but to secure the next Residentiaryship to . . . his son', thereby implying that Sterne had been a competing candidate: LETTERS, 135.

[3] LETTERS, 438. Wright is named in North Riding Deeds, AF/492–3/690.

drew from parochial duties and farming; he moved with his family to York. But, as it turned out, he did not become a canon residentiary; he became an author. The shift was, in a sense, accidental, and the cause of the accident was the ambition of Dr Francis Topham for his son.

Dr Topham doted upon his seven year old boy, Edward, who would grow up to be a journalist, playwright, dandy, and the protector of the actress, Mary Wells. 'Through life it was a feather in my friend Topham's cap', said Frederic Reynolds, 'that when a boy, he was the unconscious founder of Sterne's literary career.'[1] The unlikely chain of events arose in this wise. Archbishop Hutton, when he was still at York, revived an old practice of rewarding his favourites even before there was a suitable opening by granting them a reversionary patent to some preferment. In 1756, he gave the Reverend Francis Dodsworth, his chaplain, a reversionary patent as registrar to that wealthy spiritual, presided over by Topham, the Exchequer and Prerogative Court. Dodsworth would become the registrar upon the death of the incumbent, Thomas Sharp. Archbishop Gilbert, when he came to the see of York, decided he would not be cheated: he would give a reversionary patent to *his* favourite, Robert Bewley.[2] Dr Topham, who may have advised either or both archbishops, now began to think how he himself might take advantage of this interesting device. Why should not his own post as commissary of the court, his best preferment, be settled upon his son? He obtained an opinion from the Attorney-General that Dodsworth's patent was sound. He searched the records of the Exchequer and Prerogative Court and discovered that nine past registrars had obtained the position in this manner. True, the commissaries themselves had not; nevertheless, he thought it could be accomplished by opening his current patent and re-writing it for two lives – his and his son's.[3] He would need the help of Archbishop Gilbert and the concurrence of the dean and chapter.

The rub was the dean. On 12 August Topham wrote to Fountayne, explaining his aspirations, asking for support and dropping a hint that it might be profitable to play along: 'as I have very lately had a *private Intimation* of the Bishop of *Winchester* having just had some very alarming Symptoms, I must expect to be *able soon* to *congratulate* you on your being added to the *Bench of Bishops*.'[4] Again he had misjudged his man. The dean was very

---

[1] Quoted by CROSS, 171. On Edward Topham: DNB.
[2] CHAPTER DEEDS, 27 October 1756; 25–8 July 1758.
[3] The granting of a patent for two lives was legal according to BURN, I, 421.
[4] ANSWER, 23.

cool. Topham said later that he went immediately to the archbishop, though Fountayne denied that. In any event, Gilbert did learn of the scheme and called both men to Bishopthorpe.[1] In no uncertain terms he told Dr Topham that he would not rob his successors of this gift. He had acted differently in the case of Mr Bewley only because he was determined not to be cheated, but he had no intention of doing it again. Dr Topham would have to be disappointed. There was, of course, a sort of madness in the practice of giving away preferments before they were available. If carried to an extreme, a bishop might come into a see depleted of all its patronage. Moreover, the writing of a patent so that a son could inherit a preferment was unheard of at York. Lord Chancellor Hardwicke had been induced to sacrifice his wealthy law practice in order to serve the Crown by such a patent, but Dr Topham's services were not of that order.

The lawyer was furious. A year later his anger against the archbishop still had not abated. Dr Thomas Newton wrote from London to the Reverend John Dealtary, on 4 March 1760, that Topham was threatening to sue the archbishop for £1,000 damages for breach of promise. 'For the honor of your country,' he commented, 'if it be for the honor of it, you may reckon him too among your madmen.'[2]

In his fury with the dean, Topham began once more to talk too much, trotting out for his friends the old story of Pickering and Pocklington Court and asserting that the dean had broken his promise of that preferment. One of those friends was an indiscreet physician and man-midwife named Isaac Newton. Dr Newton soon spread the story of the broken promise all over town. The talk, now general, gave Topham an excuse to vent his wrath publicly. He went home, stammered out a pamphlet, and actually published it. On 11 December appeared *A Letter Address'd to the Reverend the Dean of York; in which is given a full Detail of some very extraordinary Behaviour of his, in relation to his Denial of a Promise made by him to Dr. Topham.*[3]

Wisely or unwisely, Fountayne replied in print, soon after 25 December, with *An Answer to a Letter address'd to the Dean of York, in the Name of Dr. Topham.* That Sterne contributed to the *Answer* cannot be proved, but it seems highly likely. Fountayne could hardly have reconstructed the events of a decade before, the main substance of the pamphlet, without the help of his friends. No doubt they thought the whole thing amusing. Dr Topham

[1] ANSWER, 30-1.
[2] DEALTARY LETTERS, fol. 133.
[3] Published by Caesar Ward, as were

ANSWER and REPLY: YORK PRESS, 256.

implied as much when he called the dean's *Answer* 'the Child and Offspring of many Parents'. 'Correcting, Revising, Ornamenting, and Embellishing', he went on, 'have been displayed in great Perfection; and *many happy Changes* have been run upon the words COMMISSARY of the DEAN, and COM-MISSARY of the DEAN and CHAPTER.'[1]

At this point Sterne began writing *A Political Romance.* There is no evidence one way or another that the dean or anyone else in the church of York knew what he was up to. He probably would have published the short first version had not Dr Topham surprised everyone by bringing out a second pamphlet, entitled *A Reply to the Answer to a Letter lately addressed to the Dean of York*, which appeared shortly after 13 January.

Meanwhile, Dr Isaac Newton, squirming under the criticism of York citizens, printed off a handbill in his own defence and foolishly distributed it. The scandalized public now opened its own attack, not on Fountayne or Topham, but on Dr Newton, whom they held responsible for starting the whole thing. There was a barrage of ephemeral printing[2] – *Mother N[ewto]n's Amazement; or, The D[octo]r Trepann'd: a New Song to the Tune of 'Twas in the Land of Cyder'*; and *The First Chapter of the Book of Isaac*, which told the story in a parody of the bible. There was *An Honorary Epitaph upon Mother N[ewto]n, who died at a large House in the Minster-yard, of a Distemper w[ch] the Physicians called 'Tremor occupat artus': and was buried in a magnificent Pamphlet Mausoleum, erected to his Memory, by the Great Leviathan of the Sp[iritua]l C[our]t*; a parody of *As You Like It*, which began 'All the Town's a Song, / And all the Men and Women turn'd to Singers'; and a ballad called *N[ewto]n's Confession:*

> Curse on my foolish babbling Tongue,
> Oh! that its Nerves had been unstrung,
> When I presum'd to prate.

Into this hubbub stepped Sterne with an enlarged *Political Romance.* Several hundred copies were printed off by Caesar Ward during the last ten days of January 1759. It is doubtful that they were ever put up for sale.

The book shows clearly the two stages in which it was written. The first part, less than half the final size, was composed after the appearance of Top-ham's original *Letter* and the dean's *Answer*: it makes fun of the part played by Topham in the events discussed in those two pamphlets. Ward actually set this version and ran off a proof. The satire takes the form of a letter,

---

[1] REPLY, 1–2. [2] The ballads and broadsides cited are in CURIOUS COLLECTION.

which Sterne originally dated from 'Cocksbull near Canterbury'. He removed the address in the final version.¹ Probably the first title was the one which has been used for many subsequent printings – *The History of a Good Warm Watch-Coat*.²

This part consists of a detailed satire of Dr Topham as Trim, the sexton of a village church. The numerous offices of the lawyer, Sterne humorously represents as Trim's parish offices – dog-whipper, clock-winder, pinder, bailiff. 'Then you begg'd the Church-Wardens to let your Wife have the Washing and Darning of the Surplice and Church-Linen, which brings you in Thirteen Shillings and Four Pence' (pp. 22–3); 'You are not only Mole-Catcher, *Trim*, but you catch STRAY CONIES too in the *Dark*; and you pretend a *Licence* for it' (p. 23). *Coney-catching* was a cant term for both swindling and fornicating. The parish, of course, represents the diocese of York, and the parson, 'the poor Gentleman, who was but in an ill State of Health' (p. 5), is Archbishop Gilbert. Dean Fountayne is John, the parish clerk; the prebendaries are represented as churchwardens, the archbishop's officers as sidesmen.

The story gets under way when Trim decides that an old watch-coat used by successive sextons of the parish (the archbishop's Exchequer and Prerogative Court) should be cut up to make an under-petticoat for his wife and a jerkin for himself (Topham's plan to rewrite his patent for his own and his son's life). The parson is at first inclined to go along until he discovers a memorandum in the parish register: the coat was given to the parish 'above two hundred Years ago, by the Lord of the Manor' (Henry VIII)

---

¹ For these and other points, I am indebted to Edward Simmen, 'Sterne's *A Political Romance*: new light from a printer's copy', *Papers of the Bibliographical Society of America*, LXIV (1970), 419–29, a study growing out of Simmen's discovery of a printer's proof of the satire in the library of Texas Christian University. Other authoritative bibliographical studies are those of Davies, YORK PRESS, 259–60, and CROSS, 598–9. I am also indebted to the unpublished MA thesis, 1970, University of Florida, by Gerald Wayne Donnelly, *A Critical Edition of Laurence Sterne's 'A Political Romance'*. Ian Jack has produced an edition for the Oxford University Press (Oxford

English Novels series), 1968, which is bound with *A Sentimental Journey* and *Journal to Eliza*; and the Scolar Press, Menston, Yorkshire, issued a facsimile reprint with an introduction by Kenneth Monkman, 1971.

² That was the title known to the author of ANONYMOUS LETTER and to the author of the biographical sketch of Sterne prefaced to *Yorick's Sentimental Journey Continued*, 1769. In the first letter appended to the final, published version, Sterne begins, 'You write me Word that the letter I wrote to you, and now stiled *The Political Romance* is printing': ROMANCE, 49.

for the use of all sextons '𝖙𝖔 𝖐𝖊𝖊𝖕 𝖙𝖍𝖊 𝖕𝖔𝖔𝖗 𝖂𝖗𝖊𝖙𝖈𝖍𝖊𝖘 𝖜𝖆𝖗𝖒' (p. 7). While he is reading, 'in pops *Trim* with the whole Subject . . . under both his Arms. – I say, under both his Arms; – for he had actually got it ripp'd and cut out ready, his own Jerkin under one Arm, and the Petticoat under the other' (p. 7). The parson orders him to put down the pieces at once, unmoved by Trim's pleading all the services he has done – 'That he had black'd the Parson's Shoes without Count, and greased his Boots above fifty Times: – That he had run for Eggs into the Town upon all Occasions; – whetted the Knives at all Hours; – catched his Horse and rubbed him down', etc. (p. 11). Disappointed, Trim blusters and threatens. But he is afraid of the parson, who is a justice; so he 'falls foul' upon John, the clerk, and the churchwardens, 'rips up the Promise of the old-cast-Pair-of-black-Plush-Breeches [Pickering and Pocklington Court], and raises an Uproar in the Town about it, notwithstanding it had slept ten Years' (p. 14). Thus the allegory moves on to the subject matter of the pamphlets – the church squabbles during the previous decade – an allegory meticulously detailed and devasting to Dr Topham.

This main portion of the satire is followed by a 'Postscript', written after Dr Topham's second pamphlet appeared: 'it seems, it is not half an Hour ago since *Trim* sallied forth again; and, having borrowed a Sow-Gelder's Horn, with hard Blowing he got the whole Town round him, and endeavoured to raise a Disturbance, and fight the whole Battle over again' (pp. 25–6). The Swiftian tone is sustained through the mock-heroic battle in which Trim takes final refuge behind the close stool (Gilbert's request to induct his brother). 'Besides, as *Trim* seems bent upon *purging* himself, and may have Abundance of foul Humours to work off, I think he cannot be better placed' (p. 28).

But Sterne could not content himself with the 'Postscript' only. He also added a 'Key', which advances explanations of the allegory other than those which, as he knows, the reader will find there. The manuscript, he explains, was accidentally dropped in the Minster Yard, picked up, and taken to a meeting of a political club where 'It was instantly agreed to, by a great Majority, That it was a *Political Romance*; but concerning what State or Potentate, could not be settled amongst them' (p. 31). The tone of the 'Key' is vastly different from that of the allegory. Sterne now turned to humorous characters, much like his 'Old Bachelor' of the essay signed 'Hamlet', written a dozen years before. A pompous President of the Night asserts that it is an allegory of the present war; but another gentleman, who has been reading the history of the wars of William and Anne, argues that the divided watch-coat represents the Partition Treaty. A gentleman geographer main-tains that the breeches mean Gibraltar, and a tailor says that the breeches look like Sicily, and the boot, Italy. A lawyer offers the opinion that the whole 'is a very fine Panegyrick upon the *Humility* of *Church-Men*', but a parson pooh-poohs him, asserting that it is a 'Panegyrick upon the *Honesty* of Attornies' (p. 41). No one pays much attention to them because – and this is Sterne's point, false though it is – 'every Man turn'd the Story to what was swim-ming uppermost in his own Brain' (p. 45). Some have thought that Sterne in the 'Key' was portraying real-life citizens of York, members of a convivial club which met at Sunton's coffee house in Coney Street,[1] but none has been identified. More probably, he was painting recognizable types drawn from a much wider range of experiences. The pipe-smoking Partition-Treaty gentle-man is especially interesting because he suggests the character of Uncle Toby – though his violent pounding of the table and his throwing away of his pipe seem more like Walter Shandy. On the eve of writing *Tristram Shandy*, Sterne warmed up with a fiction which juxtaposed the scatological satire of Swift and Pope with the 'amiable humour' of Addison and Steele.[2]

Finally, Sterne appended to the *Romance* two letters. The first, addressed to an unnamed gentleman of York – rather obviously Caesar Ward – is really an author's preface out of its expected place, as in *Tristram Shandy*. The other, addressed to Dr Topham, is Sterne's own contribution to the pamphlet war *as such*: he defends himself from charges made by Dr Topham. His argu-ment adds little or nothing to the story covered above, though it strongly supports a point which Sterne was at pains to deny – that he had helped to write the dean's *Answer*.

Having swelled the original twenty-four pages to sixty and doubled the price, Sterne took the earlier proof and the new manuscript to Ward, who printed the entire book late in January. If Sterne intended to stop the pamphlet war, he certainly accomplished that. What surprised him were the other consequences.

On 6 February the chapter gave Dean Fountayne leave to go to London to be 'one of the Lent Preachers' – says the record. Actually, he was going to see Archbishop Gilbert, who was spending the winter there. Dr Topham went to London too, as we learn from the last squeak heard on the battlefield, a broadside ballad entitled *The Baby, a New Song, To the Tune of, 'A Cobler there was, and he liv'd'*, &c.

[1] YORK PRESS, 260, n.

[2] Stuart M. Tave, *The Amiable Humorist*, Chicago, 1960.

Of a Quarrel I sing, not a Mile from a Church,
How a D[ea]n left a D[octo]r trepann'd in the Lurch;
And an Adv[oca]te nick'd made a terrible Rant,
That his *Baby* was *bobb'd* of a *lucrative Grant*.
      Derry down, &c.

  Enrag'd as they were, how they squabbled and wrote,
Asserted, evaded, deny'd, and what not?
And something let slip of a Tale of a Tub [*A Political Romance*],
Of *Whisler* [Fountayne] and *Slim* [Sterne] having out-
    witted Sc--b [Topham].
      Derry down, &c.

  How a terrified Spark [Newton] pen'd a strange Attestation,
Too publick to need any further Relation;
And when 'twas agreed that all Contest shou'd cease,
Simple Isaac no Benefit reap'd of this Peace.
      Derry down, &c.

  How the *Surplice* and *Gown* thus diverted the People,
Who had equal Regard for the *Court* and the *Steeple*;
For the Truth, as it ought, being fairly confess'd,
Few valu'd the L[a]*wy*[e]*r*, or relish'd the P[*rie*]*st*.
      Derry down, &c.

  As from *Broughton* and *Slack* [boxers], when the
    Trial begun,
Some Hits were surmis'd ere the Champions had done;
But the *Master* [of the Faculties] unsheathing, – the
    Preacher foresaw
That Blood wou'd ensue, shou'd *He* venture to draw.
      Derry down, &c.

  Thus stagger'd, He paus'd – when Peace, with a Smile,
Her Emblem presenting, reliev'd him a while:
Humility too wrought upon him to beg
For a Conference straight, – and made him a Leg.
      Derry down, &c.

> Reason, merely by chance. – tho' first of the *Quorum*,
> Pop'd in, and the Matter being open'd before 'em,
> An *Umpire* was chose from a Village near *Kent*,
> So to L[*ondon*] the Combatants hied by Consent.
> > *Derry down*, &c.

> What may there be decreed, we're at present to seek;
> But if Justice, *unaw'd*, might her Sentiments speak,
> They *Both* shou'd do Penance; and then having kiss'd,
> With a proper Rebuke from his G[race], be dismiss'd.
> > *Derry down*, &c.[1]

Very likely, Sterne also went to London and took part in the conference with the archbishop.[2] When they returned, the printed copies of *A Political Romance* were taken from Caesar Ward's shop and 'committed to the Flames'; fortunately, a few survived.[3]

Whatever was resolved in London, Sterne did not hold it against Archbishop Gilbert. He later planned to show the prelate his manuscript of *Tristram Shandy*, though it is doubtful he did.[4] According to one anecdote, 'The late archbishop of York, Dr. G[ilber]t of leaden memory, used to say, that he was so delighted with the Life and Opinions of Tristram Shandy that he read them once every six weeks.'[5]

But Sterne thought himself betrayed by John Fountayne. Probably Fountayne withdrew his support of Sterne for the residentiaryship, although we have no specific evidence one way or another. In any event, Sterne lost all

[1] In CURIOUS COLLECTION.

[2] Elizabeth, writing to Mrs Montagu in the autumn of 1761, as Curtis conjectures, said that her husband had seen Mrs Montagu 'these two last winters': CURTIS, 136–7.

[3] ANONYMOUS LETTER. Six copies are known today – listed by Simmen. Dr John Hill, in the earliest biographical account of Sterne, for the *Royal Female Magazine*, 1 May 1760, reprinted in the *London Chronicle*, 3–6 May, told a sentimental story about Sterne's throwing the manuscript into the fire to save the church of York, apparently not knowing it had been printed. John Croft gave a garbled account, confusing the original printing with a poor posthumous edition of 1769.

Croft named the man responsible for the burning – the 'present Precentor'. That would have been William Mason, the poet. Sterne assisted at Mason's induction into the prebend of Holme, 2 February 1757, but Mason spent little time in York until he was made precentor and residentiary in 1762.

[4] LETTERS, 77.

[5] CROSS, 283, who cites a footnote in the anonymous *Funeral Discourse occasioned by the . . . Death of Mr. Yorick*, 1761. Sterne probably visited the archbishop in London in 1761; at least, he saw his daughter and hostess, Emma, with whom he later corresponded: LETTERS, 127, 407.

hope of that preferment. The following autumn, when a correspondent asked him why he was turning author, he replied, 'why truly I am tired of employing my brains for other people's advantage. – 'Tis a foolish sacrifice I have made for some years to an ungrateful person' (p. 84). Almost certainly, he was referring to the dean, to whom early in 1761 he wrote a long letter of self-vindication – now lost. He sent a copy of it to Mrs Montagu, wanting to 'give some light into my hard measure – & shew You, that I was as much a protection to the Dean of York – as he to me'. True, he had received an answer from the dean which 'has made me easy with regard to my Views in the Church of York; & . . . has cemented the Dean & myself beyond the power of any future breach' (pp. 135–6), but the cement was not very strong. By the end of that year, when Sterne was preparing to leave for France, he wrote out some advice to Elizabeth, in case he should die abroad, in which he mentioned the 'long pathetic Letter' to the dean: 'I charge you, to let it be printed——'Tis equitable, You should derive that good from My Sufferings at least' (p. 147). As for the *Romance*, the manuscript of which he was leaving behind, he gave Elizabeth reluctant permission to republish it, though he hoped she would not need to.

> I have 2 Reasons why I wish it may not be wanted – first, an undeserved Compliment to One, whom I have since, found to be a very corrupt man – I knew him weak & ignorant – but thought him honest. The other reason is I have hung up Dr Topham, in the romance – in a ridiculous light – w^{ch}, upon my Soul I now doubt, whether he deserves it – so let the Romance, go to sleep, not by itself – for twil have Company.   (p. 147)

No doubt Sterne consented to the burning of *A Political Romance*, as an acquaintance of the following summer reported,[1] but he was bitterly disappointed. 'He felt it', said the acquaintance. But then, Laurence Sterne was not a man to lose heart easily: 'it was to this Disappointment that the World is indebted for Tristram Shandy.'

[1] ANONYMOUS LETTER.

14

Tristram Shandy, I–II
1759–1760

The suppression of *A Political Romance* was the greatest testimony of its effectiveness. Sterne had found his *métier*,[1] and at the very moment when his clerical career had been pulled up short. His business concerns were off his hands, and he had four months of relative freedom before he was to move his family to York. He set to work enthusiastically. Within weeks, he had produced a manuscript which he called 'The Life and Opinions of Tristram Shandy' – not the book we know today, but a satire structured along the lines of *The Memoirs of Martinus Scriblerus*.[2] This early version was a lusty, often ribald satire, and its objects were local as well as national figures. If Sterne thought to have Caesar Ward publish it, fate intervened. Ward had suddenly died on 24 April.[3] So he turned for advice to John Hinxman, the proprietor of the Sign of the Bible since John Hildyard's death three years before. Hinxman, who had done his apprenticeship under the great Robert Dodsley in London,[4] seems to have told Sterne to settle only for the best – send it to Dodsley. Sterne posted the manuscript on 23 May. 'If this 1st

[1] 'So till he had finished his Watchcoat, he says, he hardly knew that he could write at all, much less with Humour, so as to make his Reader laugh. But it is my own Opinion, that he is yet a Stranger to his own Genius, or at least that he mistakes his Fort. He is ambitious of appearing in his Fool's Coat, but he is more himself, and his Powers are much stronger, I think, in describing the tender Passions': ANONYMOUS LETTER.

[2] If one accepts at face value the dates mentioned in the published novel, one must conclude that Sterne was working on it before the *Romance* appeared in print.

In I, xiv, 37, Tristram says that he has been writing for six weeks; in I, xviii, 44, he says he is writing on 9 March: hence, he must have been writing in mid-January. However, Sterne rewrote the first volume so thoroughly that there is no certainty that he did not shift about parts. If the two statements were originally in reverse order, we would conclude that he began work early in March. (In I, xxiv, 64, he names another date, 26 March.)

[3] YORK PRESS, 260.

[4] Ralph Strauss, *Robert Dodsley*, 1910, p. 260.

Volume has a run (wch such Criticks as this Latitude affords, say it can't fail of) We may both find our Account in it.' He asked £50 for the copyright. 'The Plan', he told Dodsley, '. . . is a most extensive one, – taking in, not only, the Weak part of the Sciences, in wch the true point of Ridicule lies – but every Thing else, which I find Laugh-at-able in my way' (p. 74).[1]

We know about this amusing first version of *Tristram Shandy* primarily through the letter of an unidentified gentleman who was visiting York during June of that year, when Sterne met him for the first time. The following year, in April 1760, this man, whoever he was, wrote to another unidentified person about his evening with Sterne – a letter which eventually found its way into the newspapers.[2] Sterne and his new friend sat up an entire night with the manuscript of this first 'Tristram Shandy' spread out before them, Sterne chatting freely about his new career. 'The design', reported the gentleman,

> is to take in all Ranks and Professions. A System of Education is to be exhibited, and thoroughly discussed. For forming his future Hero . . . a private Tutor . . . no less a Person than the great and learned Dr. W[arburton]: Polemical Divines are to come in for a slap. An Allegory has been run up on the Writers on the Book of Job. The Doctor [Warburton] is the Devil who smote him from Head to Foot, and G[re]y P[ete]rs and Ch[appel]ow his miserable Comforters.

Richard Grey, prebendary of St Paul's, Leonard Chappelow, Professor of Arabic at Cambridge, and Charles Peters, a Hebrew scholar, had all attacked Warburton for his comments on *Job* in *Remarks on Several Occasional Reflections* (1744).[3]

---

[1] The holograph of this letter, No. 37 in LETTERS, is now in the collection of Robert H. Taylor of Princeton, New Jersey.

[2] ANONYMOUS LETTER. Professor Cross's edition of this letter in *Works*, from which I have taken my quotations (see Short Titles and Abbreviations), was taken from a clipping of the *St. James Chronicle*, to which it had been forwarded on 10 April 1788 by a certain G. E. G. – neither the writer nor the addressee. A second publication in the *European Magazine*, March 1792, pp. 169–70, shows only editorial differences. CROSS quotes from the letter, without documentation, but makes little use of it. I accept it without hesitation because numerous details are verified from other sources. It is faulty in only one point, probably an error of the printer or transcriber: the writer seems to say that he is the person who suggested to Sterne the idea of making Warburton the tutor to Tristram, but he then goes on to describe an episode in the manuscript before him in which Warburton is already cast in that role.

[3] The three were identified by a contributor to the *European Magazine* for October 1792. All are covered in the

A Groupe of mighty Champions in Literature is convened at Shandy-Hall. Uncle Toby and the Corporal are Thorns in the private Tutor's Side, and operate upon him as they did on Dr. Slop at reading the Sermon. All this for poor Job's Sake, whilst an Irish Bishop, a quondum Acquaintance of Sterne's, who has written on the same Subject, and loves dearly to be in a Crowd, is to come uninvited and introduce himself.

The Irish bishop was John Garnett, Bishop of Clogher, a Yorkshireman who had been a fellow of Sidney Sussex when Sterne was at Cambridge.[1]

Here were the beginnings of the comic symposia of Shandy Hall and the visitation dinner, but the mode was that of Menippean satire, not the novel. Although the setting was a Yorkshire country house, obviously Sterne made no attempt to justify the unlikely appearance there of writers and clergymen from all over England. The *Job* allegory, imposed upon the main structure, suggests *A Tale of a Tub*. The threading of satirical episodes upon a fanciful story of the birth and education of a child suggests *Martinus Scriblerus*.

The language was often bawdy. Sterne's new friend objected to 'some gross Allusions which I apprehended would be Matter of just Offense, and especially when coming from a Clergyman'. They suggested to him both the 'Dirtiness of Swift' and the 'Looseness of Rabelais'. Those writers were mentioned also by another friend who saw the manuscript, an older, unidentified clergyman who offered 'Paternal Advice'. 'I deny I have gone as farr as Swift,' Sterne answered the clergyman; 'He keeps a due distance from Rabelais – & I keep a due distance from him – Swift has said a hundred things I durst Not Say – Unless I was Dean of St. Patricks——' (p. 76).

As we know from a surviving fragment of this early version, it kept little distance from Swift or Rabelais. Lydia Sterne published a bowdlerized version of it with her father's letters, under the title 'A Fragment in the Manner of Rabelais'. The original was far more bawdy.[2] The setting of this episode,

---

DNB. Grey, who was also commissary of the archdeacon of Leicester, was a prolific pamphleteer; his *Answer to Mr. Warburton's 'Remarks on Several Occasional Reflections'*, 1744, provoked a reply from Warburton in Part II of the *Remarks*, 1745. Chappelow, Lord Almoner's Professor of Arabic at Cambridge, criticized Warburton in *Commentary on the Book of Job*,

1752. Peters published *A Critical Dissertation on the Book of Job*, 1751.

[1] DNB. Also identified in the *European Magazine* of October 1792. Among his publications was *A Dissertation on the Book of Job*, 1749.

[2] Melvyn New argues convincingly that Sterne wrote it early in 1759, kept it by him when working on *Tristram Shandy*,

though not specified, probably is the building attached to the south side of the minster which at that time housed the library, traditionally the place where the chapter members composed their sermons. In one room a group of clergy, with Rabelaisian names such as Panurge, Gymnast and Triboulet, are being harangued by Longinus Rabelaicus, who is urging them to undertake a 'Kerukopedia', a textbook on sermon writing.

> *Longinus Rabelaicus* was foreminded to usher & lead into his Dissertation, with as much Pomp & Parade as he could afford; and for my own Part, either I know no more of Greek & Latin than my Arse, or the KERUKOPÆDIA, is nothing but the Art of making 'em. . . . But what I mean, my Little Cods, says Longinus Rabelaicus (who is certainly one of the greatest Critick's in the western World, and as Rabelaic a Fellow as ever piss'd) what I mean, says he, interrupting them both, & resuming his Discourse, is this, That if all the scatter'd Rules of the KERUKOPÆDIA, could be but once carefully collected into one Code, as thick as *Panurge*'s Head, and the Whole cleanly digested – (Shite! says *Panurge*, who felt himself aggrieved –) . . .

At this point they are interrupted by the curses of their brother, Homenas, in the next room, who is rifling the sermons of Samuel Clarke, transposing whole passages into his own sermon.[1] The most indecent joke in the Homenas episode Sterne cleaned up in the manuscript itself: he removed the name of Dr John Rogers and substituted that of Dr Samuel Clarke, thereby depriving himself of such puns as the following: '*Homenas* . . . was all this while Rogering it as hard as He could drive in the very next Room.' Nevertheless, the final *Tristram Shandy* contains no imagery or expletives quite so coarse as those in the earlier manuscript.

Sterne was 'haunted with Doubts and Fears of its not taking', and with good reason. One evening he read the satire to a group of gentlemen assembled at Stillington Hall. They all fell asleep. 'Sterne was so nettled that he threw the Manuscript into the fire', but the squire rescued it.[2]

One worry he set aside: he was not going to concern himself about the threat to his career. His friend Marmaduke Fothergill, 'best of Criticks &

---

and occasionally lifted phrases and sentences from it: 'Sterne's Rabelaisian fragment: a text from the holograph manuscript', *PMLA*, LXXXVII (1972), 1083–92, from which I take quotations.

The manuscript is at the Pierpont Morgan Library.

[1] The episode is discussed above in Chapter 11.

[2] CROFT.

well wishers', was preaching to him, 'Get Your Preferment first Lory! . . . & then Write & Welcome.' 'But suppose preferment is long acoming,' answered Sterne, '. . . for aught I know I may not be preferr'd till the Resurrection of the Just' (p. 76). Moral, as distinct from professional, considerations did give him anxiety for a time. He told the older clergyman that he would be willing to show the book to the archbishop when he returned to York in the autumn. To another colleague, 'A Very Able Critick & One of my Colour too', Sterne declared his intention to 'consider the colour of My Coat', as he corrected the manuscript. The friend surprised him by answering, 'that very Idea in My head would render My Book not worth a groat' (pp. 76–7). He finally resolved the problem on aesthetic and psychological grounds. Prudence would be for him an 'understrapping Virtue'. He could afford to be cautious only to the point where it did not spoil the book by robbing 'the air and originality of it, which must resemble the Author – & I fear 'tis a Number of these slighter touches which Mark this resemblance & Identify it from all Others of the Stamp'. The comedy might indeed be 'too free & gay for the solemn colour of My coat – A meditation upon Death had been a more suiting trimming to it (I own it) – but then it Could not have been set on by Me' (p. 76). To the new friend of that summer, Sterne observed, 'an Attention to his Character would damp his Fire, and check the Flow of his Humour . . . if he went on and hoped to be read, he must not look at his Band or Cassock.' Thus resolved, Sterne never changed his stand during the rest of his life.

Early in June, Dodsley returned the manuscript. He was turning his business over to his brother, James, he explained, and did not want to burden him with so hazardous a venture.

By the time Sterne received this discouraging news, his personal life had been turned topsy-turvy. He had moved, or was in the process of moving, to the house he had hired in the Minster Yard. They were there at least by late June, though Sterne may have gone back and forth to Sutton for some months helping to break in his new curate.[1] He must have been impatient to free himself from parochial duties: he had no business, really, hiring such a curate as William Raper. Raper was a farm boy from Coxwold without a university degree. His poverty, of course, was no discredit, and there is something touching in his father's attempt, a year later, to buy him the

---

[1] Sterne's last entry in the Stillington registers was on 25 March; the first entry of his curate on 8 May. Sterne's last entry at Sutton (in the hand of his amanuensis) was on 20 June; the curate's first on 23 November.

living in Coxwold in exchange for a home-made organ. But Richard Chapman wrote of him, 'he hath a bad Character and has behaved very Ill for which Mr. Hugill Discharged him from Smeaton'.[1]

Why did Sterne decide to go ahead with the move to York even after he had lost favour with the church? Probably because he had promised his family. Elizabeth hated the country, and Lydia was growing up without the refinements of a city life. 'I have hired a small house in the Minster Yard for my wife, and daughter', he wrote to a friend. 'The latter is to begin dancing, &c. if I cannot leave her a fortune, I will at least give her an education' (p. 84). Perhaps the child was enrolled in Mrs deBoissy's school in the Minster Yard, where young ladies were instructed in English, French, writing, arithmetic, embroidery and 'all sorts of Plain-Work'. Elizabeth and Laurence were both 'very particular' about Lydia's education and rearing. One reason they took her to France three years later was, as a friend said, 'pour *finir* Miss Stern'.[2]

The couple sometimes quarrelled over their child. Elizabeth complained loudly of one incident, which may have taken place about this time.

It was agreed betwixt them [reported John Croft] to have a Strong Box with a Nick in the Top and so they were to putt in what each saved out of their private expenses towards raising a Fortune for their Daughter Lidia when unhappily M[rs] Sterne fell ill, and she espied Laurie breaking open the Strong Box. She fainted, and unluckily a Quarrel ensued. This Story M[rs] S. told herself inter alia which militated against the stability of poor Laurie.

There were health problems too, and the family may have wanted to be close to Dr John Dealtry, the prominent physician, whose house in Lendal Street, today used as the judges' lodging, was only a step from the Minster Yard.[3] Sterne, in poor health that autumn and winter, was dosing himself

[1] Chapman to Fauconberg, 16 March 1760, in NEWBURGH PAPERS. 'Old John Raper', as Chapman called his father, leased land from Lord Fauconberg at Coxwold: *Fauconberg Rentual*, 1755–71, at Beinecke Library, Yale University. Chapman added, about the son, 'he's now Curate for Mr. Sterne at Sutton.'
[2] Jean-Baptiste Tollot to Hall-Stevenson, 8 January 1764, in SEVEN LETTERS, 5. Cf. LETTERS, 186; CROFT. Mrs

deBoissy's school: advertisement in *York Courant*, 14 July 1747.
[3] The house, built by Dr Clifton Winteringham in 1720, was owned by a succession of physicians. Dr Dealtry served in the Royal Hunters and was physician to most of the wealthy families of York. Sterne presented him with an inscribed copy of *Tristram Shandy*. A sketch of him in *European Magazine*, January–June 1799, pp. 19–20.

with tar water.[1] Lydia was sickly. A few months before, Sterne had written from Sutton, 'She is very much out of all Sorts & Our Operator here, tho a very penetrating Man, Seems puzzled ab[t] her Case; If something favorable does not turn out this Day, I will send for Dealtry.' In 1762 he spoke of the 'sad asthma' which had 'martyr'd' his daughter for three winters.[2] For whatever the diagnosis may be worth, the Reverend Dr Randolph Marriott, who lived in the Minster Yard, said that Lydia suffered from epilepsy.[3] This gentleman told a story about Sterne and his daughter which in his own mind showed how devoid was Sterne of humanity and sympathy. It may not mean such to a twentieth-century reader. It does reveal the sort of strain under which the family lived in 1759 and Sterne's determination not to be overcome by their troubles. Marriott told the story to a companion, who passed it on:

> The doctor told me that his daughter had some acquaintance with Miss Sterne, and therefore that she frequently passed an afternoon at his house, that Miss Sterne was subject to violent epileptic fits, that she had been lately seized with one of these which was accompanied with such alarming symptoms as made him and his daughter apprehend that she was dying, that they therefore sent to Mr. Sterne to apprize him of the circumstances, and to come to them immediately. After waiting for some time in anxious expectation, the gentleman made his appearance, and seeing his daughter agonized upon the floor, and seemingly ready to expire, he coldly observed, that she would be well again presently, and that he could not stop a moment, being engaged to play the first fiddle at York that night. Thus he took his leave, and hastily hurried out of the house.

In May, about the time of their move, Sterne's mother died. Agnes Sterne may have ended her miserable life in her son's house in the Minster

---

[1] LETTERS, 64, 73–4, 84.

[2] LETTERS, 61, 162; cf. p. 65. Lydia had entered her signature as a witness in the Sutton marriage register on 19 January 1758 and 15 January 1759.

[3] MARRIOTT. I tentatively identify the 'Dr Marriot' who told the story as Randolph Marriott, DD, rector of Darfield, chaplain to George II, and husband to Lady Diana, daughter of Basil, Fourth Earl of Denbigh: VENN; DRUMMOND RETURNS. Darfield, where he officially resided, is close to Doncaster, but he might well have been Sterne's 'near neighbour', as he said, in the Minster Yard. If so, the story can be dated June 1759 to March 1760, the only period when Sterne lived there with his family.

Yard. We know nothing, really, except that she was buried on 5 May at St Michael le Belfry, the parish church for that corner of York.[1]

A month later, on 9 June, Uncle Jaques died. He was buried at Rise, where he had been rector for thirty-six years. Sterne, who did not appear at the visitation of Alne and Tollerton Court three days later, may have been attending the funeral. Or he may have been at a lawyer's. By a will written thirteen years before, Uncle Jaques left his entire fortune to his mistress.[2] John Croft said that Sterne was 'so offended' at his uncle's leaving him nothing 'that he did not putt on mourning tho' he had it ready, and on the contrary shewed all possible marks of disrespect to his Uncle's memory'. Probably the story is exaggerated, though Sterne must have been very disappointed. Bating the old quarrel, he was the logical choice of an heir, being the oldest of the surviving Sterne males – the only one of that name in holy orders.

And then poor Elizabeth went out of her mind. Her daughter's illness, the move into a new house, the upsetting deaths in the family, and this husband who persisted in writing obscene stories against the advice of old friends – Elizabeth broke under the strain. Perhaps also Sterne had begun to trifle with women again: according to Croft, 'his wife once caught him with the maid, when she pulled him out of bed on the Floor and soon after went out of her senses.' Elizabeth was confined 'under a Lunatick Doctor at a private house at York'. Elizabeth, Croft went on, 'fancied herself the Queen of Bohemia', and Laurence 'treated her as such, with all the supposed respect due to a crowned head'. On the surface, the story is a strange one, but schizophrenia is a strange disease. Maria Theresa, whose name was in almost every newspaper at this time, was Queen of Bohemia as well as Empress of

[1] The Reverend Dudley Rockett, curate of St Michael's and vicar choral (CHAPTER ACTS, 29 April 1758), twice served as Sterne's surrogate in the 'court' meetings for Pickering and Pocklington: *Call Book*, at Borthwick Inst. He recorded the burial only as that of 'Mrs. Sterne': *Registers of St. Michael le Belfry, York*, Part II, ed. Francis Collins (Publications of the Yorkshire Parish Register Society, XI), 1901, p. 270. It is highly unlikely that any other woman named Mrs Sterne could have been in York at this time, and the War Office records of her pension known to CURTIS, 43, indicate that Agnes did not live out the year (above, p. 120, n. 1).

[2] The date of his death is recorded in CHAPTER ACTS. His will, in CLAY, dated 17 November 1746, leaves everything, after funeral expenses, to 'Sarah Benson, now living with me, and to her heirs for ever', presumably the 'jealous Sarah' of the squib in the *York Courant* of 27 November and 4 December 1744, cited above in Chapter 8. A check of the records of the Exchequer and Prerogative Court shows that the will was not contested.

Austria. There is also a remote possibility that Elizabeth's delusions were associated with the Thompson farm in Sutton, which was named Bohemia. Croft told another fantastic story which has become the best known of all anecdotes of Sterne:

> Mrs. Shandy, fancied herself the Queen of Bohemia. Tristram, her husband, to amuse and induce her to take the air, proposed coursing, in the way practised in Bohemia; for that purpose he procured bladders, and filled them with beans, and tied them to the wheels of a single horse chair. When he drove madam into a stubble field, with the motion of the carriage and the bladders, rattle bladder, rattle; it alarmed the hares, and the greyhounds were ready to take them.

This is one of the least trustworthy stories about Sterne. Croft himself claimed no historic truth for it, having put it down, not in his letters to Caleb Whitefoord, but in his vulgar jest-book of 1792, *Scrapeana*.[1] Nevertheless, the germ of the story – Elizabeth's breakdown – is verified from other sources. Dr Thomas Newton, who succeeded Uncle Jaques as precentor and would soon be elevated to the bishopric of Bristol, wrote to the Reverend John Dealtary, on 4 March of the following year: 'I Wish Laury Sterne may have more comfort of his wife than he has had, but he has, and happy for him it is that he has, such a spring of good spirits in himself.'[2] Far less vague is the comment by the unidentified gentleman to whom Sterne showed his manuscript:

> I can say nothing to the Report you have heard about Mrs. Sterne; the few Times I have seen her she was all Life and Spirits; too much so, I thought. He told me, in a Letter last Christmas, that his Wife had lost her Senses by a Stroke of the Palsy; that the Sight of the Mother in that Condition had thrown his poor Child into a fever.

Soon after Elizabeth's collapse, Sterne began to work on his revision of *Tristram Shandy*. Croft explained, 'It was in a great measure owing to her *insane* state, which afforded him the more time for Study, and to relieve

---

[1] The story is told, not about Mrs Sterne, but 'Mrs. Shandy'. It is laid in the country, though Sterne and his family were living in York. It seems unlikely that Sterne would have had greyhounds at his disposal. Still, the story is not impossible: Sterne might have taken Elizabeth to the rural estate of some wealthy friend, perhaps to Stephen Croft's.

[2] DEALTARY LETTERS, fol. 133v. Sterne attended the chapter meeting of 20 June 1759, when Newton was elected as the new precentor.

melancholy, that he first attempted, and sett about the work of Tristram Shandy'. Sterne himself left a more dramatic account:

> He told me . . . [wrote Sterne's new friend] that in the Midst of these Afflictions, it was a strange Incident that his ludicrous Book should be printed off; but that there was a stranger still behind, which was, that every Sentence of it had been conceived and written under the greatest Heaviness of Heart, arising from some Hints the poor Creature had dropped of her Apprehensions; and that in her Illness he had found in her Pocket-Book
>
> '*Jan. 1st, Le dernier de ma vie, hélas!*'

The misfortunes of the Sterne family in 1759 probably cut the ground from under the personal satirist and lampooner, leaving Sterne in a state of mind receptive to broader ironies and more temperate humour. He would not have escaped an agony of guilt – emotions inevitably released by the death of a parent whom one does not love, heightened in Sterne's case by a second death of an antagonistic parent-image, his uncle. Elizabeth's plight would have racked his conscience, associated as it surely was with his philandering, whatever the precise details. She, poor woman, had remained chaste: 'There is not an honest Man', he later told Mrs Montagu, 'who will not do me the Justice to say, I have ever given her the Character of as moral & virtuous a woman as ever God made' (p. 136). And he was having second thoughts about the *Romance*, increasingly aware that his old allies at the minster and he himself shared the ambition for which he had punished Dr Topham. Sterne lost his appetite for pasquinades and local satire. How could he assume a pose of moral righteousness when the frailties of his flesh were so apparent? 'All locality is taken out of the book,' he wrote to Dodsley that autumn, 'the satire [made] general' (p. 81).

He worked hard that spring, writing enough to make up at least four volumes, but only half realizing that his attitudes toward the book were undergoing a change. The first twenty chapters of *Tristram Shandy* as finally printed contain numerous false starts, unfulfilled promises, and inconsistencies.[1] In the opening pages, Walter Shandy is revealed as a weak, elderly gentleman, quite capable of tearful self-pity. He shows nothing of the

---

[1] R. F. Brissenden, '"Trusting to Almighty God": another look at the composition of *Tristram Shandy*', WINGED SKULL, 258–69 – a 'corrective footnote', as Brissenden modestly calls his essay, to Wayne Booth's 'Did Sterne complete *Tristram Shandy?*', *Modern Philology*, XLVIII (1951), 172–83.

'subacid humour' and fortitude which later dominate his character. His brother, 'Mr' Toby Shandy, not yet a soldier, lacks entirely that 'unparallel'd modesty of nature' which figures so largely in the books as a whole.

As Sterne wrote on, the character of Uncle Toby, much the least static in the completed novel,[1] moved to the forefront of his mind, catalysing his imagination. The deaths of his mother and uncle would have carried Sterne's thoughts back to his distant childhood, his adored father, old Colonel Thomas Palliser, and the other soldiers he had loved. During the autumn and winter the bells had been ringing for the capture, first of Fort Louisbourg and then of Duquesne. As Sterne was burying his mother at Belfry church, the bells of the minster were ringing for the capture of Guadeloupe. In June, when his uncle was buried, they rang for the fall of Maria Galante. In August, as he poured over Tindal's *History* trying to align the events of his story with the battles of Marlborough's campaigns, the bells began to ring for the defeat of the French fleet at Lagos. Admiral Hawke was menacing Brest. Pitt's brilliant 'system'[2] was spreading and weakening the French forces, opening the way for Prince Ferdinand's victory at Minden, largely carried by six regiments of British infantry. Not since the '45 had England so admired her soldiers. Can we wonder that Captain Toby Shandy, as E. M. Forster would have put it, kicked to pieces[3] the old *Tristram Shandy* and ushered in the new?

As he wrote, Sterne found himself drifting away from biting Juvenalian satire toward fallible but lovable humorous characters of the sort he had roughly sketched in the 'Key' to the *Romance*. He did not give up satire, of course, but softened and generalized it. Walter Shandy he cast in the Horatian mould, a man who is wrong but not hateful, who typifies 'the pride of human wisdom, That the wisest of us all, should thus outwit ourselves, and eternally forego our purposes in the intemperate act of pursuing them' (V, xvi, 375). The elaborate allegory of the *Job* controversy, he abandoned, reducing his attack upon 'polemic divines' to the lightest of slaps (V, xvi, 387). His Rabelaisian spoof of sermon writers was contracted to a single paragraph about Homenas in the fourth volume (IV, xxv, 315–16). The original book, it has been argued, contained a detailed allegory of the church of York in which Sterne's own struggles and disappointments were repre-

[1] Jean-Jacques Mayoux, 'Variations on the time-sense in *Tristram Shandy*', WINGED SKULL, 3–18.
[2] Julian S. Corbett, *England in the Seven Years War*, 1907, I, 189–90; Gerald S. Graham, *Empire of the North Atlantic*, 1958, p. 169.
[3] *Aspects of the Novel*, 1927, p. 64.

sented in the character of Yorick.[1] All that remains is the history of Parson Yorick in Volume I, a novella within the novel, and the scene of the visitation dinner. Yorick's history is unlike anything else in the book – formal, restrained, Cervantic. It is a *tour de force*, Sterne's way of retaining his self-defence, but disguised and stripped of specific allusions. Instead of transparent names such as Mark Slender and Lorry Slim, we find only Gastripheres and Somnolentus.

But if Sterne intended to erase all identifying clues, he neglected one. The lawyer, Didius, was immediately recognized as Dr Francis Topham. The clue is contained in that incident in which Didius 'coax'd many of the old licensed [midwives] in the neighbourhood, to open their faculties afresh, in order to have this whim-wham of his inserted'. The whim-wham referred to so ambiguously is only a legal phrase, in a document called a 'faculty', giving the midwife her office along with all its 'rights, members, and appurtenances whatsoever' (I, vii, 12–13).[2] The master of the faculties for the Northern Province of the church was Dr Francis Topham.[3]

The identity of another character is implied from his position in Yorick's history. If it were recognized at York, no one was indiscreet enough to speak out publicly. Phutatorius must have represented originally Dr Jaques Sterne. Presumably the character figured prominently in the first satire, written before the precentor's death, though in the finished novel he appears only in the scene of the visitation dinner in Volume VI, published eighteen months after the uncle had died. Phutatorius, it will be remembered, suffered the accident of a hot chestnut's falling into an aperture in his breeches. Assuming that Parson Yorick purposely rolled it across the table at him, he hates Yorick implacably. By implication, then, Phutatorius was chiefly responsible for the 'grand confederacy' which later robbed Yorick of his

[1] Brissenden.
[2] This legal phrase, which so amused Sterne, occurred in numerous legal documents – for instance, Sterne's collation to the vicarage of Sutton, BM: Add. Chart. 16159. On the face is a statement that Sterne has been invested 'with all and singular the Rights Members and Appurtenances' of his new office; *verso* a certificate of performance signed by Philip Harland, the Reverend Richard Musgrave and Ralph Robson, a churchwarden, testifying that Sterne was inducted 'into ye real & corporal possession of ye vicarage of Sutton on ye Forest with all its fruits, profits, members & appurtenances'.

[3] The practice of licensing midwives in the spiritual courts was stopped in 1730: CHAPTER ACTS, 13 November 1730. Presumably the authority passed to the two masters of the faculties, appointees of the Archbishops of Canterbury. Dr Topham served that office for the Northern Province from 1747: VENN.

reputation and preferments (I, xii, 30). One might note, moreover, that Phutatorius wrote a treatise called *de Concubinis retinendis* – 'of keeping concubines'.

The character of Dr Slop is a different case: Sterne made no attempt at all to hide the identity of Dr John Burton. Slop, along with Walter Shandy, spouts the published theory, sometimes the exact words, of Burton's *Essay towards a Complete New System of Midwifry* (1751), and his *Letter to William Smellie, M. D.* (1753). Slop delivers the infant Tristram with the mad forceps invented by Burton and illustrated in his *Essay* – an instrument probably made for the doctor by James Dodd of York, 'Surgeons Instrument Maker', possibly displayed at Dodd's shop in the Pavement.[1] Yet Sterne did soften the satire, as one surmises from the rather clumsy omissions in the published book. He never explains the gruesome instruments in Dr Slop's bag. Though jests are made about the squirt, he gives no hint of its purpose – to baptize a fœtus before the doctor kills it. The curious distortion of Dr Burton's physical appearance accomplishes the same goal. A tall, well-made gentleman armed with murderous instruments for destroying unborn children would have been hateful. By rendering him as the 'little, squat, uncourtly figure' who waddles through *Tristram Shandy*, Sterne made him funny.

Probably Sterne represented many locally recognizable details in his original satire of Burton. Slop's Roman Catholicism – untrue of the historical man – and an allusion to the pistols which Burton had carried on his fateful journey to the rebels in 1745 suggest that Sterne originally intended to show the doctor as a Jacobite. Actually, in the published novel, there are no references to Slop's politics. This is the more surprising since Burton had just set the capstone to his long years of political intrigue: only a few months before, he and Dr Francis Drake had forced a contest in the city election – as dirty and expensive as any York had seen – for which they were repeatedly lampooned.[2] There is nothing in the published book to suggest the ludicrous fist fight between Burton and George Thompson at the Sheriff's Feast, which had so entertained the citizenry a few years before,[3] or Burton's

---

[1] Advertisement in the *York Courant*, 20 November 1744. On Dr Burton's physique, above, Chapter 8.

[2] Guard book of clippings and handbills, BM: 1875. b. 35 (4). On the election: Cedric Collyer, 'The Rockingham connection and country opinion in the early years of George III', LPS, VII (1952–5), 251–75.

[3] On the fight, which had taken place in 1754, see George Thompson, *An Account of What Passed between Mr. George Thompson . . . and Doctor John Burton . . .*, 1756; Robert Davies, 'A memoir of John Burton', YAJ, II (1877–8), 403–40. Thompson, who is noticed briefly in SKAIFE, was a York wine merchant who had served in the Royal Hunters. He was eventually convicted of assault upon Dr Burton.

antiquarian studies which had produced in 1758 the *Monasticon Eboracense*. Sterne's final treatment of Dr Slop is not a local satire at all, but another general representation of philosophic man and his blundering attempt to forestall the inexorable advance of blind fate.

Quebec, the last French bastion in North America, fell in September. 'Can one easily leave the remains of such a year as this?' wrote Horace Walpole in October. 'It is still all gold. . . . Our bells are worn threadbare with ringing for victories.'[1] The climax was yet to come. In November the great French fleet at Brest slipped away to meet an invasion force, waiting at Quiberon, to escort them to England. Hawke's fleet pounced upon them and drove them into Quiberon Bay where most of the French ships were burned or grounded. England was ecstatic. Hawke's triumph virtually assured them of the war; Pitt's strategy had brought mastery of the seas and promises of unlimited commerce.

On 29 November, a day of thanksgiving for Hawke's victory, Sterne was at the assembly rooms listening to the victory song sung by the charming new *prima donna*, Catherine Fourmantel, and 'the best Voices in Town'.[2]

AIR

All Heaven's mercies I review
   With a joyful grateful heart.
Praises still I will renew,
   Blessings still may Heav'n impart.

DUET

We'll proclaim the wond'rous story
   Of the mercies we receive,
From the day-spring's dawn of glory
   To the dewy fall of eve.
All the blessings Heaven is sending
   We'll defend.——Our ceaseless lays
To th' Almighty's throne ascending,
   Wafted on the wings of praise,
In exalted raptures joining,
   We'll employ our happy days,

[1] *Correspondence with George Montagu*, ed. W. S. Lewis and Ralph S. Brown, Jr (Yale Walpole Correspondence, IX–X), 2 vols, 1941, I, 250–1.

[2] Advertisement for the concert in CURIOUS COLLECTION, fol. 77. There is no documentary evidence that Sterne was present.

> All our grateful powers combining,
> And adore his righteous ways.

With the pretty singer, Laurence Sterne was in love. 'My dear Kitty', he was soon writing,

> If this Billet catches you in Bed, You are a lazy, sleepy little Slut – and I am a giddy foolish unthinking fellow for keeping You so late up – but this Sabbath is a day of rest – at the same time that it is a day of Sorrow – for I shall not see my dear Creature today – unless you meet me at Taylor's half an hour after twelve – but in this do as You like – I have ordered Matthew to turn thief & steal you a quart of Honey –
> What is Honey to the sweetness of thee, who art sweeter than all the flowers it comes from. – I love you to distraction Kitty – & will love you on so to Eternity – so adieu & believe what, time only will prove me, that I am
>
> Y^{rs}.   (pp. 82–3)

Catherine Fourmantel, said to be from a Huguenot family, had been singing at Ranelagh in the spring of 1758 and would return there in the summer of 1760. Little is known about her.[1] Some have assumed that she came to York in the winter of 1758–9: Tristram, in one passage, associates his 'dear *Jenny*' with a specific date – 9 March 1759 (I, xviii, 44). But the Jenny of *Tristram Shandy* is surely not Catherine Fourmantel, tradition to the contrary, but a vague general figure of the confidante and mistress. Probably Sterne met Kitty in the autumn of 1759, her earliest known appearance at York, and began seeing her while his wife was confined with the lunatic doctor. Their rendezvous were at the houses of Sterne's friends, Jack Taylor or Marmaduke Fothergill. He promised to paint her picture, 'in black which best becomes You' (p. 81), sent her honey and Calcavillo and a copy of *The Case of Elijah and the Widow of Zerephath consider'd*: 'read it my dear Kitty, & believe me,

---

[1] CURTIS's information, pp. 82, 293, 339, 465, is the most authoritative. He believes she was a connection, possibly a daughter, of Jean Berenger de Formatel, named in the registers of the French Chapel in Leicester Fields. Possibly she was related to Mrs Mary Fourmantel, 'Hair Bag Maker to his Majesty', whose house in Old Bond Street Sterne eventually made his regular London lodging. Curtis was certainly right to reject the account of her by Mrs Henry Weston, preserved in a letter at the Pierpont Morgan Library, as well as the sentimental story told by Isaac D'Israeli when he first published Sterne's letters to her in *Miscellanies of Literature*, 1884, pp. 29–33.

when I assure You, that I see something of the same kind & gentle disposition in your heart, which I have painted in the Prophet's' (p. 83).

If Sterne had an affair with Kitty, there were obstacles: her mother was with her, and the ladies lodged in the house of a respectable matron, Mrs Ann Joliffe, in Stonegate.[1] Nevertheless, by the time he went to London in the following March, he was declaring his passion in frank terms and thanking Kitty for rejecting another suitor:

> It would have stabb'd my Soul, to have thought such a fellow could have the Liberty of coming near you – I therefore take this proof of y^r Love & good principles, most kindly – & have as much faith & dependence upon You in it, as if I was at y^r Elbow. – would to God, I was at this moment, – for I am sitting solitary & alone in my bed Chamber (ten o'Clock at night, after the play) – & would give a Guinea for a Squeeze of y^r hand – I send my Soul perpetually out to see what you are a doing – wish I could convey my Body with it. (p. 97)

His declarations grew even more reckless: 'God will open a Dore, when we shall sometime be much more together, & enjoy Our Desires without fear of Interruption' (p. 104). Whether or not Kitty encouraged such expressions, she saved the letters. She soon dropped out of Sterne's life, and after 1760 her historical record vanishes. 'It is a great pity,' said Tristram Shandy,

> but 'tis certain from every day's observation of man, that he may be set on fire like a candle, at either end——provided there is a sufficient wick standing out; if there is not——there's an end of the affair; and if there is——by lighting it at the bottom, as the flame in that case has the misfortune generally to put out itself——there's an end of the affair again.   (VIII, xv, 553)

Sterne completed the first two volumes of his book in the autumn, about the time he began seeing Kitty. His scheme for publishing them did honour to his Jaques and Rawden ancestors. 'I propose', he wrote to Dodsley, 'to print a lean edition, in two small volumes, of the size of Rasselas, and on the same paper and type, at my own expense, merely to feel the pulse of the world, and that I may know what price to set upon the remaining volumes, from the reception of these.' He would correct the proof himself and see the volumes through the press. Part of the edition he would sell in Hinxman's shop; the rest he would send to Dodsley, who would have the exclusive right to market them in London. 'If my book sells and has the run our

[1] LETTERS, 97; CURTIS, 99.

critics expect, I propose to free myself of all future troubles of this kind, and bargain with you, if possible, for the rest. . . . Will you patronise my book upon these terms, and be as kind a friend to it as if you had bought the copyright?' (pp. 80–1).

During the last few days of 1759, the two volumes were printed in the shop of the late Caesar Ward, now operated by his widow, Ann. As agreed with Dodsley, about half the copies were sent to London.[1] Sterne himself took the financial risk.[2] The money was lent, said John Croft, by a Mr Lee, 'a Gentⁿ of York and a Bachelor of a liberall turn of mind'. This was William Phillips Lee, a friend of John Fountayne, William Stables and Stephen Croft, a book collector and man of cultivated taste.[3] Sterne was careful to reveal nothing on the title page about where the book was printed: too often the London buyer would pass up a provincial book. These first volumes would indeed sell well in London, and James Dodsley to bring out a second edition would pay £250 for the copyright.[4]

Next, this entrepreneur decided that he must have the support of in-fluential people in London. Who better than David Garrick? To this end, he enlisted the help of Kitty, who had a slight acquaintance with the great actor. Sterne penned a letter which Kitty, we suppose, dutifully copied, signed and sent off.[5] 'There are two Volumes just published here which

[1] Professor Curtis, following the lead of Davies in YORK PRESS, 262–3, was the first to demonstrate upon sound evidence that the first edition of Vols I–II were printed at York: 'The first printer of *Tristram Shandy*', *PMLA*, XLVII (1932), 777–89. The hesitation on the part of some scholars to accept his conclusions should now be dispelled by the recent work of Kenneth Monkman, 'The biblio-graphy of the early editions of "Tristram Shandy"', *The Library*, Fifth Series (1970), 11–39. The note by Isaac Reed, cited by Monkman, which implies that Sterne went to London in 1759 to strike his bargain with Dodsley, surely derives from Reed's misunderstanding of what Dodsley had told him about his, Dodsley's, rejection of the first version of *Tristram Shandy*. Sterne, in his second letter to Dodsley, refers to his previous correspondence with

the printer, but not to any personal con-ference between them.

[2] LETTERS, 80–1; CROFT.

[3] John Croft gave such a garbled account of the publication that one might well question his story about Mr Lee were it not for the recent information gathered about William Phillips Lee by John H. Harvey, 'A lost link with Laurence Sterne', YAJ, XLII (1967), 103–7.

[4] The agreement, in Sterne's hand, dated 8 March 1760, and signed by Sterne, James Dodsley and (as witness) Richard Berenger, is now in the Berg Collection of the New York Public Library.

[5] LETTERS, 85–6. The MS, at the Pier-pont Morgan Library, is in Sterne's hand and lacks address, salutation, or other evidence to demonstrate that it was intended for Garrick; nevertheless, that theory, first advanced by CROSS, 585, is convincing.

have made a great noise, & have had a prodigious Run', wrote Kitty. 'The Author . . . is a kind & generous friend of mine whom Providence has attachd to me in this part of the world where I came a stranger. . . . His name is Sterne, a gentleman of great Preferment & a Prebendary of the Church of York.' To add a bit of spice while maintaining the speaker's character as an *ingénue*, Sterne had Kitty add, 'the Graver People however say, tis not fit for young Ladies to read his Book. so perhaps you'l think it not fit for a young Lady to recommend it however the Nobility, & great Folks stand up mightily for it. & say tis a good Book tho' a little tawdry in some place' (pp. 85–6).

As the volumes began to disappear from Hinxman's shop, criticism began to mount among Sterne's more prudish colleagues and neighbours. It was time to prepare his defences. He edited the letter he had written during the summer to the older clergyman.[1] He carefully wrote another letter, probably for publication should the need arise, addressed to a physician of uncertain identity – possibly Sir Noah Thomas of Scarborough, or Dr Henry Goddard of Foston, near York.[2] The physician, whoever he was, had charged Sterne with cowardice and injustice for making fun of a great man who was now dead – Dr Richard Mead, the celebrated London physician. How anyone would recognize Sterne's 'Dr. Kunastrokius', who took 'the greatest delight imaginable in combing of asses tails, and plucking the dead hairs out with his teeth' (p. 13), is hard to imagine unless Dr Mead's sexual oddities were widely known.[3] Sterne wrote out a general

---

[1] Both versions in LETTERS, 75–80.

[2] CURTIS, 91, says that the *London Chronicle* of 3–6 May 1760, p. 435, identified the man as a 'doctor of the neighbourhood', and adds, 'conjecture has identified him with Dr. Noah Thomas, the "celebrated physician" at Scarborough'. Joseph Craddock, in *Literary and Miscellaneous Memoirs*, 4 vols, 1828, I, 9, tells of meeting Sterne at Dr Thomas's when he, Craddock, was a boy of about seventeen – roughly 1760. Willard Connelly, in *Laurence Sterne as Yorick*, 1958, p. 37, suggested that the correspondent was Dr Goddard. If so, Sterne's phrase in his letter to Garrick of 27 January, 'being told yesterday by Doct: Goddard, That You had actually spoke well of my Book' (p. 86), refers to the critical letter from the

physician. That letter would have come into Sterne's hand on the 26th: in his answer, dated the 30th, he says, 'I have waited four days to cool myself' (p. 88).

[3] A cancellation of the name 'Kunastrokius' in Sterne's *Journal to Eliza* suggests that his target was indeed Dr Mead: LETTERS, 347. The brief satirical jab was read as a reference to Mead's keeping in his house a young married woman for the pleasures of dalliance even when he had become impotent. Her husband was said to have lived in the house and sometimes witnessed the love-play. See *The Cornutor of Seventy-Five. Being a Genuine Narrative of the Life, Adventures, and Amours, of Don Ricardo Honeywater, Fellow of the Royal College of Physicians at Madrid* [1748]; and *Don Ricardo Honeywater Vindicated*, 1748.

defence of satire, more notable for its rhetoric than for its argument: 'Heaven forbid the stock of chastity should be lessen'd by the life and opinions of Tristram Shandy – yes, his opinions – it would certainly debauch 'em! God take them under his protection in this fiery trial' (p. 90).

He probably heard that the book was selling well in London. Late in January, he was told that Garrick had been recommending *Tristram Shandy*. He promptly sent the actor a copy, along with a letter – which he signed himself – cleverly designed to get around the guard of a man whose life was plagued by writers seeking his patronage. 'I took up my Pen twice——hang it! – I shall write a vile insinuating Letter, the english of which will be, – to beg Mr Garrick's good word for my Book, whether the Book deserves it [or] no – I will not, – the Book shall go to the Devil first.' So, he would only send his thanks for the support he had heard about. 'I know not what it was (tho "I lye abominably," because I know very well) which inclined me more to wish for your Approbation, than any Other's' (p. 86). It was deftly handled. Garrick was Sterne's champion before he set foot in London.

On 5 February the *London Chronicle* reprinted the sketch of Yorick, commenting, 'It is by some supposed to be the Character of the Author, as he himself Chuses it should be exhibited.' Exactly so. Did Sterne send it to the *Chronicle* himself? An advertisement for *Tristram Shandy* appeared in the *York Courant* of the 12th. Everyone in York was talking about Lorry Sterne's turning writer, and Lydia was being teased by the girls in her school with the names of Miss Tristram and Miss Shandy. She avenged herself, says the anecdotist, by trumping up love letters, sending them to her young tormentors, and signing them with names of actors currently playing in York. The girls, of course, were punished by their parents.[1]

There must have been a good deal of whispering and pointing and nodding of wigged heads when Sterne appeared, as we suppose, at the benefit concert for Miss Fourmantel on 15 February in the assembly rooms. 'Miss Fourmantel begs Leave', read an advertisement in the *Courant* four days later, 'to take this Way of returning her Thanks to the Ladies and Gentlemen who honored her with their presence at the Concert.' Probably in a gay mood, he went to a chapter meeting on 7 January to discuss the old problem of what constituted a residence for a residentiary. He was at another on 1

Sterne's passage provoked two dreadful pieces, supposedly comic, of 1760, *Explanatory Remarks upon the Life and Opinions of Tristram Shandy . . . by Jeremiah Kun-* astrokius; and *The Life and Opinions of Jeremiah Kunastrokius.*
[1] CROFT.

March, the last he ever attended, where, after so many long years, a regula-
tion was passed giving the dean control over substitute preachers. He may
have said a good deal that day, for no one was a greater authority upon this
topic. But he must have vowed silently never again to preach at the minster
for a fee of £1.

Next morning, when he was walking through the streets, he met Stephen
Croft, who told him that he was taking his carriage to London and asked
if he would like to come along. The squire, thinking that his friend ought to
be in London looking after his interests, offered to take him up and to defray
his expenses home again: he could have an hour to pack; then they must
be off. Sterne answered, 'all that was very kind, but he cou'd not leave his
wife in the state that she was in, to which Mᵣ C. answered that as he cou'd
not possibly do her any good by his attendance that he had better go along
with him.'[1] An hour later Sterne climbed into the carriage in the Minster
Yard, and they rattled off down Stonegate past Hinxman's shop and Kitty's
lodging into Coney Street and by the George. Then it was over Ouse
Bridge, up Micklegate, through the Bar, and on toward London.

In his pocket Sterne carried a dedication addressed to the man of the
hour, the 'Great Commoner', William Pitt. 'Never poor Wight of a Dedi-
cator had less hopes from his Dedication, than I have from this of mine . . .'
If there were a second edition in London, he would ask Mr Pitt's permission
to dedicate the book to him.[2] The Marlborough of his time, Sterne must
have thought, would be pleased with Captain Shandy and Corporal Trim.
'. . . it is written in a bye corner of the kingdom, and in a retired thatch'd
house, where I live in a constant endeavour to fence against the infirmities of
ill health, and other evils of life, by mirth; being firmly persuaded that
every time a man smiles,——but much more so, when he laughs, that it
adds something to this Fragment of Life.'

[1] CROFT.   [2] As he did: LETTERS, 103.

Appendix

Portraits of Sterne

The image of Sterne's physical person is well preserved in two excellent portraits of unquestioned authenticity – the 1760 painting by Sir Joshua Reynolds, and the bust by Joseph Nollekens (1766). But the image has been obscured. In the late eighteenth century, Wedgwood turned out many busts labelled 'Laurence Sterne' made from fanciful models supplied in 1779 by James Hoskins, and in 1781 by John Flaxman the elder. Cheap editions of Sterne's works carried bizarre engravings of Reynolds's portrait – copies at third and fourth hand. In our own times, writers have published a number of bad portraits and paintings of obscure history said to represent Sterne even though their subjects resemble not at all the man seen by Reynolds and Nollekens. The following iconography attempts to establish the authenticity of eight portraits. Two of these have been lost entirely, and three exist only as copies. The catalogue includes engravings of the genuine portraits, but inscriptions are rendered in italics regardless of the type style of the original – in accordance with the practice of Chaloner Smith. It does not include post-humous caricatures, the most amusing of which is the statuette which Percy Fitzgerald made and presented to the dean and chapter of York, to the embarrassment of that body. I am responsible for all judgements, but I am happy to acknowledge my debt to John Ingamells, Curator of the York City Art Gallery, upon whose practised eye I have often relied. I have also had the invaluable advice of J. F. Kerslake (hereinafter referred to parenthetically as JFK), Deputy Keeper of the National Portrait Gallery, and have consulted the manuscript of his forthcoming *Catalogue of the Earliest Georgian Portraits in the National Portrait Gallery, 1714–60*, which includes an iconography of Sterne.

I *Authentic Portraits*

1. THOMAS BRIDGES. Oil on canvas. Caricature of Sterne in a harlequin's costume, accompanied in the same painting by Sterne's caricature of Bridges dressed as a mountebank. Location unknown. Possibly the earliest portrait of Sterne. Painted at least by 1759 when Bridges moved to London, but probably

much earlier (above, Chapter 10). The explanation of this double portrait, 'a coarse production, in oil', was made by Dr James Atkinson of York (1759–1839), the owner, to Thomas Frognall Dibdin, who in 1838 or before had an engraving made of it (see below). Dibdin seems not to have known that the figure of Bridges was closely copied by Sterne from a comic broadside, 'The Infallible Mountebank, or Quack Doctor'. Sterne spoke of the painting in a letter to his wife of 28 December 1761: 'The 2 Pictures of the Mountebank & his Macaroni – is in a Lady's hands, who upon seeing 'em, – most cavallierly declared She would never part with them' (p. 148).

A *Engraving*

> CHARLES JOHN SMITH. *c.* 1838. Line engraving; $6\frac{1}{16}$ by $4\frac{5}{8}$ inches. In Thomas Frognall Dibdin, *Bibliographical, Antiquarian, and Picturesque Tour in the Northern Counties of England and in Scotland*, 1838, I, 213. Reproduced in Wilbur L. Cross, *Life and Times of Laurence Sterne*, New York, 1929, p. 118; and in *The Winged Skull*, ed. Arthur H. Cash and John Stedmond, 1971, p. 189. Mediocre quality. Delightful as a symbol, but of limited value as an icon.   PLATES I–II

2. CHRISTOPHER STEELE. *c.* 1756. Oil. Location unknown. George Romney, then serving as Steele's apprentice, reported that Steele painted a portrait of Sterne during the period 1756–7 when Steele had a studio in York (William Hayley, *Life of George Romney*, Chichester, 1809, pp. 26–7). Cf. below, No. 11.

3. SIR JOSHUA REYNOLDS. 1760. The 'Lansdowne portrait'. Oil on canvas, 50 by 40 inches. Signed and dated on the papers under Sterne's elbow. In this delightful portrait, Sterne peers at the observer with an expression at once searching and amused. He sits resting his right elbow on a table and leaning his head slightly on his right hand. The forefinger almost touches his wig, which is slightly askew. His left hand rests jauntily on his hip, a ring on the little finger. As an icon, the portrait is excellent, complimented and corroborated by Nollekens's bust (below, No. 7). Since Reynolds's paints tend to change colour slightly with age, Sterne's colouring may be better preserved in the best copies (below, B 1–2). The provenance is good. The artist's appointment book (at Burlington House) records Sterne's sittings on 20, 25, 29 March, 3, 6, 19, 20, 21 April 1760. In a letter of 11 November 1764, Sterne asked Robert Foley to send the Baron d'Holbach 'one of the best Impressions of my Picture from Reynolds' (p. 231). Thomas Gray alluded to the painting in a letter to Thomas Wharton, 22 April 1760: 'Tristram Shandy is still a greater object of admiration, the Man as well as the Book . . . his portrait is

done by Reynolds, and now engraving' (*Letters*, ed. Duncan C. Tovey, 1909–12, II, 137). Reynolds exhibited the painting at the Society of Artists in 1761 (82) and 1768 (97). Sometime thereafter, it seems, he sold it to John FitzPatrick, Second Earl of Upper Ossory, who was a personal acquaintance (Joseph Farington, *Diary*, ed. James Greig, 1922–8, V, 19). Ossory owned it by 1813, when he lent it for an exhibition at the British Institution (NPG records). It passed at his death in 1823 to his nephew and ward, Henry Richard Fox, Third Baron Holland; at Holland's death in 1840, it was sold to Henry Petty-FitzMaurice, Third Marquess of Lansdowne. Numbered 31 in George E. Ambrose's catalogue of Lansdowne paintings, 1897. (See James Northcote, *Life of Sir Joshua Reynolds*, 1819, I, 168–9; William Cotton, *Sir Joshua Reynolds*, 1856, p. 92; Charles Leslie and Tom Taylor, *Life and Times of Sir Joshua Reynolds*, 1865, I, 190–3; Algernon Graves and William Vine Cronin, *History of the Works of Sir Joshua Reynolds*, 1899, III, 933–4.) Reproduced as frontispiece to Curtis's edition of Sterne's *Letters*; in Sir Walter Armstrong, *Sir Joshua Reynolds*, 1900, p. 88; and in C. R. L. Fletcher and Emery Walker, *Historical Portraits, 1700–1850*, Oxford, 1919, III, 146, where it is mistakenly said to be in the collection of the Earl of Sandwich.   FRONTISPIECE

A *Engravings*. Only two engravings of the Reynolds – those by Fisher and S. W. Reynolds – were made for mounting and framing. The others are book illustrations, most of them frontispieces to various editions of Sterne printed in England and abroad during the period of 1780–1880. A search might turn up forty or more, the vast majority copies, or copies of copies, of Ravenet's rather mediocre frontispiece for the *Sermons* of 1760. Freeman O'Donoghue lists only a few in his *Catalogue of Engraved British Portraits . . . in the British Museum*, 1914, IV, 189–90. The copyists usually reversed the image of whatever they worked from. Since Ravenet's engraving was already a reverse of the painting, the first copies of Ravenet put the figure back into the original position; copies of those reverse it again, etc. By the time the copies are at fourth or fifth hand, the image of Sterne has become grotesque. The following list includes only engravings which the writer believes to be original, i.e., made directly from the painting.

(1) SIMON FRANÇOIS RAVENET. 1760. Line engraving; $6\frac{1}{4}$ by $3\frac{5}{8}$ inches; subdimensions, $5\frac{3}{4}$ by $3\frac{3}{8}$ inches. Reverse image, oval, reduced to a half-length. Frontispiece to Vol. I of Sterne's *Sermons*, which appeared on 22 May 1760. In April, probably, Sterne had written to Catherine Four-mantel, 'There is a fine print going to be done of me – so I shall make the most of myself, & sell both inside & out' (p. 105). The quality of the engraving, however, is mediocre. Ravenet exhibited a 'head of Dr.

Sterne' at the Society of Artists in 1761 (210), perhaps a preliminary drawing.

(2) EDWARD FISHER. ?1760. Mezzotinto. Probably requested or commissioned by Reynolds, who sold prints. He noted in his account book (Fitzwilliam Museum) on 26 March 1766, 'Mʳ Smart for Mʳ Sterns Print 0/5/0'. The date of 1760 cannot be assigned with certainty since Gray's comment quoted above (No. 3) might refer to the Ravenet engraving. But the date seems likely because the first inscription (*State II*, below) did not name Sterne's third living, the curacy of Coxwold, as though the engraver's informant was unaware that Sterne had been presented to a new living. Sterne was licensed to Coxwold on 29 March, while he was sitting for Reynolds. The engraving is excellent, though the right eye has a piercing look not to be found in the painting. Fisher was proud enough of his work to exhibit the engraving at the Society of Artists in 1761 (189). The engraving was popular and went through several states, the first three of which were probably Fisher's own work. John Chaloner Smith, *British Mezzotinto Portraits*, 1878–83, Pt. II, 506, described four states, and his list was corrected and expanded to five by Charles E. Russell, *English Mezzotinto Portraits and their Early States*, 1926, II, 110. The following list is longer and differs on several points.
State I. 14¾ by 10¾ inches; subdimensions, 13⅜ by 10¼ inches. No inscription; inscription space uncleaned. Described by Russell, but the location is now unknown. No doubt this is an engraver's proof.
State II. Dimensions unchanged. Inscription space cleaned and inscribed, *J. Reynolds pinxt.* | *E. Fisher fecit.* | *Laurence Sterne, A. M.* | *Prebendary of York Vicar of Sutton on the Forest and of Stillington near York* | *pʳ 5ˢ*. Called State I by Chaloner Smith, State II by Russell. These were the first prints made available to the public. Sterne may have been disappointed to discover that his new living was not mentioned in the inscription. Perhaps he himself convinced Fisher that the inscription should be changed to that we see in the next. A print of State II in the British Museum Print Room. Reproduced in Russell, I, Plate 12; and in Chaloner Smith's portfolio of plates issued with new title pages dated 1884 and sometimes found bound into the original edition. PLATE III
State III. Plate reduced to 14 by 10 inches; subdimensions, 13 by 10 inches. Inscription erased and replaced, perhaps at Sterne's urging, with a Shandian inscription that seems to acknowledge his growing list of offices: *J. Reynolds pinxt.* | *E. Fisher fecit.* | *Laurence Sterne, A. M. &c. &c. &c.* If, as Kerslake suggests, Sterne gave a print to Eliza Draper in 1767, it was probably this version. He wrote to her that spring, 'And as thou

hast fixed thy Bramin's portrait over thy writing-desk; and will consult it in all doubts and difficulties. – Grateful and good girl! Yorick smiles contentedly over all thou dost; his picture does not do justice to his own complacency!' (p. 305; see also p. 348). A few weeks later, on 6 May, Reynolds noted in his account book, 'Mr Stern for 10 Prints 2/15/0'. This state is not recognized in Chaloner Smith or Russell. Print in the Owen D. Young guardbook, Berg Collection, New York Public Library.

State IV. Plate further reduced to 13$\frac{7}{8}$ by 9$\frac{7}{8}$ inches; subdimensions, 13 by 9$\frac{7}{8}$ inches. A new inscription: *Reynolds pinx^t | E. Fisher fec^t | Laurence Sterne, A. M. &c. &c. &c. | Sold by Jno Bowles & Son at the Black Horse in Cornhill*. John Bowles operated from the Black Horse in Cornhill from *c.* 1740 until his death in 1779 (*A Dictionary of the Printers and Booksellers . . . 1726 to 1775*, Oxford, 1968). Probably this is what Chaloner Smith called State II, Russell State III, neither giving the full inscription. If so, it is difficult to understand why Chaloner Smith said it was 'retouched and the extraordinary, characteristic, and almost demoniacal expression of eyes and face wholly lost by ignorant alteration'. In the first place, the comment about the original expression is too extreme; in the second, the image shows no evidence of tampering, though it is somewhat softened by the wearing down of the plate. Chaloner Smith's remark might better apply to State VI, below. Print in the British Museum Print Room.

State V. Dimensions unchanged. Another inscription: *J. Reynolds pinx^t | E. Fisher fec^t | Laurence Sterne, A. M. &c. &c. &c. | Printed for R Sayer at the Golden Buck in Fleet Street*. Russell called this a 'very late' state and did not number it with his list. But this state could hardly be subsequent to State VI, below, which Russell included on his list. There is no evidence that the plate has been tampered with, though again the image is softened through the wearing of the plate. Robert Sayer established his business in Fleet Street in 1775; by 1780 the business was in the hands of his pupil, Laurie (*Dictionary of Printers and Booksellers*).

State VI. Dimensions unchanged. Inscribed anew, *Reynolds pinx^t | E. Fisher fec^t | Laurence Sterne, A. M. | Prebendary of York, Vicar of Sutton on the Forest and of Stillington near York. | London Printed for Robt Sayer at the Golden Buck in Fleet Street | 76*. Presumably Sayer ran off so many copies as to wear out parts of the original plate. In this state the plate has been extensively altered, including a marked change in the eyes, which are darkened and stare stupidly to the left of the observer. In all other states the eyes are focused upon the observer. Sayer's return to an inscription similar to that of State II may have been an attempt to pass off these prints as originals. The number 76, no doubt, corresponded with a number in some sale catalogue. Probably this is what Chaloner Smith described ambiguously as State III, Russell as State IV, though there may be two versions of this, without the number in the lower right corner (Chaloner Smith's III) or with it (Chaloner Smith's IV). The prints in the British Museum Print Room and the Victoria and Albert Museum bear the number. Reproduced without the inscription by Cross, frontispiece to his edition of 1929, from a print in the Morgan Library.

(3) JOHN BARLOW (called Inigo Barlow by Ulrich Thieme and Felix Becker, *Allgemeines Lexicon der Bildenden Künstler*, Leipzig, 1909). Line engraving; 4¼ by 4 inches. Reduced to a head. Frontispiece to an unidentified book, possibly to Vol. I of Sterne's *Works*, Cadell, 4 vols., 1803, a copy of which the writer has not been able to locate. Excellent quality. The clipping in the Sterne file, Print Room of the New York Public Library, is accompanied by a pencil drawing which may be Barlow's working sketch (below, C, 2). A mediocre copy of the engraving, oval, 2½ by 2 inches, inscribed lightly below, *Satchnell Del^t | London Published by Cadell & Davies Strand June 12 1803 | Widnell Sculp^t*, appears with the Fry engraving (below, 4) in Vol. I of the 1819 *Works* as the illustration for the *Memoirs*. A much better copy, unsigned, appeared as frontispiece to Foscolo's translation of *A Sentimental Journey*, Pisa, 1813 (reproduced in J. C. T. Oates, *Shandyism and Sentiment, 1760–1800*, Cambridge: Bibliographical Society, 1968). Curiously, Barlow is responsible for a bad engraving of the Ravenet type which makes Sterne appear fat – frontispiece to *Beauties of Sterne*, 1793 and subsequent editions.   PLATE IV

(4) WILLIAM THOMAS FRY. 1819. Line engraving; 3¹⁵⁄₁₆ by 3³⁄₁₆ inches. Reduced to a half-length. Frontispiece to Vol. I of Sterne's *Works*, 4 vols., 1819. Inscribed, *Laurence Sterne, A. M. | Engraved by W. T. Fry from an original Picture | by Sir Joshua Reynolds. | Published Septr 10, 1819, by T. Cadell & W. Davies, Strand, London*. Fair quality.

(5) SAMUEL WILLIAM REYNOLDS. c. 1823. Mezzotinto; 9¼ by 6⁹⁄₁₆ inches. Subdimensions, 5⅛ by 4 inches. Inscribed, *Sir Joshua Reynolds Pinx^t | S. W. Reynolds Sculp^t | L. Sterne | Proof*. Appeared as Plate 36, Vol. VII, *Engravings from the Works of Sir Joshua Reynolds . . . by S. W. Reynolds*, n. d. (in the Frick Art Reference Library; in the issue at the British

PLATE I

Thos. Bridges.   CJ Smith Sculp   Lawrence Sterne

THOS. BRIDGES AND LAWRENCE STERNE, AS MOUNTEBANKS.

PLATE II

J. Reynolds pinx.   *E.S. Fisher fecit*

Laurence Sterne. A.M.

Prebendary of York, Vicar of Sutton on the Forest and of Stillington near York.

PLATE III

L. Sterne.

PLATE IV

PLATE V

PLATE VI

PLATE VII

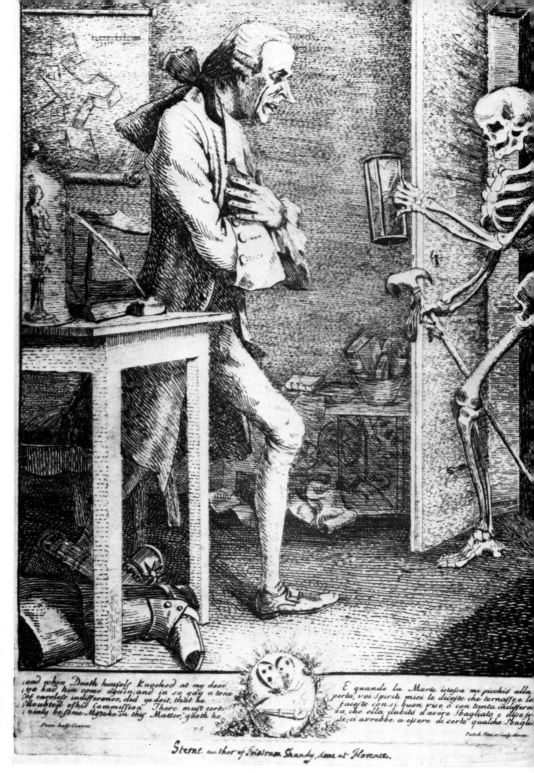

;and when Death himself Knocked at my door
;ye bad him come again;and in so gay a tone
of careless indifference, did ye doit, that he
;doubted of his Commission. There must cert:
;ainly be some Mistake in the Matter, quoth he

E quando la Morte istessa mi picchiò alla
porta, voi Spirite miei le diceste che tornasse, e lo
faceste con si buon riso, e con tanta indifferen:
za, che ella dubitò d'avere sbagliato, e dise fra
se; ci sarrebbe a essere di certo qualche sbagli

Price half-Crown

T.P.

Patch Pinx: et Sculp: Jbro

Sterne, author of Tristram Shandy, done at Florence.

PLATE VIII

PLATE IX

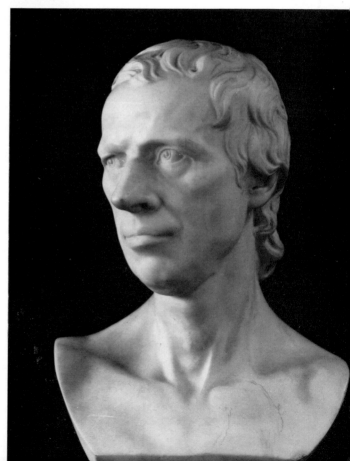

PLATE X

PLATE XI

PLATE XII

PLATE XIII

PLATE XIV

Museum Print Room, the plate appears in Vol. IV). Mediocre quality. Samuel Reynolds's collection of 357 small mezzotintos printed on folio sheets was prepared during the period 1820–6; it required the engraver to travel about England, locating and copying virtually all the known Reynolds paintings (DNB; *Bryan's Dictionary of Painters and Engravers*, ed. George C. Williamson, 1903–5). In the library of the National Portrait Gallery may be found, along with a first-state print, a later state inscribed, *Sir J. Reynolds. | S. W. Reynolds | Revᵈ Laurence Sterne | In the collection of Lord Holland | London, 1836, Hodgson & Graves, 6 Pall Mall.*

B *Copies in oil*

(1) ANON. 1768 or after. The 'Whatman painting', reported by Cross to be an original Reynolds (ed. 1929, p. 351). Oil on canvas; *c.* 31 by 26 inches; reduced to a half-length. Lacks the inkwell and plume. In a private collection. The first indication that Reynolds may have painted a second portrait of Sterne arose when this painting was shown at the Exhibition of the Royal House of Guelph, London, 1891. The exhibition catalogue, issued by the New Gallery, listed two Reynolds portraits – that of 1760 (above, No. 3) and another (305) described in the following terms:

> Half-length, seated, nearly facing, right elbow on table and right hand supporting his head, in gown and wig. Canvas 30 × 25 in. / This picture was given by Sterne to Edward Stanley, Esq., and bequeathed by him to his son-in-law, James Whatman, Esq., of Vinters [i.e., Vintner], Maidstone. / BY SIR J. REYNOLDS, P. R. A. / Lent by MRS WHATMAN.

Graves and Cronin repeated this information verbatim, and Cross, accepting their account, assigned the date of 1764 on the grounds that Reynolds's appointment book showed an entry of Sterne's name for 11 June 1764. Several considerations argue against this interpretation. First, and perhaps most important, it is unlikely that Reynolds would have painted Sterne twice in identical poses. Second, it is unlikely that he would have attempted an oil portrait in a single sitting. Third, among the papers on the table in this painting is one which shows part of the title 'A Sentimental Journey'; therefore, it was painted after 27 February 1768, when the novel appeared. To be sure, Sterne sat for Reynolds two or three times in late February and early March of that year. He was quite ill at the time and, in fact, died on 18 March. Since in the Whatman painting Sterne appears healthy, it is difficult to identify it with anything Reynolds might have painted of a dying man.

Presumably, Reynolds did not finish the portrait of 1768 (see below, No. 18). Lastly, the history of the painting given in the Guelph catalogue, probably a family tradition, has not been corroborated. There is no evidence to link Sterne with the Whatman ancestor, Edward Stanley (1718–89). Curtis hypothesized that Stanley was the mysterious 'Mr S.' to whom Sterne addressed one letter, but his speculation rested upon his unquestioned acceptance of Graves and Cronin's description of the Whatman painting (*Letters*, pp. 284–5). Furthermore, there is no reliable evidence that Reynolds ever gave Sterne a portrait. In 1865 Leslie and Taylor quoted a letter (repeated in a note by Graves and Cronin) in which Sterne speaks of receiving a portrait from Reynolds, but the letter is spurious. All in all, it seems best to regard the Whatman painting as a good contemporary copy of the 1760 Reynolds with minor variations – the best copy of the figure itself in the opinion of Kerslake, who has examined the painting. It passed out of the Whatman family some time after the Guelph exhibition and was eventually acquired by Asher Wertheimer (d. 1918), a well-known antique art dealer, who believed it to be an original. As such, it was sold at Christie's from the Wertheimer Collection (the Christie's catalogue clearly identifying the Whatman painting) on 18 June 1920, lot 48, to Wertheimer's son, C. J. Conway (name changed, 1916). In 1953 it was authenticated as an original Reynolds by Kingsley Adams of the National Portrait Gallery, and is believed to be an original by its present owner.

(2) Attributed to R. HOLME, said to have been a pupil of Reynolds, but otherwise unidentified. At Jesus College, Cambridge. John Croft, writing in 1795, said, 'Sterne's Picture hangs in the Combination Room of that College' (*Whitefoord Papers*, ed. W. A. S. Hewins, Oxford, 1898, p. 229), but he must have been referring to another picture, probably a print. The Holme copy was in the collection of Beriah Botfield in 1848 (*Catalogue of Pictures in the Possession of Beriah Botfield, Esq. at Norton Hall*, 1848, p. 19). Botfield, who seems not to have known the painting was a copy, lent it for an exhibition at the British Institution in 1857 (128). Good quality.

(3) ANON. Oil on copper; circular. At the Irish National Portrait Gallery. Bought at the Earl of Lonsdale's sale, 1887 (NPG records). Poor quality.

(4) ANON. At York Minster Library on loan from the York City Art Gallery. Mediocre quality.

(5) ANON. In the collection of Dr F. Hermann, Norfolk, Virginia. Poor quality (NPG records).

(6) Attributed to JAMES NORTHCOTE. Location unknown. Exhibited, 1868, in the Yorkshire Worthies section of the National Exhibition of Works of Art, Leeds (3179), on loan from the collection of Mrs Wallis. The attribution, made in the exhibition catalogue, is doubtful.

(7) JAMES LONSDALE. c. 1826. Location unknown. Lonsdale, portrait painter and copyist, spoke of offering the painting to the Duke of Sussex in a letter addressed to Mrs Ryves, 12 January 1826 (Berg Collection).

C *Copies in pencil*

(1) HENRY BONE. 1814. $8\frac{1}{4}$ by $6\frac{2}{3}$ inches. In the National Portrait Gallery Library. An original working drawing for an enamel, on cross-lined paper, dated 1814, mounted with other such drawings in a two-volume folio, called on the spine *Bone Drawings*, II, f. 96. The enamel itself, measuring $8\frac{1}{4}$ by $6\frac{5}{8}$ inches, was sold at Christie's on 30 June 1832, lot 34, to Sir J. Farqueher (Christie's records). By 1957 the enamel was in the collection of Mrs John Hales-Took: photograph in *Connoisseur Year Book*, 1957, p. 68, Plate 6.

(2) Attributed to SIR JOSHUA REYNOLDS. 5 by $3\frac{7}{8}$ inches. Head. In the Sterne file, Print Room, New York Public Library. Formerly in the Ford Collection. The attribution, made in a note pencilled on the drawing, is doubtful. Probably a working drawing for an engraving, possibly for Barlow's engraving (above, No. 3, A (3), which accompanies it in the file. The quality is excellent. Brought to light by Gardner D. Stout, Jr, and reproduced as frontispiece to his edition of *A Sentimental Journey*, Berkeley and Los Angeles, 1967.

(3) SIMON FRANÇOIS RAVENET. See above, No. 3, A (1).

4. LOUIS CARROGIS, *dit* CARMONTELLE. 1762. Location unknown. Spoken of by Sterne in a letter to Garrick, 19 March 1762: 'The Duke of Orleans has suffered my portrait to be added to the number of some odd men in his collection; and a gentleman who lives with him has taken it most expressively, at full length – I propose to obtain an etching of it, and to send it you' (pp. 157–8). No etching, however, is known.

A *Copies*. Probably it was a copy of the Carmontelle which was owned by Sterne's banker in Paris, Robert Foley. Sterne wrote to him from Montpellier on 5 October 1763, 'I believe I shall beg leave to get a copy of my own [picture] from yours, when I come in *propria persona*' (p. 202). He wrote again from York on 11 November 1764,

> Is it possible for you to get me over a Copy of my picture anyhow? – If so – I would write to Mlle Navarre to make as good a Copy from it as She possibly could – with a view to do her Service here – & I w^d remit her 5 Louis – I really believe, twill be the parent of a dozen portraits to her – if she executes it with the spirit of the Original in y^r hands – for it will be seen by half London – and as my Phyz – is as remarkable as myself——if she preserves the Character of both, 'twill do her honour & service too.   (p. 231)

The copyist Sterne referred to was Mlle Geneviève Navarre, residing in rue Beaurepaire, Paris, who painted pastel portraits and miniatures. She was a member of the Académie Saint-Luc and on 29 October 1764 was registered as a Master Painter in the Corporation of Paris (Georges Wildenstein, *Mélanges*, Paris, 1925–6, II, 202; *Livrets des Expositions de L'Académie de Saint-Luc*, Paris, 1872, pp. 11, 136, 160). Neither copy described below can be shown to be by Mlle Navarre. Kerslake points out that Carmontelle himself may have made copies, but both those now known are disappointing compared to other Carmontelle portraits. Since neither treats well Sterne's 'Phyz' perhaps neither was the painting owned by Foley.

(1) ANON. Water colour and chalk, 10⅜ by 6⅞ inches. At the National Portrait Gallery, No. 2785. Full-length profile, facing left, standing cross-legged and leaning on a chair with right forearm, left hand in pocket, wearing white wig, black clerical dress, and white ruffles and bands. By 1890 in possession, possibly on loan, of P. & D. Colnaghi & Co., London (Percy Fitzgerald, *Life*, 1896, II, 2). Purchased by the National Portrait Gallery, 1935, from Paul Wallraf, Paris, out of the collection of H. E. Powell (NPG records). The face is of limited iconographic value, though the full figure is well represented.   PLATE V

(2) ANON. Water colour. At Musée Condé, Chantilly. Similar to the above, but not demonstrably the original. Formerly in the collection of the duc d'Aumale (1822–97), grandson of the duc d'Orléans, for whom Carmontelle painted the original, but not descended to him; he pur-

chased this copy at Sotheby's, 30 April 1885, lot 292, from the collection of Edward Cheney (F.-A. Gruyer, *Les Portraits de Carmontelle*, Condé Museum at Chantilly, Paris, 1902, pp. 302–3).

(3) ANOTHER OR ONE OF THE ABOVE, 'in water colours', sold at Christie's 20 May 1859 (fourth day of sale), lot 536, from the collection of J. B. Jarman (Christie's records).

(4) ANON. 1762. Miniature, presumably though not certainly of the Carmontelle. Location unknown. On 12 [May] 1762, Sterne sent instructions from Paris to his friend and printer, Thomas Becket, asking him to pack and forward to Mrs Sterne two snuff boxes which were being brought to England by Charles Tollet – 'they are of Value – in one is my Portrait, done here – & the Other full of Garnets' (p. 167). They were duly delivered by Tollet (p. 176) and presumably arrived in York and remained in Elizabeth Sterne's hands until she sold the picture for 10 guineas after Sterne's death (p. 441).

B *Lithograph*

P. & D. COLNAGHI & CO. *c.* 1890. Print in the British Museum. Reproduced in black and white by Cross, ed. 1929, p. 308; and in colour by Lewis Melville (i.e., Lewis Saul Benjamin) as frontispiece to *Life and Letters of Laurence Sterne*, [1911], Vol. I.

5. ANON. Oil on canvas; 17⅛ by 13⅝ inches. At National Portrait Gallery, No. 2022. Three-quarter length, seated in a pink damask chair, torso a quarter to the left, face forward, right hand in lap, left arm hanging over arm of chair; white wig, black clerical dress with pale pink undergarment, white ruffles, and white bands; in a circular niche above and behind to the left, a classical head in sculpture labelled 'Rablais' (*sic*). Purchased 1924 from Arthur Morrison, who bought it at an unidentified auction near Swiss Cottage, London. Not known to Morrison as a portrait of Sterne, but identified by the Museum staff on the basis of comparison with other portraits of Sterne. The identification is strongly supported by the recently discovered engraving described below, which antedates 1780 and includes as part of the original engraving the name of Laurence Sterne. Accepted as a portrait of Sterne by Kerslake and, reluctantly, by the present writer. This is an unflattering portrait lacking the tension of body and vitality of face seen in others. The pallid skin may have led to Cross's opinion that it represented Sterne 'wasted by disease' (ed. 1929, p. xxi). Kerslake thinks it was done late in Sterne's life when he was weakened by haemorrhages of the lungs. But the figure is not gaunt, as in the Patch, and

does not suggest a man 'worn down to a shadow', as Sterne described himself at least four times during his last year (pp. 326, 328, 342, 408). Furthermore, Sterne's illness, if that is what is represented, will not explain the excessively long, ungainly limbs, large hands, and sloping shoulders. Sterne's hands appear large in Patch's caricature, but nowhere else, and his shoulders in the Patch, as in the Carmontelle, are quite square. In the Reynolds and Bridges, Sterne's shoulders and limbs seem almost comely. The face lacks the long nose so prominently displayed by Nollekens and Patch, and the cheek bones, compared to the Reynolds and Nollekens, are too broad. The eyes are humourless and soft. The entire figure suggests moral, more than physical, weakness. The painting is poorly executed in some other respects: the left hand is only indicated crudely, and the arm of the chair does not seem attached to the back. Yet curiously the background panelling and doors are well drawn. Perhaps, as Kerslake suggests, the painter did not normally paint portraits. The painting style, the interior background, and the chair appear to be English, though the chair could be American colonial (JFK, who cites the opinion of P. Thornton, Keeper, Department of Furniture and Woodwork, Victoria and Albert Museum).   PLATE VI

A *Engraving*

> ANON. Before 1780. Mezzotinto; 14¾ by 10¾ inches; subdimensions, 13⅝ by 10¾ inches. In the Owen D. Young guardbook, Berg Collection. This appears to be an engraver's proof before the final inscription has been added. There is, however, the simple inscription, *Laurence Sterne*. The paper, in the opinion of Allen D. Hazen, antedates 1780. Verso, a pencilled note, 'Unique proof. Not described in Chaloner Smith. Painter & engraver unknown.' No other prints are known. The engraving is carefully done, capturing the original in every detail, but compensating for some of the faults of the painting: the eyes are darker and have more expression, and the left hand is finished.

6. THOMAS PATCH. 1765. Oil on canvas; 21¾ by 16½ inches; signed 'Patch'. At Jesus College. Caricature of Sterne greeting Death. Painted at Florence, where Patch lived, between 18 December 1765, and 1 January 1766, the day Sterne left that city. Misdated on the frame, 1766. For Sir Horace Mann's comment on how the painting came to be made, see below, A. Sterne, facing left, hands to his breast, bows to Death as a skeleton entering the door. Sterne, in black clerical dress with white bands, wears, nevertheless, a sword. Death trails a scythe in his left hand and in the right holds an hourglass flanked by bat's wings. A masterful comic treatment of so serious a topic, but when considered as an icon, allowances must be made for Patch's exaggerations, especi-

ally of the nose. Formerly in the possession of Sir William Fitzherbert, Bart.; donated to the college in 1939 by J. A. Henderson of Mamhead Grange, Exeter (F. J. B. Watson, 'Thomas Patch . . . Notes on His Life . . .', *Walpole Society*, XXVIII, 1939–40, pp. 15–50; JFK). Reproduced as frontispiece to Willard Connely, *Laurence Sterne as Yorick*, 1958.   PLATE VII

A *Engraving*

THOMAS PATCH. *c.* 1766. Line engraving; 16¼ by 12 inches; signed with initials (Watson). A reverse engraving with a table in the foreground blocking out the sword. An elaborated background with symbols of Sterne's career about the room, including a machine for shredding books. Horace Walpole's print, in the W. S. Lewis Collection, Farmington, Connecticut, bears a note in Walpole's hand: 'Sterne, author of Tristram Shandy, done at Florence'. Reproduced in Curtis's edition of Sterne's *Letters*, p. 266, and in the Yale Walpole *Correspondence*, XXIII, 5. Sir Horace Mann, Envoy to the Court of Florence, wrote to Walpole on 15 March 1768, 'I send you a *caricatura* which wants no explanation as to the principal figure. The rest is too complicated to be explained. It was done here by an Englishman who has made most excellent caricatures of most of our countrymen who have passed by here, by their own desire and in societies.'   PLATE VIII

B *Etching*

THOMAS PATCH. 1769. 14 1/16 by 6⅝ inches; subdimensions, 13 15/16 by 6½ inches; dated and signed, 'P'. No. 20 in Patch's *Twenty-Five Caricatures*, 1769 (Watson). Also a reverse image, Sterne again wearing the sword. Only the hand of Death with the hourglass shows. Inscribed, upper left, *Dr Stern. | alias | Tristram Shandy*. A print in the Kenneth Monkman Collection, Shandy Hall.

7. JOSEPH NOLLEKENS. 1766. Bust, life size, 15½ inches high without the socle. Bare neck and shoulders. Original not identified or located, though it may have been the terra cotta bust said to have been in the collection of the Fourth Earl of Yarborough (DNB; Cross, ed. 1909, p. xi). Although no record appears in the family papers, a bust said to be the original was sold at Christie's *c.* 1928 out of the Yarborough Collection (JFK). Sculpted at Rome during one or both of Sterne's visits there, 11–25 January and 17 March–5 April 1766. This and another bust, of Garrick, also done at Rome, were the first busts Nollekens attempted professionally. They remained his best-known works and are generally thought to have launched him upon his highly successful

career as a portrait sculptor. He exhibited a 'busto of the Rev. Dr. Sterne' at the Society of Artists in 1767 (309). 'With this performance', said his friend, John Thomas Smith, 'Nollekens continued to be pleased even to his second childhood' (Smith, *Nollekens and His Times*, ed. Edmund Gosse, 1894, p. 34). Smith also told of going with Nollekens to deliver a plaster cast of Sterne's bust to Sterne's friend, Ignatius Sancho, the black former slave (pp. 51–2). The bust is an exact likeness, made, in all probability, by taking exact measurements of Sterne's face and head. But the hair is conventionalized in the manner of Roman busts; no doubt Sterne shaved his head. When Sterne's remains were exhumed in London in 1969 to be reburied in Coxwold churchyard, the skull was identified, not only by its location, but by evidences of autopsy and by measurements of the skull compared by an anatomist to the Nollekens bust in the possession of Kenneth Monkman (*Winged Skull*, p. ix).

A *Copies*

> Sterne's friend and printer, Thomas Becket, ran an advertisement in the *Public Advertiser* of 12 February 1771, offering for sale copies of the bust 'done from a Marble one which he sat to at Rome, executed by the famous Noliken. It is the greatest Likeness that can possibly be conceived. . . . The Price in plain Plaister is One Guinea, or if done in Imitation of Marble, or bronzed, they will be Six Shillings more.' It is quite possible that Nollekens's studio produced these copies. During this century, a number of copies in plaster and marble have been sold from London shops. No doubt, the following list is incomplete.

(1) In the collection of Kenneth Monkman, Shandy Hall. Marble. Photograph in *Winged Skull*, p. 205.   PLATE IX

(2) At the National Portrait Gallery, No. 1891. Marble. The gift of Lieutenant-Colonel Croft-Lyons, 1920; acquired by him from Armor of St James Street (JFK). Photographs in *Connoisseur*, LXV (March 1923), 135; and in Cross, ed. 1929, p. 404.   PLATE X

(3) At the Huntington Library and Art Gallery. Marble. Purchased, 1924, from the Anderson Galleries, New York. Said to have been in the collection of Lord Taunton, Quantock Lodge (JFK).

(4) In a private collection. Marble. Owned originally by John Hall-Stevenson. Exhibited at Manchester, 1857, with the next. Photograph in Cross, ed. 1909, p. 381.

(5) Location unknown. Exhibited at the Manchester Exhibition, 1857 (112),

from the collection of the Rt Hon. H. Labouchère (W. Durrant Cooper, N&Q, Second Series VIII, 1859, p. 15; JFK).

(6) Location unknown. Sold at Christie's 3 July 1823, to Mrs Russell Palmer; sold again at her sale, 23 March 1847, to Graves (NPG records).

(7) Location unknown. Sold at Christie's 1 February 1923 (44), to Guinness, the subject mistakenly identified as Addison, from the collection of Sir J. G. Thorbold, Bart., of Syston Park, Grantham (Christie's records; JFK).

(8) In the collection of R. A. Lee. Sold at Sotheby's 18 June 1965, from the collection of Lord Hore-Belisha (NPG records).

(9) See below, No. 21.

B *Engraving*

JAMES CALDWALL. 1775. Frontispiece to Vol. I of Sterne's *Letters*, 1775, edited by Sterne's daughter, Lydia Sterne Medalle. Caldwall's engraving, after a painting by Benjamin West (location unknown), depicts Mrs Medalle placing a garland upon a Nollekens bust.

II *Unauthentic Portraits*

8. Attributed to FRANCIS COTES. Oval crayon drawing accompanied by another said to be of Sterne's wife. In the collection of Dr Calvin H. Plimpton, Riverdale, New York. The man, facing front, head and shoulders showing, has dark eyebrows and is dressed in a white wig, blue-black coat, blue vest with white bands. The woman, facing three-quarters left, head and shoulder showing, is in a white dress with a red collar, her hair piled high with a red bow on top. Formerly in the collection of Reverend Canon G. W. Blenkin of St Albans (Walter Sichel, *Sterne, A Study*, 1910, pp. 29, 77; NPG records); by 1925 in the collection of George A. Plimpton. Cross, ed. 1929, pp. xx–xxi, dated the portrait of the man 1759, that of the woman 1761, a dating which indicates an unorthodox pair. Reproduced in Cross, p. 52; Sichel, pp. 29, 77; Melville, I, 33. Cross, in accepting these as genuine, identified them with portraits seen in a dealer's shop in Boston, England, by Nathaniel Hawthorne and mentioned in his 'Pilgrimage to Old Boston', in *Our Old Home* (centenary ed. of *Works*, Columbus, Ohio, 1970, V, 159–60). One must reject the identification of Sterne on grounds of little or no resemblance to authentic portraits. It is harder to reject that of Elizabeth Sterne since no authentic portrait of her is

known, but it seems probable that the pair was put together by some dealer and passed off as Sterne and his wife.   PLATE XI

9. Attributed to THOMAS GAINSBOROUGH. Oil on canvas; 18 by 14 inches. At the Peel Park Museum and Art Gallery, Salford. The attribution and identification were made originally by George William Fulcher, *Life of Thomas Gainsborough*, 1856, pp. 87, 219; and the attribution was repeated at Christie's, 14 April 1864, in the posthumous sale of Thomas Turton, Bishop of Ely (JFK). The identification of Sterne was disproved by one of the Peel Park Museum keepers who detected on the book held by the figure the name of *Evelina*, Fanny Burney's novel published in 1778 (Paul Kaufman, 'A True Image of Laurence Sterne', *Bulletin of the New York Public Library*, LXVI, 1962, pp. 653–6). No longer regarded as a Gainsborough by the museum staff. Reproduced by Kaufman; Melville, II, 140; and as frontispiece to Cross, ed. 1909.
                                                              PLATE XII

10. Attributed to ALLAN RAMSAY. Oil on canvas; 30 by 25 inches. Spuriously dated and signed, 'A Ramsay 1774'. At Jesus College. Presented to the college *c.* 1900 by Hugh Shield. Believed to be a Ramsay, but not of Sterne, by Alastair Smart, *Life and Art of Allan Ramsay*, 1952, p. 140. Reproduced by Melville, II, 335; and Cross, ed. 1909, p. 36.   PLATE XIII

11. Attributed to CHRISTOPHER STEELE. Oil; 29 by 24 inches. In 1910 in the possession of Theodore Blake Wirgman. Attribution and identification, both highly unlikely, were made at Christie's, 7 June 1912, lot 60 (Christie's records). By 1935 in the stock of Herman Kellerman Co., Weimar (NPG records). Reproduced as frontispiece to Sichel and in *Bookman*, July 1913, p. 154. Cf. No. 2, above.   PLATE XIV

12. D. DODD (perhaps the Daniel Dodd listed in Thieme–Becker and *Bryan's Dictionary*, who exhibited for the Society of Artists, 1761–80). Location unknown. Probably a posthumous drawing for purposes of the engraving described below.

A *Engravings*

WALKER. Circle bust, profile facing right, 1¾ inches diameter; below a scene of Sterne in the pulpit preaching to a fashionable audience in a gothic church; line engraving. Frontispiece of an edition of Sterne's *Sermons*, Joseph Wenman, London, 1785. Pirated by CASPER WEIN- RAUCH and used as frontispiece for an edition of *Letters to His Most Intimate Friends . . . between Yorick and Eliza . . .*, R. Sammer, Vienna,

1797. Reproduced in Boswell's *Life of Johnson*, 1907, ed. Roger Ingpen, II, 952. Clippings at NPG and in the author's collection. Pirated also by an unidentified artist and used as frontispiece to some unidentified book – a crude copy which was reproduced by Melville, II, 226.

13. Attributed to JOHN OPIE. Oil on canvas; *c.* 20 by 24 inches. Called an Opie on the frame. In the collection of Mrs Parnell Rucker in 1965. Attribution doubtful; identification fanciful (NPG records).

14. Attributed to ANDREA SOLDI. Oil on canvas. At the Henry E. Huntington Library and Art Gallery. Acquired by Huntington before 1928. The identification, made in 1934 by C. H. Collins Baker, is plausible so long as one considers the work to be a Soldi: the painter did several portraits at Coxwold of Sterne's patron, Lord Fauconberg, and his family. But neither Robert Wark, Curator of Art at the Huntington, nor John Ingamells, currently researching Soldi paintings, believes that Soldi painted this picture. The resemblance of the subject to Sterne as seen in the Reynolds is marginal.

15. Attributed to JOHN ZOFFANY. Oil. Bust-length oval. In 1964 in the collection of Sir George Bellew. Attribution and identification highly doubtful (NPG records).

16. NATHANIEL HONE. Drawing in black and red crayon of head facing right. Identification fanciful. Photograph sent by Gerard Sterne, New York, in the National Portrait Gallery library.

17. ANON. *c.* 1750. Oil; 50 by 40 inches. Inscribed in oil, top right, at a later date, *Laurence Sterne 1713/68* | *Author of 'Tristram Shandy'* | *and 'Sentimental Journey'* | *'From my Lord Spencer.'* The figure is identified in National Portrait Gallery files as Ralph Allen. Sold at Sotheby's 11 April, 1973, lot 100, to Mrs Filmer.

III *Unfinished or Never Executed*

18. SIR JOSHUA REYNOLDS. 1764. See above, the 'Whatman painting', No. 3, B (1).

19. SIR JOSHUA REYNOLDS. 1768. Unfinished, presumably destroyed. Reynolds's jumbled appointment book for 1768 seems to indicate appointments for Sterne on 23 February, 1 March and 9 March (the latter indistinct and uncertain; Leslie and Taylor found only two appointments, 22 February and 4 March, dates accepted by Cross). Sterne, who was seriously ill, was

confined to his bed early in March and died on 18 March. If Reynolds had actually begun a portrait, it is unlikely he finished it.

20. LOUIS-FRANÇOIS ROUBILIAC. Bust. Christie's catalogue for the Garrick sale, 23 June 1823, lists a Roubiliac bust of Sterne (73), sold for 9 guineas to Jameson. W. T. Tiffin in *Gossip about Portraits*, 1866, p. 72 – not a very reliable source – speaks of the 1760 Reynolds portrait of Sterne and a 'bust of him by Roubiliac, taken at a later period of his life'. Roubiliac died on 11 January 1762, only twenty months after Sterne sat for Reynolds. Moreover, Tiffin speaks of an engraving of the bust. The only known engraving of a Sterne bust is Caldwall's engraving of Lydia Sterne Medalle, which includes the Nollekens bust (above, No. 7, B). Cross, ed. 1925, although he said nothing about Tiffin, reported the Christie's sale. It was reported again by Katherine A. Esdaile in *Life and Works of Louis-François Roubiliac*, Oxford, 1928, p. 110. Since then most scholars have assumed there was indeed a Roubiliac of Sterne, now lost. Kenneth Monkman, however, points out that there is no other corroborating evidence, no contemporary reference, no advertisement, no other sales record; and he argues convincingly that Christie's, as Tiffin, had mistaken a Nollekens bust for a Roubiliac.

21. DEATH MASK. The mask at Princeton University Library, the gift of Laurence Hutton along with his collection of death masks, was made from a copy of the Nollekens bust. It shows the open eyes, incised pupils and irises, and a portion of the conventionalized hair – features which could not be captured in a genuine death mask. Hutton had doubts about its authenticity (Isabel Moore, *Talks in a Library with Laurence Hutton*, New York, 1907, pp. 167–8, 210–11). Photographs in *Life*, 27 August 1951, p. 74; and in William V. Holtz, *Image and Immortality*, Providence, R. I., 1970, p. 81.

Index

This is a selective index. It includes the names of most historic persons who touched upon Sterne's life, but not the names of scholars, critics, authorities, or owners of manuscripts and portraits. Information in the footnotes is indexed rarely, and then only when the reader could not be expected to find it by looking up related material on the corresponding page. Books discussed in the text are indexed by author (except Sterne's own works), but source materials, whether books or manuscripts, are not included. Under the entry, 'Sterne, Laurence,' the reader will find only items which he could not readily locate by tracing out the chronology of Sterne's life.

Catholicism, *see* Roman Catholics
Catton, Yorks., 65, 265
Centlivre, Susannah, *Busy Body*, 207
Cervantes Saavedra, Miguel de, 51, 200, 289
Chaloner, Anne, of Guisborough, 58, 188
Chaloner, Mary, of Guisborough, 189
Chambers, Ephraim, *Cyclopaedia*, 201–2
Chambers, Sir William, 188–9
Chancery Court, *see* spiritual courts
Chapman, Richard, steward, 127, 147, 264, 283
Chappelow, Leonard, professor, 279
Charles Edward, Prince, son of the pretender, 155–6, 159–64 *passim*
Chester, 66, 119–21, 145–6
Cholmley, Nathaniel, of Whitby, 144
Chudleigh's regiment, 1–2, 8–9, 13–22, 36–9
Church Farm, Sutton, 68, 116
Cibber, Colley: *Letter to Pope*, 199, 203; *Provok'd Husband*, 207
Cicero, 51
Clarke, Reverend Dr Samuel, 51–2, 196, 206, 218–19, 281
Clément, Abbé Denis-Xavier, 126
Cleveland Archdeaconry Court, *see* spiritual courts
Clive, Robert, 262
Clonmel, Co. Tipperary, 2–3
Clough, John, assistant registrar, 138, 143, 252
Coates, William, apparator, 128
Coley Chapel, *see* Hipperholme
Collier, Jane, *Art of Ingeniously Tormenting*, 199
Combe, William, xiii, 50–1
Common Sense, London newspaper, 100–1
Cope, General Sir John, 155–6
Cornwallis, Colonel, of Hayes's regiment, 38
Costobadie, Jacob, registrar, 39 n. 2, 119, 252–3
Cotes, Francis, painter, 313–14
Country Interest party: at Halifax, 31–4;

at Sutton, 67–8; at York, 73, 77–8, 90–112 *passim*, 165–7, 177
Cowper, Mrs, née Hoyland, 133, 265
Cowper, Reverend Charles, 112, 265, 268
Coxwold: Shandy Hall, 67; seat of Lord Fauconberg, 122; Richard Wilkinson preferred to curacy, 257; S preferred to curacy, 257, 261, 302; S's preaching there, 127, 217; S reburied there, 312; William Raper, curate, from, 282–3
Crébillon, Claude-Prosper Jolyot de, 199
Croft, Sir Christopher, 143
Croft, Henrietta, née Thompson, 144
Croft, John: youth, 145; his memoir of S, xii, xx, 145; his stories of 'Mr S' in *Scrapeana*, 86 n.1; *not indexed as a source of information or anecdotes*
Croft, Stephen: portrait by Reynolds, xvii, 144 n. 2; family and house, 143–4; politics, 140, 144; and enclosure, 261 n. 2; friendship with S, 133, 145; lends S money, 149, 239; rescues MS of *Tristram Shandy*, 281; takes S to London, 297; mentioned, 139 n. 3, 224, 294
Cross, Wilbur L.: his biography of S, xii–xiii, xx; his hypothesis about the gaoling of Agnes Sterne, 238
Culloden, battle of, 174–5
Cumberland, Duke of, 163, 175–6, 184
Curtis, L. P., his studies of S, xiii

Daily Gazetteer, 100, 103
D'Arcy, Sir Conyers, 156
Dashwood, Sir Francis, 62, 188 n. 4, 193
Davis, Cuthbert, of Lancaster, 180
Dawson, Reverend William, 138, 146–7
Dealtary, Reverend John, xx, 73, 78–9, 270, 286
Dealtry, Dr John, 183, 283–4
Dean and Chapter Peculiar Court, *see* spiritual courts
Deanery Peculiar Court, *see* spiritual